500 BEST
muffin
RECIPES

500 BEST muffin RECIPES

Esther Brody

Robert
ROSE

Dedication

To my son, Leonard Jason, who spent so many
hours of his very busy law practice and seminar
schedules to make all of this possible for me.

To my daughter, Lisa Michelle, a wonderful cook
in her own right, and for the birth of my beautiful
granddaughter, "Natty," the love of my life.

To my little granddaughter, Natalie Arielle,
a beautiful little person inside and out, who
has brought such joy, happiness, caring
and unconditional love into my life.

In memory of my mother and father, Mary and
Louis Goldstein, who were wonderful parents
and who gave so much to us, their children.

To Bob Dees and staff of Robert Rose Inc.,
for their guidance, expertise and hard
work to make my books such a success.

For complete cataloguing information, see page 360.

Disclaimer
The recipes in this book have been carefully tested by our kitchen and our tasters. To the best of our knowledge, they are safe and nutritious for ordinary use and users. For those people with food or other allergies, or who have special food requirements or health issues, please read the suggested contents of each recipe carefully and determine whether or not they may create a problem for you. All recipes are used at the risk of the consumer.

We cannot be responsible for any hazards, loss or damage that may occur as a result of any recipe use.

For those with special needs, allergies, requirements or health problems, in the event of any doubt, please contact your medical adviser prior to the use of any recipe.

Design & Production: PageWave Graphics Inc.
Photography: Mark T. Shapiro
Art Direction (cover): PageWave Graphics Inc.
Art Direction (inside photopages): Sharon Matthews
Food Stylist: Kate Bush
Prop Stylist: Charlene Ericson
Index: Barbara Schon

We acknowledge the financial support of the Government of Canada through the Book Publishing Industry Development Program (BPIDP) for our publishing activities.

Published by: Robert Rose Inc.
120 Eglinton Ave. E., Suite 800, Toronto, Ontario, Canada M4P 1E2
Tel: (416) 322-6552   Fax: (416) 322-6936

Printed in Canada
1 2 3 4 5 6 7 8 9 10   FP   09 08 07 06 05 04 03

Contents

Acknowledgments

To the many friends, in many places, who so willingly and graciously shared their family or special recipes with me, I want to express my thanks and deep appreciation.

To my dear friends and the most wonderful, caring and giving people I know, Colleen and John Stienstra, I thank for their friendship and encouragement over many years.

In memory of my dear friend, Arlene Kushner, who is gone but not forgotten, and who was always so encouraging and excited over every book I wrote.

To my sister, Betty Shapiro and family, Randy Shapiro and Cara Shapiro for their encouragement.

To my niece and family, Shauna, David, Drew and Brandon Jackson, for their encouragement, love, generosity and always caring about everything I undertake.

To my twin sister, Cecille Shtabsky and family, husband Aaron, and daughters Marla, Karen, Wendy and Leslie Shtabsky for their encouragement.

— Esther

Introduction

I REALLY DON'T REMEMBER HOW MY MUFFIN CAREER BEGAN, BUT IT was long before muffin specialty shops and franchises started appearing.

Muffins have always seemed healthier than danishes, doughnuts and cinnamon buns — although I love all three. They are good to eat at any time of the day and can be made with a wide variety of healthy, nutritious ingredients such as bran, whole wheat, oats, and wheat germ — as well as not-so-healthy (but oh-so-good) things like chocolate.

Muffins are endlessly adaptable; you can vary their flavor and appearance by adding fruit (such as dates, raisins, blueberries, apples), chopped nuts or chocolate chips. You can use brown or white flour, sugar or syrup. Muffins can be sprinkled with various toppings, split in half and covered with favorite spreads and served warm or cold. They make wonderful additions to children's or adult's lunches. And they're always a welcome snack. With a high fiber content, muffins can be a part of any well-balanced diet. Who says being healthy has to be dull?

Most muffin recipes can be put together from ingredients you usually have on hand and need to use up, such as overripe bananas or other perishable fruits such as strawberries, peaches or nectarines.

To some people, baking muffins sounds simple: just measure the ingredients, mix well and bake. Well, the procedure is simple — at least, once you've mastered the basic techniques and have learned how to avoid the pitfalls that can come along the way.

In this book, I have attempted to pull together everything that I have learned over the years — all the secret tips, general baking information, as well as all my favorite recipes so that you, too, can bake big, beautiful, moist and tasty muffins. To me, making "good" muffins is an art and if you master the correct techniques to proper muffin baking, you should have no problems.

This book is the direct result of all the positive feedback that my muffins have received over the years. In fact, I have lost track of the number of times that people have raved about my muffins' moistness, large uniform size and shape, and their flavor. So a few years ago, when some delis and smoke shops asked me to supply them with my muffins, I decided to give it a try.

I recall once meeting a truck driver who said he didn't eat muffins anymore because they all seemed so dry, small and tasteless. So I gave him a complimentary bag of muffins to take on his drive back to British Columbia and was thrilled to receive a long distance call a few days later telling me how great they were and that he was a muffin fan again. His company and fellow workers wanted me to consider shipping muffins to them weekly, but I had to decline, since I was having enough trouble keeping up with demands in my own city!

Another incident I recall fondly occurred in a building to which I delivered muffins daily, and where there was great demand for my rhubarb muffins. It was so great, in fact, that my small garden was soon unable to supply the fresh rhubarb required. Well, it wasn't long before the people in that building were bringing me bags of fresh rhubarb from their gardens; attached were notes asking me to keep making muffins!

At times, I had asked some of my distributors to specify which muffin varieties their customers like best, since I often didn't have time to make as many flavors as I'd like. But they always told me that their customers loved all the different flavors and were happy to buy whatever I brought in. It was a wonderful compliment, but very frustrating for me having to decide which of my hundreds of muffin recipes would please the greatest number of people. Still, it was great knowing people trusted me enough to supply what I felt was best.

Over the years, I have come to be known as "The Muffin Lady." In fact, to this day, some people still don't know my real name! People have sent me their favorite recipes from all over, including the United States and Europe. Some have given me permission to use their names but others preferred I didn't, so I have decided to eliminate names completely. It also became a kind of hobby for me to collect recipes from newspapers and magazines, as well as restaurants I have been to that were kind enough to share their special recipes with me.

Some years ago, I began to realize that I just couldn't keep up with the demand all by myself. I had responsibilities as a single parent with a house to run and a full-time job. I eventually had to inform my customers that I was retiring. To this day, I still get calls from people asking me to supply them with muffins or to share my muffin recipes and secrets. So, I decided to write a book as a special thanks to all those people whose compliments I have cherished and who have provided me with so much encouragement.

There is no such thing, I believe, as an original muffin recipe. Good recipes are handed down in families, given over to friends, and people usually adapt recipes to suit their own tastes. Every time I have come upon a new recipe, I have tried it out in one or two shops. If it was good, it went in my "yes" file, if not it was discarded. I wish now that I had kept notes on all these recipes so that I could have shared my thoughts and opinions with you. In some 20 years of muffin making I have obviously made so many kinds of muffins that it is hard to remember exactly what I liked about each one — and I never thought I'd be writing a cookbook!

Tired of the same old bran, blueberry and carrot muffins? Well, I think the variety of recipes in this book will awaken your interests again.

So pick a recipe — and bake away to your heart's content!

— *Esther Brody*

10 Steps to Perfect Muffins

To achieve perfect baking results, just follow these basic steps:

1 Read the recipe carefully and check the required ingredients, oven temperature and baking time.

2 Remove shortening, butter or margarine from the refrigerator 1 hour before mixing. Unless the recipe states otherwise, take milk and eggs out of the refrigerator as you start mixing.

3 Adjust the oven racks to the desired level. I always bake muffins or cakes in the middle of the oven on the center rack.

4 Preheat oven thoroughly to the recommended temperature in your recipe. This is important for maximum rise as a too cool temperature will result in nearly flat muffins.

5 Collect all of the utensils that you will require.

6 Set out the remaining ingredients that you will require.

7 Prepare the muffin tins. You can grease them, spray them with vegetable spray or I prefer to line the tins with paper baking cups.

8 Check the recipe again for the method of baking to be used.

9 Spoon the batter into greased or paper-lined muffin tins, filling two-thirds to three-quarters full. Any cups not filled with batter should be filled halfway with water. This will not only save the muffin pans but will add moisture to the oven, enlarging the muffins and allowing for even baking.

10 Bake as your recipe directs. Muffins are done when they are golden brown, firm to the touch, come away from the sides of the pan and a toothpick inserted in the center comes out clean and dry.

Muffin Baking Techniques

SUCCESSFUL MUFFIN MAKING depends on three important activities — measuring, mixing and baking. Let's look at each of these in turn.

Measuring

For best baking results, it is essential to measure ingredients accurately each time.

Have measuring cups for both dry and liquid ingredients ready — it saves time to have large measures also.

Make sure that your measuring spoons are in good shape, not warped, bent or dented, as you can't get perfect measurements if they are.

Dry Ingredients

Use measuring cups with a flat rim so the ingredients can easily be leveled off.

Use aluminum or plastic sets that hold the exact amount needed when leveled off.

For less than $\frac{1}{4}$ cup (50 mL) use your standard measuring spoons.

Fill standard measuring cups or spoons to overflowing, then level off using a straight-edged knife or spatula — do not pack or bang on table.

Flour. I find that the best way to measure flour is to choose a measure of the correct size with a flush rim for leveling. Fill it to overflowing by dipping it into the package directly, or use a scoop or spoon to add flour to the measuring cup. Do not bang the measuring cup on the table, but level off with the straight edge of a knife or spatula.

Older cookbooks call for flour to be sifted before measuring but today most flours are pre-sifted. If a recipe calls for "sifting the dry ingredients together," there is no need to sift the flour prior to measuring. Just sift all pre-measured dry ingredients together and proceed with the recipe.

Baking powder and baking soda. Dip measuring spoon into container and level off with the edge of a knife.

To measure $\frac{1}{8}$ tsp (0.5 mL), halve $\frac{1}{4}$ tsp (1 mL) with the tip of a knife.

Dry ingredients such as baking soda, baking powder and cocoa sometimes have a tendency to pack down in their containers so before measuring, stir to loosen.

Brown sugar. If a recipe calls for "firmly packed" brown sugar, spoon into a measuring cup, pack it down firmly with the back of a spoon and then level off.

Liquid Ingredients

Always use a see-through glass or plastic measure with volume amounts marked on the outside.

Place glass measuring cup on a flat surface. Bend down so that you can read the measure at eye level.

Make sure that your liquid measuring cup has a safety rim above the full cup mark in order to get an accurate measurement without spilling a drop.

Oil or melted fat. Dip measuring spoon into the oil and then lift out carefully. The spoon should be so full that it will not hold another drop.

Shortening. To measure an amount that is less than 1 cup (250 mL) partly fill a measuring cup with water, leaving space for the amount of shortening to be measured. Add shortening until the water moves up to the 1 cup (250 mL) mark. Or, press the shortening firmly into a fractional cup so that no air holes are left. Level off and scoop out.

Mixing

There are two common methods for mixing muffins:

The Standard Method
1. Sift the dry ingredients into a large bowl and make a well or depression in the center. Remember to mix dry ingredients together well in order to distribute the baking powder and baking soda evenly.
2. Combine the egg (slightly beaten), milk and oil or melted shortening (cool the melted butter or shortening first).
3. Add the liquid ingredients all at once to the dry ingredients.
4. Stir quickly only until the dry ingredients are moist. The batter will be slightly lumpy.
5. Spoon batter into prepared muffin tins.
6. Bake as directed.

The Biscuit Method
1. Cut shortening into the sifted dry ingredients until crumbly.
2. Combine the egg and milk. Add all at once to the flour mixture.
3. Stir just until moist.
4. Spoon batter into prepared muffin tins.
5. Bake as directed.

A key factor in producing successful muffins is the mixing. Your muffins will be lighter when you mix them together quickly and lightly as this produces the best rising effect.

When a muffin batter is overmixed it is too smooth and flows readily leaving the spoon in a long ribbon-like strand. This will result in tough muffins with funnels and a pronounced peak. Muffins should always be light and tender and baked to a golden brown. The secret for accomplishing this is not to overmix or stir. Use as few strokes as possible — the batter should look lumpy. I stir and mix my muffin batter with a "folding-in" movement using a large stainless steel spoon, not a spatula as you would normally when "folding" in a recipe.

In most of my muffin recipes I fill the muffin tins full, right to the top, unless I am adding a filling or topping, to produce large and even-sized muffins.

I prefer to use the standard mixing method (above) with most of my recipes, unless the recipe states otherwise. I find it the easiest way.

Dry ingredients should be thoroughly mixed in one bowl and liquid ingredients in another bowl. When separated like this they can be left indefinitely. But as soon as you combine the two of them, you have to work quickly, stirring just to enough to moisten and combine. Then spoon immediately into muffin tins.

The batter for muffins is usually stirred but may be creamed.

For a stirred batter, the dry ingredients are mixed together in order to evenly distribute the baking powder and baking soda. If the leavening is unevenly distributed, the muffins may have a bitter taste.

For a creamed batter, the shortening and sugar are beaten

together before adding the other ingredients. The muffins are usually sweeter and have a cake-like texture.

Once the muffin batter has been prepared and put into the muffin tins it should go into the oven quickly. The idea is for the batter to start rising in the oven not on the counter. That is why I prepare the muffin tins before I start mixing the recipe and I have all of the ingredients ready, including any grating.

Baking

Most muffin recipes suggest baking at 375°F (190°C) or 400°F (200°C). I have found that baking at 425°F (220°C) for 20 minutes works best for many of my muffins. If the muffins brown too quickly turn your oven down.

Muffins bake best on the middle rack in the oven. On the lowest shelf the bottoms burn too quickly and on the highest shelf the tops brown too soon.

I set my timer for 15 minutes and then I turn the muffin pan around in the oven, putting front to back. Then I set the timer for 5 minutes and bake for the remaining 5 minutes.

Most ovens cook unevenly, but I have found that my method of turning for the last 5 minutes of baking produces a more evenly baked and browned muffin.

Check the accuracy of your oven often and make any necessary adjustments. It is quite normal for ovens to vary. Also, ovens often bake faster at the back, that is why I turn the muffin pan around for a more even baking.

Muffins straight from the hot oven are very fragile so allow the pan to cool for about 5 to 10 minutes before removing the muffins. The steam from the pan should loosen them. If they still stick, loosen the muffins by running a knife around the edge of the cup. Often you can simply turn the pan upside-down and the muffins will fall out.

If you are baking fruit-filled muffins, cool completely before removing them from the tins.

If you wish to keep muffins hot for serving, loosen them and tilt to one side of the muffin tin slightly. It is a good idea to place them in the warm, turned off oven until you are ready to serve.

General Muffin Tips

BECAUSE MUFFINS ARE GREAT warm, you can reheat them by wrapping loosely in foil and placing in the oven at 400°F (200°C) for about 5 to 10 minutes. If frozen, heat for about 15 to 20 minutes.

Muffins can be heated in the microwave by covering with a damp paper towel. Heat for about 30 seconds or just until warm. But be careful, microwaves heat very quickly.

Muffins can be baked successfully in the microwave using special microwave muffin pans or glass custard cups. Be sure to follow the manufacturer's directions that come with your microwave oven for proper baking time and power levels. See the Microwave Muffins chapter (pages 221 to 236) for some great recipes.

The yield amount in most recipes is based on filling the muffin tins about two-thirds full. If you fill tins to the top you will have 2 or 3 fewer muffins.

For smaller muffins, use medium-sized paper baking cups. The yield will be 3 or 4 muffins greater. You should reduce the baking time slightly, usually up to 5 minutes.

Whether I plan on freezing the muffins or eating them in the next few days, I wrap each muffin separately in plastic wrap. Once wrapped, they have a terrific shelf life of 3 to 5 days. They will stay moist and fresh and ready to go.

I do not store muffins in the refrigerator as they become stale and dry faster. Keep them on the counter or in the freezer.

Muffins freeze well for up to 6 months or more if wrapped properly. To freeze muffins, cool completely first. Wrap in plastic and place on a foil or styrofoam tray. Place tray in a large airtight freezer bag and tie securely. This double wrap prevents the freezer taste you sometimes get when foods thaw.

To heat frozen muffins, unwrap and thaw. Place muffins in greased muffin tins and heat slowly at 300°F (150°C) or until just warm.

Instead of baking muffin batter immediately you can freeze it by spooning the batter into paper baking cups. Place cups in the freezer. When frozen, place the cups into airtight containers or freezer bags and return to the freezer. To bake, unwrap and place the paper cups and frozen batter into ungreased muffin tins. Bake in a preheated oven 300°F (150°C) until well risen. Then increase oven temperature to 425°F (220°C) and finish baking for 15 to 20 minutes or until golden brown. If you wish to thaw the muffin batter first, it usually takes about 1 hour. Bake thawed muffins in preheated oven 425°F (220°C) for 15 to 20 minutes or until golden brown.

If you begin to find that seeing so many muffin recipes gets confusing, check for ingredients you know and like and then try that particular recipe.

Muffin Troubleshooting

IF YOUR MUFFINS ARE LESS THAN perfect, here are some important tips:

Muffins are too hard.

- There is too much flour and not enough liquid. Try using ¼ cup (50 mL) less flour.
- You may have stirred too long and hard. Try mixing for only 10 seconds.

Muffins are flat or spreading.

- If they are spreading out all over the top of the tins, don't fill as full.
- There could be too much liquid in the batter. Try using ¼ cup (50 mL) less liquid.

Muffins are tough and soggy, peaks in center.

- You have probably overmixed which toughens the batter.
- Underbaking could be causing the problem as ovens vary in temperatures. Try turning up your oven 25°F (10°C) and shorten the baking time.

Muffins rise high, fall flat in center.

- There is not enough flour. Increase the amount by about ¼ cup (50 mL). Sometimes the eggs are so large that they increase the ratio of liquid ingredients. Use large eggs but not extra large.

Muffins do not brown.

- If they do not brown easily, your oven rack is too high or too low.
- If muffins are baked on the lowest rack, they may burn on the bottom before being done on top.
- If muffins are baked on the highest rack, they will get too brown on top.
- Always use the middle rack for an even browning.

Muffins are coarse-textured.

- This is usually caused from insufficient stirring and baking at too low a temperature.

Classic Muffins

Basic Muffin

2 cups	all-purpose flour	500 mL
4 tsp	baking powder	20 mL
1/2 tsp	salt	2 mL
2 tbsp	granulated sugar	25 mL
1 cup	milk	250 mL
2	eggs, beaten	2
3 tbsp	melted butter or margarine or shortening	45 mL

◆ *Preheat oven to 400°F (200°C)*
◆ *Muffin tin, lightly greased*

1. In a large bowl sift together flour, baking powder, salt and sugar. Make a well in the center.

2. In another bowl combine milk, beaten eggs and melted butter. Pour into dry ingredients. Mix just until blended, no more than 15 to 20 strokes. Do not overmix.

3. Spoon batter into prepared muffin tin, filling two-thirds full. Bake in preheated oven for 15 to 18 minutes or until golden brown.

Variations

◆ *Apple Cinnamon Muffins:* Add 1 tsp (5 mL) cinnamon, 2 tbsp (25 mL) butter and 1 1/2 cups (375 mL) finely chopped apples.

◆ *Bacon Muffins:* Fry 5 strips side bacon until crisp; crumble. Set aside to cool. Substitute bacon and drippings for the melted butter.

◆ *Blueberry Muffins:* Substitute brown sugar for granulated sugar. Dredge 1 1/2 cups (375 mL) frozen blueberries in 2 tbsp (25 mL) of flour taken from Basic recipe. (This prevents blueberries from sinking.) Fold berries into batter.

◆ *Cheese Muffins:* Add 1 cup (250 mL) grated sharp cheese to dry ingredients.

◆ *Cornmeal Muffins:* Use 3/4 cup (175 mL) cornmeal and 1 1/4 cups (300 mL) all-purpose flour instead of 2 cups (500 mL) all-purpose flour. Add 1 tbsp (15 mL) more granulated sugar (or omit sugar completely). Use 1 egg instead of 2 eggs.

◆ *Double Top Muffins:* Place 1 cooked, dried apricot half in bottom of each greased muffin cup; fill two-thirds full with batter. Top with a crumb mixture of 1/2 cup (125 mL) firmly packed brown sugar, 1/2 cup (125 mL)

softened butter or margarine, 1/3 cup (75 mL) all-purpose flour and 1 tsp (5 mL) cinnamon.

◆ *Dried Fruit and Nut Muffins:* Add 1/2 cup (125 mL) dried fruit (raisins, figs, chopped pitted dates) and/or nuts.

◆ *Oatmeal Muffins:* Substitute 1 cup (250 mL) quick-cooking oats (uncooked) for 1 cup (250 mL) flour. Add 1/4 cup (50 mL) more flour.

◆ *Orange Muffins:* Add 1 tbsp (15 mL) grated orange zest to dry ingredients. Substitute orange juice for milk.

◆ *Pumpkin Muffins:* Add 1 tsp (5 mL) cinnamon and 1/2 tsp (2 mL) nutmeg to dry ingredients. Add 2/3 cup (150 mL) canned pumpkin with the milk.

◆ *Rice Muffins:* Use 1 cup (250 mL) flour and 1 cup (250 mL) cold boiled rice. Use 1 egg instead of 2 eggs and 2/3 cup (150 mL) milk instead of 1 cup (250 mL). Add rice last, mixing in lightly. Bake for about 30 minutes.

◆ *Quick Tea Cake Muffins:* Increase sugar to 1/2 cup (125 mL) and eggs to 3 eggs. Reduce milk to 3/4 cup (175 mL). Bake at 425°F (220°C) for about 15 minutes.

Rich Biscuit-Style Muffins

2 cups	all-purpose flour	500 mL
2½ tsp	baking powder	12 mL
2 tbsp	granulated sugar	25 mL
½ tsp	salt	2 mL
½ cup	shortening	125 mL
1	egg, well beaten	1
¾ cup	milk	175 mL

◆ *Preheat oven to 400°F (200°C)*
◆ *Muffin tin, greased*

1. In a bowl sift together flour, baking powder, sugar and salt. Using a pastry blender, cut in shortening.
2. In another bowl combine egg and milk. Add to dry ingredients; stir until moistened. Spoon better into prepared muffin tin. Bake in preheated oven for 25 minutes.

Variations

◆ Cranberry-Cube Muffins: Fill muffin tins one-third full. Cut 1 cup (250 mL) canned jellied cranberry sauce into ½-inch (1 cm) cubes. Sprinkle over batter. Spoon in remaining batter.

◆ *Cheese-Caraway Muffins:* Add 1 cup (250 mL) shredded sharp processed cheese and 1 tsp (5 mL) caraway seed to flour mixture.

◆ *Bacon Muffins:* Add ½ cup (125 mL) crumbled crisp bacon to dry ingredients.

◆ *Raisin, Nut or Date Muffins:* Add ½ to ¾ cup (125 mL to 175 mL) raisins, chopped nuts or coarsely cut dates.

Apple Crunch Muffins

1½ cups	all-purpose flour	375 mL
⅓ cup	granulated sugar	75 mL
2 tsp	baking powder	10 mL
½ tsp	salt	2 mL
½ cup	dry non-fat milk	125 mL
1 tsp	cinnamon	5 mL
¼ cup	softened shortening	50 mL
1	egg	1
½ cup	water	125 mL
1 cup	finely chopped peeled apples	250 mL

TOPPING

⅓ cup	firmly packed brown sugar	75 mL
⅓ cup	finely chopped nuts	75 mL

◆ *Preheat oven to 375°F (190°C)*
◆ *Muffin tin, greased*

1. In a bowl combine flour, sugar, baking powder, salt, milk and ½ tsp (2 mL) cinnamon; mix well. Add shortening, egg, water and apples. Mix quickly, just until blended. Spoon batter into prepared muffin tin, filling two-thirds full.

2. In a bowl combine remaining cinnamon, brown sugar and nuts; sprinkle over muffins. Bake in preheated oven for 20 to 25 minutes.

Esther's Special Banana Muffins

1 cup	granulated sugar	250 mL
2	eggs	2
1/2 cup	softened margarine	125 mL
2 cups	all-purpose flour	500 mL
2 tsp	baking soda	10 mL
3 or 4	medium bananas, mashed	3 or 4

MUFFIN STUFF:
I always mix batter in stainless steel bowls.
Ripe bananas are best to use.
If you plan to double the recipe, use only
1 1/2 cups (375 mL) sugar.

◆ *Preheat oven to 425°F (220°C)*
◆ *Large muffin tin, paper-lined*

1. In a bowl cream together sugar and eggs until well mixed. Add margarine; blend well. Add flour and baking soda; mix until a loose dough forms.
2. Add bananas; stir just until moist. Spoon batter into prepared muffin tin, filling to top.
3. Bake in preheated oven for 15 to 20 minutes or until golden brown. After 15 minutes, turn pans around, back to front, for last 5 minutes of baking.

Banana Muffins Plus

1 cup	granulated sugar	250 mL
1/2 cup	butter or shortening	125 mL
1	egg	1
3	mashed bananas	3
1/2 tsp	salt	2 mL
2 tbsp	orange juice or milk	25 mL
1 1/2 tsp	baking powder	7 mL
1/2 tsp	baking soda	2 mL
2 cups	all-purpose flour	500 mL
1/2 cup	chocolate chips (optional)	125 mL

◆ *Preheat oven to 350°F (180°C)*
◆ *Muffin tin, greased or paper-lined*

1. In a bowl cream together sugar, butter and egg; mix well. Add bananas, salt, orange juice, baking powder, baking soda, flour and chocolate chips; stir well.
2. Spoon batter into prepared muffin tin, filling to top. Bake in preheated oven for 20 to 30 minutes.

Banana Bran Muffins

½ cup	granulated sugar	125 mL
1 cup	brown sugar	250 mL
1 cup	vegetable oil	250 mL
3	eggs	3
1 tsp	vanilla	5 mL
1½ cups	mashed banana	375 mL
3 cups	natural bran	750 mL
1½ cups	buttermilk	375 mL
3 cups	all-purpose flour	750 mL
3 tsp	baking powder	15 mL
3 tsp	baking soda	15 mL
1 tsp	salt	5 mL
1 cup	raisins	250 mL

- *Preheat oven to 375°F (190°C)*
- *Muffin tin, greased or paper-lined*

1. In a bowl combine granulated sugar, brown sugar and oil. Beat in eggs, one at a time. Add vanilla and banana; mix well. Add bran and buttermilk.
2. In another bowl combine flour, baking powder, baking soda and salt. Add to banana mixture; stir until ingredients are just mixed. Do not overmix. Fold in raisins.
3. Spoon batter into prepared muffin tin, filling to top. Bake in preheated oven for 15 to 20 minutes.

> **MUFFIN STUFF:** This recipe makes about 30 to 36 muffins. If that's too many, feel free to halve the recipe. Or simply freeze the muffins and use as needed.

Banana Date-Nut Muffins

1	pkg (7 oz/210 g) bran muffin mix with dates or corn muffin mix	1
1 cup	mashed ripe bananas	250 mL
2	eggs	2
⅓ cup	chopped walnuts or pecans	75 mL

- *Preheat oven to 400°F (200°C)*
- *Muffin tin, greased or paper-lined*

1. In a bowl combine muffin mix, bananas, eggs and walnuts; mix just until blended.
2. Spoon batter into prepared muffin tin, filling to top. Bake in preheated oven for 15 to 20 minutes or until done.

Variation

- Use plain bran muffin mix instead of bran muffin mix with dates and add ½ cup (125 mL) chopped dates.

Honey Bran Muffins

1¼ cups	all-purpose flour	300 mL
¾ tsp	baking soda	4 mL
½ tsp	baking powder	2 mL
½ tsp	salt	2 mL
1½ cups	bran flakes cereal	375 mL
1¼ cups	buttermilk	300 mL
¼ cup	oil	50 mL
¼ cup	honey	50 mL
1	egg	1
½ cup	dark raisins	125 mL

◆ *Preheat oven to 400°F (200°C)*
◆ *12-cup muffin tin*

1. In a bowl combine flour, baking soda, baking powder, salt and bran flakes.
2. In another bowl combine buttermilk, oil, honey and egg; whisk well. Pour into flour mixture; stir just until moist and blended.
3. Fold in raisins. Spoon batter into muffin tin, filling three-quarters full. Bake in preheated oven for 15 to 20 minutes.

Nutritious Raisin Bran Muffins

1 cup	all-bran or natural bran cereal	250 mL
1 cup	milk	250 mL
1	egg	1
3 tbsp	butter or margarine or shortening, melted	45 mL
1 tsp	vanilla	5 mL
1 cup	raisins	250 mL
1 cup	all-purpose flour	250 mL
3 tsp	baking powder	15 mL
½ cup	brown sugar	125 mL
1 tsp	cinnamon	5 mL
½ tsp	salt	2 mL

◆ *Preheat oven to 400°F (200°C)*
◆ *12-cup muffin tin, greased*

1. In a bowl combine bran and milk. Add egg, butter and vanilla; mix well. Stir in raisins.
2. In another bowl sift together flour and baking powder. Add brown sugar, cinnamon and salt; mix well. Make a well in the center; add bran mixture. Stir just until blended.
3. Spoon batter into prepared muffin tin. Bake in preheated oven for 15 to 20 minutes.

Esther's Favorite Blueberry Muffins

¼ cup	softened butter or margarine	50 mL
¾ cup	granulated sugar	175 mL
1	egg, beaten	1
1½ cups	pastry flour	375 mL
½ tsp	salt	2 mL
2 tsp	baking powder	10 mL
½ cup	milk	125 mL
1 cup	fresh or frozen blueberries	250 mL

♦ *Preheat oven to 400°F (200°C)*
♦ *12-cup muffin tin, greased or paper-lined*

1. In a bowl cream together butter and sugar. Add egg; mix well.

2. In another bowl sift together flour, salt and baking powder. Add to creamed mixture alternately with milk; stir just until moistened. Fold in blueberries.

3. Spoon batter into prepared muffin tin, filling to top. Bake in preheated oven for 15 to 20 minutes or until browned.

Old-Fashioned Blueberry Muffins

2	eggs	2
1¼ cups	milk	300 mL
½ cup	melted butter or margarine	125 mL
1 tsp	grated lemon zest	5 mL
1½ cups	all-purpose flour	375 mL
1 cup	whole wheat flour	250 mL
½ cup	granulated sugar	125 mL
1 tbsp	baking powder	15 mL
½ tsp	salt	2 mL
1½ cups	fresh or frozen blueberries	375 mL

♦ *Preheat oven to 400°F (200°C)*
♦ *12-cup muffin tin, greased or paper-lined*

1. In a bowl combine eggs, milk, butter and lemon zest; whisk well.

2. In another bowl combine all-purpose flour, whole wheat flour, sugar, baking powder and salt; mix well. Make a well in the center. Pour in egg mixture; stir just until ingredients are moistened.

3. Spoon batter into prepared muffin tin, dividing evenly. Bake in preheated oven for 15 to 20 minutes.

Blueberry-Orange Muffins

1¾ cups	all-purpose flour	425 mL
½ cup	granulated sugar	125 mL
1 tsp	grated orange zest	5 mL
1 tbsp	baking powder	15 mL
1 cup	fresh or frozen blueberries	250 mL
1 cup	milk	250 mL
½ cup	melted butter	125 mL
1	egg	1
½ tsp	salt	2 mL
TOPPING		
2 tbsp	melted butter	25 mL
¼ cup	orange juice	50 mL
¼ cup	granulated sugar	50 mL

- *Preheat oven to 350°F (180°C)*
- *12-cup muffin tin, greased*

1. In a bowl sift together flour, sugar, orange zest and baking powder. Add blueberries; toss to combine well.

2. In another bowl whisk together milk, butter, egg and salt. Add to flour mixture; stir quickly just until all ingredients are moistened. Spoon batter into prepared muffin tin, dividing evenly. Bake in preheated oven for 15 to 18 minutes or until golden brown.

3. In a bowl combine butter and orange juice. Pour sugar into another bowl. When muffins are ready, remove from tins. Dip tops into butter mixture and then into sugar.

Best-Ever Bran Muffins

2½ cups	all-purpose flour	625 mL
¾ cup	brown sugar	175 mL
1½ cups	natural bran	375 mL
1½ tsp	cinnamon	7 mL
1 tsp	nutmeg	5 mL
2 tsp	baking soda	10 mL
½ tsp	salt	2 mL
2	eggs	2
¾ cup	vegetable oil	175 mL
2 cups	buttermilk	500 mL
¼ cup	molasses	50 mL
1 cup	raisins (dark or yellow)	250 mL

◆ *Preheat oven to 375°F (190°C)*
◆ *18-cup muffin tin, greased*

1. In a bowl combine flour, brown sugar, bran, cinnamon, nutmeg, baking soda and salt. Make a well in the center.
2. In another bowl whisk together eggs, oil, buttermilk and molasses. Pour into flour mixture; stir just until blended. Fold in raisins.
3. Spoon batter into prepared muffin tins, filling to top. Bake in preheated oven for 20 to 25 minutes.

Carrot Pineapple Streusel Muffins

STREUSEL TOPPING		
¼ cup	lightly packed brown sugar	50 mL
¼ cup	chopped walnuts	50 mL
MUFFINS		
1	pkg (15 oz/450 g) carrot raisin loaf cake mix	1
1 cup	undrained crushed pineapple	250 mL
1	egg	1
3 tbsp	oil	45 mL

◆ *Preheat oven to 400°F (200°C)*
◆ *12-cup muffin tin, greased or paper-lined*

1. In a bowl combine sugar and walnuts; set aside.
2. In another bowl combine cake mix, pineapple, egg and oil; mix until smooth.
3. Spoon batter into prepared muffin tins, filling three-quarters full. Sprinkle with topping. Bake in preheated oven for 20 minutes.

MUFFIN STUFF: These are quick and easy to make – delicious!

Creamy Rice Muffins

2 cups	milk or water	500 mL
1 cup	rice (not instant) or 2 cups (500 mL) cooked rice	250 mL
4 tbsp	butter or margarine	60 mL
4 tbsp	granulated sugar	60 mL
2	eggs	2
1 cup	sour cream	250 mL
¾ cup	all-purpose flour	175 mL
1 tsp	baking powder	5 mL
¼ tsp	salt	1 mL

- ◆ *Preheat oven to 350°F (180°C)*
- ◆ *Muffin tin, greased*

1. In a saucepan over medium-high heat, bring milk to a boil; add rice. Cook, covered, until thick and milk is absorbed. Set aside to cool.
2. In a bowl cream together butter, sugar, eggs and sour cream. Add flour, baking powder and salt; mix well. Add cooled rice; stir just until blended.
3. Spoon batter into prepared muffin tins, filling to top. Bake in preheated oven for about 45 minutes.

MUFFIN STUFF: Delicious served warm with sour cream and sliced strawberries.

Special Carrot Puddings

¾ cup	shortening	175 mL
½ cup	brown sugar	125 mL
1	egg	1
1¼ cups	all-purpose flour	300 mL
½ tsp	baking soda	2 mL
1 tsp	baking powder	5 mL
1 tsp	salt	5 mL
1 tbsp	water	15 mL
1 tbsp	lemon juice	15 mL
1 tsp	vanilla	5 mL
2 cups	grated carrots	500 mL

- ◆ *Preheat oven to 400°F (200°C)*
- ◆ *Muffin tin, greased*

1. In a bowl combine shortening and brown sugar; mix well. Add egg, flour, baking soda, baking powder, salt, water, lemon juice, vanilla and carrots. Do not overmix.
2. Heat prepared muffin tin in oven for a few minutes. Spoon in batter, filling cups to top. Bake in preheated oven for 20 minutes.

MUFFIN STUFF: I serve these with meat dinners or with a green salad.

Carrot Plus Muffins

3 cups	all-purpose flour	750 mL
1 tsp	baking powder	5 mL
½ tsp	baking soda	2 mL
½ tsp	salt	2 mL
½ tsp	cloves	2 mL
½ tsp	nutmeg	2 mL
1 tbsp	chopped candied ginger	15 mL
½ cup	granulated sugar	125 mL
½ cup	brown sugar	125 mL
½ cup	vegetable oil	125 mL
2	eggs	2
½ cup	apricot juice or orange juice	125 mL
1	can (14 oz/425 g) apricots, drained or 8 fresh ripe apricots, reserving some slices for topping	1
1 cup	grated carrots	250 mL
1 cup	grated rutabaga	250 mL
½ cup	chopped pecans	125 mL
TOPPING (OPTIONAL)		
1	pkg (8 oz/250 g) soft cream cheese	1
¼ cup	apricot juice or orange juice	50 mL
½ cup	icing sugar	125 mL

◆ *Preheat oven to 400°F (200°C)*
◆ *Muffin tin, greased*

1. In a bowl combine 2¾ cups (675 mL) flour, baking powder, baking soda, salt, cloves and nutmeg.

2. In another bowl combine ginger and remaining flour; mix well. Add to clove mixture.

3. In another bowl combine granulated sugar, brown sugar and oil. Add eggs one at a time; whisk in juice. Pour into flour mixture, stirring just until moistened. Add apricots, carrots, rutabaga and pecans.

4. Spoon batter into prepared muffin tin, filling three-quarters full. Bake in preheated oven for 20 to 25 minutes or until toothpick inserted in center comes out clean.

5. In a bowl combine cream cheese, juice and icing sugar; mix well. Spread onto cooled muffins. Top with a slice of apricot.

MUFFIN STUFF: Rutabaga and carrots make a great combination. The end result is a dense, moist muffin.

Esther's Savory Cheese Muffins

2 cups	all-purpose flour	500 mL
3 tbsp	granulated sugar	45 mL
1 tbsp	baking powder	15 mL
½ tsp	grated lemon zest (optional)	2 mL
1	egg, slightly beaten	1
1 cup	milk	250 mL
¼ cup	melted butter or margarine	50 mL
1 cup	shredded Cheddar cheese	250 mL

◆ *Preheat oven to 425°F (220°C)*
◆ *Muffin tin, greased or paper-lined*

1. In a bowl combine flour, sugar, baking powder and lemon zest. Make a well in center of mixture.
2. In another bowl combine egg, milk and butter; whisk well. Stir into flour mixture. Reserve 2 tbsp (25 mL) cheese for topping; add remaining cheese to flour mixture. Mix until moist and blended.
3. Spoon batter into prepared muffin tin, filling three-quarters full. Sprinkle tops with reserved cheese.
4. Bake in preheated oven for 20 minutes or until golden brown.

Variations

◆ This recipe originally called for ¾ tsp (4 mL) garlic salt. I don't use it, but you might want to give it a try.
◆ You can replace the 1 cup (250 mL) milk with ½ cup (125 mL) milk and ½ cup (125 mL) plain yogurt.

Cottage Cheese Muffins

1	pkg (12 oz/375 g) dry cottage cheese	1
3 tbsp	granulated sugar	45 mL
2	eggs, slightly beaten	2
1/2 cup	melted butter or margarine	125 mL
Pinch	salt	Pinch
2 tsp	baking powder	10 mL
1 cup	all-purpose flour	250 mL

MUFFIN STUFF: Delicious served warm with sour cream and thawed frozen strawberries.

◆ *Preheat oven to 400°F (200°C)*
◆ *Muffin tin, greased*

1. In a bowl combine cottage cheese, sugar, eggs and butter; mix well. Add salt, baking powder and flour; stir just until blended.
2. Spoon batter into prepared muffin tin, filling three-quarters full. Bake in preheated oven for 20 to 25 minutes or until lightly browned.

Variation
◆ Use 2 cups (500 mL) dry cottage cheese and 1/2 cup (125 mL) creamed cottage cheese.

Parmesan Muffins

1	egg	1
1/2 cup	plain yogurt or sour cream	125 mL
1 cup	milk	250 mL
1/2 cup	melted butter or margarine	125 mL
2 1/2 cups	all-purpose flour	625 mL
1/2 cup	grated Parmesan cheese	125 mL
1/4 cup	granulated sugar	50 mL
1 tbsp	baking powder	15 mL
1 tsp	salt	5 mL
1/2 tsp	dried basil	2 mL

◆ *Preheat oven to 400°F (200°C)*
◆ *12-cup muffin tin, greased or paper-lined*

1. In a bowl combine egg, yogurt, milk and butter; whisk well.
2. In another bowl combine flour, cheese, sugar, baking powder, salt and basil. Make a well in center of mixture; pour in egg mixture. Stir just until blended.
3. Spoon batter into prepared muffin tin, dividing equally. Bake in preheated oven for about 20 minutes.

Variations
◆ Replace basil with 1/4 tsp (1 mL) rosemary. Add 4 tbsp (50 mL) yellow cornmeal to the dry ingredients.

◆ Replace basil with package of fine herbs from a store-bought pizza mix.

Chocolate Cheesecake Muffins

FILLING

1	pkg (3 oz/75 g) softened cream cheese	1
2 tbsp	granulated sugar	25 mL

MUFFINS

1 cup	all-purpose flour	250 mL
½ cup	granulated sugar	125 mL
3 tbsp	unsweetened cocoa	45 mL
2 tsp	baking powder	10 mL
½ tsp	salt	2 mL
1	egg, beaten	1
¾ cup	milk	175 mL
⅓ cup	oil	75 mL
	Icing sugar (optional)	

◆ *Preheat oven to 375°F (190°C)*
◆ *Muffin tin, greased or paper-lined*

1. In a bowl combine cream cheese and sugar; beat until light and fluffy. Set aside.
2. In another bowl combine flour, sugar, cocoa, baking powder and salt. Make a well in center of mixture.
3. In another bowl combine egg, milk and oil. Pour into flour mixture; stir just until lumpy and moist.
4. Spoon batter into prepared muffin tin, filling cups half full. Add 1 tsp (5 mL) cheese filling; top with remaining batter.
5. Bake in preheated oven for 20 minutes. Dust with icing sugar, if desired.

Chocolate Chipit Snackin' Muffins

1½ cups	all-purpose flour	375 mL
1 cup	granulated sugar	250 mL
2 tbsp	cocoa	25 mL
1 tsp	baking powder	5 mL
1 tsp	baking soda	5 mL
½ tsp	salt	2 mL
¼ cup	oil	50 mL
1 tsp	vanilla	5 mL
1 tbsp	vinegar	15 mL
1 cup	warm water	250 mL
½ cup	chocolate chips	125 mL

◆ *Preheat oven to 400°F (200°C)*
◆ *Muffin tin, paper-lined*

1. In a bowl combine flour, sugar, cocoa, baking powder, baking soda and salt. Make a well in the center. Add oil, vanilla, vinegar and warm water. Stir just until moist. Add chocolate chips.
2. Spoon batter into prepared muffin tin, filling to top. Bake in preheated oven for 15 to 20 minutes.

Variation

◆ Before putting in oven, sprinkle chocolate chips over top.

Chocolate Date Muffins

2 cups	all-purpose flour	500 mL
4 tsp	baking powder	20 mL
½ tsp	salt	2 mL
½ cup	granulated sugar	125 mL
½ cup	cocoa	125 mL
½ cup	sliced dates	125 mL
1 cup	milk	250 mL
1	egg, beaten	1
2 tbsp	shortening, melted	25 mL

♦ *Preheat oven to 350°F (180°C)*
♦ *12-cup muffin tin, greased*

1. In a bowl sift together flour, baking powder, salt, sugar and cocoa. Add dates; mix with your fingers. Add milk, egg and shortening; stir just until blended.

2. Spoon batter into prepared muffin tin, filling two-thirds full. Bake in preheated oven for 20 minutes.

Chunky Chocolate Orange Muffins

½ cup	softened butter	125 mL
1 cup	granulated sugar	250 mL
2	eggs	2
½ cup	sour cream	125 mL
	Grated zest of 2 oranges	
½ cup	orange juice	125 mL
2 cups	all-purpose flour or 2 ¼ cups (550 mL) cake and pastry flour	500 mL
1 tsp	baking powder	5 mL
½ tsp	baking soda	2 mL
3	squares semi-sweet chocolate, chopped or ½ cup (125 mL) chocolate chips	3
1	square semi-sweet chocolate, melted	1

♦ *Preheat oven to 400°F (200°C)*
♦ *Muffin tin, greased*

1. In a bowl combine butter and sugar; cream until light and fluffy. Add eggs one at a time; beat well. Add sour cream, orange zest and orange juice; mix well.

2. In another bowl combine flour, baking powder, baking soda and chopped chocolate. Add to creamed mixture; stir gently just until blended.

3. Spoon batter into prepared muffin tin, filling three-quarters full. Bake in preheated oven for 18 to 22 minutes or until top springs back when lightly touched. Set aside to cool. Drizzle with melted chocolate.

Coffee Cake Muffins

TOPPING		
1/3 cup	granulated sugar	75 mL
1 1/2 tsp	cinnamon	7 mL
1 tbsp	margarine, melted	15 mL
MUFFINS		
3 tbsp	softened butter	45 mL
3/4 cup	granulated sugar	175 mL
1	egg	1
2 cups	flour	500 mL
3 tsp	baking powder	15 mL
Pinch	salt	Pinch
3/4 cup	milk	175 mL
1 cup	raisins	250 mL

◆ *Preheat oven to 375°F (190°C)*
◆ *Muffin tin, greased or paper-lined*

1. In a bowl combine sugar, cinnamon and margarine; mix well. Set aside.
2. In another bowl beat butter. Add sugar and egg; beat well.
3. In another bowl combine flour, baking powder and salt. Add to creamed mixture alternately with milk; blend well. Fold in raisins.
4. Spoon batter into prepared muffin tin, dividing evenly. Sprinkle with topping. Bake in preheated oven for 20 minutes.

Coffee Walnut Muffins

1 tbsp	instant coffee	15 mL
1/2 cup	hot water	125 mL
1/2 cup	milk or cream	125 mL
1	egg, beaten	1
1/2 cup	melted shortening or oil	125 mL
1 1/2 cups	all-purpose flour	375 mL
3 tsp	baking powder	15 mL
1/3 cup	granulated sugar	75 mL
1 tsp	salt	5 mL
1/2 cup	chopped walnuts	125 mL

◆ *Preheat oven to 375°F (190°C)*
◆ *Muffin tin, greased*

1. In a bowl dissolve coffee in hot water. Add milk, egg and shortening; stir to combine well.
2. In another bowl combine flour, baking powder, sugar and salt. Add walnuts; stir well. Add coffee mixture; stir just until moist.
3. Spoon batter into prepared muffin tin, dividing evenly. Bake in preheated oven for 15 to 20 minutes.

Coffee-Raisin Spice Muffins

TOPPING

1 cup	icing sugar	250 mL
2 to 3 tsp	grated lemon zest	10 to 15 mL
4 to 5 tsp	lemon juice	20 to 25 mL

MUFFINS

1 cup	coffee	250 mL
1 cup	granulated sugar or packed brown sugar	250 mL
1½ cups	chopped raisins	375 mL
⅓ cup	butter or margarine or shortening	75 mL
½ tsp	ground cloves	2 mL
1 tsp	cinnamon	5 mL
1 tsp	nutmeg	5 mL
½ tsp	salt	2 mL
½ tsp	baking powder	2 mL
1 tsp	baking soda	5 mL
2 cups	all-purpose flour	500 mL

- *Preheat oven to 400°F (200°C)*
- *Muffin tin, paper-lined*

1. In a bowl combine icing sugar, lemon zest and lemon juice; mix well. Set aside.
2. In a saucepan over medium-high heat combine coffee, sugar, raisins, butter, cloves, cinnamon and nutmeg; bring to a boil. Cook for 3 minutes. Set aside to cool.
3. When cool add salt, baking powder, baking soda and flour; mix well.
4. Spoon batter into prepared muffin tin, filling two-thirds full. Bake in preheated oven for 15 to 20 minutes or until toothpick inserted in center comes out clean. Set aside to cool. Drizzle with topping.

Date Muffins

⅓ cup	shortening	75 mL
1	egg, beaten	1
¾ cup	milk	175 mL
2 cups	all-purpose flour	500 mL
3 tsp	baking powder	15 mL
½ tsp	salt	2 mL
1 cup	chopped pitted dates	250 mL

- *Preheat oven to 400°F (200°C)*
- *Muffin tin, greased*

1. In a bowl cream shortening. Add egg and milk; beat well.
2. In another bowl sift together flour, baking powder and salt. Add to creamed mixture; blend well. Add dates.
3. Spoon batter into prepared muffin tin, dividing evenly. Bake in preheated oven for about 25 minutes.

Variation
- For sweet muffins add ¼ cup (50 mL) sugar.

Sweet Raisin Muffins

1 cup	raisins	250 mL
1 tbsp	grated orange zest	15 mL
1 cup	boiling water	250 mL
1/2 tsp	baking soda	2 mL
1/2 cup	granulated sugar	125 mL
2 tbsp	margarine	25 mL
1	egg	1
1¾ cups	all-purpose flour	425 mL
2 tsp	baking powder	10 mL
1/2 tsp	cinnamon	2 mL
1/4 tsp	nutmeg	1 mL

♦ *Preheat oven to 425°F (220°C)*
♦ *12-cup muffin tin, greased*

1. In a bowl combine raisins and orange zest. Add boiling water and baking soda. Set aside to cool.
2. In another bowl cream together sugar and margarine. Add egg; beat well. Add raisin mixture; beat well.
3. In another bowl combine flour, baking powder, cinnamon and nutmeg. Fold into creamed mixture; stir just until moist.
4. Spoon batter into prepared muffin tin, filling three-quarters full. Bake in preheated oven for 20 minutes or until toothpick inserted in center comes out clean.

Quick Bake Muffins

1 cup	self-rising flour	250 mL
3 tbsp	mayonnaise	45 mL
1/2 cup	milk	125 mL

HINT: If you don't have self-rising flour, use 1½ tsp (7 mL) baking powder to 1 cup (250 mL) all-purpose flour.

♦ *Preheat oven to 400°F (200°C)*
♦ *Muffin tin, greased or paper-lined*

1. In a bowl combine flour and mayonnaise. Add milk, a little at a time, stirring just until moistened.
2. Form dough into balls; place into prepared muffin tin. Bake in preheated oven for about 20 minutes.

Jam-Filled Muffins

1½ cups	all-purpose flour	375 mL
¼ cup	granulated sugar	50 mL
2 tsp	baking powder	10 mL
½ tsp	baking soda	2 mL
½ tsp	salt	2 mL
1	egg	1
½ tsp	vanilla	2 mL
¼ cup	butter or margarine, melted	50 mL
1 cup	plain yogurt	250 mL
¼ cup	milk	50 mL
	Jam or jelly	
¼ cup	nuts (optional)	50 mL

- *Preheat oven to 425°F (220°C)*
- *Muffin tin, greased*

1. In a large bowl combine flour, sugar, baking powder, baking soda and salt.
2. In another bowl beat together egg and vanilla. Add butter, yogurt and milk; mix well. Add to flour mixture; stir just until blended.
3. Spoon batter into prepared muffin tin, filling half full. Add 1 tsp (5 mL) of your favorite jam or jelly to each; top with remaining batter. Add nuts, if desired. Bake in preheated oven for 15 to 20 minutes.

Lemon Tea Muffins

1 cup	cake and pastry flour or all-purpose flour	250 mL
½ cup	granulated sugar	125 mL
1½ tsp	baking powder	7 mL
1 tsp	salt	5 mL
2	eggs	2
½ cup	lemon juice	125 mL
¼ cup	melted margarine	50 mL
2 tsp	grated lemon zest	10 mL
TOPPING		
¼ cup	melted margarine	50 mL
1 tbsp	lemon juice	15 mL
	Granulated sugar	

- *Preheat oven to 375°F (190°C)*
- *Muffin tin, greased or paper-lined*

1. In a bowl combine flour, sugar, baking powder and salt.
2. In another bowl whisk together eggs, lemon juice, margarine and lemon zest. Add to flour mixture; stir just until moist and blended.
3. Spoon batter into prepared muffin tin, filling to top. Bake in preheated oven for 15 to 20 minutes. Remove muffins from pan while still warm.
4. In a bowl combine margarine and lemon juice. Dip muffin tops in juice mixture; dip in sugar.

The Muffin Lady's Special Mincemeat Muffins

¾ cup	oil	175 mL
1 cup	granulated sugar	250 mL
2	eggs, beaten	2
2 cups	all-purpose flour	500 mL
1 cup	milk	250 mL
1 cup	all-bran cereal or whole bran cereal	250 mL
2 tsp	baking powder	10 mL
1 tsp	salt	5 mL
1 tsp	baking soda	5 mL
1 cup	mincemeat	250 mL

◆ *Preheat oven to 350°F (180°C)*
◆ *24-cup muffin tin, greased or paper-lined*

1. In a bowl combine oil, sugar, eggs, flour, milk, cereal, baking powder, salt, baking soda and mincemeat; mix well.
2. Spoon batter into prepared muffin tin, filling to top. Bake in preheated oven for 20 to 25 minutes.

MUFFIN STUFF: If you don't want to use all the batter, it can be stored in the refrigerator for about 2 weeks.

Golden Oatmeal Muffins

1 cup	rolled oats or quick-cooking oatmeal	250 mL
1 cup	buttermilk or sour cream	250 mL
½ cup	vegetable oil or melted shortening	125 mL
½ cup	firmly packed brown sugar	125 mL
1	egg, beaten	1
1 cup	all-purpose flour	250 mL
1 tsp	baking powder	5 mL
½ tsp	baking soda	2 mL
1 tsp	salt	5 mL

◆ *Preheat oven to 400°F (200°C)*
◆ *Muffin tin, greased*

1. In a bowl combine oats and buttermilk; let stand for 5 minutes. Add oil, brown sugar and egg.
2. In another bowl combine flour, baking powder, baking soda and salt. Add to oat mixture, stirring just until moistened.
3. Spoon batter into prepared muffin tin, filling to top. Bake in preheated oven for 15 to 20 minutes or until golden brown.

Peanut Butter Muffins

1/3 cup + 2 tsp	self-rising flour	75 mL + 10 mL
1 tbsp	superfine sugar	15 mL
1/4 cup	skim milk	50 mL
1	egg, lightly beaten	1
3 tbsp	chunky-style peanut butter, room temperature	45 mL
1 tsp	margarine, melted	5 mL

MUFFIN STUFF: These muffins are great served with any flavor jam.

♦ *Preheat oven to 400°F (200°C)*
♦ *Muffin tin, paper-lined*

1. In a bowl sift together flour and sugar. Add milk, egg, peanut butter and margarine; stir just until blended (batter will be lumpy).
2. Spoon batter into prepared muffin tin, filling three-quarters full. Bake in preheated oven for 20 minutes or until toothpick inserted in center comes out clean.

Peanut Butter Crunch Muffins

TOPPING		
3 tbsp	peanut butter	45 mL
4 tbsp	granulated sugar	60 mL
2 tbsp	all-purpose flour	25 mL
1/8 tsp	salt	0.5 mL
MUFFINS		
2 cups	all-purpose flour	500 mL
1 tbsp	baking powder	15 mL
1/2 tsp	salt	2 mL
2 tbsp	granulated sugar	25 mL
1	egg, beaten	1
1 cup	milk	250 mL
1/3 cup	melted butter or margarine	75 mL

♦ *Preheat oven to 400°F (200°C)*
♦ *Muffin tin, greased*

1. In a bowl combine peanut butter, sugar, flour and salt; mix with a fork. Set aside.
2. In another bowl combine flour, baking powder, salt and sugar. Make a well in the center.
3. In another bowl whisk together egg, milk and butter. Add to dry ingredients; stir quickly just until blended.
4. Spoon batter into prepared muffin tin, filling two-thirds full. Sprinkle with topping. Bake in preheated oven for 20 minutes.

Peanut Butter Jelly Muffins

1½ cups	all-purpose flour	375 mL
½ cup	brown sugar	125 mL
1 tsp	baking powder	5 mL
½ tsp	baking soda	2 mL
½ tsp	salt	2 mL
½ cup	smooth peanut butter	125 mL
2	eggs, beaten	2
¾ cup	milk	175 mL
1 tsp	vanilla	5 mL
4 tbsp	margarine, melted	60 mL
	Grape jelly or apricot jam	

◆ *Preheat oven to 375°F (190°C)*
◆ *Muffin tin, greased*

1. In a bowl sift together flour, brown sugar, baking powder, baking soda and salt. Make a well in the center.
2. In another bowl combine peanut butter and eggs; beat well. Add milk, vanilla and margarine; mix thoroughly. Add to dry ingredients; mix until moist.
3. Spoon batter into prepared muffin tin, filling three-quarters full. Make an indentation in the center of each; spoon 1 tsp (5 mL) either grape jelly or apricot jam into each muffin. Bake in preheated oven for about 20 minutes.

MUFFIN STUFF: The contrasting colors of grape and apricot make a sweet, colorful arrangement.

Pecan Muffins

1½ cups	all-purpose flour	375 mL
½ cup	granulated sugar	125 mL
½ cup	chopped pecans	125 mL
2 tsp	baking powder	10 mL
½ tsp	salt	2 mL
1	egg, slightly beaten	1
½ cup	milk	125 mL
¼ cup	vegetable oil	50 mL

◆ *Preheat oven to 400°F (200°C)*
◆ *Muffin tin, greased or paper-lined*

1. In a bowl combine flour, sugar, pecans, baking powder and salt. Make a well in the center.
2. In another bowl combine egg, milk and oil. Add to dry ingredients; stir just until moist.
3. Spoon batter into prepared muffin tin, filling two-thirds full. Bake in preheated oven for 15 to 20 minutes.

Mom's Old-Fashioned Oatmeal Muffins

1½ cups	quick oatmeal	375 mL
1 cup	all-purpose flour	250 mL
1 tsp	baking powder	5 mL
1 tsp	baking soda	5 mL
½ tsp	salt	2 mL
1 tsp	cinnamon	5 mL
¾ cup	brown sugar	175 mL
1	egg, lightly beaten	1
¼ cup	oil	50 mL
1 cup	plain yogurt	250 mL
½ cup	raisins	125 mL

◆ *Preheat oven to 350°F (180°C)*
◆ *Muffin tin, greased*

1. In a bowl combine oatmeal, flour, baking powder, baking soda, salt, cinnamon and brown sugar. Make a well in the center.
2. In another bowl, whisk together egg, oil and yogurt. Add to dry ingredients; stir just until blended. Fold in raisins.
3. Spoon batter into prepared muffin tin. Bake in preheated oven for 20 to 25 minutes.

Esther's Famous Poppyseed Muffins

¼ cup	vegetable oil	50 mL
¾ cup	granulated sugar	175 mL
2	eggs	2
½ cup	poppy seeds	125 mL
1 cup	sour cream	250 mL
¼ cup	milk	50 mL
2 cups	all-purpose flour	500 mL
½ tsp	baking soda	2 mL
2 tsp	baking powder	10 mL
½ tsp	salt	2 mL

◆ *Preheat oven to 425°F (220°C)*
◆ *12-cup muffin tin, paper-lined*

1. In a bowl cream together oil, sugar and eggs. Add poppy seeds, sour cream, milk, flour, baking soda, baking powder and salt. Stir just until moist and still lumpy. The mixture will be quite thick and heavy.
2. Spoon batter into prepared muffin tin, filling to top. Bake in preheated oven for 15 to 20 minutes or until toothpick inserted in center comes out clean.

Poppyseed Muffins

1 cup	milk	250 mL
½ cup	poppy seeds	125 mL
¼ cup	butter or margarine	50 mL
3 tbsp	granulated sugar	45 mL
1	egg	1
1 tsp	vanilla	5 mL
2 cups	all-purpose flour	500 mL
3 tsp	baking powder	15 mL
¾ tsp	salt	4 mL

MUFFIN STUFF: Here is another version of poppy seed muffins that I know you'll enjoy.

◆ *Preheat oven to 400°F (200°C)*
◆ *Muffin tin, greased*

1. In a bowl combine milk and poppy seeds. Let stand for about 10 minutes.
2. In another bowl combine butter, sugar and egg; beat well. Add vanilla; blend thoroughly. Add poppy seed mixture.
3. In another bowl combine flour, baking powder and salt; mix thoroughly. Make a well in the center. Add liquid ingredients; stir just until moist.
4. Spoon batter into prepared muffin tin, filling three-quarters full. Bake in preheated oven for 20 to 25 minutes. Serve warm.

Pumpkin Muffins

1	can (14 oz/398 mL) pumpkin	1
4	eggs	4
1½ cups	granulated sugar	375 mL
1½ cups	oil	375 mL
3 cups	all-purpose flour	750 mL
3 tsp	cinnamon	15 mL
2 tsp	baking soda	10 mL
2 tsp	baking powder	10 mL
1 tsp	salt	5 mL
1 cup	raisins	250 mL

MUFFIN STUFF: Most of the time I try to reduce the amount of sugar and oil used to 1 cup (250 mL) or less.

◆ *Preheat oven to 400°F (200°C)*
◆ *Muffin tin, greased*

1. In a bowl combine pumpkin and eggs. Add sugar and oil; mix well.
2. In another bowl combine flour, cinnamon, baking soda, baking powder, salt and raisins. Add to pumpkin mixture, stirring just until blended.
3. Spoon batter into prepared muffin tin, filling to top. Bake in preheated oven for 20 to 25 minutes.

The Muffin Lady's Famous Rhubarb Muffins

1½ cups	brown sugar	375 mL
¼ cup	oil	50 mL
2	eggs	2
2 tsp	vanilla	10 mL
1 cup	buttermilk	250 mL
1½ cups	finely diced rhubarb	375 mL
½ cup	chopped walnuts or pecans	125 mL
2½ cups	all-purpose flour	625 mL
1 tsp	baking powder	5 mL
1 tsp	baking soda	5 mL
½ tsp	salt	2 mL
TOPPING		
⅓ cup	granulated sugar	75 mL
1½ tsp	cinnamon	7 mL
1 tbsp	margarine, melted	15 mL

- ◆ *Preheat oven to 425°F (220°C)*
- ◆ *Muffin tin, greased or paper-lined*

1. In a bowl whisk together brown sugar, oil, eggs and vanilla; mix well. Add buttermilk, rhubarb and walnuts.
2. In another bowl combine flour, baking powder, baking soda and salt. Add to rhubarb mixture; stir just until moist.
3. In another bowl combine sugar, cinnamon and margarine.
4. Spoon batter into prepared muffin tin, filling three-quarters full. Sprinkle with topping. Bake in preheated oven for about 20 minutes.

Raisin Muffins

1 cup	raisins	250 mL
1½ cups	water	375 mL
⅔ cup	brown sugar	160 mL
½ cup	shortening	125 mL
1	egg, beaten	1
1 tsp	vanilla	5 mL
1½ cups	all-purpose flour	375 mL
1 tsp	salt	5 mL
1 tsp	baking soda	5 mL
1 tsp	baking powder	5 mL

- ◆ *Preheat oven to 350°F (180°C)*
- ◆ *Muffin tin, greased or paper-lined*

1. In a saucepan over medium-high heat, combine raisins and water; bring to a boil. Cook for 20 minutes. Set aside to cool (keep in water).
2. In a bowl cream together brown sugar, shortening and egg. Add cooled raisins with water and vanilla.
3. In another bowl sift together flour, salt, baking soda and baking powder. Add to creamed mixture; stir just until blended.
4. Spoon batter into prepared muffin tin. Bake in preheated oven for about 20 minutes.

Spicy Raisin Muffins

1½ cups	raisins	375 mL
1 cup	water	250 mL
½ cup	brown sugar	125 mL
½ cup	butter or margarine	125 mL
1	egg, beaten	1
1½ cups	all-purpose flour	375 mL
1 tsp	baking soda	5 mL
¼ tsp	mace	1 mL
1 tsp	cinnamon	5 mL
¼ tsp	cloves	1 mL

- *Preheat oven to 350°F (180°C)*
- *16-cup muffin tin, greased or paper-lined*

1. In a saucepan over medium-high heat, bring raisins and water to a boil. Simmer for 20 minutes. Set aside to cool. Retain ¾ cup (175 mL) water; discard rest.
2. In a bowl cream together brown sugar and butter. Add egg and raisin water; beat well. Add raisins, flour, baking soda, mace, cinnamon and cloves; stir just until blended.
3. Spoon batter into prepared muffin tin, filling to top. Bake in preheated oven for about 15 minutes.

Raisin Nut Muffins

½ cup	softened butter	125 mL
1 cup	granulated sugar	250 mL
3	eggs	3
2 cups	all-purpose flour	500 mL
2 tsp	baking powder	10 mL
¼ tsp	nutmeg	1 mL
⅔ cup	milk	150 mL
1 cup	chopped walnuts	250 mL
1 cup	raisins, dredged in flour	250 mL

- *Preheat oven to 400°F (200°C)*
- *Muffin tin, greased or paper-lined*

1. In a bowl cream butter. Add sugar; beat slowly until well blended.
2. In another bowl beat eggs until light. Add to creamed mixture.
3. In another bowl sift together flour, baking powder and nutmeg. Add to batter alternately with milk; mix well. Fold in walnuts and raisins.
4. Spoon batter into prepared muffin tin, filling two-thirds full. Bake in preheated oven for 15 to 20 minutes.

Rice Pudding Muffins

1½ cups	all-purpose flour	375 mL
¼ cup	granulated sugar	50 mL
1½ tsp	baking powder	7 mL
½ tsp	baking soda	2 mL
¼ tsp	salt	1 mL
1 tsp	cinnamon	5 mL
1 tsp	nutmeg	5 mL
1 cup	cooked white rice, cooled	250 mL
1	egg	1
2 tbsp	butter, melted	25 mL
1¼ cups	buttermilk	300 mL
	Icing sugar	

◆ *Preheat oven to 400°F (200°C)*
◆ *Muffin tin, greased*

1. In a bowl combine flour, sugar, baking powder, baking soda, salt, cinnamon and nutmeg. Add rice.
2. In another bowl whisk together egg, butter and buttermilk. Add to flour mixture; stir just until moist.
3. Spoon batter into prepared muffin tin, dividing evenly. Bake in preheated oven for 15 to 20 minutes. Remove from tins; sprinkle with icing sugar.

Self-Iced Muffins

1 cup	brown sugar	250 mL
1 cup	margarine	250 mL
2 cups	all-purpose flour	500 mL
1	egg, beaten	1
1 cup	milk	250 mL
1 tsp	vinegar	5 mL
1 tsp	baking soda	5 mL
1 cup	dates, dredged in flour	250 mL
1 cup	raisins, dredged in flour	250 mL
1 tsp	cinnamon	5 mL
1 tsp	vanilla	5 mL

◆ *Preheat oven to 375°F (190°C)*
◆ *Muffin tin, paper-lined*

1. In a bowl combine sugar and margarine; beat well. Add flour. Set aside ¾ cup (175 mL) of this mixture for topping.
2. To remaining mixture add egg, milk, vinegar and baking soda; combine well. Add dates, raisins, cinnamon and vanilla.
3. Spoon batter into prepared muffin tin, filling two-thirds full. Sprinkle with reserved mixture. Bake in preheated oven for 20 to 30 minutes.

Southern Biscuit Muffins

2½ cups	all-purpose flour	625 mL
¼ cup	granulated sugar	50 mL
1½ tbsp	baking powder	20 mL
¾ cup	chilled butter or margarine	175 mL
1 cup	cold milk	250 mL

MUFFIN STUFF: Delicious with jam, jelly or honey, these muffins are just like baking powder biscuits.

♦ *Preheat oven to 400°F (200°C)*
♦ *12-cup muffin tin, greased*

1. In a bowl combine flour, sugar and baking powder. Add butter; mix until crumbly. Add milk; stir just until moist.
2. Spoon batter into prepared muffin tin, dividing evenly. Bake in preheated oven for 20 minutes or until golden brown.

Sour Cream Raisin Bran Muffins

4 oz	butter or margarine	125 g
¾ cup	brown sugar	175 mL
1	egg, slightly beaten	1
1 cup	all-purpose flour	250 mL
½ tsp	baking soda	2 mL
½ cup	bran flour or natural bran	125 mL
1 cup	sour cream	250 mL
1 tsp	vanilla	5 mL
¾ cup	raisins	175 mL

♦ *Preheat oven to 375°F (190°C)*
♦ *Muffin tin, greased or paper-lined*

1. In a bowl cream together butter, brown sugar and egg. Add all-purpose flour, baking soda, bran flour, sour cream, vanilla and raisins; stir just until moist and blended.
2. Spoon batter into prepared muffin tin, filling to top. Bake in preheated oven for 20 to 25 minutes.

Wheat Germ Muffins

2 cups	all-purpose flour	500 mL
2 tbsp	baking powder	25 mL
1 tsp	baking soda	5 mL
1½ cups wheat germ		375 mL
1 cup	firmly packed brown sugar	250 mL
2	eggs	2
1½ cups milk		375 mL
½ cup	vegetable oil	125 mL

◆ *Preheat oven to 400°F (200°C)*
◆ *Muffin tin, greased or paper-lined*

1. In a bowl combine flour, baking powder, baking soda, wheat germ and brown sugar; mix until well blended.
2. In another bowl whisk together eggs, milk and oil. Pour into dry ingredients; stir just until blended.
3. Spoon batter into prepared muffin tin, dividing evenly. Bake in preheated oven for 15 to 20 minutes.

Wholesome Wheat Germ Muffins

1½ cups all-purpose flour		375 mL
¼ cup	brown sugar	50 mL
3 tsp	baking powder	15 mL
½ tsp	salt	2 mL
⅔ cup	wheat germ	160 mL
½ cup	raisins	125 mL
1 cup	milk	250 mL
1	egg	1
2 tbsp	melted margarine, cooled	25 mL

◆ *Preheat oven to 400°F (200°C)*
◆ *12-cup muffin tin, greased*

1. In a bowl combine flour, brown sugar, baking powder and salt; mix well. Add wheat germ and raisins.
2. In another bowl whisk together milk, egg and margarine. Add to dry ingredients; stir just until moistened. Do not overmix.
3. Spoon batter into prepared muffin tin, filling three-quarters full. Bake in preheated oven for about 20 minutes.

> **MUFFIN STUFF:** Here's another wheat germ recipe. The raisins add a nice sweetness.

Wholesome Healthy Muffins

continued on next page

Basic Bran Muffin

1 cup	all-purpose flour	250 mL
½ cup	packed brown sugar	125 mL
¼ tsp	salt	1 mL
1½ tsp	baking powder	7 mL
½ tsp	baking soda	2 mL
1½ cups	natural bran	375 mL
½ cup	raisins	125 mL
½ cup	chopped nuts (optional)	125 mL
2	eggs, beaten	2
1 cup	milk	250 mL
¼ cup	molasses	50 mL
½ cup	margarine, melted	125 mL

- *Preheat oven to 400°F (200°C)*
- *12-cup muffin tin, greased or paper-lined*

1. In a bowl combine flour, brown sugar, salt, baking powder, baking soda, bran, raisins and nuts. Make a well in the center.
2. In another bowl beat together eggs, milk, molasses and margarine. Add to flour mixture; stir just until moistened. Do not overmix (batter will be lumpy).
3. Spoon batter into prepared muffin tins, dividing evenly. Bake in preheated oven for 18 to 20 minutes.

Variations

- *Banana Bran:* Replace molasses and raisins with 1 cup (250 mL) mashed bananas. Decrease milk to ½ cup (125 mL) and add 1 tsp (5 mL) cinnamon.

- *Applesauce Bran:* Replace molasses with ¾ cup (175 mL) applesauce. Decrease milk to ½ cup (125 mL) and add 1 tsp (5 mL) cinnamon or nutmeg.

- *Carrot Bran:* Add 1 cup (250 mL) grated carrots and 1 tsp (5 mL) cinnamon to dry ingredients.

All-Bran Cereal Muffins

1 cup	all-bran cereal	250 mL
1 cup	milk	250 mL
1	egg	1
¼ cup	melted shortening	50 mL
½ cup	raisins or chopped dates	125 mL
1 cup	all-purpose flour	250 mL
2½ tsp	baking powder	12 mL
½ tsp	salt	2 mL
¼ cup	granulated sugar	50 mL
1 tsp	cinnamon	5 m L
½ tsp	nutmeg	2 mL

- *Preheat oven to 400°F (200°C)*
- *12-muffin tin, greased*

1. In a bowl combine cereal and milk; mix well. Let stand until milk is absorbed. Add egg and shortening; beat well. Stir in raisins.
2. In another bowl sift together flour, baking powder, salt, sugar, cinnamon and nutmeg. Add to cereal mixture; blend well.
3. Spoon batter into prepared muffin tin, dividing evenly. Bake in preheated oven for 20 to 25 minutes.

Apple Bran Muffins

1 cup	all-purpose flour	250 mL
1 tsp	baking soda	5 mL
1 tsp	baking powder	5 mL
½ tsp	salt	2 mL
3 tbsp	brown sugar	45 mL
1 cup	natural bran	250 mL
1	egg	1
1 cup	buttermilk or sour milk	250 mL
¼ cup	vegetable oil	50 mL
2 tbsp	molasses	25 mL
1	small apple, peeled and finely chopped	1

- *Preheat oven to 400°F (200°C)*
- *12-cup muffin tin, greased*

1. In a bowl combine flour, baking soda, baking powder, salt and sugar; mix well. Add bran; stir well with a fork. Make a well in the center.
2. In another bowl beat together egg, buttermilk, oil and molasses; add apple. Pour into dry ingredients; stir just until blended.
3. Spoon batter into prepared muffin tin, dividing evenly. Bake in preheated oven for about 15 minutes.

Applesauce Bran Muffins

3 cups	applesauce	750 mL
2 cups	buttermilk or sour milk	500 mL
1 cup	packed brown sugar	250 mL
¾ cup	molasses	175 mL
¾ cup	vegetable oil	175 mL
1 tbsp	vanilla	15 mL
3	eggs	3
3 cups	natural bran	750 mL
6 cups	all-purpose flour	1.5 L
1 tbsp	baking soda	15 mL
1 tbsp	cinnamon	15 mL
1 tbsp	salt	15 mL
3 cups	raisins or chopped dates	750 mL

- *Preheat oven to 375°F (190°C)*
- *Muffin tin, greased*

1. In a bowl whisk together applesauce, buttermilk, brown sugar, molasses, oil, vanilla and eggs. Stir in bran; let stand for 5 to 10 minutes.
2. In another bowl combine flour, baking soda, cinnamon and salt; mix well. Add applesauce mixture; stir just until blended. Fold in raisins.
3. Spoon batter into prepared muffin tin, filling to top (makes about 36 muffins; bake in batches). Bake in preheated oven for about 25 minutes.

Easy Breakfast Bran Muffins

1 cup	natural bran	250 mL
1/2 cup	granulated sugar	125 mL
1 cup	all-purpose flour	250 mL
1 tsp	baking powder	5 mL
1 tsp	baking soda	5 mL
1/2 tsp	salt	2 mL
1	egg	1
6 tbsp	oil	90 mL
1 cup	boiling water	250 mL
1/3 cup	raisins or dates	75 mL

◆ *Preheat oven to 375°F (190°C)*
◆ *Muffin tin, paper-lined*

1. In a bowl combine bran, sugar, flour, baking powder, baking soda and salt. Make a well in the center.
2. In another bowl beat together egg and oil. Add raisins and boiling water; mix well. Pour into dry ingredients; stir just until blended.
3. Spoon batter into prepared muffin tin. Bake in preheated oven for about 20 to 25 minutes.

Surprise Brownie Muffins

1 3/4 cups	all-purpose flour	425 mL
5 tsp	baking powder	25 mL
1 tsp	salt	5 mL
1 cup	granulated sugar (can be reduced to 1/2 cup/ 125 mL or to taste)	250 mL
2/3 cup	cocoa or carob powder	150 mL
1 1/4 cups	natural bran	300 mL
2	eggs, beaten	2
1 cup	milk	250 mL
1/2 tsp	vanilla	2 mL
2/3 cup	oil	150 mL

◆ *Preheat oven to 350°F (180°C)*
◆ *Muffin tin, paper-lined*

1. In a bowl combine flour, baking powder, salt, sugar, cocoa powder and bran. Make a well in the center.
2. In another bowl combine eggs, milk, vanilla and oil; mix well. Pour into dry ingredients; stir just until moist and blended.
3. Spoon batter into prepared muffin tin. Bake in preheated oven for 18 to 20 minutes.

Buttermilk Bran Muffins

1/3 cup	shortening	75 mL
1/2 cup	firmly packed brown sugar	125 mL
1	egg	1
1 cup	all-purpose flour	250 mL
1 tsp	baking powder	5 mL
1/2 tsp	baking soda	2 mL
1 tsp	salt	5 mL
3 cups	shredded bran cereal	750 mL
1 cup	buttermilk	250 mL

♦ *Preheat oven to 400°F (200°C)*
♦ *12-cup muffin tin, greased or paper-lined*

1. In a bowl cream together shortening, brown sugar and egg.
2. In another bowl sift together flour, baking powder, baking soda, salt and bran; mix well. Add to creamed mixture alternately with buttermilk; stir just until blended.
3. Spoon batter into prepared muffin tin, filling to top. Bake in preheated oven for about 20 minutes.

Spiced Carrot Bran Muffins

1 cup	all-bran cereal	250 mL
1 cup	buttermilk or sour milk	250 mL
1	egg, beaten	1
3/4 cup	finely shredded carrots (about 2 medium)	175 mL
3 tbsp	oil	45 mL
1 cup	all-purpose flour	250 mL
1/4 cup	packed brown sugar	50 mL
2 tsp	baking powder	10 mL
3/4 tsp	cinnamon or allspice	4 mL
1/2 tsp	baking soda	2 mL
1/2 tsp	salt	2 mL

♦ *Preheat oven to 400°F (200°C)*
♦ *12-cup muffin tin, greased or paper-lined*

1. In a bowl combine bran cereal and buttermilk. Let stand for about 5 minutes. Add egg, carrots and oil; mix well.
2. In another bowl combine flour, brown sugar, baking powder, cinnamon, baking soda, salt and bran mixture; stir just until blended.
3. Spoon batter into prepared muffin tin, dividing evenly. Bake in preheated oven for 15 to 20 minutes or until browned.

Crunchy Cheddar Bran Muffins

1 cup	all-bran cereal	250 mL
1¼ cups	buttermilk or sour milk	300 mL
¼ cup	shortening	50 mL
⅓ cup	granulated sugar	75 mL
1	egg	1
1½ cups	all-purpose flour	375 mL
1½ tsp	baking powder	7 mL
½ tsp	salt	2 mL
¼ tsp	baking soda	1 mL
1 cup	shredded sharp Cheddar cheese	250 mL

- ◆ *Preheat oven to 400°F (200°C)*
- ◆ *12-cup muffin tin, greased*

1. In a bowl cover bran with buttermilk. Let stand until softened.
2. In another bowl combine shortening and sugar; cream until light and fluffy. Beat in egg.
3. In another bowl sift together flour, baking powder, salt and baking soda. Add to creamed mixture alternately with bran mixture; stir in cheese.
4. Spoon batter into prepared muffin tin, filling three-quarters full. Bake in preheated oven for about 30 minutes.

Chocolate Chip Bran Muffins

½ cup	softened shortening	125 mL
⅔ cup	granulated sugar	150 mL
1	egg	1
1 tsp	vanilla	5 mL
1½ cups	all-purpose flour	375 mL
½ tsp	baking soda	2 mL
3 tbsp	cocoa	45 mL
½ tsp	salt	2 mL
1 cup	buttermilk or sour milk	250 mL
½ cup	bran cereal	125 mL
½ cup	chocolate or carob chips	125 mL

- ◆ *Preheat oven to 350°F (180°C)*
- ◆ *12-cup muffin tin, paper-lined*

1. In a bowl cream together shortening, sugar, egg and vanilla.
2. In another bowl combine flour, baking soda, cocoa and salt. Add to creamed mixture alternately with buttermilk; stir just until blended. Add bran cereal and chocolate chips; stir well.
3. Spoon batter into prepared muffin tin, filling to top. Bake in preheated oven for about 25 minutes.

Cream Cheese Bran Muffins

TOPPING		
1	pkg (8 oz/250 g) softened cream cheese	1
1/4 cup	granulated sugar	50 mL
1	egg, beaten	1
MUFFINS		
1 1/4 cups	all-bran cereal	300 mL
1 cup	milk	250 mL
1/4 cup	vegetable oil	50 mL
1	egg, beaten	1
1 1/4 cups	all-purpose flour	300 mL
1/2 cup	granulated sugar	125 mL
1 tbsp	baking powder	15 mL
1/2 tsp	salt	2 mL
1/2 cup	raisins	125 mL

◆ *Preheat oven to 375°F (190°C)*
◆ *Muffin tin, greased or paper-lined*

1. In a bowl combine cream cheese, sugar and egg; mix until blended well. Set aside.
2. In another bowl combine bran cereal and milk. Let stand for 2 minutes.
3. In another bowl combine oil and egg. Add to cereal mixture; mix well. Add flour, sugar, baking powder and salt; stir just until moist and blended. Fold in raisins.
4. Spoon batter into prepared muffin tin, filling three-quarters full. Drop 1 tbsp (15 mL) topping onto each muffin. Bake in preheated oven for 25 minutes.

All-Bran Sour Cream Muffins

1 cup	unsifted pastry flour	250 mL
3 tsp	baking powder	15 mL
1/2 tsp	baking soda	2 mL
1/2 tsp	salt	2 mL
1/4 cup	packed brown sugar	50 mL
3/4 cup	all-bran cereal	175 mL
2	egg whites	2
1/4 cup	dark molasses	50 mL
3/4 cup	sour cream	175 mL
3 tbsp	vegetable oil	45 mL

◆ *Preheat oven to 425°F (220°C)*
◆ *12-cup muffin tin, greased*

1. In a bowl sift together flour, baking powder, baking soda and salt. Add brown sugar and cereal; blend well.
2. In another bowl combine egg whites, molasses, sour cream and oil; beat well. Add to flour mixture; stir just until blended.
3. Spoon batter into prepared muffin tin, filling three-quarters full. Bake in preheated oven for 15 to 20 minutes.

Double Bran Fig Muffins

¾ cup	whole wheat flour	175 mL
½ cup	natural bran	125 mL
½ cup	oat bran	125 mL
⅓ cup	wheat germ	75 mL
⅓ cup	packed brown sugar	75 mL
1 tsp	baking powder	5 mL
½ tsp	baking soda	2 mL
½ tsp	cinnamon	2 mL
¼ tsp	salt	1 mL
1	egg	1
1 cup	buttermilk	250 mL
¼ cup	vegetable oil	50 mL
1 cup	chopped figs	250 mL

◆ *Preheat oven to 375°F (190°C)*
◆ *8-cup muffin tin, greased*

1. In a bowl combine whole wheat flour, natural bran, oat bran, wheat germ, brown sugar, baking powder, baking soda, cinnamon and salt. Make a well in the center.

2. In another bowl whisk together egg, buttermilk and oil. Set aside 2 tbsp (25 mL) figs; add remaining figs to egg mixture. Pour into dry ingredients; stir just until blended. Do not overmix.

3. Spoon batter into prepared muffin tin; top with reserved figs. Bake in preheated oven for 20 to 25 minutes.

Surprise-Inside Muffins

1½ cups	all-purpose flour	375 mL
2½ tsp	baking powder	12 mL
¼ tsp	salt	1 mL
1 cup	oat bran	250 mL
½ cup	packed light brown sugar	125 mL
1 cup	milk	250 mL
⅓ cup	vegetable oil	75 mL
2	eggs, lightly beaten	2
1 tsp	vanilla	5 mL
1	pkg (3 oz/75 g) cream cheese, cut into 12 pieces	1
¾ cup	apricot-pineapple jam	175 mL

◆ *Preheat oven to 425°F (220°C)*
◆ *12-cup muffin tin, greased*

1. In a bowl sift together flour, baking powder and salt. Add oat bran and brown sugar. Set aside.

2. In another bowl combine milk, oil, eggs and vanilla. Add to dry ingredients; stir just until moist.

3. Spoon batter into prepared muffin tin, filling one-third full. Add 1 tbsp (15 mL) jam to each; top with 1 piece cream cheese. Spoon remaining batter over jam and cheese, dividing evenly. Bake in preheated oven for 14 to 16 minutes or until browned.

> **MUFFIN STUFF:** These muffins are perfect for a special brunch or buffet.

Honey Bran Muffins

½ cup	natural bran	125 mL
½ cup	toasted wheat germ	125 mL
½ cup	raisins	125 mL
1 cup	whole wheat flour	250 mL
2½ tsp	baking powder	12 mL
½ tsp	baking soda	2 mL
½ tsp	salt	2 mL
¼ tsp	cinnamon	1 mL
Pinch	nutmeg	Pinch
Pinch	allspice	Pinch
1	egg	1
3 tbsp	molasses	45 mL
¼ cup	liquid honey	50 mL
⅓ cup	vegetable oil	75 mL
1¼ cups	milk	300 mL

◆ *Preheat oven to 400°F (200°C)*
◆ *12-cup muffin tin, greased or paper-lined*

1. In a bowl combine bran, wheat germ, raisins, flour, baking powder, baking soda, salt, cinnamon, nutmeg and allspice; mix well. Make a well in the center.

2. In another bowl whisk together egg, molasses, honey, oil and milk. Pour into dry ingredients; stir just until moistened (batter will be runny).

3. Spoon batter into prepared muffin tin, filling three-quarters full. Bake in preheated oven for about 15 minutes.

Sour Cream-Raisin Muffins

1	egg	1
1 cup	sour cream	250 mL
½ cup	milk	125 mL
½ cup	raisins	125 mL
1¾ cups	all-purpose flour	425 mL
2 tbsp	granulated sugar	25 mL
1 tsp	baking powder	5 mL
½ tsp	baking soda	2 mL
½ tsp	salt	2 mL
1 tsp	nutmeg	5 mL

◆ *Preheat oven to 400°F (200°C)*
◆ *12-cup muffin tin, greased or paper-lined*

1. In a bowl combine egg, sour cream and milk; beat well. Add raisins.

2. In another bowl sift together flour, sugar, baking powder, baking soda, salt and nutmeg. Add egg mixture; stir just until moist and blended. Do not overmix.

3. Spoon batter into prepared muffin tin, filling three-quarters full. Bake in preheated oven for 15 to 20 minutes.

Prune Bran Muffins

1½ cups	all-purpose flour	375 mL
½ cup	granulated sugar	125 mL
1 tbsp	baking powder	15 mL
1 tsp	salt	5 mL
1½ cups	whole bran cereal	375 mL
1 cup	milk	250 mL
½ cup	chopped pitted prunes	125 mL
1	egg	1
⅓ cup	oil	75 mL

◆ *Preheat oven to 400°F (200°C)*
◆ *12-cup muffin tin, greased*

1. In a bowl combine flour, sugar, baking powder and salt.
2. In another bowl combine cereal, milk and prunes. Let stand for 2 minutes. Add egg and oil; beat well. Add to flour mixture; stir just until moist and blended. Do not overmix.
3. Spoon batter into prepared muffin tin, filling two-thirds or three-quarters full. Bake in preheated oven for 15 to 20 minutes or until golden brown.

Bran Oat Muffins

2	eggs, beaten	2
1 cup	brown sugar	250 mL
¾ cup	oil	175 mL
2 cups	milk	500 mL
⅓ cup	bran	75 mL
⅓ cup	oatmeal	75 mL
⅓ cup	wheat germ	75 mL
1 tsp	baking soda	5 mL
2 tsp	baking powder	10 mL
1 tsp	salt	5 mL
2 cups	all-purpose flour	500 mL
1 cup	raisins or dates	250 mL
¼ cup	walnuts (optional)	50 mL
1 tsp	cinnamon	5 mL
1 tsp	vanilla	5 mL

◆ *Preheat oven to 350°F (180°C)*
◆ *Muffin tin, greased or paper-lined*

1. In a bowl combine eggs, sugar, oil and milk; whisk until well blended. Add bran, oatmeal, wheat germ, baking soda, baking powder, salt, flour, raisins, walnuts, cinnamon and vanilla. Stir just until moist and blended.
2. Spoon batter into prepared muffin tin. Bake in preheated oven for 15 to 20 minutes.

Tangerine Bran Muffins

1 cup	all-bran cereal	250 mL
3/4 cup	milk	175 mL
2 tsp	grated tangerine zest	10 mL
1/3 cup	freshly squeezed tangerine juice	75 mL
1	egg, beaten	1
1/4 cup	oil	50 mL
1 1/4 cups	all-purpose flour	300 mL
1/4 cup	granulated sugar	50 mL
3 tsp	baking powder	15 mL
1/4 tsp	baking soda	1 mL
1/4 tsp	salt	1 mL
1	tangerine, divided into sections	1

◆ *Preheat oven to 400°F (200°C)*
◆ *Muffin tin, greased or paper-lined*

1. In a bowl combine bran cereal, milk, zest, juice, egg and oil; blend well.
2. In another bowl sift together flour, sugar, baking powder, baking soda and salt. Add to bran mixture; stir just until moist and blended.
3. Spoon batter into prepared muffin tin, filling three-quarters full. Top each with an orange section. Bake in preheated oven for 20 to 25 minutes.

Cereal Breakfast Muffins

2 cups	all-purpose flour	500 mL
1/2 cup	granulated sugar or brown sugar	125 mL
1 tbsp	baking powder	15 mL
1 tsp	cinnamon	5 mL
1/4 tsp	nutmeg	1 mL
1/2 tsp	salt	2 mL
1 cup	milk	250 mL
1	egg	1
1 tsp	vanilla	5 mL
1/3 cup	vegetable oil	75 mL
1	medium apple or pear, peeled and coarsely chopped	1
1/2 cup	raisins	125 mL
2 cups	dry cereal	500 mL

◆ *Preheat oven to 375°F (190°C)*
◆ *12-cup muffin tin, paper-lined*

1. In a bowl combine flour, sugar, baking powder, cinnamon, nutmeg and salt. Make a well in the center.
2. In another bowl beat together milk, egg, vanilla and oil. Add apple, raisins and cereal. Pour into dry ingredients; stir just until moistened.
3. Spoon batter into prepared muffin tin. Bake in preheated oven for 25 to 30 minutes.

Chocolate Chipit Snackin' Muffins ➤
(page 37)

Spicy Bran-Sweet Potato Muffins

CRUMB TOPPING		
¾ cup	crushed bran flakes cereal	175 mL
2 tbsp	butter or margarine, melted	25 mL
2 tbsp	light brown sugar	25 mL
MUFFINS		
1 cup	vegetable oil	250 mL
¾ cup	firmly packed light brown sugar	175 mL
2	eggs	2
1 tsp	vanilla	5 mL
½ cup	crushed bran flakes cereal	125 mL
1 cup	all-purpose flour	250 mL
1½ tsp	baking soda	7 mL
½ tsp	salt	2 mL
½ tsp	cinnamon	2 mL
¼ tsp	ginger	1 mL
⅛ tsp	cloves	0.5 mL
⅛ tsp	allspice	0.5 mL
1 tsp	grated orange zest	5 mL
1½ cups	pared shredded sweet potato	375 mL
1 cup	chopped almonds	250 mL

◆ *Preheat oven to 350°F (180°C)*
◆ *16-cup muffin tin, greased*

1. In a bowl combine ¾ cup (175 mL) cereal, butter and sugar. Set aside.
2. In another bowl combine oil, brown sugar, eggs and vanilla; beat on high for 2 minutes.
3. In another bowl combine ½ cup (125 mL) crushed cereal, flour, baking soda, salt, cinnamon, ginger, cloves and allspice; mix well. Add orange zest. Add to oil mixture; stir just until blended. Fold in sweet potato and almonds.
4. Spoon batter into prepared muffin tin, filling two-thirds full. Sprinkle topping evenly over tops. Bake in preheated oven for about 20 minutes.

Upside-Down Honey Bran Muffins

1 cup	honey	250 mL
½ cup	water	125 mL
½ cup	walnuts	125 mL
1 cup	whole wheat flour	250 mL
1 cup	natural bran	250 mL
1 cup	bran cereal	250 mL
1 tsp	baking soda	5 mL
3 tsp	baking powder	15 mL
1 tsp	salt	5 mL
2	eggs	2
1 cup	sour cream	250 mL
1 cup	raisins	250 mL

◆ *Preheat oven to 350°F (180°C)*
◆ *18-cup muffin tin, greased*

1. In a saucepan over low heat, combine honey and water; gently warm until blended.
2. Spoon 1 tbsp (15 mL) walnuts into each muffin cup; cover with 1 tbsp (15 mL) warm honey mixture.
3. In a bowl combine flour, natural bran, bran cereal, baking soda, baking powder and salt.
4. In another bowl whisk together eggs and sour cream; fold in raisins. Add remaining warm honey mixture. Add to flour mixture; stir quickly just until moist and blended.
5. Spoon batter into muffin tin, filling to top. Bake in preheated oven for about 25 minutes. Cool slightly; invert pan over a large plate or tray so that honey mixture is now a topping.

Apple-Filled Bran Muffins

⅓ cup	chopped apple	75 mL
¼ cup	chopped walnuts	50 mL
2 tbsp	packed brown sugar	25 mL
1 tbsp	softened butter	15 mL
½ tsp	cinnamon	2 mL
1¼ cups	all-purpose flour	300 mL
⅓ cup	granulated sugar	75 mL
1 tbsp	baking powder	15 mL
¼ tsp	salt	1 mL
1 cup	whole bran cereal	250 mL
1 cup	milk	250 mL
1	egg, beaten	1
2 tbsp	vegetable oil	25 mL

◆ *Preheat oven to 400°F (200°C)*
◆ *12-cup muffin tin, paper-lined*

1. In a small bowl combine apple, walnuts, brown sugar, butter and cinnamon. Set aside.
2. In a large bowl combine flour, sugar, baking powder and salt.
3. In another bowl combine cereal and milk. Let stand for 5 to 10 minutes. Stir in egg and oil. Add to flour mixture, stirring just until blended.
4. Spoon batter into prepared muffin tin, filling cups only half full. Spoon in 1 tsp (5 mL) apple filling and then top with remaining batter. Bake in preheated oven for 20 minutes or until golden brown.

Apple Bran Streusel Muffins

¼ cup	all-purpose flour	50 mL
¼ cup	packed brown sugar	50 mL
½ tsp	cinnamon	2 mL
2 tbsp	cold butter	25 mL
2 cups	all-purpose flour	500 mL
1 cup	natural bran	250 mL
¾ cup	lightly packed brown sugar	175 mL
1 tbsp	baking powder	15 mL
½ tsp	baking soda	2 mL
1 tsp	cinnamon	5 mL
1 tsp	salt	5 mL
2	large apples, unpeeled and chopped	2
1 cup	milk	250 mL
½ cup	vegetable oil	125 mL
2	eggs	2

HINT: Store brown sugar, raisins, nuts, bran, etc. in glass jars to keep fresh.

- ◆ *Preheat oven to 400°F (200°C)*
- ◆ *Muffin tin, greased or paper-lined*

1. In a small bowl combine flour, ¼ cup (50 mL) brown sugar and cinnamon. With a pastry blender, cut in butter until mixture is crumbly. Set aside.

2. In a large bowl combine flour, bran, ¾ cup (175 mL) brown sugar, baking powder, baking soda, cinnamon and salt. Fold in chopped apples.

3. In another bowl beat together milk, oil and eggs. Pour into apple mixture and stir just until blended.

4. Spoon batter into prepared muffin tin, filling cups three-quarters full. Sprinkle with topping and bake in preheated oven for 25 to 30 minutes.

Branicot Pecan Muffins

1 cup	boiling water	250 mL
2 cups	100% bran cereal	500 mL
1/2 cup	butter or margarine	125 mL
1	egg	1
1/2 cup	milk	125 mL
2 tbsp	molasses	25 mL
1 1/2 cups	all-purpose flour	375 mL
1 cup	chopped dried apricots	250 mL
1 cup	chopped pecans	250 mL
1/2 cup	firmly packed brown sugar	125 mL
1 tbsp	baking powder	15 mL
1/2 tsp	salt	2 mL

HINT: For stale nuts, place in a 250°F (120°C) oven for 5 to 10 minutes. The heat will freshen them.

♦ *Preheat oven to 400°F (200°C)*
♦ *Muffin tin, greased or paper-lined*

1. In a small bowl pour boiling water over cereal and butter. Stir until butter melts and set aside to cool.
2. In another bowl combine egg, milk and molasses. Stir in cooled cereal mixture.
3. In a large bowl combine flour, apricots, pecans, brown sugar, baking powder and salt. Add cereal mixture, stirring just until moistened and blended.
4. Spoon batter into prepared muffin tin, filling cups to the top. Bake in preheated oven for 15 to 20 minutes or until golden brown.

Double Cheese Bran Muffins

1 cup	boiling water	250 mL
1½ cups	100% bran cereal	375 mL
¼ cup	butter or margarine	50 mL
½ cup	milk	125 mL
1	egg	1
1½ cups	all-purpose flour	375 mL
¼ cup	granulated sugar	50 mL
1 tbsp	baking powder	15 mL
½ tsp	salt	2 mL
1½ cups	shredded old Cheddar cheese	375 mL
2 tbsp	grated Parmesan cheese	25 mL

♦ *Preheat oven to 400°F (200°C)*
♦ *12-cup muffin tin, greased or paper-lined*

1. In a medium bowl pour boiling water over cereal and butter. Stir until butter melts. Set aside to cool. Stir in milk and egg.
2. In a large bowl combine flour, sugar, baking powder and salt. Stir in 1¼ cups (300 mL) Cheddar cheese and Parmesan cheese. Add cereal mixture, stirring just until moist and blended.
3. Spoon batter into prepared muffin tin, filling cups three-quarters full. Sprinkle with remaining Cheddar cheese. Bake in preheated oven for 20 to 25 minutes or until golden brown.

Date Bran Muffins

1½ cups	natural bran	375 mL
¾ cup	all-purpose flour or cake-and-pastry flour	175 mL
1 tsp	baking soda	5 mL
1 tsp	salt	5 mL
1	egg	1
½ cup	lightly packed brown sugar	125 mL
1 tbsp	vegetable oil	15 mL
1 cup	buttermilk or sour milk	250 mL
1 cup	chopped dates	250 mL
1 cup	hot water	250 mL
½ cup	lightly packed brown sugar	125 mL
1 tsp	lemon juice	5 mL

♦ *Preheat oven to 375°F (190°C)*
♦ *Muffin tin, greased or paper-lined*

1. In a large bowl combine bran, flour, baking soda and salt.
2. In another bowl beat together egg, brown sugar, oil and buttermilk. Pour into dry ingredients and stir just until blended.
3. In another bowl combine dates, hot water, brown sugar and lemon juice. Add to batter, stirring just until blended.
4. Spoon batter into prepared muffin tin, filling cups three-quarters full. Bake in preheated oven for 20 to 25 minutes.

HINT: Dates, marshmallows and any sticky ingredients can be cut easily with scissors dipped in hot water.

Sunburst Bran Muffins

2 cups	all-purpose flour	500 mL
1 tbsp	baking powder	15 mL
1/2 tsp	salt	2 mL
1	egg	1
1 1/4 cups	milk	300 mL
1 1/2 cups	100% bran cereal	375 mL
1/3 cup	margarine, melted	75 mL
1/2 cup	raisins (optional)	125 mL
1/2 cup	firmly packed brown sugar	125 mL
1 tsp	grated orange zest	5 mL
1/2 cup	orange juice	125 mL

- *Preheat oven to 400°F (200°C)*
- *Muffin tin, greased or paper-lined*

1. In a large bowl combine flour, baking powder and salt. Make a well in the center.
2. In another bowl beat egg with a fork. Stir in milk, cereal, margarine, raisins (if using), sugar, zest and juice. Mix well. Add to flour mixture, stirring just until blended and moistened.
3. Spoon batter into prepared muffin tin, filling cups to the top. Bake in preheated oven for about 20 minutes.

Lemon Yogurt-Cranberry Muffins

2/3 cup	honey	150 mL
1/3 cup	oil	75 mL
4	eggs	4
1 1/2 tsp	lemon extract	7 mL
1 3/4 cups	all-purpose flour	425 mL
3/4 cup	whole wheat flour	175 mL
2 1/2 tsp	baking powder	12 mL
1 cup	lemon yogurt	250 mL
1 cup	coarsely chopped cranberries	250 mL
1 tbsp	grated lemon zest	15 mL

- *Preheat oven to 400°F (200°C)*
- *Muffin tin, greased or paper-lined*

1. In a bowl beat together honey and oil until creamy. Add eggs and lemon extract; blend well.
2. In another bowl combine all-purpose flour, whole wheat flour and baking powder. Add to egg mixture alternately with yogurt, beginning and ending with flour mixture. Fold in cranberries and lemon zest. Do not overmix.
3. Spoon batter into prepared muffin tin, filling to top. Bake in preheated oven for 15 to 20 minutes.

Applesauce Cheese Muffins

2 cups	whole wheat flour	500 mL
1/4 cup	wheat germ	50 mL
2 tbsp	granulated sugar	25 mL
1 tbsp	baking powder	15 mL
1/2 tsp	baking soda	2 mL
1/4 tsp	salt	1 mL
1/4 cup	softened butter or margarine	50 mL
1 1/2 cups	grated Cheddar cheese	375 mL
2	eggs, lightly beaten	2
3/4 cup	milk	175 mL
3/4 cup	applesauce	175 mL

◆ *Preheat oven to 400°F (200°C)*
◆ *12-cup muffin tin, greased*

1. In a bowl combine flour, wheat germ, sugar, baking powder, baking soda and salt. Cut in butter with a pastry blender until mixture is crumbly. Add cheese.

2. In another bowl combine remaining ingredients. Pour all at once into dry ingredients and stir just until blended.

3. Spoon batter into prepared muffin tin, filling three-quarters full. Bake in preheated oven for 18 to 20 minutes.

Beer and Cheese Muffins

2 cups	all-purpose flour	500 mL
2 tbsp	granulated sugar	25 mL
1 tsp	baking powder	5 mL
1/4 tsp	dry mustard	1 mL
1 cup	beer	250 mL
1/4 cup	oil	50 mL
1	egg, beaten	1
1 1/4 cups	grated sharp Cheddar cheese	300 mL

◆ *Preheat oven to 400°F (200°C)*
◆ *Muffin tin, greased or paper-lined*

1. In a bowl combine flour, sugar, baking powder and mustard. Make a well in the center.

2. In another bowl combine beer, oil, egg and cheese. Add to dry ingredients; stir just until blended.

3. Spoon batter into prepared muffin tin, filling three-quarters full. Bake in preheated oven for 20 to 25 minutes.

Cheddar Cheese Apple Muffins

1	egg	1
1¼ cups	milk	300 mL
¼ cup	melted margarine	50 mL
2½ cups	all-purpose flour	625 mL
¼ cup	granulated sugar	50 mL
1 tbsp	baking powder	15 mL
1 tsp	salt	5 mL
1 cup	grated unpeeled apple	250 mL
1¼ cups	grated old Cheddar cheese	300 mL

- *Preheat oven to 400°F (200°C)*
- *12-cup muffin tin, greased or paper-lined*

1. In a bowl beat egg lightly with a fork. Add milk and margarine; stir well.
2. In a bowl combine flour, sugar, baking powder and salt. Add egg mixture; stir just until blended. Fold in apple and 1 cup (250 mL) cheese.
3. Spoon batter into prepared muffin tin, dividing equally. Sprinkle with remaining cheese. Bake in preheated oven for about 20 minutes or until golden brown.

Cheese and Mustard Muffins

2 tbsp	minced green onions	25 mL
2 tbsp	minced red bell pepper	25 mL
4 tbsp	unsalted butter	50 mL
1 cup	all-purpose flour	250 mL
1 cup	whole wheat pastry flour	250 mL
2½ tsp	baking powder	12 mL
½ tsp	salt	2 mL
2	eggs	2
1 cup	milk	250 mL
2 tbsp	Dijon mustard	25 mL
1 tbsp	granulated sugar	15 mL
1 cup	grated Cheddar cheese	250 mL

- *Preheat oven to 375°F (190°C)*
- *Muffin tin, greased*

1. In a saucepan over medium-high heat, combine onions, pepper and butter. Sauté until soft; set aside.
2. In a bowl combine all-purpose flour, whole wheat flour, baking powder and salt; mix well.
3. In another bowl combine eggs, milk, mustard and sugar; whisk well. Stir in cheese. Add onion mixture and flour mixture; stir just until moist and blended.
4. Spoon batter into prepared muffin tin, dividing evenly. Bake in preheated oven for 20 to 25 minutes.

Cheesy Tuna 'n' Rice Muffins

2 cups	cooked rice	500 mL
1 cup	shredded Cheddar cheese	250 mL
1	can (7½ oz/213 g) drained flaked tuna	1
¾ cup	black olives, sliced into thirds	175 mL
1 tbsp	chopped onion	15 mL
1 tbsp	parsley flakes	15 mL
1 tsp	seasoned salt	5 mL
2	eggs, beaten	2
2 tbsp	milk	25 mL
TANGY BUTTER SAUCE		
¼ cup	melted butter or margarine	50 mL
1 tbsp	lemon juice	15 mL
½ tsp	seasoned salt	2 mL
½ tsp	parsley flakes	2 mL

- *Preheat oven to 375°F (190°C)*
- *6-cup muffin tin, greased*

1. In a bowl combine rice, cheese, tuna, olives, onion, parsley and salt. Add eggs and milk; mix thoroughly.
2. Spoon batter into prepared muffin tin, dividing evenly. Bake in preheated oven for 15 minutes or until lightly browned.
3. Meanwhile, in a bowl combine butter, lemon juice, salt and parsley; mix well. Spoon over warm muffins.

Potato Cheese Muffins

2 cups	all-purpose flour	500 mL
1/2 cup	granulated sugar	125 mL
4 tsp	baking powder	20 mL
1 tsp	salt	5 mL
2	eggs	2
1 1/2 cups milk		375 mL
1/2 cup	cooled mashed potatoes	125 mL
1/2 cup	shredded Cheddar cheese	125 mL
1/3 cup	melted shortening	75 mL

- ◆ *Preheat oven to 400°F (200°C)*
- ◆ *Muffin tin, greased or paper-lined*

1. In a bowl combine flour, sugar, baking powder and salt. Make a well in the center.
2. In another bowl beat eggs well. Add milk, potatoes, cheese and shortening; mix well. Add to flour mixture, stirring just until moistened.
3. Spoon batter into prepared muffin tin, dividing evenly. Bake in preheated oven for 25 minutes or until lightly browned.

MUFFIN STUFF: A great way to use today's leftover potatoes for tomorrow's lunch.

Cheesy Mushroom Muffins

3 tbsp	butter or margarine	45 mL
3 cups	finely chopped mushrooms	750 mL
1 cup	whole wheat flour	250 mL
1 cup	all-purpose flour	250 mL
3 tsp	baking powder	15 mL
2 tsp	granulated sugar	10 mL
1/2 tsp	salt	2 mL
1 cup	grated old Cheddar cheese	250 mL
3/4 cup	milk	175 mL
2	eggs	2

- ◆ *Preheat oven to 375°F (190°C)*
- ◆ *Muffin tin, greased*

1. In a skillet heat butter over medium-high heat. Add mushrooms; cook quickly until golden brown and no moisture is left.
2. In a bowl sift together whole wheat flour, all-purpose flour, baking powder, sugar and salt. Add cheese; toss to coat well.
3. In another bowl beat together milk and eggs. Add to flour mixture; mix well. Add mushrooms.
4. Spoon batter into prepared muffin tin, dividing evenly. Bake in preheated oven for 30 minutes.

Cheddar Bacon Muffins

2 cups	all-purpose flour	500 mL
2 tbsp	granulated sugar	25 mL
1 tbsp	baking powder	15 mL
¼ tsp	salt	1 mL
½ cup	grated Cheddar cheese	125 mL
4 or 5	slices bacon, cooked crisp and crumbled	4 or 5
1	egg, slightly beaten	1
1 cup	milk	250 mL
¼ cup	vegetable oil	50 mL

- *Preheat oven to 400°F (200°C)*
- *Muffin tin, greased or paper-lined*

1. In a large bowl combine flour, sugar, baking powder, salt, cheese and bacon. Blend well and make a well in the center.
2. In another bowl whisk together egg, milk and oil. Pour into dry ingredients and stir just until moist and lumpy.
3. Spoon batter into prepared muffin tin, filling cups to the top. Bake in preheated oven for 20 to 25 minutes.

Variations

- Increase grated Cheddar cheese to 1 cup (250 mL). Use the added ½ cup (125 mL) to sprinkle over tops before baking.
- Replace milk with 1 can (10 oz/284 mL) of any cream soup such as mushroom or chicken.
- Omit the bacon and substitute ⅔ cup (150 mL) chopped cooked ham. Substitute Swiss cheese for Cheddar and increase oil to ⅓ cup (75 mL).

Bran 'n' Cheese Muffins

1 cup	all-bran cereal	250 mL
1¼ cups	buttermilk or sour milk	300 mL
1	egg	1
¼ cup	vegetable oil	50 mL
1½ cups	all-purpose flour	375 mL
¼ cup	granulated sugar	50 mL
1½ tsp	baking powder	7 mL
½ tsp	baking soda	2 mL
½ tsp	salt	2 mL
1 cup	grated sharp Cheddar cheese	250 mL

HINT: To prevent a block of cheese from becoming moldy, wrap a cloth saturated in white vinegar around the cheese.

- ◆ *Preheat oven to 400°F (200°C)*
- ◆ *Two 8-cup muffin tins, greased or paper-lined*

1. In a small bowl combine cereal and buttermilk. Let stand 5 minutes.
2. In another bowl beat egg. Add oil and cereal mixture.
3. In a large bowl combine flour, sugar, baking powder, baking soda, salt and cheese. Add egg mixture, stirring just until moistened and lumpy.
4. Spoon batter into prepared muffin tins, filling cups three-quarters full. Bake in preheated oven for 20 to 25 minutes.

Cheddar Cheese Muffins with Apple Butter

2 cups	all-purpose flour	500 mL
½ cup	granulated sugar	125 mL
1 tbsp	baking powder	15 mL
½ tsp	salt	2 mL
½ tsp	baking soda	2 mL
2 cups	grated Cheddar cheese	500 mL
1 cup	plain yogurt	250 mL
¼ cup	butter or margarine, melted	50 mL
2	eggs, beaten	2
APPLE BUTTER		
½ cup	softened butter	125 mL
½ cup	apple jelly	125 mL
¼ tsp	cinnamon	1 mL

- ◆ *Preheat oven to 400°F (200°C)*
- ◆ *Muffin tin, greased or paper-lined*

1. In a large bowl combine flour, sugar, baking powder, salt and baking soda. Stir in cheese, mixing well. Make a well in the center.
2. In another bowl whisk together yogurt, butter and eggs. Add quickly to dry ingredients, stirring just until blended and lumpy.
3. Spoon batter into prepared muffin tin, filling to the top. Bake in preheated oven for 18 to 20 minutes or until golden brown.
4. Meanwhile, prepare Apple Butter. In a bowl beat butter until creamy. Add jelly and cinnamon, blending well. Serve with warm muffins.

Cheddar Brunch Muffins

2 cups	all-purpose flour	500 mL
2 tbsp	granulated sugar	25 mL
2½ tsp	baking powder	12 mL
½ tsp	salt	2 mL
1½ cups	shredded Cheddar cheese	375 mL
1	egg	1
1 cup	milk	250 mL
¼ cup	melted butter	50 mL

◆ *Preheat oven to 400°F (200°C)*
◆ *Muffin tin, greased or paper-lined*

1. In a large bowl sift together flour, sugar, baking powder and salt. Fold in cheese, making sure to coat well with flour. Add unbeaten egg, milk and butter, stirring quickly just until blended. Do not overmix.

2. Spoon batter into prepared muffin tin, filling cups three-quarters full. Bake in preheated oven for 20 to 30 minutes.

HINT: A dull knife works much better than a sharp one for slicing cheese.

Cottage Marmalade Muffins

½ cup + 1 tbsp	all-purpose flour	125 mL + 15 mL
1 tsp	baking powder	5 mL
⅛ tsp	salt	0.5 mL
1	egg, lightly beaten	1
⅔ cup	small-curd cottage cheese	150 mL
1 tbsp	vegetable oil	15 mL
1 tsp	honey	5 mL
2 tbsp	orange marmalade	25 mL

◆ *Preheat oven to 400°F (200°C)*
◆ *6-cup muffin tin, greased or paper-lined*

1. In a large bowl sift together flour, baking powder and salt. Make a well in the center.

2. In another bowl whisk together egg, cheese, oil and honey. Add to dry ingredients, stirring just until moistened.

3. Spoon batter into prepared muffin tin, filling cups half full. Add 1 tsp (5 mL) marmalade to each cup and top with remaining batter. Bake in preheated oven for 15 to 20 minutes.

Cheesy Lemony Muffins

1½ cups	all-purpose flour	375 mL
¼ cup	granulated sugar	50 mL
1½ tsp	baking powder	7 mL
½ tsp	baking soda	2 mL
½ tsp	salt	2 mL
1	small lemon	1
1 cup	creamed cottage cheese	250 mL
1 cup	all-bran cereal	250 mL
2 tbsp	milk	25 mL
2	eggs	2
¼ cup	butter or margarine, melted	50 mL
¼ cup	liquid honey	50 mL

◆ *Preheat oven to 400°F (200°C)*
◆ *12-cup muffin tin, greased or paper-lined*

1. In a large bowl combine flour, sugar, baking powder, baking soda and salt. Make a well in the center.

2. Peel lemon very thinly to remove zest. Then remove white pith, seeds and inner membranes from the rest of the lemon. Put zest and pulp into a food processor or blender and process until smooth. Add cottage cheese and process again. Stir in cereal and milk. Let stand for 5 minutes.

3. Stir in eggs, margarine and honey. Pour into flour mixture, stirring just until moistened and lumpy.

4. Spoon batter into prepared muffin tin, filling cups to the top. Bake in preheated oven for 20 minutes or until golden brown and firm to the touch.

Mashed Potato Muffins

10	medium-sized potatoes	10
1 tsp	salt	5 mL
½ tsp	pepper	2 mL
2 tbsp	oil	25 mL
4	eggs, beaten	4
2	onions, chopped	2

◆ *Preheat oven to 400°F (200°C)*
◆ *2 12-cup muffin tins, greased*

1. In a saucepan of boiling water, cook potatoes until soft. In a bowl combine cooked potatoes, salt, pepper and oil; mash until smooth. Add eggs; mix well.

2. In a frying pan over medium-high heat, cook onions for about 2 minutes. Add to potato mixture; stir well.

3. In preheated oven heat prepared muffin tin. Spoon batter into hot tin. Bake in preheated oven for 30 to 40 minutes.

Cornmeal Bacon Muffins

6	bacon slices, chopped	6
1½ cups	all-purpose flour	375 mL
½ cup	cornmeal	125 mL
1 tbsp	baking powder	15 mL
½ tsp	salt	2 mL
Pinch	cayenne red pepper (optional)	Pinch
1¼ cups	coarsely grated Cheddar cheese	300 mL
1	egg	1
1 cup	milk	250 mL
¼ cup	melted butter or margarine	50 mL
TOPPING		
⅓ cup	coarsely grated Cheddar cheese	75 mL

- Preheat oven to 425°F (220°C)
- 12-cup muffin tin, greased or paper-lined

1. In a skillet over medium-high heat, cook bacon until crisp; drain. Set aside to cool.
2. In a bowl combine flour, cornmeal, baking powder, salt, cayenne (if desired), Cheddar cheese and bacon.
3. In another bowl whisk egg; add milk and melted butter. Add to flour mixture; stir just until moist and blended.
4. Spoon batter into prepared muffin tin, filling three-quarters full. Sprinkle with cheese topping. Bake in preheated oven for 20 minutes or until golden brown.

Tangy Cottage Cheese Muffins

1	egg, slightly beaten	1
¼ cup	vegetable oil	50 mL
½ cup	milk	125 mL
1 cup	cottage cheese	250 mL
2 tbsp	chopped green onions	25 mL
2 tsp	finely chopped fresh dill	10 mL
½ tsp	Worcestershire sauce	2 mL
2 cups	all-purpose flour	500 mL
1 tbsp	baking powder	15 mL
½ tsp	seasoned salt	2 mL

- Preheat oven to 400°F (200°C)
- 12-cup muffin tin, greased

1. In a bowl combine egg, oil, milk, cheese, onions, dill and Worcestershire sauce; stir well. Add flour, baking powder and salt; stir just until moist and blended.
2. Spoon batter into prepared muffin tin, dividing evenly. Bake in preheated oven for 20 minutes.

Cheese Danish Muffins

1	pkg (4 oz/125 g) softened cream cheese	1
2 tbsp	granulated sugar	25 mL
1 tbsp	lemon juice	15 mL
1	egg	1
1¼ cups	milk	300 mL
½ cup	melted margarine	125 mL
1 tsp	grated lemon zest	5 mL
2½ cups	all-purpose flour	625 mL
½ cup	granulated sugar	125 mL
3½ tsp	baking powder	17 mL
1 tsp	salt	5 mL

◆ *Preheat oven to 400°F (200°C)*
◆ *12-cup muffin tin, greased or paper-lined*

1. In a bowl cream together cheese, sugar and lemon juice. Set aside.
2. In another bowl beat egg lightly with a fork; add milk, margarine and zest.
3. In another bowl combine flour, sugar, baking powder and salt. Add egg mixture; stir just until blended.
4. Spoon batter into prepared muffin tin, filling half full. Place 1 tbsp (15 mL) cheese mixture over each; top with remaining batter. Bake in preheated oven for 20 minutes.

Cheese and Rice Muffins

8 oz	dry cottage cheese	250 g
¾ cup	cooked rice	175 mL
1 tbsp	butter or margarine, melted	15 mL
1 tbsp	oil	15 mL
3 tbsp	granulated sugar	45 mL
3 tbsp	sour cream	45 mL
3	eggs, beaten	3
¾ cup	all-purpose flour	175 mL
2 tsp	baking powder	10 mL

◆ *Preheat oven to 425°F (220°C)*
◆ *12-cup muffin tin, greased*

1. In a bowl combine cottage cheese, rice, butter, oil, sugar, sour cream, eggs, flour and baking powder.
2. Place empty prepared muffin tin in preheated oven; heat until sizzling. Remove from oven. Spoon batter into hot tin, dividing evenly. Bake in preheated oven for 20 to 25 minutes.

Nutritious Health Muffins

4	eggs	4
1½ cups	canola oil	375 mL
2½ cups	brown sugar	625 mL
1 tbsp	salt	15 mL
2½ cups	milk	625 mL
1 tbsp	baking soda	15 mL
3 tbsp	molasses	45 mL
½ cup	applesauce	125 mL
¾ cup	walnut pieces or 1 apple, peeled and grated	175 mL
1 cup	chopped dates	250 mL
1 cup	raisins	250 mL
5½ cups	whole wheat flour	1.375 L

♦ *Preheat oven to 375°F (190°C)*
♦ *Muffin tin, greased or paper-lined*

1. In a bowl beat together eggs and oil. Add brown sugar; mix well. Gradually add salt, milk, baking soda, molasses, applesauce, walnut pieces, dates, raisins and whole wheat flour; stir just until blended.
2. Spoon batter into prepared muffin tins, dividing evenly (makes 30 to 36 muffins). Bake in preheated oven for about 25 minutes.

Fresh Herb Muffins

1½ cups	all-purpose flour	375 mL
1 tbsp	granulated sugar	15 mL
1½ tsp	baking powder	7 mL
½ tsp	baking soda	2 mL
Pinch	salt	Pinch
1 tsp	garlic powder	5 mL
⅓ cup	grated Parmesan cheese	75 mL
½ cup	finely chopped fresh herbs (oregano or basil)	125 mL
1	egg	1
2 tbsp	butter, melted	25 mL
1¼ cups	buttermilk	300 mL

♦ *Preheat oven to 400°F (200°C)*
♦ *12-cup muffin tin, greased or paper-lined*

1. In a bowl sift together flour, sugar, baking powder, baking soda, salt and garlic powder. Add cheese and herbs; stir well.
2. In another bowl beat egg lightly with a fork; add butter and buttermilk. Add to dry ingredients; mix quickly just until moistened.
3. Spoon batter into prepared muffin tin, filling three-quarters full. Bake in preheated oven for 15 to 20 minutes.

Double Good Oat Bran Muffins

1 cup	quick oats	250 mL
1 cup	all-purpose flour	250 mL
1 cup	oat bran	250 mL
1 tsp	baking soda	5 mL
1 tbsp	baking powder	15 mL
1/2 tsp	salt	2 mL
1/2 cup	chopped pecans	125 mL
1/2 cup	chopped almonds	125 mL
1 cup	plain yogurt	250 mL
1 cup	buttermilk	250 mL
1	egg	1
1 tsp	vanilla	5 mL
4 tbsp	butter or margarine, melted or oil	50 mL
1/2 cup	dark brown sugar	125 mL

- *Preheat oven to 400°F (200°C)*
- *18-cup muffin tin, greased*

1. In a bowl combine oats, flour, oat bran, baking soda, baking powder, salt, pecans and almonds; mix well.
2. In another bowl whisk together yogurt, buttermilk, egg, vanilla, butter and brown sugar. Add to dry ingredients; stir just until blended.
3. Spoon batter into prepared muffin tin, dividing evenly. Bake in preheated oven for 18 to 20 minutes.

Banana-Raisin Oat Bran Muffins

1 cup	whole wheat flour	250 mL
1 tsp	baking powder	5 mL
1 tsp	baking soda	5 mL
1 cup	oat bran	250 mL
1/2 cup	raisins	125 mL
1	egg, lightly beaten	1
1/4 cup	oil	50 mL
1/2 cup	granulated sugar	125 mL
1 cup	mashed bananas	250 mL
1 tsp	vanilla	5 mL

- *Preheat oven to 400°F (200°C)*
- *12-cup muffin tin, paper-lined*

1. In a bowl combine flour, baking powder, baking soda, oat bran and raisins.
2. In another bowl combine egg, oil, sugar, bananas and vanilla. Add to flour mixture; stir just until blended.
3. Spoon batter into prepared muffin tin, dividing evenly. Bake in preheated oven for 20 to 25 minutes.

Carrot Chipit Oat Bran Muffins

1¼ cups	whole wheat flour	300 mL
1 cup	oat bran	250 mL
½ cup	firmly packed brown sugar	125 mL
1 tsp	baking soda	5 mL
1 cup	butterscotch chips or chocolate chips	250 mL
1 cup	grated carrots	250 mL
¾ cup	plain yogurt	175 mL
½ cup	chopped pecans	125 mL
½ cup	melted butter	125 mL
1½ tsp	grated orange zest	7 mL
2	eggs	2

◆ *Preheat oven to 400°F (200°C)*
◆ *12-cup muffin tin, greased or paper-lined*

1. In a bowl combine flour, bran, brown sugar, baking soda and butterscotch chips; mix well.
2. In another bowl combine carrots, yogurt, pecans, butter, zest and eggs. Add to dry ingredients; stir just until blended.
3. Spoon batter into prepared muffin tin, filling three-quarters full. Bake in preheated oven for 25 to 30 minutes.

Oat Bran Fruit Muffins

2¼ cups	oat bran	550 mL
½ cup	packaged mixed dried diced fruit	125 mL
1 tsp	cinnamon	5 mL
1 tsp	baking powder	5 mL
½ tsp	baking soda	2 mL
¼ tsp	salt	1 mL
2	egg whites	2
1 cup	unsweetened applesauce	250 mL
½ cup	packed brown sugar	125 mL
½ cup	buttermilk or plain yogurt	125 mL
2 tbsp	vegetable oil	25 mL

◆ *Preheat oven to 350°F (180°C)*
◆ *Muffin tin, greased*

1. In a bowl combine oat bran, dried fruit, cinnamon, baking powder, baking soda and salt.
2. In another bowl whisk together egg whites, applesauce, brown sugar, buttermilk and oil. Add to dry ingredients; stir just until blended.
3. Spoon batter into prepared muffin tin, filling three-quarters full. Bake in preheated oven for 30 to 35 minutes.

Honey-Nut Oat Bran Muffins

2 cups	oat bran cereal	500 mL
1/3 cup	all-purpose flour	75 mL
2 tbsp	packed brown sugar	25 mL
1/4 cup	chopped nuts	50 mL
1/4 cup	raisins	50 mL
1 tbsp	baking powder	15 mL
1/2 tsp	salt	2 mL
1/4 tsp	cinnamon	1 mL
1 cup	milk	250 mL
2	eggs, beaten	2
1/3 cup	honey or molasses	75 mL
2 tbsp	vegetable oil	25 mL

◆ *Preheat oven to 425°F (220°C)*
◆ *Muffin tin, greased or paper-lined*

1. In a bowl combine cereal, flour, brown sugar, nuts, raisins, baking powder, salt and cinnamon. Make a well in the center. Add milk, eggs, honey and oil; stir just until moist and blended.

2. Spoon batter into prepared muffin tin, filling three-quarters full. Bake in preheated oven for 15 to 20 minutes or until golden brown.

Orange Oat Bran Muffins

1 cup	oat bran	250 mL
1 cup	whole wheat flour	250 mL
3/4 cup	all-purpose flour	175 mL
1/2 cup	quick-cooking oats	125 mL
1 tbsp	baking powder	15 mL
1/2 tsp	cinnamon	2 mL
1/4 tsp	salt	1 mL
2	eggs, lightly beaten	2
1 cup	orange juice	250 mL
2 tsp	grated orange zest	10 mL
1/2 cup	honey	125 mL
1/3 cup	oil	75 mL
1/4 cup	skim milk	50 mL

◆ *Preheat oven to 400°F (200°C)*
◆ *12-cup muffin tin, lightly greased*

1. In a bowl combine oat bran, whole wheat flour, all-purpose flour, oats, baking powder, cinnamon and salt; blend well. Make a well in the center.

2. In another bowl combine eggs, juice, zest, honey, oil and milk; blend well. Add to dry ingredients; stir just until blended.

3. Spoon batter into prepared muffin tin, filling to top. Bake in preheated oven for 15 to 20 minutes.

Vegetable Oat Bran Muffins

4 cups	oat bran	1 L
1 cup	all-purpose flour	250 mL
2 tbsp	baking powder	25 mL
2 tbsp	cornstarch	25 mL
½ tsp	salt	2 mL
2 tbsp	cinnamon	25 mL
½ tsp	nutmeg	2 mL
2 cups	skim milk	500 mL
½ cup	brown sugar	125 mL
4 tbsp	vegetable oil	60 mL
2	eggs	2
1 tbsp	vanilla	15 mL
2 tbsp	corn syrup	25 mL
2 cups	grated carrots, zucchini or apple or mashed banana or 1 can (14 oz/398 mL) pumpkin	500 mL
1½ cups	raisins or currants or chopped dates (or a mixture)	375 mL

- ◆ *Preheat oven to 425°F (220°C)*
- ◆ *Muffin tin, greased*

1. In a bowl combine oat bran, flour, baking powder, cornstarch, salt, cinnamon and nutmeg. Make a well in the center.
2. In another bowl, combine milk, brown sugar, oil, eggs, vanilla, corn syrup, carrots and raisins; blend well. Add to dry ingredients; stir just until moistened.
3. Spoon batter into prepared muffin tin, dividing evenly. Bake in preheated oven for 15 to 20 minutes.

Easy Oat Bran Muffins

1¼ cups	all-purpose flour	300 mL
½ cup	packed brown sugar	125 mL
¾ cup	oat bran	175 mL
¼ cup	granulated sugar	50 mL
2 tsp	baking powder	10 mL
½ tsp	salt	2 mL
¼ tsp	cinnamon	1 mL
1	egg, slightly beaten	1
1 cup	milk	250 mL
¼ cup	vegetable oil	50 mL
¼ cup	liquid honey	50 mL

♦ *Preheat oven to 400°F (200°C)*
♦ *Muffin tin, greased or paper-lined*

1. In a large bowl, mix together flour, brown sugar, oat bran, sugar, baking powder, salt and cinnamon. Make a well in the center. Add egg, milk, oil and honey. Mix just until moist and blended.

2. Spoon batter into prepared muffin tin, filling cups three-quarters full. Bake in preheated oven for 20 to 25 minutes.

Oldtime Classic Oat Bran Muffins

1½ cups	oat bran	375 mL
1 cup	buttermilk	250 mL
1	egg	1
⅓ cup	vegetable oil	75 mL
½ cup	packed brown sugar	125 mL
½ tsp	vanilla	2 mL
1 cup	all-purpose flour	250 mL
1 tsp	baking powder	5 mL
1 tsp	baking soda	5 mL
½ tsp	salt	2 mL
½ tsp	cinnamon	2 mL
½ cup	raisins	125 mL

♦ *Preheat oven to 375°F (190°C)*
♦ *12-cup muffin tin, greased or paper-lined*

1. In a large bowl combine oat bran and buttermilk. Let stand.

2. In another bowl beat egg lightly. Add oil, sugar and vanilla. Stir into bran mixture.

3. In another bowl sift together flour, baking powder, baking soda, salt and cinnamon. Stir into bran mixture just until moistened. Fold in raisins.

4. Spoon batter into prepared muffin tin, filling cups three-quarters full. Bake in preheated oven for 15 to 20 minutes or until firm to the touch.

Applesauce Oat Bran Muffins

1 cup	oat bran	250 mL
1 cup	all-purpose flour	250 mL
1/4 cup	granulated sugar	50 mL
1 tbsp	baking powder	15 mL
1/2 tsp	salt	2 mL
1/4 cup	raisins	50 mL
2	eggs	2
1 cup	unsweetened applesauce	250 mL
3 tbsp	milk	45 mL
3 tbsp	vegetable oil	45 mL
TOPPING		
1 tbsp	granulated sugar	15 mL
1/2 tsp	cinnamon	2 mL
1/4 cup	chopped walnuts	50 mL

◆ *Preheat oven to 425°F (220°C)*
◆ *12-cup muffin tin, greased or foil-lined*

1. In a large bowl combine oat bran, flour, sugar, baking powder, salt and raisins.
2. In another bowl beat eggs lightly with a fork. Stir in applesauce, milk and oil. Pour into dry ingredients. Stir just until moist and blended.
3. Spoon batter into prepared muffin tin, filling cups three-quarters full. Sprinkle with sugar, cinnamon and walnuts. Bake in preheated oven for 20 minutes.

> **HINT:** Here's a great way to crush nuts and avoid messy clean-ups: Place nuts in a plastic bag or between sheets of wax paper and crush with a rolling pin.

Apple Walnut Oat Bran Muffins

1 cup	all-purpose flour	250 mL
1 cup	whole-wheat flour	250 mL
1 cup	oat bran	250 mL
1 tbsp	baking powder	15 mL
1 1/2 tsp	baking soda	7 mL
1 tsp	cinnamon	5 mL
1 cup	chopped walnuts	250 mL
1 cup	grated unpeeled apple	250 mL
1/2 cup	packed brown sugar	125 mL
1 1/2 cups	buttermilk	375 mL
3	egg whites	3
5 tbsp	vegetable oil	75 mL

◆ *Preheat oven to 400°F (200°C)*
◆ *Muffin tin, greased or paper-lined*

1. In a large bowl combine all-purpose flour, whole-wheat flour, oat bran, baking powder, baking soda, cinnamon, walnuts and apple.
2. In another bowl dissolve brown sugar in buttermilk. Add egg whites and oil, beating lightly with a fork until well blended. Add to dry ingredients, stirring just until moistened. Do not overmix.
3. Spoon batter into prepared muffin tin, filling cups to the top. Bake in preheated oven for 20 minutes.

Banana Oat Bran Muffins

1¼ cups	all-purpose flour	300 mL
¾ cup	oat bran	175 mL
1 tsp	baking powder	5 mL
1 tsp	baking soda	5 mL
¼ tsp	salt	1 mL
1	egg	1
⅓ cup	vegetable oil	75 mL
⅓ cup	lightly packed brown sugar	75 mL
1 cup	mashed banana	250 mL
½ cup	buttermilk or sour milk	125 mL
2 tbsp	molasses	25 mL
¾ cup	raisins	175 mL

- *Preheat oven to 375°F (190°C)*
- *12-cup muffin tin, greased or paper-lined*

1. In a large bowl combine flour, oat bran, baking powder, baking soda and salt.
2. In another bowl whisk together egg, oil, brown sugar, banana, buttermilk, molasses and raisins. Add to dry ingredients, stirring just until blended and lumpy.
3. Spoon batter into prepared muffin tin, filling cups three-quarters full. Bake in preheated oven for 20 to 25 minutes.

Berry Oat Bran Muffins

1	egg, slightly beaten	1
½ cup	milk or yogurt	125 mL
¼ cup	vegetable oil	50 mL
¼ cup	honey	50 mL
⅔ cup	applesauce	150 mL
1 tsp	vanilla	5 mL
1 cup	whole-wheat flour	250 mL
1 tsp	baking powder	5 mL
1 tsp	baking soda	5 mL
1 cup	oat bran	250 mL
1 cup	berries (Saskatoon or any other)	250 mL

- *Preheat oven to 375°F (190°C)*
- *Muffin tin, greased or paper-lined*

1. In a blender or food processor combine egg, milk, oil, honey, applesauce and vanilla. Mix well and transfer to a large bowl.
2. In another bowl combine flour, baking powder, baking soda, oat bran and berries. Stir into egg mixture just until blended. Do not overmix.
3. Spoon batter into prepared muffin tin. Bake in preheated oven for about 15 minutes.

Buttermilk Oat Bran Muffins

1 cup	all-purpose flour	250 mL
1 cup	oat bran	250 mL
1/3 cup	granulated sugar	75 mL
1 tsp	baking powder	5 mL
1 tsp	baking soda	5 mL
1/2 tsp	cinnamon	2 mL
1/4 tsp	salt	1 mL
1	egg	1
3/4 cup	buttermilk	175 mL
1/4 cup	corn oil	50 mL
1 tbsp	grated orange zest	15 mL
2 tbsp	orange juice	25 mL
1 cup	raisins or chopped dates	250 mL

- ◆ *Preheat oven to 400°F (200°C)*
- ◆ *12-cup muffin tin, greased*

1. In a large bowl combine flour, oat bran, sugar, baking powder, baking soda, cinnamon and salt. Mix well and make a well in the center.
2. In another bowl whisk together egg, buttermilk, oil, zest and juice. Pour into dry ingredients and stir just until moist and blended. Fold in raisins.
3. Spoon batter into prepared muffin tin, dividing evenly. Bake in preheated oven for 20 to 25 minutes or until top springs back when lightly touched.

HINT: If you have leftover raisins and nuts, chop them together for a great snack and healthy treat.

Carrot Pecan Oat Bran Muffins

1 cup	all-purpose flour	250 mL
1 cup	oat bran	250 mL
2 tsp	baking soda	10 mL
1 tsp	baking powder	5 mL
1/2 tsp	salt	2 mL
2 tsp	cinnamon	10 mL
1 cup	packed brown sugar	250 mL
1 1/2 cups	shredded carrots	375 mL
2	large apples, shredded	2
1/2 cup	raisins	125 mL
1 cup	chopped pecans	250 mL
1/4 cup	vegetable oil	50 mL
1/2 cup	skim milk	125 mL
2	eggs, lightly beaten	2
1 tsp	vanilla	5 mL

- ◆ *Preheat oven to 375°F (190°C)*
- ◆ *18-cup muffin tin, greased*

1. In a large bowl combine flour, oat bran, baking soda, baking powder, salt and cinnamon. Add sugar and mix well. Stir in carrots, apples, raisins and pecans. Make a well in the center. Add oil, milk, eggs and vanilla, stirring just until moist and blended.
2. Spoon batter evenly into prepared muffin tin. Bake in preheated oven for about 20 minutes.

Honey Date Oat Bran Muffins

2 cups	oat and wheat cereal (such as Kellogg's Common Sense)	500 mL
1¼ cups	skim milk	300 mL
¼ cup	liquid honey	50 mL
2	egg whites	2
3 tbsp	vegetable oil	45 mL
¾ cup	chopped pitted dates	175 mL
1¼ cups	all-purpose flour	300 mL
1 tbsp	baking powder	15 mL
¼ tsp	salt	1 mL
¾ tsp	cinnamon	4 mL
¼ tsp	nutmeg	1 mL

◆ *Preheat oven to 400°F (200°C)*
◆ *12-cup muffin tin, greased*

1. In a large bowl combine cereal, milk, honey, egg whites, oil and dates.

2. In another bowl combine flour, baking powder, salt, cinnamon and nutmeg. Add to cereal mixture, stirring just until well blended. Batter will be lumpy.

3. Spoon batter into prepared muffin tin. Bake in preheated oven for 15 to 20 minutes or until golden brown.

Lemon Banana Oat Bran Muffins

1½ cups	all-purpose flour	375 mL
¾ cup	oat bran cereal	175 mL
1 tsp	baking soda	5 mL
½ tsp	salt	2 mL
1 cup	granulated sugar	250 mL
½ cup	margarine or butter	125 mL
1 cup	mashed ripe bananas	250 mL
2	eggs	2
½ tsp	grated lemon zest	2 mL
⅓ cup	milk	75 mL
1 tsp	lemon juice	5 mL
½ cup	chopped nuts	125 mL

◆ *Preheat oven to 400°F (200°C)*
◆ *Muffin tin, greased or paper-lined*

1. In a bowl combine flour, cereal, baking soda and salt. Mix together well.

2. In a large bowl cream together sugar and margarine until light and fluffy. Stir in bananas, eggs and zest.

3. In another bowl combine milk and juice. Add to banana mixture alternately with flour mixture, stirring after each addition. Fold in nuts.

4. Spoon batter into prepared muffin tin, filling cups to the top. Bake in preheated oven for 15 to 20 minutes.

Oat Bran Raisin Muffins

2 cups	oat bran	500 mL
¼ cup	packed brown sugar	50 mL
2 tsp	baking powder	10 mL
½ cup	raisins	125 mL
1 cup	plain yogurt	250 mL
2	egg whites, slightly beaten	2
¼ cup	milk	50 mL
¼ cup	honey or molasses	50 mL
2 tbsp	vegetable oil	25 mL
1 tsp	grated orange zest	5 mL

- *Preheat oven to 400°F (200°C)*
- *12-cup muffin tin, greased or paper-lined*

1. In a large bowl combine oat bran, sugar, baking powder and raisins. Make a well in the center. Add yogurt, egg whites, milk, honey, oil and zest, stirring just until blended.
2. Spoon batter into prepared muffin tin. Bake in preheated oven for 20 minutes.

Grandma's Old-Fashioned Oatmeal Muffins

¾ cup	regular rolled oats	175 mL
¾ cup + 2 tbsp	all-purpose flour	175 mL + 25 mL
2 tbsp	firmly packed light brown sugar	25 mL
1½ tsp	baking powder	7 mL
½ tsp	baking soda	2 mL
½ tsp	salt	2 mL
1 tsp	cinnamon	5 mL
¼ cup	butter or margarine	50 mL
1	egg	1
¾ cup	buttermilk	175 mL
TOPPING		
⅓ cup	granulated sugar	75 mL
1½ tsp	cinnamon	7 mL
1 tbsp	margarine, melted	15 mL

- *Preheat oven to 425°F (220°C)*
- *Muffin tin, greased or paper-lined*

1. In a bowl combine oats, flour, brown sugar, baking powder, baking soda, salt and cinnamon; mix well. Cut in butter; mix until crumbly.
2. In another bowl beat together egg and buttermilk. Pour into dry ingredients; stir just until blended.
3. In another bowl combine sugar, cinnamon and margarine; mix well.
4. Spoon batter into prepared muffin tin, filling two-thirds full. Sprinkle with topping. Bake in preheated oven for 15 to 20 minutes.

Maple Oat Muffins

1 cup	maple oats	250 mL
1 cup	sour cream	250 mL
1 cup	all-purpose flour	250 mL
½ cup	brown sugar	125 mL
1 tsp	baking powder	5 mL
½ tsp	baking soda	2 mL
½ tsp	salt	2 mL
1	egg, beaten	1
¼ cup	vegetable oil	50 mL

◆ *Preheat oven to 400°F (200°C)*
◆ *Muffin tin, paper-lined*

1. In a bowl combine oats and sour cream. Set aside.
2. In another bowl combine flour, brown sugar, baking powder, baking soda and salt.
3. Add egg and oil to oat mixture; blend well. Add dry ingredients; mix together quickly just until moist. Do not overmix (batter will be lumpy).
4. Spoon batter into prepared muffin tin, filling two-thirds full. Bake in preheated oven for 15 to 20 minutes.

Scrumptious Blueberry Oat Muffins

1 cup	oats	250 mL
1 cup	buttermilk	250 mL
1	egg, beaten	1
¼ cup	butter or margarine, melted	50 mL
1 cup	all-purpose flour	250 mL
1 tsp	baking powder	5 mL
½ tsp	baking soda	2 mL
½ tsp	salt	2 mL
¾ cup	lightly packed brown sugar	175 mL
1 cup	fresh blueberries or frozen blueberries, thawed and drained	250 mL

◆ *Preheat oven to 400°F (200°C)*
◆ *12-cup muffin tin, greased*

1. In a bowl combine oats and buttermilk; mix well. Let stand for 5 to 10 minutes. Add egg and butter; blend well.
2. In another bowl combine flour, baking powder, baking soda, salt and brown sugar. Add oat mixture; stir just until moist and blended. Fold in blueberries.
3. Spoon batter into prepared muffin tin, dividing evenly. Bake in preheated oven for 15 to 20 minutes.

Buttermilk Oatmeal Muffins

1 cup	quick-cooking oats	250 mL
1 cup	buttermilk	250 mL
1	egg, beaten	1
½ cup	brown sugar	125 mL
¼ cup	melted shortening, cooled or vegetable oil	50 mL
½ cup	all-purpose flour	125 mL
½ cup	whole wheat pastry flour	125 mL
1½ tsp	baking powder	7 mL
½ tsp	baking soda	2 mL
½ tsp	salt	2 mL

◆ *Preheat oven to 400°F (200°C)*
◆ *12-cup muffin tin, greased*

1. In a bowl combine oats and buttermilk. Let stand for 50 to 60 minutes.
2. In another bowl combine egg, brown sugar and shortening; mix well. Add to oat mixture; blend well. Add all-purpose flour, whole wheat flour, baking powder, baking soda and salt; stir just until moist and blended.
3. Spoon batter into prepared muffin tin, dividing evenly. Bake in preheated oven for 15 to 20 minutes or until browned.

Chocolate Chip Oatmeal Muffins

1 cup	old-fashioned oats	250 mL
2 cups	buttermilk	500 mL
2	lightly beaten eggs	2
1⅔ cups	whole wheat flour	410 mL
1 tsp	baking soda	5 mL
1 tsp	salt	5 mL
2 tbsp	vegetable oil	25 mL
1 cup	chocolate chips	250 mL

◆ *Muffin tin, greased or paper-lined*

1. In a bowl combine oats and buttermilk. Cover; refrigerate overnight. The next day, add beaten eggs; whisk well.
2. In another bowl sift together flour, baking soda, salt and oil. Add to oat mixture; stir just until blended. Fold in chocolate chips.
3. Spoon batter into prepared muffin tin, filling to the top. Bake at 400°F (200°C) for 15 to 20 minutes.

Garden Oatmeal Muffins

1½ cups	quick-cooking oats	375 mL
1½ cups	milk	375 mL
1	egg	1
½ cup	margarine, melted	125 mL
1 cup	all-purpose flour	250 mL
1 cup	whole wheat flour	250 mL
½ cup	firmly packed brown sugar	125 mL
3½ tsp	baking powder	17 mL
1 tsp	salt	5 mL
1 tsp	cinnamon	5 mL
½ tsp	nutmeg	2 mL
1 cup	grated carrots	250 mL
1 cup	grated zucchini	250 mL

- ◆ *Preheat oven to 400°F (200°C)*
- ◆ *12-cup muffin tin, greased or paper-lined*

1. In a bowl cover oats with milk. Let stand for 5 minutes. Add egg and margarine; blend well.
2. In another bowl combine all-purpose flour, whole wheat flour, brown sugar, baking powder, salt, cinnamon and nutmeg; blend well. Add oat mixture; stir just until moist. Fold in carrots and zucchini.
3. Spoon batter into prepared muffin tin, filling to top. Bake in preheated oven for about 20 minutes.

Pineapple Oatmeal Muffins

1	can (8 oz/250 g) crushed pineapple, not drained	1
1 cup	sour cream	250 mL
1	egg	1
¼ cup	butter or margarine, melted	50 mL
1½ cups	all-purpose flour	375 mL
1 cup	old-fashioned oats	250 mL
½ cup	granulated sugar	125 mL
1 tbsp	baking powder	15 mL
1 tsp	cinnamon	5 mL
½ tsp	nutmeg	2 mL
½ tsp	salt	2 mL
1 cup	raisins (optional)	250 mL

- ◆ *Preheat oven to 350°F (180°C)*
- ◆ *12-cup muffin tin, greased or paper-lined*

1. In a bowl combine pineapple, sour cream, egg and butter; blend well.
2. In another bowl combine flour, oats, sugar, baking powder, cinnamon, nutmeg, salt and raisins. Add to pineapple mixture; stir just until moist.
3. Spoon batter into prepared muffin tin, dividing evenly. Bake in preheated oven for 30 to 35 minutes or until lightly browned.

Quick Oatmeal Muffins

1 cup	all-purpose flour	250 mL
¼ cup	granulated sugar	50 mL
3 tsp	baking powder	15 mL
½ tsp	salt	2 mL
1 cup	quick-cooking oats	250 mL
1	egg, slightly beaten	1
1 cup	milk	250 mL
3 tbsp	vegetable oil	45 mL

◆ *Preheat oven to 425°F (220°C)*
◆ *Muffin tin, greased or paper-lined*

1. In a large bowl combine flour, sugar, baking powder, salt, oats, egg, milk and oil. Stir just until moist and blended.
2. Spoon batter into prepared muffin tin, filling cups three-quarters full. Bake in preheated oven for about 15 minutes.

> **HINT:** Olive oil will stay fresh longer if you add a cube of sugar to the bottle.

Apple Date Oatmeal Muffins

⅔ cup + 2 tbsp	quick oats	150 mL + 25 mL
1 tsp	firmly packed light brown sugar	5 mL
¼ tsp	cinnamon	1 mL
1 cup less 1 tbsp	all-purpose flour	250 mL less 15 mL
2 tbsp	granulated sugar	25 mL
2 tsp	baking powder	10 mL
1 tbsp	grated orange zest	15 mL
½ cup	orange juice	125 mL
1	egg	1
¼ cup	margarine, melted	50 mL
1	small apple, cored and chopped	1
8	dates, pitted and chopped	8

◆ *Preheat oven to 400°F (200°C)*
◆ *8-cup muffin tin, paper-lined*

1. In a small skillet over medium heat, cook ⅓ cup (75 mL) oats, stirring often, for 3 to 4 minutes or until golden. Remove from heat and stir in brown sugar and cinnamon. Set aside for topping.
2. In a large bowl combine remaining oats, flour, sugar and baking powder. Make a well in the center.
3. In another bowl combine zest, juice, egg and margarine. Add to the flour mixture, stirring just until moistened. Fold in apple and dates.
4. Spoon batter into prepared muffin tin, filling cups two-thirds full. Sprinkle with topping. Bake in preheated oven for 20 to 25 minutes.

Apricot Oatmeal Muffins

¾ cup	boiling water	175 mL
1 cup	quick-cooking oats	250 mL
½ cup	chopped dried apricots	125 mL
½ cup	margarine or butter	125 mL
1	egg	1
1 cup	milk	250 mL
2½ cups	all-purpose flour	625 mL
½ cup	firmly packed brown sugar	125 mL
1 tbsp	baking powder	15 mL
½ tsp	salt	2 mL

◆ *Preheat oven to 400°F (200°C)*
◆ *Muffin tin, greased or paper-lined*

1. In a medium bowl pour boiling water over oats, apricots and margarine. Stir until margarine melts. Set aside to cool. Add egg and milk.
2. In a large bowl combine flour, brown sugar, baking powder and sàlt. Add oat mixture, stirring just until blended and moistened. Do not overmix.
3. Spoon batter into prepared muffin tin, filling cups to the top. Bake in preheated oven for about 20 minutes.

Cranberry Oatmeal Muffins

½ cup	finely chopped walnuts	125 mL
½ cup	dried cranberries	125 mL
1½ cups	all-purpose flour	375 mL
1 tbsp	baking powder	15 mL
¾ tsp	salt	4 mL
¾ cup	old-fashioned oats	175 mL
3 tbsp	softened butter or margarine	45 mL
¾ cup	firmly packed light brown sugar	175 mL
¾ cup	milk	175 mL
1	egg	1

◆ *Preheat oven to 350°F (180°C)*
◆ *Muffin tin, greased*

1. In a small bowl toss together nuts, cranberries and 1 tsp (5 mL) flour. Set aside.
2. In a large bowl combine remaining flour, baking powder and salt. Stir in oats.
3. In another bowl whisk together butter, sugar, milk and egg, blending well. Add to flour mixture, stirring just until evenly moist and blended. Fold in nut mixture.
4. Spoon batter into prepared muffin tin, filling cups to the top. Bake in preheated oven for about 20 minutes.

Berry Oat Bran Muffins ➤
(page 88)

Oatmeal Date Muffins

1 cup	all-purpose flour	250 mL
2 tsp	baking powder	10 mL
½ tsp	baking soda	2 mL
½ tsp	salt	2 mL
1 cup	old-fashioned rolled oats	250 mL
1 cup	buttermilk	250 mL
½ cup	packed dark brown sugar	125 mL
1	egg, beaten	1
½ cup	butter or margarine, melted	125 mL
½ cup	chopped moist dates	125 mL

♦ *Preheat oven to 375°F (190°C)*
♦ *12-cup muffin tin, greased or paper-lined*

1. In a medium bowl sift together flour, baking powder, baking soda and salt.
2. In a large bowl combine oats and buttermilk. Let stand for 5 minutes. Add sugar, egg and butter, mixing well. Fold in dates. Add to flour mixture, stirring just until moist and blended.
3. Spoon batter into prepared muffin tin, filling cups three-quarters full. Bake in preheated oven for 25 to 30 minutes.

Fruity Oatmeal Muffins

1 cup	all-purpose flour	250 mL
1 tsp	baking powder	5 mL
¼ tsp	pumpkin pie spice	1 mL
1 cup	packaged dried fruit	250 mL
½ cup	softened butter or margarine	125 mL
⅔ cup	granulated sugar	150 mL
6	eggs	6
1 tsp	vanilla	5 mL
⅓ cup	rolled oats	75 mL

♦ *Preheat oven to 350°F (180°C)*
♦ *12-cup muffin tin, greased or paper-lined*

1. In a small bowl combine flour, baking powder and pumpkin pie spice. Take 1 tbsp (15 mL) of this flour mixture and toss in another bowl, with dried fruit.
2. In a large bowl beat butter and sugar on medium speed until light and fluffy. Beat in eggs and blend well. Reduce speed to low and add vanilla. Gradually add flour mixture, beating just until blended. Stir in fruit mixture and oats.
3. Spoon batter into prepared muffin tin, filling cups three-quarters full. Bake in preheated oven for 20 minutes or until golden brown.

◄ Peachy Oatmeal Muffins (page 101)

Whole-Wheat Honey Oatmeal Muffins

1 cup	whole-wheat flour	250 mL
1 cup	rolled oats	250 mL
1½ tsp	baking powder	7 mL
1 tsp	baking soda	5 mL
½ tsp	salt	2 mL
¼ tsp	cinnamon	1 mL
¼ cup	packed brown sugar	50 mL
1	egg	1
¼ cup	butter or margarine, melted and cooled	50 mL
¼ cup	honey	50 mL
1¼ cups	buttermilk	300 mL

◆ *Preheat oven to 400°F (200°C)*
◆ *Muffin tin, greased or paper-lined*

1. In a large bowl combine flour, oats, baking powder, baking soda, salt, cinnamon and brown sugar.
2. In another bowl whisk together egg, butter, honey and buttermilk. Pour into flour mixture, stirring just until moistened and blended.
3. Spoon batter into prepared muffin tin, filling cups to the top. Bake in preheated oven for 15 minutes.

> **HINT:** Use a muffin pan for a manicure tray. Put bottles of base, topcoat, various colors nail polish, cotton, etc. into each cup.

Orange Date Oatmeal Muffins

1¼ cups	milk	300 mL
1 cup	quick-cooking oats	250 mL
1	medium orange, cut into quarters and seeded	1
1	egg	1
¾ cup	firmly packed brown sugar	175 mL
½ cup	butter or margarine, melted	125 mL
½ cup	chopped dates	125 mL
2 cups	all-purpose flour	500 mL
1 tbsp	baking powder	15 mL
½ tsp	salt	2 mL

◆ *Preheat oven to 400°F (200°C)*
◆ *12-cup muffin tin, greased or paper-lined*

1. In a bowl pour milk over oats. Let stand for 5 minutes.
2. In a food processor or blender, process orange until finely chopped. Stir into oat mixture. Add egg, sugar, butter and dates.
3. In a large bowl combine flour, baking powder and salt. Add oat mixture, stirring just until blended. Do not overmix.
4. Spoon batter into prepared muffin tin, dividing evenly. Bake in preheated oven for 20 to 25 minutes or until golden brown.

Whole Wheat Oatmeal Muffins

½ cup	all-purpose flour	125 mL
½ cup	whole wheat flour	125 mL
1 cup	old-fashioned oats	250 mL
2 tsp	baking powder	10 mL
½ tsp	salt	2 mL
2	eggs	2
¾ cup	packed brown sugar	175 mL
¾ cup	milk	175 mL
¼ cup	butter or margarine, melted	50 mL
1 tsp	vanilla	5 mL

♦ *Preheat oven to 400°F (200°C)*
♦ *Muffin tin, greased*

1. In a bowl combine all-purpose flour, whole wheat flour, oats, baking powder and salt; blend well.
2. In another bowl whisk together eggs, brown sugar, milk, butter and vanilla. Add to dry mixture; stir just until blended.
3. Spoon batter into prepared muffin tin, filling three-quarters full. Bake in preheated oven for 15 to 20 minutes.

Lemon-Glazed Apple Oatmeal Muffins

1¼ cups	all-purpose flour	300 mL
½ cup	packed light brown sugar	125 mL
1½ tsp	baking powder	7 mL
1 tsp	baking soda	5 mL
1 tsp	cinnamon	5 mL
½ tsp	salt	2 mL
¼ tsp	ground nutmeg	1 mL
1	egg	1
½ cup	milk	125 mL
¼ cup	vegetable oil	50 mL
2 tbsp	lemon juice	25 mL
¾ cup	quick-cooking oats	175 mL
1 cup	finely chopped apples	250 mL
½ cup	chopped nuts	125 mL
LEMON GLAZE		
½ cup	icing sugar	125 mL
1 tbsp	lemon juice	15 mL
1 tbsp	butter or margarine, melted	15 mL

◆ *Preheat oven to 400°F (200°C)*
◆ *Muffin tin, greased or paper-lined*

1. In a medium bowl combine flour, sugar, baking powder, baking soda, cinnamon, salt and nutmeg.
2. In a large bowl beat egg. Add milk, oil and lemon juice. Stir in oats and mix well. Add flour mixture, blending well. Add apples and nuts, stirring just until moistened and lumpy. Do not overmix.
3. Spoon batter into prepared muffin tin, filling cups three-quarters full. Bake in preheated oven for 20 minutes or until golden brown.
4. Meanwhile, in a small bowl, combine icing sugar, juice and butter. Remove muffins from tin and place on a plate. Drizzle with lemon glaze.

> **HINT:** If you reduce or eliminate salt in recipes, use more herbs and spices to enhance the flavor. Experiment with small amounts at first, such as ¼ tsp (1 mL).

Peachy Oatmeal Muffins

2 cups	whole-wheat flour	500 mL
1 cup	rolled oats	250 mL
½ cup	unprocessed wheat bran	125 mL
½ cup	packed brown sugar	125 mL
1½ tsp	baking soda	7 mL
1 tsp	salt	5 mL
2	eggs	2
1½ cups	buttermilk	375 mL
¼ cup	vegetable oil	50 mL
3 tsp	orange zest	15 mL
1½ tsp	cinnamon	7 mL
3	fresh peaches, finely chopped	3

- *Preheat oven to 400°F (200°C)*
- *Muffin tin, paper-lined*

1. In a large bowl combine flour, oats, wheat bran, sugar, baking soda and salt. Make a well in the center.
2. In another bowl whisk together eggs, buttermilk and oil. Stir in zest and cinnamon. Add to dry ingredients, stirring just until moistened. Fold in peaches.
3. Spoon batter into prepared muffin tin, filling cups three-quarters full. Bake in preheated oven for about 20 minutes.

Variations
- You could replace peaches with 2 cups (500 mL) fresh chopped pears, plums or nectarines.

Oatmeal Raisin Breakfast Muffins

½ cup	raisins	125 mL
¼ cup	all-purpose flour	50 mL
¼ cup	butter or margarine	50 mL
⅓ cup	granulated sugar	75 mL
2	eggs	2
⅔ cup	milk	150 mL
¾ cup	all-purpose flour	175 mL
3 tsp	baking powder	15 mL
¾ tsp	salt	4 mL
1 cup	rolled oats	250 mL

- *Preheat oven to 400°F (200°C)*
- *12-cup muffin tin, greased*

1. In a small bowl toss together raisins and ¼ cup (50 mL) flour. Set aside.
2. In a large bowl cream together butter and sugar. Add eggs one at a time, beating after each addition. Add milk.
3. In another bowl combine ¾ cup (175 mL) flour, baking powder and salt. Pour into wet ingredients. Add oats, stirring just until blended. Fold in dredged raisins.
4. Spoon batter into prepared muffin tin, dividing evenly. Bake in preheated oven for 20 to 25 minutes.

> **HINT:** In baking only, you can use 1 cup (250 mL) shortening plus ½ tsp (2 mL) salt to replace 1 cup (250 mL) butter.

Banana Wheat Germ Muffins

2	small ripe bananas or 1 large banana, mashed	2
½ cup	granulated sugar or brown sugar	125 mL
⅓ cup	vegetable oil	75 mL
1	egg	1
1 tsp	vanilla	5 mL
½ cup	wheat germ	125 mL
1½ cups	all-purpose flour	375 mL
1 tsp	baking powder	5 mL
1 tsp	baking soda	5 mL
½ cup	milk	125 mL

*   *Preheat oven to 375°F (190°C)*
*   *12-cup muffin tin, greased or paper-lined*

1. In a bowl combine bananas, sugar, oil, egg and vanilla; beat until smooth. Add wheat germ; blend well.
2. In another bowl sift together flour, baking powder and baking soda. Add to banana mixture alternately with milk; stir just until blended.
3. Spoon batter into prepared muffin tin, filling to top. Bake in preheated oven for 20 to 25 minutes.

Wheat Germ Oat Muffins

½ cup	wheat germ	125 mL
½ cup	quick-cooking oats	125 mL
1 cup	all-purpose flour	250 mL
3 tsp	baking powder	15 mL
½ tsp	salt	2 mL
¾ tsp	cinnamon	4 mL
Pinch	nutmeg	Pinch
½ cup	brown sugar	125 mL
⅓ cup	shortening	75 mL
1	egg, slightly beaten	1
1 cup	milk	250 mL
1 tsp	vanilla	5 mL

*   *Preheat oven to 425°F (220°C)*
*   *12-cup muffin tin, greased or paper-lined*

1. In a bowl combine wheat germ, oats, flour, baking powder, salt, cinnamon, nutmeg and brown sugar; blend well. With a pastry blender or 2 knives, cut in shortening; mix until crumbly. Add egg, milk and vanilla; stir just until moist.
2. Spoon batter into prepared muffin tin, filling three-quarters full. Bake in preheated oven for 15 to 20 minutes.

Orange-Glazed Wheat Germ Muffins

ORANGE GLAZE		
½ cup	icing sugar	125 mL
1 tbsp	orange juice	15 mL
MUFFINS		
1½ cups	all-purpose flour	375 mL
½ cup	wheat germ	125 mL
¼ cup	granulated sugar	50 mL
1 tbsp	baking powder	15 mL
½ tsp	salt	2 mL
1 tbsp	grated orange zest	15 mL
⅔ cup	milk	150 mL
⅓ cup	margarine, melted	75 mL
2	eggs	2

◆ *Preheat oven to 400°F (200°C)*
◆ *12-cup muffin tin, greased or paper-lined*

1. In a bowl combine sugar and orange juice; blend well. Set aside.
2. In another bowl combine flour, wheat germ, sugar, baking powder, salt and zest; mix well. Make a well in the center.
3. In another bowl combine milk, margarine and eggs. Add to dry ingredients; stir just until moist and blended.
4. Spoon batter into prepared muffin tin, filling to top. Bake in preheated oven for 20 to 25 minutes. Let cool; drizzle with glaze.

Favorite Wheat Germ Muffins

1 cup	all-purpose flour	250 mL
1 cup	toasted wheat germ	250 mL
4 tsp	baking powder	20 mL
¼ tsp	baking soda	1 mL
½ tsp	salt	2 mL
1	egg	1
2 tbsp	softened butter or margarine	25 mL
¼ cup	packed brown sugar	50 mL
	Grated zest of 1 orange	
¼ cup	orange juice	50 mL
¾ cup	plain yogurt	175 mL

◆ *Preheat oven to 425°F (200°C)*
◆ *Muffin tin, greased or paper-lined*

1. In a large bowl combine flour, wheat germ, baking powder, baking soda and salt. Make a well in the center.
2. In another bowl cream together egg, butter and sugar. Stir in zest and orange juice, mixing well. Add yogurt. Add to dry ingredients, stirring just until blended. Do not overmix.
3. Spoon batter into prepared muffin tin, filling cups to the top. Bake in preheated oven for about 15 minutes.

Apple Streusel Wheat Germ Muffins

TOPPING

¼ cup	granulated sugar	50 mL
½ tsp	cinnamon	2 mL
⅓ cup	chopped nuts	75 mL
2 tbsp	butter or margarine, melted	25 mL

MUFFINS

1½ cups	all-purpose flour	375 mL
½ cup	wheat germ	125 mL
¼ cup	granulated sugar	50 mL
1 tbsp	baking powder	15 mL
¾ tsp	cinnamon	4 mL
½ tsp	salt	2 mL
1 cup	chopped peeled apple	250 mL
1	egg	1
1 cup	milk	250 mL

- ◆ *Preheat oven to 400°F (200°C)*
- ◆ *Muffin tin, greased or paper-lined*

1. In a bowl combine sugar, cinnamon, nuts and butter. Set aside.
2. In a large bowl combine flour, wheat germ, sugar, baking powder, cinnamon and salt. Stir in apple.
3. In another bowl whisk together egg, milk and oil. Add to dry ingredients, stirring just until moistened.
4. Spoon batter into prepared muffin tin, filling cups two-thirds full. Sprinkle with topping. Bake in preheated oven for 20 to 25 minutes or until browned.

Blueberry Wheat Germ Muffins

1¾ cups	all-purpose flour	425 mL
⅓ cup	wheat germ	75 mL
⅓ cup	granulated sugar	75 mL
1 tbsp	baking powder	15 mL
1½ tsp	grated lemon zest	7 mL
½ tsp	salt	2 mL
1	egg	1
1 cup	milk	250 mL
¼ cup	vegetable oil	50 mL
1 cup	fresh blueberries or frozen blueberries, drained	250 mL

- ◆ *Preheat oven to 400°F (200°C)*
- ◆ *Muffin tin, greased or paper-lined*

1. In a large bowl combine flour, wheat germ, sugar, baking powder, zest and salt. Make a well in the center.
2. In another bowl whisk together egg, milk and oil. Add to dry ingredients, stirring just until moist and blended. Fold in berries.
3. Spoon batter into prepared muffin tin, filling cups three-quarters full. Bake in preheated oven for 20 to 25 minutes.

Orange Wheat Germ Muffins

1 cup	all-purpose flour	250 mL
¾ cup	wheat germ	175 mL
½ cup	wheat bran	125 mL
3 tsp	baking powder	15 mL
½ tsp	salt	2 mL
½ cup	brown sugar	125 mL
½ cup	raisins	125 mL
1	egg	1
1 cup	milk	250 mL
¼ cup	vegetable oil	50 mL
2 tsp	grated orange zest	10 mL

♦ *Preheat oven to 400°F (200°C)*
♦ *Muffin tin, greased or paper-lined*

1. In a large bowl combine flour, wheat germ, bran, baking powder, salt, sugar and raisins.
2. In another bowl whisk together egg, milk, oil and zest. Add to dry ingredients, stirring just until moist and blended.
3. Spoon batter into prepared muffin tin, dividing evenly. Bake in preheated oven for 15 to 20 minutes or until tests done.

HINT: For plumper raisins, soak in orange juice and store in the refrigerator.

Spicy Whole Wheat Muffins

2 cups	whole wheat flour	500 mL
¾ cup	all-purpose flour	175 mL
⅔ cup	packed brown sugar	150 mL
2 tsp	baking soda	10 mL
1 tsp	pumpkin pie spice	5 mL
2 cups	buttermilk	500 mL
¾ cup	raisins	175 mL

♦ *Preheat oven to 350°F (180°C)*
♦ *Muffin tin, greased or paper-lined*

1. In a bowl combine whole wheat flour, all-purpose flour, brown sugar, baking soda and pumpkin pie spice; blend well. Add buttermilk; stir just until moist. Fold in raisins.
2. Spoon batter into prepared muffin tin, dividing evenly. Bake in preheated oven for 35 to 40 minutes.

Apricot Whole Wheat Muffins

1	can (14 oz/398 mL) apricot halves, well drained	1
1 cup	all-purpose flour	250 mL
¾ cup	whole wheat flour	175 mL
2½ tsp	baking powder	12 mL
½ tsp	baking soda	2 mL
¾ tsp	salt	4 mL
Pinch	ginger	Pinch
⅓ cup	brown sugar	75 mL
1	egg	1
¼ cup	oil	50 mL
½ cup	milk	125 mL
¼ cup	dried apricot halves, cut into tiny pieces	50 mL

♦ *Preheat oven to 400°F (200°C)*
♦ *12-cup muffin tin, greased or paper-lined*

1. In a blender purée canned apricots. Set aside.

2. In a bowl combine all-purpose flour, whole wheat flour, baking powder, baking soda, salt, ginger and brown sugar; mix well. Make a well in the center.

3. In another bowl whisk together egg, oil and milk. Add 1 cup (250 mL) apricot purée and dried apricots. Add to flour mixture; stir just until moist and blended.

4. Spoon batter into prepared muffin tin, dividing evenly. Bake in preheated oven for about 15 minutes.

Orange Marmalade Wheat Muffins

¾ cup	whole wheat flour	175 mL
¾ cup	all-purpose flour	175 mL
⅓ cup	granulated sugar	75 mL
2 tsp	baking powder	10 mL
½ tsp	baking soda	2 mL
¼ tsp	salt	1 mL
2 tsp	ginger	10 mL
2	eggs	2
⅓ cup	sour cream	75 mL
⅓ cup	orange juice	75 mL
7 tbsp	butter, melted	105 mL
1 tbsp	grated orange zest	15 mL
	Orange marmalade	

♦ *Preheat oven to 400°F (200°C)*
♦ *16-cup muffin tin, greased*

1. In a bowl combine whole wheat flour, all-purpose flour, sugar, baking powder, baking soda, salt and ginger. Make a well in the center.
2. In another bowl whisk together eggs, sour cream, orange juice, butter and orange zest. Pour into dry ingredients; stir quickly just until moist and blended.
3. Spoon batter into prepared muffin tin, filling three-quarters full. Add about 1 tsp (5 mL) orange marmalade to center of each. Bake in preheated oven for about 20 minutes.

Walnut Crunch Wheat Muffins

1 cup	whole wheat flour	250 mL
1 cup	all-purpose flour	250 mL
½ tsp	salt	2 mL
1 tbsp	baking powder	15 mL
1 tsp	baking soda	5 mL
½ cup	brown sugar	125 mL
1 cup	coarsely chopped walnuts	250 mL
1 cup	buttermilk	250 mL
2	eggs, beaten	2
⅓ cup	melted butter	75 mL

♦ *Preheat oven to 425°F (220°C)*
♦ *18-cup muffin tin, greased or paper-lined*

1. In a bowl sift together whole wheat flour, all-purpose flour, salt, baking powder, baking soda and brown sugar; mix well. Add walnuts; make a well in the center.
2. In another bowl whisk together buttermilk, eggs and butter. Pour into flour mixture; stir only until moist and blended.
3. Spoon batter into prepared muffin tin, filling three-quarters full. Bake in preheated oven for about 15 minutes.

Wheat Muffins

1 cup	all-purpose flour	250 mL
1 cup	unsifted whole-wheat flour	250 mL
2 tsp	baking powder	10 mL
1 tsp	salt	5 mL
1	egg, slightly beaten	1
¼ cup	molasses	50 mL
1 cup	milk	250 mL
¼ cup	butter or margarine, melted	50 mL

◆ *Preheat oven to 400°F (200°C)*
◆ *Muffin tin, greased or paper-lined*

1. In a large bowl combine all-purpose flour, whole-wheat flour, baking powder and salt. Make a well in the center.
2. In another bowl combine egg, molasses, milk and butter. Add to flour mixture, stirring just until blended. Do not overmix.
3. Spoon batter into prepared muffin tin, filling cups three-quarters full. Bake in preheated oven for 25 minutes or until golden brown.

Apple Whole-Wheat Muffins

1½ cups	whole-wheat flour	375 mL
½ cup	all-purpose flour	125 mL
2½ tsp	baking powder	12 mL
¾ tsp	salt	4 mL
1	egg, beaten	1
¾ cup	milk	175 mL
⅓ cup	vegetable oil	75 mL
⅓ cup	honey	75 mL
1 cup	chopped apples	250 mL

◆ *Preheat oven to 400°F (200°C)*
◆ *Muffin tin, greased or paper-lined*

1. In a large bowl combine whole-wheat flour, all-purpose flour, baking powder and salt.
2. In another bowl whisk together egg, milk, oil and honey. Add to flour mixture, stirring just until moist and blended. Do not overmix. Fold in apples.
3. Spoon batter into prepared muffin tin, filling cups three-quarters full. Bake in preheated oven for 18 to 20 minutes or until a toothpick inserted in center comes out clean and dry.

Whole-Wheat Date Muffins

1 cup	chopped pitted dates	250 mL
1 tsp	baking soda	5 mL
¾ cup	boiling water	175 mL
1	egg	1
½ cup	granulated sugar	125 mL
1 tsp	salt	5 mL
1 tsp	vanilla	5 mL
1½ cups	whole-wheat flour	375 mL
1 tsp	baking powder	5 mL
½ cup	chopped walnuts	125 mL
¼ cup	butter, melted	50 mL

> **HINT:** Store shelled nuts (and coconut) in tightly covered containers in the fridge or freezer to prevent from becoming rancid. When ready to use, heat thoroughly at 350°F (180°C).

◆ *Preheat oven to 375°F (190°C)*
◆ *Muffin tin, greased or paper-lined*

1. In a large bowl toss together dates and baking soda. Pour boiling water over top. Mix well and set aside to cool.

2. In another bowl whisk together egg, sugar, salt and vanilla. Add to date mixture. Stir in flour, baking powder and walnuts. Add melted butter, stirring just until blended.

3. Spoon batter into prepared muffin tin, filling cups three-quarters full. Bake in preheated oven for 15 to 20 minutes.

Herbed Whole-Wheat Muffins

1 cup	whole-wheat flour	250 mL
1 cup	all-purpose flour	250 mL
1/3 cup	granulated sugar	75 mL
2 tsp	baking powder	10 mL
1/2 tsp	baking soda	2 mL
1/2 tsp	salt	2 mL
1/2 tsp	dried basil leaves	2 mL
1/4 tsp	dried marjoram leaves	1 mL
1/4 tsp	dried oregano leaves	1 mL
1/8 tsp	dried thyme leaves	.5 mL
3/4 cup	raisins	175 mL
1 cup	buttermilk	250 mL
2 tbsp	butter or margarine, melted	25 mL
1	egg, beaten	1
2 tbsp	wheat germ	25 mL

- *Preheat oven to 400°F (200°C)*
- *Muffin tin, greased or paper-lined*

1. In a large bowl combine whole-wheat flour, all-purpose flour, sugar, baking powder, baking soda, salt, basil, marjoram, oregano, thyme and raisins.
2. In another bowl whisk together buttermilk, butter and egg. Add to flour mixture, stirring just until moistened and blended.
3. Spoon batter into prepared muffin tin, filling cups two-thirds full. Sprinkle with wheat germ. Bake in preheated oven for 15 to 20 minutes or until browned.

Honey Whole-Wheat Muffins

1 cup	whole-wheat flour	250 mL
1 cup	all-purpose flour	250 mL
3 tsp	baking powder	15 mL
1 tsp	salt	5 mL
1	egg	1
1 cup	milk	250 mL
1/4 cup	vegetable oil	50 mL
1/4 cup	honey	50 mL

- *Preheat oven to 400°F (200°C)*
- *12-cup muffin tin, greased or paper-lined*

1. In a large bowl combine whole-wheat flour, all-purpose flour, baking powder and salt. Make a well in the center.
2. In another bowl whisk together egg, milk and oil. Add the honey. Stir into flour mixture until moist and lumpy.
3. Spoon batter into prepared muffin tin, dividing evenly. Bake in preheated oven for 20 to 25 minutes or until lightly browned.

Peanut Butter Wheat Muffins

1¼ cups	whole-wheat flour	300 mL
1 tsp	baking powder	5 mL
1 tsp	baking soda	5 mL
½ tsp	salt	2 mL
⅓ cup	packed brown sugar	75 mL
1	egg	1
½ cup	peanut butter	125 mL
1 cup	buttermilk	250 mL
½ tsp	vanilla	2 mL
½ cup	peanut halves (optional)	125 mL

◆ *Preheat oven to 400°F (200°C)*
◆ *Muffin tin, greased or paper-lined*

1. In a large bowl mix together flour, baking powder, baking soda, salt and brown sugar. Make a well in the center.
2. In another bowl whisk together egg and peanut butter. Whisk in milk and vanilla. Add to dry ingredients, stirring just until moistened.
3. Spoon batter into prepared muffin tin, filling cups three-quarters full. If desired, sprinkle with peanut halves. Bake in preheated oven for 15 to 18 minutes.

Raisin Bran Wheat Muffins

1 cup	wheat bran	250 mL
1 cup	buttermilk	250 mL
½ cup	raisins	125 mL
½ cup	honey	125 mL
¼ cup	molasses	50 mL
⅓ cup	butter, melted or vegetable oil	75 mL
2	eggs	2
1 tsp	vanilla	5 mL
2 cups	whole-wheat flour	500 mL
1 tsp	baking powder	5 mL
1 tsp	baking soda	5 mL
¼ tsp	cinnamon	1 mL
Pinch	salt	Pinch

◆ *Preheat oven to 400°F (200°C)*
◆ *Muffin tin, greased or paper-lined*

1. In a small bowl combine bran, buttermilk and raisins. Set aside to soak.
2. In another bowl whisk together honey, molasses, butter, eggs and vanilla. Add bran mixture.
3. In another bowl sift together flour, baking powder, baking soda, cinnamon and salt. Add to liquid ingredients, stirring just until blended. Do not overmix.
4. Spoon batter into prepared muffin tin, filling cups to the top. Bake in preheated oven for 20 to 25 minutes.

> **HINT:** Use baking soda to remove coffee and tea stains from plastic cups and dishes.

Yogurt-Honey Muffins

1¼ cups	whole wheat flour	300 mL
1 cup	all-purpose flour	250 mL
¼ cup	brown sugar	50 mL
1½ tsp	baking powder	7 mL
1 tsp	baking soda	5 mL
1 tsp	salt	5 mL
Pinch	cinnamon	Pinch
Pinch	nutmeg	Pinch
1½ cups	plain yogurt	375 mL
¼ cup	honey	50 mL
¼ cup	melted butter	50 mL
1	egg	1
1 cup	raisins (optional)	250 mL

◆ *Preheat oven to 400°F (200°C)*
◆ *12-cup muffin tin, greased*

1. In a bowl combine whole wheat flour, all-purpose flour, brown sugar, baking powder, baking soda, salt, cinnamon and nutmeg; mix well. Make a well in the center.

2. In another bowl whisk together yogurt, honey, butter and egg. Pour into dry ingredients. Fold in raisins; stir just until moist and blended.

3. Spoon batter into prepared muffin tin. Bake in preheated oven for about 15 minutes.

Apricot Bran Yogurt Muffins

1¼ cups	all-purpose flour	300 mL
1¼ cups	natural bran	300 mL
¾ cup	packed brown sugar	175 mL
1 tbsp	baking powder	15 mL
1 tsp	baking soda	5 mL
¼ tsp	cinnamon	1 mL
¼ tsp	salt	1 mL
1 cup	chopped dried apricots	250 mL
1 cup	low-fat yogurt	250 mL
¼ cup	vegetable oil	50 mL
1	egg	1
1½ tsp	vanilla	7 mL

◆ *Preheat oven to 375°F (190°C)*
◆ *Muffin tin, greased or paper-lined*

1. In a large bowl combine flour, bran, sugar, baking powder, baking soda, cinnamon and salt.

2. Set aside 2 tbsp (25 mL) of the apricots and add remaining apricots to flour mixture.

3. In another bowl whisk together yogurt, oil, egg and vanilla. Add to flour mixture, stirring just until blended. Do not overmix.

4. Spoon batter into prepared muffin tin, filling cups three-quarters full. Sprinkle with reserved apricots. Bake in preheated oven for 20 to 25 minutes.

Savory Yogurt Muffins

1 cup	rolled oats	250 mL
1/3 cup	oat bran	75 mL
1 cup	boiling water	250 mL
1 cup	granulated sugar	250 mL
1/3 cup	oil	75 mL
2	eggs	2
2 cups	low-fat yogurt	500 mL
1 cup	whole wheat flour	250 mL
1 cup	all-purpose flour	250 mL
3 tsp	baking soda	15 mL
2 cups	bran cereal	500 mL

MUFFIN STUFF: If you only want to use half the batter, keep the remainder covered in your refrigerator for up to 2 weeks.

◆ *Preheat oven to 375°F (190°C)*
◆ *Muffin tin, greased or paper-lined*

1. In a bowl combine oats, bran and water. Let stand for 5 minutes. Add sugar, oil, eggs and yogurt; blend well. Add whole wheat flour, all-purpose flour, baking soda and bran cereal; stir just until blended. Do not overmix.

2. Spoon batter into prepared muffin tin, filling to top. Bake in preheated oven for about 15 minutes.

Variations

For every 2 cups (500 mL) batter, you can add:

◆ 1 cup (250 mL) fresh or frozen berries (blueberries, raspberries or cranberries) and 1 tbsp (15 mL) grated orange zest.

◆ 1 cup (250 mL) chopped fruit (dates, raisins, prunes, apricots), 1/2 cup (125 mL) chopped nuts (walnuts or almonds) and 1 tsp (5 mL) pumpkin pie spice.

Blueberry Bran Yogurt Muffins

2 cups	yogurt	500 mL
2 tsp	baking soda	10 mL
1½ cups	packed brown sugar	375 mL
2	eggs	2
1 cup	vegetable oil	250 mL
2 cups	natural bran	500 mL
2 tsp	vanilla	10 mL
2 cups	all-purpose flour	500 mL
4 tsp	baking powder	20 mL
½ tsp	salt	2 mL
1 cup	fresh blueberries or frozen blueberries, unsweetened	250 mL

◆ *Preheat oven to 350°F (180°C)*
◆ *Muffin tin, greased or paper-lined*

1. In a bowl combine yogurt and baking soda. Set aside.
2. In a large bowl whisk together sugar, eggs and oil. Add bran and vanilla.
3. In another bowl sift together flour, baking powder and salt. Add to bran mixture alternately with yogurt mixture. Fold in blueberries.
4. Spoon batter into prepared muffin tin, filling cups three-quarters full. Bake in preheated oven for 30 to 35 minutes or until toothpick inserted in center comes out clean.

> **HINT:** When a recipe tells you to fold in egg whites, fruit or other ingredients, use a rubber spatula. Gently cut down through the center of the mixture, across the bottom and up the side, heaping mixture from bottom to top. Repeat, turning bowl slightly each time.

Orange-Glazed Yogurt Muffins

2½ cups	all-purpose flour	625 mL
1 tsp	baking powder	5 mL
1 tsp	baking soda	5 mL
½ tsp	salt	2 mL
⅔ cup	butter or margarine	150 mL
2	eggs	2
½ cup	plain yogurt	125 mL
½ cup	orange juice	125 mL
1 tbsp	grated orange zest	15 mL
ORANGE GLAZE		
3 to 4 tsp	orange juice	15 to 20 mL
½ cup	sifted icing sugar	125 mL

- *Preheat oven to 400°F (200°C)*
- *Muffin tin, greased or paper-lined*

1. In a bowl sift together flour, baking powder, baking soda and salt.
2. In a large mixer bowl beat together butter and sugar until light and fluffy. Add eggs, yogurt, juice and zest, beating until smooth. Fold in flour mixture and stir just until blended. Do not overmix.
3. Spoon batter into prepared muffin tin, filling cups to the top. Bake in preheated oven for 15 to 20 minutes. Set aside to cool.
4. In a bowl combine juice and icing sugar to make a fairly thick glaze. Drizzle over cooled muffins.

Lemon Yogurt Cranberry Muffins

⅔ cup	honey	150 mL
⅓ cup	vegetable oil	75 mL
4	eggs	4
1½ tsp	lemon extract	7 mL
1¾ cups	all-purpose flour	425 mL
¾ cup	whole-wheat flour	175 mL
2½ tsp	baking powder	12 mL
1 cup	lemon yogurt	250 mL
1 cup	coarsely chopped cranberries	250 mL
1 tbsp	grated lemon zest	15 mL

◆ *Preheat oven to 400°F (200°C)*
◆ *Muffin tin, greased or paper-lined*

1. In a large mixer bowl beat together honey and oil until creamy. Beat in eggs and lemon extract.

2. In another bowl combine all-purpose flour, whole-wheat flour and baking powder. Add to egg mixture alternately with yogurt, beginning and ending with flour mixture. Fold in cranberries and zest, stirring just until moistened. Do not overmix.

3. Spoon batter into prepared muffin tin, filling cups to the top. Bake in preheated oven for 15 to 20 minutes.

Delicious Vegetable Muffins

2⅓ cups	all-purpose flour	575 mL
4 tbsp	grated Parmesan cheese	60 mL
2 tbsp	granulated sugar	25 mL
1 tbsp	baking powder	15 mL
¾ tsp	salt	4 mL
¾ tsp	dried thyme	4 mL
⅛ tsp	nutmeg	0.5 mL
1 cup	milk	250 mL
¼ cup	vegetable oil	50 mL
1	egg	1
½ cup	chopped spinach leaves	125 mL
½ cup	grated carrots	125 mL
1	scallion, chopped	1
2 tbsp	sliced pimento	25 mL

◆ *Preheat oven to 350°F (180°C)*
◆ *Muffin tin, greased*

1. In a bowl combine flour, 2 tbsp (25 mL) Parmesan cheese, sugar, baking powder, salt, thyme and nutmeg.

2. In another bowl combine milk, oil and egg. Add to flour mixture; stir just until moist. Add spinach, carrots, scallion and pimento.

3. Spoon batter into prepared muffin tin, filling three-quarters full. Sprinkle with remaining Parmesan cheese. Bake in preheated oven for 20 to 25 minutes or until toothpick inserted in center comes out clean and dry.

Two-Tone Muffins

2 cups	all-purpose flour	500 mL
½ cup	granulated sugar	125 mL
1 tbsp	baking powder	15 mL
1 tsp	salt	5 mL
¾ cup	roasted diced almonds	175 mL
¾ cup	orange juice	175 mL
⅓ cup	almond oil or vegetable oil	75 mL
1	egg, beaten	1
¼ cup	cocoa powder	50 mL
1 tsp	grated orange zest	5 mL

- ◆ *Preheat oven to 400°F (200°C)*
- ◆ *12-cup muffin tin, paper-lined*

1. In a bowl combine flour, sugar, baking powder and salt. Add almonds, reserving some for garnish.
2. In another bowl combine orange juice, oil and egg. Add to flour mixture; stir just until moist.
3. In another bowl combine half the batter and cocoa powder. Set aside. To remaining batter add orange zest; mix well.
4. Spoon orange zest batter into one side of prepared muffin cups, dividing evenly. Spoon cocoa powder batter into other side of cups, dividing evenly. Sprinkle with reserved almonds. Bake in preheated oven for 20 minutes or until toothpick inserted in center comes out clean and dry.

Wild Rice Muffins

2 cups	water	500 mL
1/3 cup	wild rice	75 mL
2	large eggs	2
1 cup	milk	250 mL
1/2 cup	melted butter, cooled	125 mL
1 1/2 cups	all-purpose flour	375 mL
1/2 cup	natural bran	125 mL
1/3 cup	packed brown sugar	75 mL
1 tbsp	baking powder	15 mL
1/4 tsp	salt	1 mL
1/4 tsp	nutmeg	1 mL
1/2 cup	chopped toasted pecans	125 mL
1/2 cup	sliced dates	125 mL
1/4 cup	slivered apricots	50 mL
2 tsp	grated orange zest	10 mL

♦ *Preheat oven to 375°F (190°C)*
♦ *Muffin tin, paper-lined*

1. In a saucepan over high heat, bring water to a boil. Reduce heat to medium; add rice. Cook, covered, for 45 minutes or until tender. Drain well; set aside to cool.

2. In a bowl whisk eggs. Add rice, milk and butter; mix well.

3. In another bowl combine flour, bran, brown sugar, baking powder, salt and nutmeg. Add to rice mixture; blend well. Add pecans, dates, apricots and orange zest; mix just until moist.

4. Spoon batter into prepared muffin tin, dividing evenly. Bake in preheated oven for 20 to 25 minutes or until golden brown.

Low-Fat Muffins

All-Bran Muffins

1¼ cups	all-bran cereal	300 mL
1 cup	buttermilk	250 mL
1	egg	1
½ cup	vegetable oil	125 mL
2 tbsp	molasses	25 mL
2 tsp	vanilla	10 mL
1 cup	all-purpose flour	250 mL
1 tsp	baking powder	5 mL
1 tsp	baking soda	5 mL
Pinch	salt	Pinch

◆ *Preheat oven to 425°F (220°C)*
◆ *Muffin tin, paper-lined*

1. In a bowl cover cereal with buttermilk. Set aside.
2. In another bowl vigorously beat together egg, oil, molasses and vanilla.
3. In another bowl combine flour, baking powder, baking soda and salt. Add to egg mixture; stir just until blended. Add cereal mixture; blend well.
4. Spoon batter into prepared muffin tin, filling three-quarters full. Bake in preheated oven for 15 to 20 minutes.

> **MUFFIN STUFF:** As a substitute for 1 cup (250 mL) buttermilk, you can combine 3 tbsp (45 mL) powdered buttermilk with about ¾ cup (175 mL) lukewarm water.

Apricot Orange Muffins

1 cup	orange juice	250 mL
½ cup	chopped dried apricots	125 mL
½ cup	raisins	125 mL
1	egg	1
1	egg white	1
2 tbsp	butter, melted	25 mL
1½ tsp	vanilla	7 mL
2 cups	all-purpose flour	500 mL
¾ cup	granulated sugar	175 mL
2 tsp	baking powder	10 mL
1 tsp	baking soda	5 mL
Pinch	nutmeg	Pinch

◆ *Preheat oven to 350°F (180°C)*
◆ *12-cup muffin tin, lightly sprayed with vegetable spray or paper-lined*

1. In a bowl combine orange juice, apricots, raisins, egg, egg white, butter and vanilla.
2. In another bowl combine flour, sugar, baking powder, baking soda and nutmeg. Add liquid ingredients; stir just until moist and blended.
3. Spoon batter into prepared muffin tin, filling three-quarters full. Bake in preheated oven for 20 to 25 minutes or until golden brown.

Easy Bran Muffins

2 tbsp	canola oil	25 mL
1/4 cup	firmly packed brown sugar	50 mL
1/4 cup	molasses	50 mL
2	egg whites	2
1 cup	skim or 1% milk	250 mL
1 1/2 cups	bran	375 mL
1 cup	all-purpose flour	250 mL
1 1/2 tsp	baking powder	7 mL
1/2 tsp	baking soda	2 mL
3/4 tsp	salt	4 mL
1/2 cup	raisins	125 mL

- *Preheat oven to 400°F (200°C)*
- *12-cup muffin tin, lightly sprayed with vegetable spray or paper-lined*

1. In a bowl beat together oil, brown sugar, molasses and egg whites. Add milk and bran; blend well.
2. In another bowl combine flour, baking powder, baking soda and salt. Add to liquid ingredients; stir just until moist. Add raisins; blend.
3. Spoon batter into prepared muffin tin, dividing evenly. Bake in preheated oven for 18 to 20 minutes.

Variations
- Ginger Bran Muffins: Add 1 tbsp (15 mL) finely chopped crystalized ginger to batter.

Old-Fashioned Bran Muffins

1 1/2 cups	skim milk or non-fat dry milk	375 mL
1 cup	whole bran cereal	250 mL
1 1/4 cups	all-purpose flour	300 mL
2 tbsp	granulated sugar	25 mL
4 tsp	double-acting baking powder	20 mL
3/4 tsp	salt	4 mL
1	egg	1
3 tbsp	shortening, melted	45 mL

- *Preheat oven to 400°F (200°C)*
- *18-cup muffin tin, lightly sprayed with vegetable spray or paper-lined*

1. In a bowl cover bran cereal with milk. Let stand for 5 minutes.
2. In another bowl combine flour, sugar, baking powder and salt. Make a well in the center.
3. Add egg and shortening to bran mixture; blend well. Pour into flour mixture; stir just until moist and blended.
4. Spoon batter into prepared muffin tin, dividing evenly. Bake in preheated oven for 25 minutes or until brown.

Banana Bran Muffins

2½ cups	whole wheat flour	625 mL
½ cup	coarsely chopped dates	125 mL
½ cup	coarsely chopped prunes	125 mL
3 cups	bran	750 mL
1 cup	boiling water	250 mL
1 cup	raisins	250 mL
2½ tsp	baking soda	12 mL
1 cup	buttermilk or low-fat milk	250 mL
¾ cup	honey	175 mL
2	ripe bananas, mashed	2
⅓ cup	oil	75 mL
½ cup	egg substitute	125 mL
½ cup	chopped walnuts (optional)	125 mL

- *Preheat oven to 350°F (180°C)*
- *20-cup muffin tin, lightly sprayed with vegetable spray or paper-lined*

1. In a food processor combine 1 cup (250 mL) flour, dates and prunes; process until finely chopped. In a bowl combine fruit mixture, bran, water and raisins. Let stand for 10 minutes.

2. In another bowl combine remaining flour and baking soda.

3. In another bowl combine buttermilk, honey, bananas, oil, egg substitute and walnuts; blend well. Add to flour mixture; combine well. Add bran mixture; stir just until moist and blended.

4. Spoon batter into prepared muffin tin, filling three-quarters full. Bake in preheated oven for 20 to 25 minutes.

Raisin Bran Muffins

½ cup	whole wheat flour	125 mL
¼ cup + 3 tbsp	all-purpose flour	50 mL + 45 mL
6 tsp	sugar substitute	30 mL
1 tbsp	baking powder	15 mL
¼ tsp	salt	1 mL
1½ cups	unprocessed bran	375 mL
1½ cups	uncooked quick-cooking rolled oats	375 mL
¾ cup	buttermilk	175 mL
¼ cup	frozen, concentrated apple juice	50 mL
2 tbsp	vegetable oil	25 mL
2	egg whites	2
2½ tsp	honey	12 mL
¼ cup + 2 tbsp	raisins	50 mL + 25 mL
½ cup	hot water	125 mL

- *Preheat oven to 400°F (200°C)*
- *12-cup muffin tin, lightly sprayed with vegetable spray or paper-lined*

1. In a bowl sift together whole wheat flour, all-purpose flour, sugar substitute, baking powder and salt; blend well. Add bran and oats.
2. In a blender combine buttermilk, apple juice, oil, egg whites and honey; process until well blended. Pour into dry ingredients; stir just until moist. Add raisins and hot water.
3. Spoon batter into prepared muffin tin, filling three-quarters full. Bake in preheated oven for 20 minutes or until lightly browned and firm to the touch.

Blueberry Muffins

1¾ cups	all-purpose flour	425 mL
3 tsp	baking powder	15 mL
½ tsp	salt	2 mL
3 tbsp	granulated sugar	45 mL
1	egg white	1
1 tsp	lemon juice	5 mL
1 cup	skim milk	250 mL
¼ cup	corn oil margarine, melted	50 mL
1 cup	frozen unsweetened blueberries, not thawed	250 mL

- *Preheat oven to 400°F (200°C)*
- *Muffin tin, lightly sprayed with vegetable spray or paper-lined*

1. In a bowl sift together flour, baking powder, salt and sugar.
2. In another bowl beat together egg white and lemon juice until stiff.
3. Add milk and margarine to flour mixture; blend with a fork just until mixed. Fold in beaten egg white. Add blueberries.
4. Spoon batter into prepared muffin tin, filling three-quarters full. Bake in preheated oven for 25 minutes.

Blueberry Buttermilk Bran Muffins

3 cups	bran	750 mL
2 cups	whole wheat flour	500 mL
¾ cup	granulated sugar	175 mL
1 tbsp	baking powder	15 mL
1 tsp	baking soda	5 mL
2	eggs, beaten	2
2 cups	buttermilk	500 mL
½ cup	vegetable oil	125 mL
½ cup	molasses	125 mL
1 cup	fresh or frozen blueberries	250 mL

◆ *Preheat oven to 375°F (190°C)*
◆ *Muffin tin, paper-lined*

1. In a bowl combine bran, flour, sugar, baking powder and baking soda.
2. In another bowl combine eggs, buttermilk, oil and molasses. Pour into dry ingredients; stir just until moist. Do not overmix. Fold in blueberries.
3. Spoon batter into prepared muffin tin, filling three-quarters full. Bake in preheated oven for about 25 minutes.

Blueberry Oatmeal Muffins

1¾ cups	all-purpose flour	425 mL
1 cup	quick-cooking rolled oats	250 mL
¼ cup	firmly packed brown sugar	50 mL
1 tbsp	baking powder	15 mL
½ tsp	salt	2 mL
1 tsp	cinnamon	5 mL
1 cup	skim milk	250 mL
1	egg, beaten	1
3 tbsp	oil	45 mL
1 cup	fresh or frozen blueberries, unsweetened	250 mL

◆ *Preheat oven to 425°F (220°C)*
◆ *12-cup muffin tin, paper-lined*

1. In a bowl combine flour, oats, brown sugar, baking powder, salt and cinnamon; blend well. Add milk, egg and oil; stir until blended. Fold in berries.
2. Spoon batter into prepared muffin tin, dividing evenly. Bake in preheated oven for 20 to 25 minutes.

Herbed Brown Rice Muffins

1¾ cups + 2 tbsp	all-purpose flour	425 mL + 25 mL
1 cup	cooked brown rice	250 mL
1 tbsp	baking powder	15 mL
2 tsp	granulated sugar	10 mL
½ tsp	salt	2 mL
¼ cup	minced fresh basil	50 mL
2 tbsp	chopped fresh dill	25 mL
1 cup	skim milk	250 mL
¼ cup	water	50 mL
1	egg	1
3 tbsp	vegetable oil	45 mL

◆ *Preheat oven to 400°F (200°C)*
◆ *12-cup muffin tin, paper-lined*

1. In a bowl combine flour, rice, baking powder, sugar, salt, basil and dill; blend well with a fork.
2. In another bowl combine milk, water, egg and oil. Add to flour mixture; stir just until blended.
3. Spoon batter into prepared muffin tin, dividing evenly. Bake in preheated oven for 20 to 25 minutes.

Carrot Orange Muffins

1 cup	all-purpose flour	250 mL
1 cup	whole wheat flour	250 mL
2 tsp	baking powder	10 mL
1 tsp	cinnamon	5 mL
¼ tsp	salt	1 mL
1 tsp	grated orange zest	5 mL
½ cup + 2 tbsp	fresh orange juice	125 mL + 25 mL
½ cup	skim milk	125 mL
¼ cup	vegetable oil	50 mL
2 tbsp	honey	25 mL
2	egg whites	2
1 cup	coarsely grated carrots	250 mL

◆ *Preheat oven to 400°F (200°C)*
◆ *Muffin tin, lightly sprayed with vegetable spray or paper-lined*

1. In a bowl combine all-purpose flour, whole wheat flour, baking powder, cinnamon and salt.
2. In another bowl whisk together orange zest, orange juice, milk, oil, honey and egg whites (mixture will look curdled). Add carrots; pour into flour mixture. Fold with spatula just until moist.
3. Spoon batter into prepared muffin tin, filling three-quarters full. Bake in preheated oven for 20 to 25 minutes or until golden brown.

Carrot Raisin Muffins

½ cup	all-purpose flour	125 mL
½ cup	whole wheat flour	125 mL
1 tsp	baking powder	5 mL
½ tsp	baking soda	2 mL
1 tsp	cinnamon	5 mL
¼ tsp	salt	1 mL
4	egg whites	4
⅔ cup	granulated sugar	160 mL
¼ cup	vegetable oil	50 mL
½ tsp	vanilla	2 mL
1½ cups	shredded carrots	375 mL
½ cup	raisins	125 mL

◆ *Preheat oven to 375°F (190°C)*
◆ *12-cup muffin tin, paper-lined*

1. In a bowl combine all-purpose flour, whole wheat flour, baking powder, baking soda, cinnamon and salt.
2. In another bowl whisk together egg whites, sugar, oil and vanilla. Add dry ingredients; stir just until moist. Add carrots and raisins.
3. Spoon batter into prepared muffin tin, filling three-quarters full. Bake in preheated oven for about 20 minutes.

Cinnamon Raisin Muffins

2¼ cups	all-purpose flour	550 mL
¼ cup	granulated sugar	50 mL
2 tsp	baking powder	10 mL
1 tsp	cinnamon	5 mL
½ tsp	baking soda	2 mL
½ tsp	salt	2 mL
¾ cup	dark raisins	175 mL
1 cup + 2 tbsp	buttermilk	250 mL + 25 mL
1	egg, lightly beaten	1

◆ *Preheat oven to 375°F (190°C)*
◆ *12-cup muffin tin, paper-lined*

1. In a bowl combine flour, sugar, baking powder, cinnamon, baking soda and salt; blend well. Add raisins, buttermilk and egg, mixing just until blended.
2. Spoon batter into prepared muffin tin, filling three-quarters full. Bake in preheated oven for about 20 minutes or until lightly browned.

Quick Cornmeal Muffins

1 cup	cornmeal	250 mL
½ cup	whole wheat flour	125 mL
½ cup	unbleached flour	125 mL
1 tbsp	baking powder	15 mL
1 tsp	dried sage	5 mL
1 cup	skim milk	250 mL
¼ cup	fat-free egg substitute	50 mL
2 tbsp	honey	25 mL
2 tbsp	oil	25 mL

+ *Preheat oven to 450°F (230°C)*
+ *12-cup muffin tin, sprayed with vegetable spray*

1. In a bowl combine cornmeal, whole wheat flour, unbleached flour, baking powder and sage; blend well. Make a well in the center.

2. In another bowl whisk together milk, egg substitute, honey and oil. Pour into dry ingredients; stir until well blended.

3. Spoon batter into prepared muffin tin, filling two-thirds full. Bake in preheated oven for 15 minutes or until golden brown.

Low-Cal Cornmeal Muffins

¾ cup	cornmeal	175 mL
¼ cup	all-purpose flour	50 mL
½ tsp	salt	2 mL
1½ tsp	baking powder	7 mL
¼ tsp	baking soda	1 mL
¾ cup	buttermilk	175 mL
1	egg	1
2 tbsp	butter or margarine, melted or vegetable oil	25 mL
2 tbsp	sugar substitute	25 mL

+ *Preheat oven to 425°F (220°C)*
+ *Muffin tin, paper-lined*

1. In a bowl sift together cornmeal, flour, salt, baking powder and baking soda; blend well. Add buttermilk, egg, butter and sugar substitute; beat for 1 minute with rotary beater (mixture will be loose).

2. Spoon batter into prepared muffin tin, filling three-quarters full. Bake in preheated oven for 20 to 25 minutes.

Johnny Appleseed Muffins

1 cup	whole wheat flour	250 mL
½ cup	unbleached flour	125 mL
1 cup	bran flakes cereal	250 mL
1 tbsp	baking powder	15 mL
½ tsp	baking soda	2 mL
1 tsp	cinnamon	5 mL
½ tsp	grated nutmeg	2 mL
½ tsp	ground cloves	2 mL
1¼ cups	applesauce	300 mL
½ cup	fat-free egg substitute	125 mL
⅓ cup	honey	75 mL
2 tbsp	oil	25 mL
1	medium apple, shredded	1

◆ *Preheat oven to 425°F (220°C)*
◆ *12-cup muffin tin, sprayed with vegetable spray or paper-lined*

1. In a bowl combine whole wheat flour, unbleached flour, cereal, baking powder, baking soda, cinnamon, nutmeg and cloves; mix well.

2. In another bowl whisk together applesauce, egg substitute, honey and oil; blend well. Add apple; pour into flour mixture. Stir just until moist.

3. Spoon batter into prepared muffin tin. Bake in preheated oven for about 20 minutes.

Blueberry Muffins ➤
(page 123)

Maple Muffins

1 cup	whole wheat flour	250 mL
1 cup	unbleached flour	250 mL
¼ cup	coarsely chopped pecans	50 mL
2 tsp	baking powder	10 mL
⅔ cup	low-fat milk	160 mL
⅔ cup	maple syrup	160 mL
½ cup	fat-free egg substitute	125 mL
2 tbsp	oil	25 mL

♦ *Preheat oven to 375°F (190°C)*
♦ *12-cup muffin tin, sprayed with vegetable spray*

1. In a bowl combine whole wheat flour, unbleached flour, pecans and baking powder.
2. In another bowl whisk together milk, maple syrup, egg substitute and oil. Pour into dry ingredients; stir just until blended.
3. Spoon batter into prepared muffin tin, filling three-quarters full. Bake in preheated oven for 15 to 20 minutes.

Maple Pecan Muffins

1 cup	all purpose flour	250 mL
½ cup	whole wheat flour	125 mL
¼ cup	chopped pecans	50 mL
2	egg yolks	2
½ cup	skim milk	125 mL
¼ cup	maple syrup	50 mL
2 tbsp	unsalted butter or margarine, melted	25 mL
4	egg whites	4
3 tbsp	granulated sugar	45 mL

♦ *Preheat oven to 400°F (200°C)*
♦ *Muffin tin, paper-lined*

1. In a bowl combine all-purpose flour, whole wheat flour and pecans. Set aside.
2. In another bowl combine egg yolks, milk, maple syrup and melted butter. Set aside.
3. In another bowl beat egg whites at high speed, gradually adding sugar, until stiff peaks form.
4. Beat milk mixture until well blended. Add to flour mixture; stir until moist. Gently fold in egg whites until blended.
5. Spoon batter into prepared muffin tin, filling to top. Bake in preheated oven for 20 minutes or until lightly browned.

Orange Currant Oat Bran Muffins

2½ cups	oat bran	625 mL
½ cup	currants	125 mL
1 tbsp	baking powder	15 mL
1 tsp	grated orange zest	5 mL
⅓ cup	granulated sugar	75 mL
½ cup	fresh orange juice	125 mL
¼ cup	vegetable oil	50 mL
3	egg whites	3

◆ *Preheat oven to 375°F (190°C)*
◆ *Muffin tin, sprayed with vegetable spray*

1. In a bowl combine oat bran, currants, baking powder, orange zest and ¼ cup (50 mL) sugar; blend well. Add orange juice and oil; stir until well blended.

2. In a bowl beat egg whites; slowly add remaining sugar until soft peaks form. Gently add to oat bran mixture; blend well.

3. Spoon batter into prepared muffin tin, dividing evenly. Bake in preheated oven for about 20 minutes or until browned.

Orange Fig Fiber Muffins

1	small orange, cut into quarters and seeds removed	1
¾ cup	water	175 mL
5	large dried figs, cut into quarters	5
¼ cup	margarine, cut into pieces	50 mL
¼ cup + 2 tbsp	frozen orange juice concentrate	50 mL + 25 mL
2	egg whites	2
2 cups less 2 tbsp	all-purpose flour	500 mL less 25 mL
1 tsp	baking powder	5 mL
½ tsp	baking soda	2 mL
½ tsp	salt	2 mL
2½ tsp	sunflower seeds	12 mL

◆ *Preheat oven to 350°F (180°C)*
◆ *Muffin tin, paper-lined*

1. In a blender or food processor combine orange, water, figs, margarine, orange juice concentrate and egg whites. Process for 1 minute or until well blended and peel is finely ground. Transfer to a bowl.

2. In another bowl sift together flour, baking powder, baking soda and salt. Add to orange mixture; stir just until blended. Fold in sunflower seeds.

3. Spoon batter into prepared muffin tin, dividing evenly. Bake in preheated oven for about 35 minutes.

Sunny Boy Cereal Muffins

1 cup	sifted whole wheat flour	250 mL
1 cup	Sunny Boy cereal	250 mL
1/2 cup	raisins or chopped dates	125 mL
1/2 tsp	salt	2 mL
1/2 cup	honey	125 mL
2 tbsp	safflower oil	25 mL
1	egg	1
1 tsp	baking soda	5 mL
1 cup	buttermilk or sour milk	250 mL

- *Preheat oven to 375°F (190°C)*
- *Muffin tin, paper-lined*

1. In a bowl combine flour, cereal, raisins and salt; blend well.
2. In another bowl combine honey, oil and egg; mix well.
3. In another bowl combine baking soda and buttermilk; blend well. Add to honey mixture; mix well. Add to flour mixture; stir just until moist.
4. Spoon batter into prepared muffin tin, dividing evenly. Bake in preheated oven for about 25 minutes.

Pineapple Bran Muffins

4	egg whites	4
1	can (8 oz/227 mL) crushed pineapple, in juice	1
1/2 cup	granulated sugar	125 mL
1/3 cup	skim or 1% milk	75 mL
3 tbsp	vegetable oil	45 mL
3 tbsp	molasses	45 mL
1 1/2 cups	wheat bran or all-bran cereal or whole bran flakes	375 mL
3/4 cup	all-purpose flour	175 mL
3/4 cup	whole wheat flour	175 mL
2 tsp	baking powder	10 mL
1/2 tsp	ginger	2 mL
1/2 tsp	salt	2 mL

- *Preheat oven to 375°F (190°C)*
- *12-cup muffin tin, sprayed with vegetable spray*

1. In a bowl whisk together egg whites, pineapple (with juice), sugar, milk, oil and molasses; blend well. Add bran. Let stand for 5 minutes.
2. In another bowl combine all-purpose flour, whole wheat flour, baking powder, ginger and salt. Add to bran mixture; stir just until blended.
3. Spoon batter into prepared muffin tin. Bake in preheated oven for 20 to 25 minutes.

Prune Muffins

1 cup	prune paste	250 mL
2 cups	brown sugar	500 mL
2	eggs	2
2 tbsp	molasses	25 mL
2¾ cups all-purpose flour		675 mL
1½ cups wheat bran		375 mL
2 tsp	baking powder	10 mL
½ tsp	salt	2 mL
1 cup	raisins	250 mL
2 tsp	baking soda	10 mL
2 cups	buttermilk	500 mL

◆ *Preheat oven to 375°F (190°C)*
◆ *18-cup muffin tin, sprayed with vegetable spray or paper-lined*

1. In a bowl beat together prune paste and sugar. Add eggs and molasses; beat well.

2. In another bowl combine flour, bran, baking powder and salt. Add to prune mixture; stir just until blended. Add raisins.

3. In another bowl combine baking soda and buttermilk; mix well. Add to batter; stir just until blended.

4. Spoon batter into prepared muffin tin, filling two-thirds full. Bake in preheated oven for about 20 minutes.

Fruit and Vegetable Muffins

continued on next page

Apple Muffins

2¼ cups	sifted cake flour	550 mL
3½ tsp	baking powder	17 mL
½ tsp	salt	2 mL
½ tsp	cinnamon	2 mL
½ tsp	nutmeg	2 mL
4 tbsp	shortening	60 mL
½ cup	granulated sugar	125 mL
1	egg, beaten	1
1 cup	milk	250 mL
1 cup	finely chopped peeled apples	250 mL
2 tbsp	granulated sugar	25 mL

◆ *Preheat oven to 425°F (220°C)*
◆ *Muffin tin, greased or paper-lined*

1. In a bowl sift together flour, baking powder, salt, ¼ tsp (1 mL) cinnamon and ¼ tsp (1 mL) nutmeg; blend well.
2. In another bowl cream together shortening and sugar. Add egg; stir well. Add flour mixture alternately with milk; combine well. Fold in apples.
3. Spoon batter into prepared muffin tin, filling three-quarters full. Sprinkle tops with sugar and remaining cinnamon and nutmeg. Bake in preheated oven for 20 to 25 minutes.

Cheesy Apple Bacon Muffins

2 cups	all-purpose flour	500 mL
¼ cup	granulated sugar	50 mL
4 tsp	baking powder	20 mL
¾ tsp	salt	4 mL
1 cup	milk	250 mL
⅓ cup	melted butter	75 mL
1	egg, slightly beaten	1
½ cup	finely chopped unpeeled apples	250 mL
¾ cup	grated old Cheddar cheese	175 mL
⅔ cup	crumbled crisp bacon (about 8 slices)	150 mL

◆ *Preheat oven to 400°F (200°C)*
◆ *18-cup muffin tin, greased or paper-lined*

1. In a bowl combine flour, sugar, baking powder and salt; blend well.
2. In another bowl combine milk, butter and egg; mix well. Add to flour mixture; stir just until blended. Fold in apples, cheese and bacon.
3. Spoon batter into prepared muffin tin, dividing evenly. Bake in preheated oven for 15 to 20 minutes or until browned.

Spicy Apple Bran Muffins

4	eggs	4
1½ cups	milk	375 mL
1 cup	packed brown sugar	250 mL
½ cup	vegetable oil	125 mL
2 tsp	vanilla	10 mL
3 cups	bran cereal	750 mL
2 cups	grated peeled apples	500 mL
1 cup	raisins	250 mL
1 cup	chopped walnuts	250 mL
3 cups	all-purpose flour	750 mL
2 tbsp	baking powder	25 mL
2 tsp	baking soda	10 mL
1½ tsp	cinnamon	7 mL
½ tsp	nutmeg	2 mL
1 tsp	salt	5 mL

◆ *Preheat oven to 375°F (190°C)*
◆ *Muffin tin, greased or paper-lined*

1. In a bowl beat eggs. Add milk, brown sugar, oil and vanilla; blend well. Add bran cereal, apples, raisins and walnuts; mix well.

2. In another bowl combine flour, baking powder, baking soda, cinnamon, nutmeg and salt. Add bran mixture; mix well. Add to flour mixture; stir just until blended.

3. Spoon batter into prepared muffin tin, dividing evenly. Bake in preheated oven for 20 minutes or until firm to the touch.

Applecrisp Muffins

1	egg	1
1¼ cups	milk	300 mL
½ cup	melted margarine	125 mL
⅓ cup	liquid honey	75 mL
1½ cups	graham cracker crumbs	375 mL
1½ cups	all-purpose flour	375 mL
1 tbsp	baking powder	15 mL
1 tsp	cinnamon	5 mL
½ tsp	salt	2 mL
1 cup	grated peeled apples	250 mL

◆ *Preheat oven to 400°F (200°C)*
◆ *12-cup muffin tin, greased or paper-lined*

1. In a bowl beat egg with a fork. Add milk, margarine and honey; blend well. Add graham crumbs.

2. In another bowl combine flour, baking powder, cinnamon and salt. Add honey mixture; stir just until moist. Fold in apples.

3. Spoon batter into prepared muffin tin, filling to top. Bake in preheated oven for 20 minutes.

Apple Cinnamon Muffins

2 cups	all-purpose flour	500 mL
½ cup	granulated sugar	125 mL
3 tsp	baking powder	15 mL
½ tsp	cinnamon	2 mL
½ tsp	salt	2 mL
½ cup	butter or margarine	125 mL
1	large apple, peeled and diced	1
¼ cup	finely chopped walnuts	50 mL
1	egg	1
⅔ cup	milk	150 mL
1 tsp	cinnamon	5 mL
1 tbsp	brown sugar	15 mL

◆ *Preheat oven to 425°F (220°C)*
◆ *16-cup muffin tin, greased*

1. In a bowl sift together flour, sugar, baking powder, cinnamon and salt. With a pastry blender or 2 knives cut in butter. Measure out ¼ cup (50 mL) mixture; reserve for topping. Add apple and walnuts to remaining flour mixture.

2. In a bowl beat egg. Add milk; blend well. Add to flour mixture; stir just until blended (batter should be lumpy).

3. Spoon batter into prepared muffin tin, filling two-thirds full. Add cinnamon and brown sugar to reserved topping mixture; sprinkle over batter. Bake in preheated oven for 15 to 20 minutes or until toothpick inserted in center comes out clean.

Apple Pecan Streusel Muffins

STREUSEL TOPPING		
½ cup	brown sugar	125 mL
¼ cup	butter	50 mL
½ cup	chopped pecans	125 mL
MUFFINS		
2 cups	all-purpose flour	500 mL
2 tsp	baking powder	10 mL
2 tsp	baking soda	10 mL
1 tsp	salt	5 mL
1 tsp	cinnamon	5 mL
½ tsp	allspice	2 mL
Pinch	cloves	Pinch
1	egg	1
1 cup	brown sugar	250 mL
¼ cup	oil	50 mL
1 cup	applesauce	250 mL

◆ *Preheat oven to 375°F (190°C)*
◆ *12-cup muffin tin, greased*

1. In a bowl combine brown sugar, butter and pecans; mix until crumbly. Set aside.

2. In another bowl combine flour, baking powder, baking soda, salt, cinnamon, allspice and cloves.

3. In another bowl beat together egg, brown sugar, oil and applesauce. Add to flour mixture; stir just until moist.

4. Spoon batter into prepared muffin tin, filling three-quarters full. Sprinkle with topping. Bake in preheated oven for 20 to 25 minutes or until browned.

Spiced Apple Muffins

2 cups	all-purpose flour	500 mL
1 cup	bran flakes	250 mL
2/3 cup	packed brown sugar	150 mL
3 tsp	baking powder	15 mL
1 tsp	salt	5 mL
1/2 tsp	cinnamon	2 mL
1/4 tsp	nutmeg	1 mL
2	eggs	2
2/3 cup	milk	150 mL
1/4 cup	oil	50 mL
1 cup	grated peeled apples	250 mL

◆ *Preheat oven to 400°F (200°C)*
◆ *16-cup muffin tin, greased*

1. In a bowl combine flour, bran flakes, brown sugar, baking powder, salt, cinnamon and nutmeg; blend with a fork. Make a well in the center.
2. In another bowl beat eggs slightly. Add milk, oil and apples; mix well. Add to dry ingredients; stir quickly just until moist (batter will be lumpy).
3. Spoon batter into prepared muffin tin, filling three-quarters full. Bake in preheated oven for 15 to 20 minutes.

Oatmeal Raisin Applesauce Muffins

1/2 cup	butter or margarine	125 mL
3/4 cup	lightly packed light brown sugar	175 mL
1	egg	1
1 cup	all-purpose flour	250 mL
1/2 tsp	ground cardamom or cinnamon	2 mL
1 tsp	baking powder	5 mL
1/4 tsp	baking soda	1 mL
1/4 tsp	salt	1 mL
3/4 cup	applesauce	175 mL
1/2 cup	golden raisins	125 mL
1 cup	quick-cooking rolled oats (not instant)	250 mL
1/2 cup	chopped nuts	125 mL
	Icing sugar (optional)	

◆ *Preheat oven to 350°F (180°C)*
◆ *12-cup muffin tin, greased or paper-lined*

1. In a bowl cream together butter and brown sugar until light and fluffy. Add egg; beat well.
2. In another bowl combine flour, cardamom, baking powder, baking soda and salt. Add to creamed mixture alternately with applesauce; blend well. Add raisins, oats and nuts.
3. Spoon batter into prepared muffin tin, filling three-quarters full. Bake in preheated oven for 25 to 30 minutes. Let cool. Remove muffins from pan. If desired, sprinkle with icing sugar.

Apple Streusel Muffins

STREUSEL TOPPING

1/3 cup	packed brown sugar	75 mL
2 tbsp	all-purpose flour	25 mL
1/2 tsp	cinnamon	2 mL
2 tbsp	softened butter	25 mL
1/3 cup	chopped pecans (optional)	75 mL

MUFFINS

1 1/2 cups	all-purpose flour	375 mL
1/4 cup	granulated sugar	50 mL
2 tsp	baking powder	10 mL
1/2 tsp	cinnamon	2 mL
1/4 tsp	salt	1 mL
1/8 tsp	nutmeg	0.5 mL
1 cup	shredded peeled apples	250 mL
1/2 cup	milk	125 mL
1/4 cup	vegetable oil	50 mL
1	egg, beaten	1

◆ *Preheat oven to 400°F (200°C)*
◆ *12-cup muffin tin, greased or paper-lined*

1. In a bowl combine brown sugar, flour, cinnamon, butter and pecans; mix until crumbly. Set aside.
2. In another bowl sift together flour, sugar, baking powder, cinnamon, salt and nutmeg; blend well. Add apples. Make a well in the center.
3. In another bowl combine milk, oil and egg. Add to dry ingredients; stir just until moist.
4. Spoon batter into prepared muffin tin, filling half full. Sprinkle with topping, reserving 3 tbsp (45 mL). Top with remaining batter; sprinkle with remaining topping. Bake in preheated oven for 20 to 25 minutes.

Pumpernickel Applesauce Muffins

1 cup	unsweetened applesauce	250 mL
1/4 cup	vegetable oil	50 mL
1	large egg	1
2 tbsp	packed brown sugar	25 mL
2	slices packaged soft pumpernickel bread, torn into small pieces	2
2/3 cup	fine graham cracker crumbs, crushed	150 mL
1/3 cup	all-purpose flour	75 mL
1 tsp	baking soda	5 mL

◆ *Preheat oven to 400°F (200°C)*
◆ *Muffin tin, greased or paper-lined*

1. In a food processor combine applesauce, oil, egg and brown sugar; process until well blended. Add bread; continue to process until smooth, stopping once to scrape down sides of container. Add crumbs, flour and baking soda; process until smooth.
2. Spoon batter into prepared muffin tin, filling two-thirds full. Bake in preheated oven for 15 to 20 minutes or until toothpick inserted in center comes out clean.

Lemony Apricot Jam Muffins

1½ cups	all-purpose flour	375 mL
½ cup	granulated sugar	125 mL
½ tsp	grated lemon zest	2 mL
1½ tsp	baking powder	7 mL
½ tsp	baking soda	2 mL
½ tsp	salt	2 mL
1	egg, beaten	1
4 tbsp	butter, melted	50 mL
1 cup	buttermilk	250 mL
2 tsp	lemon juice	10 mL
TOPPING		
	Apricot jam	
¼ cup	chopped almonds	50 mL

- ◆ *Preheat oven to 400°F (200°C)*
- ◆ *Muffin tin, greased or paper-lined*

1. In a bowl combine flour, sugar, lemon zest, baking powder, baking soda and salt. Make a well in the center.
2. In another bowl whisk together egg, butter, buttermilk and lemon juice. Add to dry ingredients; stir just until blended.
3. Spoon batter into prepared muffin tin, filling half full. Drop a bit of apricot jam into each tin. Top with remaining batter; sprinkle with almonds. Bake in preheated oven for 15 to 20 minutes or until golden brown.

Iced Banana Muffins

1 cup	granulated sugar	250 mL
1 tsp	baking soda	5 mL
2 tsp	baking powder	10 mL
2 cups	all-purpose flour	500 mL
Pinch	salt	Pinch
½ cup	melted butter	125 mL
2	eggs	2
4 tbsp	milk	60 mL
3	bananas, mashed	3
ICING		
1½ cups	icing sugar	375 mL
2 tbsp	butter, melted	25 mL
1 tsp	vanilla	5 mL
1¼ tbsp	milk	19 mL

- ◆ *Preheat oven to 350°F (180°C)*
- ◆ *Muffin tin, greased or paper-lined*

1. In a bowl sift together sugar, baking soda, baking powder, flour and salt; blend well. Add butter, eggs and milk; stir just until blended. Add bananas.
2. Spoon batter into prepared muffin tin, filling three-quarters full. Bake in preheated oven for 25 minutes. Set aside to cool.
3. In a bowl combine icing sugar, butter, vanilla and milk; mix well. Spread over muffins.

Easy Banana Bran Muffins

1 cup	all-purpose flour	250 mL
3 tbsp	granulated sugar	45 mL
2½ tsp	baking powder	12 mL
½ tsp	salt	2 mL
1 cup	all-bran cereal	250 mL
1	egg, beaten	1
1 cup	mashed ripe banana	250 mL
¼ cup	milk	50 mL
2 tbsp	salad oil	25 mL

♦ *Preheat oven to 400°F (200°C)*
♦ *12-cup muffin tin, greased or paper-lined*

1. In a bowl sift together flour, sugar, baking powder and salt. Add bran.
2. In another bowl combine egg, banana, milk and oil; blend well. Add to dry ingredients; stir just until moist.
3. Spoon batter into prepared muffin tin, filling three-quarters full. Bake in preheated oven for 20 to 25 minutes.

Breakfast Special Banana Chip Muffins

¼ cup	granulated sugar	50 mL
¼ cup	vegetable oil	50 mL
1 cup	mashed bananas	250 mL
1	egg	1
1 tsp	vanilla	5 mL
½ cup	all-bran cereal	125 mL
½ cup	all-purpose flour	125 mL
½ cup	whole wheat flour	125 mL
1 tsp	baking powder	5 mL
1 tsp	baking soda	5 mL
½ tsp	salt	2 mL
½ cup	chocolate chips	125 mL

♦ *Preheat oven to 375°F (190°C)*
♦ *Muffin tin, greased or paper-lined*

1. In a bowl combine sugar, oil, bananas, egg, vanilla and cereal. Let stand for 5 minutes.
2. In another bowl combine all-purpose flour, whole wheat flour, baking powder, baking soda and salt. Add to bran mixture; stir just until blended. Fold in chocolate chips.
3. Spoon batter into prepared muffin tin, filling three-quarters full. Bake in preheated oven for 20 to 25 minutes.

Chocolate 'n' Banana Muffins

1/3 cup	vegetable oil	75 mL
1/2 cup	granulated sugar	125 mL
1	egg	1
1 cup	mashed bananas	250 mL
1	pkg (10 oz/300 g) semi-sweet chocolate chips	1
1 cup	all-purpose flour	250 mL
1 tsp	baking soda	5 mL
1/2 tsp	salt	2 mL
1/2 tsp	cinnamon	2 mL

◆ *Preheat oven to 350°F (180°C)*
◆ *12-cup muffin tin, greased or paper-lined*

1. In a bowl whisk together oil, sugar and egg. Add bananas and half chocolate chips; mix well.

2. In another bowl combine flour, baking soda, salt and cinnamon. Add to liquid ingredients; stir just until blended.

3. Spoon batter into prepared muffin tin, filling three-quarters full. Sprinkle evenly with remaining chips. Bake in preheated oven for 15 to 20 minutes.

Banana Nut Muffins

1¾ cups	all-purpose flour	425 mL
1/3 cup	granulated sugar	75 mL
3 tsp	baking powder	15 mL
1/2 tsp	salt	2 mL
1/2 tsp	nutmeg	2 mL
1/2 cup	chopped nuts	125 mL
1 cup	mashed ripe bananas	250 mL
1/3 cup	salad oil	75 mL
1/4 cup	milk	50 mL
1	egg	1
2 tsp	lemon juice	10 mL

◆ *Preheat oven to 400°F (200°C)*
◆ *12-cup muffin tin, greased*

1. In a bowl combine flour, sugar, baking powder, salt and nutmeg; blend well. Add nuts; stir.

2. In another bowl combine bananas, oil, milk, egg and lemon juice. Beat slightly with a rotary beater. Add to dry ingredients; mix just until moist.

3. Spoon batter into prepared muffin tin. Bake in preheated oven for 20 to 25 minutes.

Banana 'n' Peanut Muffins

1½ cups	whole wheat flour	375 mL
2 tsp	baking powder	10 mL
½ tsp	baking soda	2 mL
½ tsp	salt	2 mL
Pinch	cinnamon	Pinch
Pinch	nutmeg	Pinch
½ cup	brown sugar	125 mL
1½ cups	mashed bananas	375 mL
1	egg	1
⅓ cup	melted butter, cooled	75 mL
½ cup	coarsely chopped peanuts	125 mL

◆ *Preheat oven to 400°F (200°C)*
◆ *Muffin tin, greased or paper-lined*

1. In a bowl combine flour, baking powder, baking soda, salt, cinnamon, nutmeg and brown sugar; stir with a fork until well blended. Make a well in the center.
2. In another bowl whisk together bananas, egg and butter. Add to dry ingredients; fold in nuts. Stir just until moist (batter will be lumpy).
3. Spoon batter into prepared muffin tin, filling three-quarters full. Bake in preheated oven for about 15 minutes or until toothpick inserted in center comes out clean.

Chunky Peanut-Banana Muffins

1	egg	1
1½ cups	milk	375 mL
½ cup	crunchy peanut butter	125 mL
½ cup	firmly packed brown sugar	125 mL
¼ cup	vegetable oil	50 mL
1 cup	all-bran cereal	250 mL
2	medium whole bananas, cut into chunks	2
2 cups	all-purpose flour	500 mL
1 tbsp	baking powder	15 mL
¼ tsp	salt	1 mL

◆ *Preheat oven to 400°F (200°C)*
◆ *Muffin tin, greased or paper-lined*

1. In a bowl combine egg, milk, peanut butter, brown sugar and oil; beat until well-blended. Add cereal. Let stand for 5 to 10 minutes. Add bananas.
2. In another bowl combine flour, baking powder and salt. Add cereal mixture; stir just until moist and blended. Batter will be lumpy; do not overmix.
3. Spoon batter into prepared muffin tin, filling to top. Bake in preheated oven for 20 minutes or until golden brown.

Banana Pineapple Muffins

½ cup	granulated sugar	125 mL
½ cup	softened shortening	125 mL
½ cup	mashed overripe bananas	125 mL
½ cup	crushed pineapple, with juice	125 mL
1	egg, beaten	1
1 tsp	baking soda	5 mL
1 tsp	baking powder	5 mL
1½ cups	all-purpose flour	375 mL
Pinch	salt	Pinch

◆ *Preheat oven to 400°F (200°C)*
◆ *12-cup muffin tin, greased*

1. In a bowl cream together sugar and shortening. Add bananas and pineapple; mix well. Add egg (batter will look curdled). Add baking soda, baking powder, flour and salt; blend well.

2. Spoon batter into prepared muffin tin, dividing evenly. Bake in preheated oven for 15 minutes.

Pineapple-Choco-Banana Muffins

1 cup	all-purpose flour	250 mL
¾ cup	whole wheat flour	175 mL
½ cup	granulated sugar	125 mL
1 cup	semi-sweet chocolate chips	250 mL
1 tbsp	baking powder	15 mL
½ tsp	salt	2 mL
1	egg	1
½ cup	mashed ripe banana	125 mL
1	can (14 oz/398 mL) crushed pineapple, drained, reserve juice	1
½ cup	vegetable oil	125 mL

◆ *Preheat oven to 375°F (190°C)*
◆ *Muffin tin, greased or paper-lined*

1. In a bowl combine all-purpose flour, whole wheat flour, sugar, chocolate chips, baking powder and salt.

2. In another bowl beat egg. Add bananas, pineapple, reserved juice and oil; stir just until blended. Add to dry ingredients; stir until moist.

3. Spoon batter into prepared muffin tin, filling to top. Bake in preheated oven for 20 to 25 minutes.

Very Ripe Banana Muffins

1 cup	mashed overripe bananas	250 mL
¼ cup + 2 tbsp	vegetable oil	50 mL + 25 mL
½ cup	granulated sugar or brown sugar	125 mL
½ tsp	salt	2 mL
1	egg	1
1 tsp	vanilla	5 mL
1½ cups	all-purpose flour	375 mL
1 tsp	baking soda	5 mL
1 tsp	baking powder	5 mL
½ cup	chopped walnuts or pecans (optional)	125 mL

♦ *Preheat oven to 350°F (180°C)*
♦ *Muffin tin, greased or paper-lined*

1. In a bowl combine bananas, oil, sugar and salt; blend well. Add egg and vanilla; beat well.
2. In another bowl combine flour, baking soda, baking powder and walnuts. Add to banana mixture; stir just until moist. Do not overmix.
3. Spoon batter into prepared muffin tin, dividing evenly. Bake in preheated oven for 15 to 20 minutes.

Banana Yogurt Muffins

1⅔ cups	all-purpose flour	410 mL
1 tsp	baking powder	5 mL
1 tsp	baking soda	5 mL
½ cup	softened butter	125 mL
⅔ cup	natural bran	150 mL
½ cup	chopped nuts	125 mL
1	egg	1
⅔ cup	puréed bananas	160 mL
½ cup	plain yogurt	125 mL
½ cup	packed brown sugar	125 mL
1 tbsp	molasses	15 mL

♦ *Preheat oven to 375°F (190°C)*
♦ *12-cup muffin tin, greased*

1. In a bowl combine flour, baking powder and baking soda. With a pastry blender cut in butter until mixture is crumbly. Add bran and nuts.
2. In another bowl combine egg, bananas, yogurt, sugar and molasses. Add to dry ingredients; stir just until blended.
3. Spoon batter into prepared muffin tin, dividing evenly. Bake in preheated oven for 20 to 25 minutes or until a toothpick inserted in center comes out clean.

Wheat Germ Banana Muffins

1¼ cups	all-purpose flour	300 mL
½ cup	natural bran	125 mL
⅓ cup	wheat germ	75 mL
1 tsp	baking powder	5 mL
1 tsp	baking soda	5 mL
Pinch	salt	Pinch
½ cup	butter or margarine	125 mL
½ cup	lightly packed brown sugar	125 mL
1	egg	1
⅔ cup	mashed bananas	150 mL
½ cup	buttermilk or sour milk	125 mL
1 tbsp	molasses	15 mL
¾ cup	raisins	175 mL
⅓ cup	chopped nuts	75 mL

◆ *Preheat oven to 375°F (190°C)*
◆ *12-cup muffin tin, greased or paper-lined*

1. In a bowl combine flour, bran, wheat germ, baking powder, baking soda and salt; blend well.
2. In another bowl cream together butter, brown sugar and egg. Add bananas, buttermilk and molasses; mix well. Add to flour mixture; stir just until blended. Add raisins and nuts.
3. Spoon batter into prepared muffin tin, filling to top. Bake in preheated oven for 20 to 25 minutes.

Simplified Blueberry Muffins

1	egg	1
	Milk	
1½ cups	self-rising flour	375 mL
½ cup	granulated sugar	125 mL
¼ cup	softened butter or margarine	50 mL
1 cup	fresh or frozen blueberries, partially thawed	250 mL

◆ *Preheat oven to 400°F (200°C)*
◆ *12-cup muffin tin, greased*

1. In a measuring cup combine egg and enough milk to make 1 cup (250 mL).
2. In a bowl combine flour and sugar. With a pastry blender cut in butter until crumbly. Add egg mixture; stir just until moist. Fold in blueberries.
3. Spoon batter into prepared muffin tin, filling three-quarters full. Bake in preheated oven for 20 to 25 minutes or until golden brown.

Blueberry Almond Muffins

2 cups	all-purpose flour	500 mL
1 cup	granulated sugar	250 mL
2 tsp	baking powder	10 mL
1/2 tsp	salt	2 mL
2	eggs	2
1/2 cup	milk	125 mL
1/3 cup	melted butter or margarine	75 mL
1 tsp	grated lemon zest	5 mL
1 tsp	lemon juice	5 mL
1	pkg (10 oz/300 g) frozen unsweetened blueberries, divided	1
TOPPING		
2 tbsp	granulated sugar	25 mL
1/4 cup	sliced almonds	50 mL

* Preheat oven to 400°F (200°C)
* Muffin tin, greased or paper-lined

1. In a bowl combine flour, sugar, baking powder, salt, eggs, milk, butter, lemon zest and lemon juice. Blend on low speed just until moist. Beat on medium speed for 2 minutes. Add 1 cup (250 mL) blueberries; stir well.

2. Spoon batter into prepared muffin tin, filling two-thirds full. Sprinkle with remaining blueberries, sugar and almonds. Bake in preheated oven for 20 to 25 minutes or until golden brown.

Grandma's Blueberry Gems

2 1/4 cups	all-purpose flour	550 mL
3/4 cup	granulated sugar	175 mL
3 tsp	baking powder	15 mL
3/4 tsp	salt	4 mL
6 tbsp	butter or margarine	90 mL
3/4 cup	milk	175 mL
3/4 cup	water	175 mL
2	small eggs	2
	Grated zest of 1 lemon	
	Juice of 1/2 lemon	
1 1/2 cups	frozen blueberries, not thawed	375 mL

* Preheat oven to 400°F (200°C)
* Muffin tin, greased or paper-lined

1. In a bowl sift together flour, sugar, baking powder and salt. Add butter, milk, water, eggs, lemon zest and lemon juice; blend well. Using a spatula, fold in blueberries.

2. Spoon batter into prepared muffin tin, filling three-quarters full or to the top. Bake in preheated oven for 25 minutes or until golden brown.

Blueberry Lemon Muffins

1 cup	fresh blueberries or frozen blueberries, thawed	250 mL
2 cups	all-purpose flour	500 mL
3 tsp	baking powder	15 mL
½ tsp	salt	2 mL
¼ tsp	nutmeg	1 mL
¾ cup	granulated sugar	175 mL
	Grated zest of 1 lemon	
1	egg	1
¼ cup	vegetable oil	50 mL
1¼ cups	milk	300 mL
½ cup	chopped walnuts	125 mL

MUFFIN STUFF: If using frozen berries, thaw and gently pat dry on paper towels.

♦ *Preheat oven to 425°F (220°C)*
♦ *Muffin tin, greased or paper-lined*

1. In a bowl combine blueberries and 2 tbsp (25 mL) flour: toss until lightly coated. Set aside.

2. In another bowl combine remaining flour, baking powder, salt, nutmeg and sugar; stir with a fork until well blended. Sprinkle with lemon zest.

3. In another bowl beat together egg, oil and milk. Add to flour mixture; stir just until moist and blended. Add walnuts and berries; blend well.

4. Spoon batter into prepared muffin tin, filling three-quarters full. Bake in preheated oven for 20 minutes.

Variation

♦ You can make a loaf with this batter. Spoon into a greased loaf pan. Bake at 350°F (180°C) for about 1 hour and 10 minutes.

Glazed Blueberry Orange Muffins

1½ cups	all-purpose flour	375 mL
1 cup	whole wheat flour	250 mL
1 tbsp	baking powder	15 mL
1 tsp	cinnamon	5 mL
½ tsp	salt	2 mL
1	egg	1
1¼ cups	milk	300 mL
⅓ cup	vegetable oil	75 mL
⅓ cup	liquid honey or maple syrup	75 mL
1 tsp	grated orange zest	5 mL
1½ cups	fresh blueberries or frozen blueberries, not thawed	375 mL
GLAZE		
½ cup	icing sugar	125 mL
2 to 3 tsp	orange juice	10 to 15 mL
1 tsp	grated orange zest	5 mL

♦ *Preheat oven to 400°F (200°C)*
♦ *12-cup muffin tin, greased or paper-lined*

1. In a bowl combine all-purpose flour, whole wheat flour, baking powder, cinnamon and salt.
2. In another bowl combine egg, milk, oil, honey and orange zest. Add to dry ingredients; stir just until blended. Do not overmix. Fold in blueberries.
3. Spoon batter into prepared muffin tin, filling to the top. Bake in preheated oven for about 20 minutes or until golden brown.
4. In a bowl combine icing sugar, orange juice and orange zest; mix until smooth. Spread over warm muffins.

MUFFIN STUFF: Omit the glaze if you are freezing the muffins.

Blueberry Muffins with Crunchy Pecan Topping

TOPPING		
1/2 cup	chopped pecans	125 mL
2/3 cup	packed brown sugar	150 mL
2 tbsp	all-purpose flour	25 mL
1/2 tsp	cinnamon	2 mL
2 tbsp	melted butter	25 mL
MUFFINS		
1/2 cup	butter	125 mL
1 cup	granulated sugar	250 mL
1 tsp	vanilla	5 mL
3	eggs	3
2 cups	all-purpose flour	500 mL
1/2 tsp	salt	2 mL
1 tsp	baking powder	5 mL
1 tsp	baking soda	5 mL
1 1/4 cups	sour cream	300 mL
2 cups	frozen blueberries, thawed and patted dry	500 mL

◆ *Preheat oven to 400°F (200°C)*
◆ *Muffin tin, paper-lined*

1. In a bowl combine pecans, brown sugar, flour and cinnamon; mix well. Add melted butter; stir. Set aside.

2. In a bowl combine butter and sugar; cream until light and fluffy. Add vanilla; continue to beat. Add eggs one at a time; beat well.

3. In another bowl combine flour, salt, baking powder and baking soda. Add one-third of this mixture to creamed mixture; mix well. Add half sour cream and one-third flour mixture; blend well. Add remaining sour cream and remaining flour mixture; mix well.

4. Spoon batter into prepared muffin tin, filling half full. Add blueberries; top with remaining batter. Sprinkle with topping. Bake in preheated oven for 20 to 25 minutes.

Blueberry Sour Cream Muffins

1 cup	fresh or frozen blueberries	250 mL
2 tbsp	all-purpose flour	25 mL
¼ cup	butter or margarine	50 mL
¾ cup	granulated sugar	175 mL
2	eggs	2
1¼ cups	all-purpose flour	300 mL
½ tsp	baking soda	2 mL
¼ tsp	salt	1 mL
¾ cup	sour cream	175 mL
½ tsp	vanilla	2 mL

- *Preheat oven to 450°F (230°C)*
- *Muffin tin, greased or paper-lined*

1. In a bowl combine blueberries and flour; toss to coat well. Set aside.
2. In a bowl combine butter and sugar; cream until light. Add eggs one at a time; beat well.
3. In another bowl sift together flour, baking soda and salt. Add to creamed mixture alternately with sour cream; mix well. Add blueberries and vanilla.
4. Spoon batter into prepared muffin tin, filling three-quarters full. Bake in preheated oven for about 15 minutes.

Black Cherry Muffins

2 cups	all-purpose flour	500 mL
1 tbsp	baking powder	15 mL
¼ tsp	salt	1 mL
1 cup	coarsely chopped pitted black cherries	250 mL
6 tbsp	softened butter or margarine	90 mL
⅔ cup	granulated sugar	150 mL
2	eggs	2
1 tsp	vanilla	5 mL
½ cup	milk	125 mL

- *Preheat oven to 400°F (200°C)*
- *12-cup muffin tin, greased or paper-lined*

1. In a bowl combine flour, baking powder and salt. In another bowl combine 1 tbsp (15 mL) flour mixture and cherries; toss well. Set aside.
2. In another bowl combine butter and sugar; beat until light and fluffy. Add eggs and vanilla; beat for 3 minutes. Add remaining flour mixture alternately with milk; beat well. Add cherries.
3. Spoon batter into prepared muffin tin, filling three-quarters full. Bake in preheated oven for 20 to 25 minutes or until golden.

Marmalade Muffins

Peel of 1 grapefruit, chopped		
Peel of 1 orange, chopped		
1½ cups	buttermilk	375 mL
1 cup	granulated sugar	250 mL
1 tsp	salt	5 mL
½ cup	margarine	125 mL
1¾ cups	all-purpose flour	425 mL
2 tsp	baking powder	10 mL
½ tsp	baking soda	2 mL

♦ *Preheat oven to 375°F (190°C)*
♦ *Muffin tin, greased or paper-lined*

1. In a food processor or blender combine grapefruit peel, orange peel and buttermilk; process until finely ground. Add sugar, salt and margarine; process.
2. In a bowl combine flour, baking powder and baking soda. Add peel mixture; stir just until moist.
3. Spoon batter into prepared muffin tin, dividing evenly. Bake in preheated oven for 20 minutes.

Orange Surprise Muffins

3 tbsp	shortening	45 mL
2 cups	all-purpose flour	500 mL
1 tbsp	baking powder	15 mL
½ tsp	salt	2 mL
¾ cup	milk	175 mL
1	egg	1
½ cup	orange marmalade	125 mL
3 tbsp	granulated sugar	45 mL

♦ *Preheat oven to 400°F (200°C)*
♦ *Muffin tin, greased*

1. In a saucepan heat shortening over medium-high heat. Set aside to cool.
2. In a bowl sift together flour, baking powder and salt.
3. In a blender or food processor combine milk, egg, marmalade and sugar. Add cooled shortening; blend until thoroughly mixed.
4. Make a well in the center of dry ingredients. Add marmalade mixture; stir quickly just until moist.
5. Spoon batter into prepared muffin tin, filling two-thirds full. Bake in preheated oven for 30 to 35 minutes or until golden brown.

Quick Lemon Muffins

6 tbsp	butter	90 mL
1 cup	granulated sugar	250 mL
2	eggs	2
1½ cups	all-purpose flour	375 mL
½ cup	milk	125 mL
	Grated zest of 1½ lemons	
¼ tsp	salt	1 mL
1½ tsp	baking powder	7 mL
TOPPING		
	Juice of 1½ lemons	
⅓ cup	granulated sugar	75 mL

◆ *Preheat oven to 400°F (200°C)*
◆ *Muffin tin, greased*

1. In a bowl cream together butter, sugar and eggs. Add flour, milk, lemon zest, salt and baking powder; mix well.
2. Spoon batter into prepared muffin tin, filling three-quarters full. Bake in preheated oven for 15 to 20 minutes.
3. Meanwhile in a bowl combine lemon juice and sugar. When muffins are done, prick tops with a fork. Drizzle with topping.

Lemon Poppyseed Muffins

1 cup	lemonade	250 mL
½ tsp	grated lemon zest	2 mL
¼ cup	poppy seeds	50 mL
¼ cup	butter	50 mL
¼ cup	granulated sugar	50 mL
1	egg	1
1 tsp	vanilla	5 mL
2 cups	all-purpose flour	500 mL
1 tbsp	baking powder	15 mL
1 tsp	salt	5 mL
GLAZE		
2 tbsp	freshly squeezed lemon juice	25 mL
2 tsp	granulated sugar	10 mL

◆ *Preheat oven to 375°F (190°C)*
◆ *Muffin tin, greased*

1. In a saucepan heat lemonade over medium-high heat. When just about to boil, remove from heat. Add lemon zest and poppy seeds. Set aside to cool.

2. In a bowl combine butter and sugar; beat well. Add egg and vanilla; mix thoroughly.

3. In another bowl combine flour, baking powder and salt. Add to butter mixture; mix well. Add lemonade mixture; stir to moisten thoroughly.

4. Spoon batter into prepared muffin tin, filling three-quarters full. Bake in preheated oven for 20 to 25 minutes or until golden brown.

5. In a saucepan over medium-high heat, combine lemon juice and sugar. Heat, stirring constantly, just until sugar has completely dissolved. With a cake tester or metal skewer, prick the surface of each muffin all over; drizzle with glaze.

Raisin Lemon Muffins

1½ cups	all-purpose flour	375 mL
1 tbsp	baking powder	15 mL
½ tsp	salt	2 mL
¼ tsp	nutmeg	1 mL
¾ cup	brown sugar	175 mL
1 cup	rolled oats	250 mL
	Finely grated zest of 1 lemon	
1	egg	1
¼ cup	vegetable oil	50 mL
1 cup	milk	250 mL
½ cup	raisins	125 mL

◆ Preheat oven to 400°F (200°C)
◆ 12-cup muffin tin, greased or paper-lined

1. In a bowl combine flour, baking powder, salt, nutmeg and brown sugar; mix well. Add oats and lemon zest. Make a well in the center.
2. In another bowl whisk together egg, oil and milk. Add to dry ingredients; stir just until moist. Fold in raisins.
3. Spoon batter into prepared muffin tin, filling three-quarters full. Bake in preheated oven for 15 to 20 minutes.

Lemon Yogurt Muffins

1¾ cups	all-purpose flour	425 mL
¾ cup	granulated sugar	175 mL
	Grated zest of 1 large lemon	
1 tsp	baking powder	5 mL
¾ tsp	baking soda	4 mL
¼ tsp	salt	1 mL
8 oz	lemon yogurt	250 g
6 tbsp	melted butter, cooled	90 mL
1	egg	1
1 to 2 tbsp	fresh lemon juice	15 to 25 mL

◆ Preheat oven to 400°F (200°C)
◆ 12-cup muffin tin, greased

1. In a bowl combine flour, sugar, lemon zest, baking powder, baking soda and salt.
2. In another bowl whisk together lemon yogurt, butter, egg and lemon juice. Add to flour mixture; stir just until blended.
3. Spoon batter into prepared muffin tin, dividing evenly. Bake in preheated oven for 20 to 25 minutes.

Great Lemonade Muffins

1¾ cups	sifted all-purpose flour	425 mL
¼ cup	granulated sugar	50 mL
2½ tsp	baking powder	12 mL
¾ tsp	salt	4 mL
1	egg, well-beaten	1
1	can (6 oz/175 g) frozen lemonade concentrate, thawed	1
¼ cup	milk	50 mL
⅓ cup	cooking oil	75 mL
½ cup	chopped walnuts	125 mL
	Granulated sugar	

- *Preheat oven to 400°F (200°C)*
- *12-cup muffin tin, greased or paper-lined*

1. In a bowl sift together flour, sugar, baking powder and salt. Make a well in the center.
2. In another bowl combine egg, ½ cup (125 mL) lemonade, milk and oil. Add to flour mixture quickly; stir just until moist and blended. Add walnuts; stir gently.
3. Spoon batter into prepared muffin tin, dividing evenly. Bake in preheated oven for 25 minutes. Remove from tins. While still hot brush muffins with remaining lemonade; sprinkle with sugar.

Orange Muffins

2	oranges, cut into 8 pieces	2
½ cup	orange juice	125 mL
½ cup	dates or raisins	125 mL
1	egg	1
½ cup	margarine	125 mL
¼ cup	wheat germ or bran	50 mL
1½ cups	all-purpose flour	375 mL
1 tsp	baking powder	5 mL
1 tsp	baking soda	5 mL
¾ cup	granulated sugar	175 mL
Pinch	salt	Pinch

- *Preheat oven to 400°F (200°C)*
- *Muffin tin, greased or paper-lined*

1. In a blender or food processor combine oranges, orange juice, dates, egg and margarine; process until well blended. Scrape down edges of blender. Add wheat germ; process again.
2. In a bowl sift together flour, baking powder, baking soda, sugar and salt. Add orange mixture; blend well.
3. Spoon batter into prepared muffin tin, dividing evenly. Bake in preheated oven for about 15 minutes.

Orangeberry Muffins

1	medium-sized orange, cut into pieces	1
1/3 cup	shortening	75 mL
1	egg	1
1/2 cup	milk	125 mL
1 1/2 cups	all-purpose flour	375 mL
3/4 cup	granulated sugar	175 mL
2 tsp	baking powder	10 mL
1 tsp	baking soda	5 mL
1 cup	fresh or frozen blueberries	250 mL

◆ *Preheat oven to 375°F (190°C)*
◆ *12-cup muffin tin, greased*

1. In a blender or food processor combine orange pieces, shortening, egg and milk. Blend until orange is finely chopped. Set aside.
2. In a bowl combine flour, sugar, baking powder and baking soda. Make a well in the center. Add orange mixture; stir just until moist and blended. Fold in blueberries.
3. Spoon batter into prepared muffin tin, dividing evenly. Bake in preheated oven for 22 to 25 minutes or until golden brown.

Orange Chocolate Chip Muffins

1	egg	1
1 cup	milk	250 mL
1/2 cup	melted margarine	125 mL
1/2 tsp	grated orange zest	2 mL
1/4 cup	orange juice	50 mL
1 1/2 cups	all-purpose flour	375 mL
1 cup	whole wheat flour	250 mL
1/2 cup	granulated sugar	125 mL
1 tbsp	baking powder	15 mL
1/2 tsp	salt	2 mL
1/2 cup	semi-sweet chocolate chips	125 mL

◆ *Preheat oven to 400°F (200°C)*
◆ *12-cup muffin tin, greased or paper-lined*

1. In a bowl beat egg with a fork. Add milk, margarine, orange zest and orange juice.
2. In another bowl combine all-purpose flour, whole wheat flour, sugar, baking powder and salt. Add egg mixture; stir just until moist. Fold in chocolate chips.
3. Spoon batter into prepared muffin tin, filling to the top. Bake in preheated oven for about 20 minutes.

Cinnamon Nut Orange Muffins

1½ cups	all-purpose flour	375 mL
1½ tsp	baking powder	7 mL
¼ tsp	salt	1 mL
¼ tsp	nutmeg	1 mL
¼ cup	pecans	50 mL
⅓ cup	butter	75 mL
½ cup	granulated sugar	125 mL
1	egg	1
½ tsp	vanilla	2 mL
1 tsp	orange zest	5 mL
½ cup	milk	125 mL
CINNAMON TOPPING		
¼ cup	melted butter	50 mL
½ cup	granulated sugar	125 mL
1 tsp	cinnamon	5 mL

◆ *Preheat oven to 375°F (190°C)*
◆ *Muffin tin, greased*

1. In a bowl combine flour, baking powder, salt, nutmeg and pecans.
2. In another bowl cream together butter and sugar. Beat in egg, vanilla and orange zest; blend well. Add flour mixture alternately with milk, stirring just until blended.
3. Spoon batter into prepared muffin tin, filling three-quarters full. Bake in preheated oven for 20 to 25 minutes.
4. Remove muffins from tins. While still hot dip tops in butter; roll in sugar and cinnamon.

Orange Date Muffins

1¼ cups	whole wheat flour	300 mL
1 cup	all-purpose flour	250 mL
¾ cup	lightly packed brown sugar	175 mL
2 tsp	baking powder	10 mL
1 tsp	baking soda	5 mL
½ tsp	salt	2 mL
¾ cup	chopped dates	175 mL
1 tsp	grated orange zest	5 mL
2	eggs	2
½ cup	orange juice	125 mL
⅓ cup	melted butter	75 mL

◆ *Preheat oven to 400°F (200°C)*
◆ *12-cup muffin tin, paper-lined*

1. In a bowl combine whole wheat flour, all-purpose flour, brown sugar, baking powder, baking soda and salt; mix well. Add dates and orange zest.
2. In another bowl beat eggs. Add orange juice and butter; blend well. Add to dry ingredients; stir with a fork just until moist.
3. Spoon batter into prepared muffin tin, dividing evenly. Bake in preheated oven for 15 to 20 minutes.

Mandarin Orange Muffins

1½ cups	all-purpose flour	375 mL
½ cup	granulated sugar	125 mL
2½ tsp	baking powder	12 mL
¼ tsp	salt	1 mL
¼ tsp	allspice	1 mL
½ tsp	nutmeg	2 mL
1	egg	1
¾ cup	milk	175 mL
⅓ cup	melted butter	75 mL
1 cup	mandarin orange segments, each cut into 4 pieces	250 mL
2 tbsp	granulated sugar	25 mL

◆ *Preheat oven to 400°F (200°C)*
◆ *12-cup muffin tin, paper-lined*

1. In a bowl sift together flour, sugar, baking powder, salt, allspice and nutmeg.
2. In another bowl beat egg. Add milk and melted butter; blend well. Add to flour mixture; stir just until moist. Add orange pieces; stir gently.
3. Spoon batter into prepared muffin tin, dividing evenly. Sprinkle with sugar. Bake in preheated oven for about 20 minutes.

Pineapple Orange Muffins

2 cups	all-purpose flour	500 mL
½ tsp	salt	2 mL
4 tsp	baking powder	20 mL
¼ cup	granulated sugar	50 mL
1	egg	1
1 cup	unsweetened pineapple juice	250 mL
¼ cup	melted shortening	50 mL
½ cup	well-drained crushed pineapple	125 mL
TOPPING		
2 tbsp	granulated sugar	25 mL
1 tsp	grated orange zest	5 mL

◆ *Preheat oven to 400°F (200°C)*
◆ *Muffin tin, greased or paper-lined*

1. In a bowl sift together flour, salt, baking powder and sugar.
2. In another bowl beat together egg and pineapple juice. Add shortening; blend well. Add to flour mixture; stir just until moist and blended. Fold in pineapple.
3. In a bowl combine sugar and orange zest.
4. Spoon batter into prepared muffin tin, filling two-thirds full. Sprinkle with topping. Bake in preheated oven for 25 minutes.

Old-Fashioned Orange Tea Cakes

2 cups	sifted cake flour	500 mL
2 tsp	baking powder	10 mL
2 tbsp	butter or shortening	25 mL
1 cup	granulated sugar	250 mL
1	egg	1
1 tbsp	grated orange zest	15 mL
¼ cup	milk	50 mL
½ cup	orange juice	125 mL

◆ *Preheat oven to 350°F (180°C)*
◆ *Muffin tin, paper-lined*

1. In a bowl combine flour and baking powder.
2. In another bowl cream together butter and sugar. Add egg; beat until light and fluffy. Add orange zest; blend well. Add flour mixture alternately with milk and orange juice; beat until smooth.
3. Spoon batter into prepared muffin tin, filling two-thirds full. Bake in preheated oven for 25 minutes.

Peaches 'n' Cream Muffins

2	eggs	2
1¼ cups	milk	300 mL
⅓ cup	liquid honey	75 mL
¼ cup	melted margarine	50 mL
1 tsp	grated lemon zest	5 mL
1½ cups	all-bran cereal	375 mL
2 cups	all-purpose flour	500 mL
1 tbsp	baking powder	15 mL
1 tsp	cinnamon	5 mL
½ tsp	salt	2 mL
1	can (14 oz/398 mL) sliced peaches, drained and cut into cubes	1
4 oz	cream cheese, cut into cubes	125 g

◆ *Preheat oven to 400°F (200°C)*
◆ *12-cup muffin tin, greased or paper-lined*

1. In a bowl beat eggs lightly. Add milk, honey, margarine, lemon zest and cereal; stir well.
2. In another bowl combine flour, baking powder, cinnamon and salt. Add cereal mixture; stir just until blended. Fold in peaches and cheese.
3. Spoon batter into prepared muffin tin, dividing evenly. Bake in preheated oven for 20 to 25 minutes or until golden brown.

Chili-Pepper Corn Muffins ➤
(page 179)

Peach Melba Dessert Muffins

1 cup	diced peaches	250 mL
½ tsp	cinnamon	2 mL
2 cups	all-purpose flour	500 mL
½ cup	granulated sugar	125 mL
2½ tsp	baking powder	12 mL
½ tsp	salt	2 mL
½ cup	chopped walnuts	125 mL
1	egg	1
1 cup	milk	250 mL
⅓ cup	melted butter or margarine	75 mL
2 tbsp	brandy	25 mL
	Raspberry jam	

◆ *Preheat oven to 400°F (200°C)*
◆ *12-cup muffin tin, greased or paper-lined*

1. In a bowl combine peaches and cinnamon. Set aside.
2. In a bowl sift together flour, sugar, baking powder and salt. Add walnuts; blend well. Make a well in the center.
3. In another bowl whisk together egg, milk, butter and brandy. Add peach mixture; blend well. Add to dry ingredients; stir just until moist.
4. Spoon batter into prepared muffin tin, filling half full. Add about 1 tsp (5 mL) raspberry jam; cover with remaining batter. Bake in preheated oven for 20 to 25 minutes.

Special Pear Cheese Muffins

2 cups	all-purpose flour	500 mL
⅓ cup	granulated sugar	75 mL
1 tbsp	baking powder	15 mL
½ tsp	salt	2 mL
¼ tsp	pumpkin pie spice	1 mL
1 cup	shredded Colby cheese	250 mL
2	medium-sized pears, peeled and cut into large chunks	2
1 cup	milk	250 mL
2	eggs	2
¼ cup	melted butter	50 mL

◆ *Preheat oven to 425°F (220°C)*
◆ *15-cup muffin tin, paper-lined*

1. In a bowl combine flour, sugar, baking powder, salt and spice. Make a well in the center.
2. In a blender or food processor combine cheese, pears, milk, eggs and butter; process until pears are finely chopped. Add to flour mixture; stir just until moist and blended.
3. Spoon batter into prepared muffin tin, filling three-quarters full. Bake in preheated oven for 20 to 25 minutes.

Pineapple Muffins

2 cups	all-purpose flour	500 mL
1/2 cup	granulated sugar	125 mL
3 tsp	baking powder	15 mL
1/2 tsp	salt	2 mL
1	egg	1
1/4 cup	cooking oil	50 mL
1 cup	milk	250 mL
1/2 cup	well-drained crushed pineapple	125 mL

♦ *Preheat oven to 400°F (200°C)*
♦ *18-cup muffin tin, greased*

1. In a bowl combine flour, sugar, baking powder and salt. Make a well in the center.
2. In another bowl beat egg. Add oil, milk and pineapple; mix well. Add to dry ingredients; stir just until moist.
3. Spoon batter into prepared muffin tin, dividing evenly. Bake in preheated oven for 20 to 25 minutes.

Pineapple Coconut Delights

1 1/2 cups	all-purpose flour	375 mL
1 tsp	baking powder	5 mL
1/2 tsp	baking soda	2 mL
1/2 tsp	salt	2 mL
1/4 cup	softened butter	50 mL
1/2 cup	granulated sugar	125 mL
1	egg	1
1 cup	sour cream	250 mL
1 tsp	rum extract	5 mL
1 cup	drained crushed pineapple	250 mL
1/2 cup	flaked coconut	125 mL

♦ *Preheat oven to 375°F (190°C)*
♦ *12-cup muffin tin, greased or paper-lined*

1. In a bowl combine flour, baking powder, baking soda and salt.
2. In another bowl beat together butter, sugar, egg, sour cream and rum. Add to flour mixture; stir just until blended. Add pineapple and coconut.
3. Spoon batter into prepared muffin tin, filling three-quarters full. Bake in preheated oven for 20 to 25 minutes.

Pineapple Upside-Down Muffins

¼ cup	melted butter	50 mL
⅓ cup	brown sugar	75 mL
8 oz	drained crushed pineapple	250 g
1½ cups	all-purpose flour	375 mL
½ cup	granulated sugar	125 mL
¼ tsp	salt	1 mL
½ tsp	baking soda	2 mL
1 tsp	baking powder	5 mL
1 tsp	cinnamon	5 mL
2	eggs, beaten	2
1 cup	buttermilk	250 mL
2 tbsp	melted butter	25 mL

◆ *Preheat oven to 375°F (190°C)*
◆ *12-cup muffin tin, greased*

1. Spoon melted butter evenly into prepared muffin tin. Sprinkle brown sugar over top. Spoon pineapple over brown sugar. Set aside.
2. In a bowl combine flour, sugar, salt, baking soda, baking powder and cinnamon. Make a well in the center.
3. In another bowl whisk together eggs, buttermilk and butter. Add quickly to flour mixture; stir just until moist and blended.
4. Spoon batter into muffin cups over pineapple. Bake in preheated oven for 20 to 25 minutes.
5. When cool, remove muffins from pan. Serve pineapple-side up.

Tropical Treat Muffins

2 cups	all-purpose flour	500 mL
2 tsp	baking powder	10 mL
½ tsp	baking soda	2 mL
½ tsp	salt	2 mL
½ cup	brown sugar	125 mL
1	egg, well-beaten	1
1 cup	sour cream	250 mL
1	can (8 oz/250 g) crushed pineapple, with juice	1
⅓ cup	oil or melted shortening	75 mL
½ cup	chopped pecans	125 mL

◆ *Preheat oven to 400°F (200°C)*
◆ *18-cup muffin tin, greased*

1. In a bowl sift together flour, baking powder, baking soda and salt. Add brown sugar.
2. In another bowl combine egg and sour cream; mix well. Add pineapple (with juice), oil and pecans. Add to flour mixture; stir just until moist.
3. Spoon batter into prepared muffin tin, dividing evenly. Bake in preheated oven for 20 minutes.

Favorite Raspberry Muffins

1½ cups	all-purpose flour	375 mL
½ cup	quick-cooking rolled oats or oatmeal	125 mL
½ cup	packed brown sugar	125 mL
¼ tsp	salt	1 mL
2 tsp	baking powder	10 mL
1 tsp	baking soda	5 mL
1 cup	frozen raspberries, not thawed	250 mL
2	eggs	2
½ cup	buttermilk	125 mL
½ cup	melted margarine	125 mL
TOPPING		
¼ cup	softened butter	50 mL
¼ cup	brown sugar	50 mL
¼ cup	quick-cooking rolled oats or oatmeal	50 mL
¼ cup	all-purpose flour	50 mL
1 tsp	cinnamon	5 mL

◆ *Preheat oven to 400°F (200°C)*
◆ *Muffin tin, greased or paper-lined*

1. In a bowl combine flour, oats, brown sugar, salt, baking powder and baking soda. Add frozen raspberries; blend well.

2. In another bowl whisk together eggs, buttermilk and margarine. Add to flour mixture; stir just until moist and blended.

3. In a bowl cream together butter and brown sugar. Add oats, flour and cinnamon; mix well.

4. Spoon batter into prepared muffin tin, filling two-thirds full. Spoon topping over muffins evenly. Bake in preheated oven for 15 to 20 minutes.

Raspberry Almond Muffins

½ cup	butter (room temperature)	125 mL
¾ cup	granulated sugar	175 mL
2	eggs	2
1 tsp	baking powder	5 mL
½ tsp	baking soda	2 mL
1 tsp	almond extract	5 mL
2 cups	all-purpose flour	500 mL
1 cup	plain yogurt or buttermilk	250 mL
¼ cup	raspberry preserves	50 mL
5 oz	almond paste	150 g

◆ *Preheat oven to 350°F (180°C)*
◆ *Muffin tin, paper-lined*

1. In a bowl combine butter and sugar; cream until light and fluffy. Beat in eggs one at a time. Add baking powder, baking soda and almond extract; mix well. Fold in 1 cup (250 mL) flour. Add yogurt and remaining flour; mix well.

2. Spoon batter into prepared muffin tin, filling half full. Top each with 1 tsp (5 mL) raspberry preserves and piece of almond paste. Top with remaining batter. Bake in preheated oven for 25 to 30 minutes or until lightly browned.

Raspberry-Blueberry-Cornmeal Muffins

1 cup	yellow cornmeal	250 mL
1 cup	all-purpose flour	250 mL
⅓ cup	granulated sugar	75 mL
2 tsp	baking powder	10 mL
¼ tsp	salt	1 mL
1 cup	buttermilk	250 mL
6 tbsp	melted butter	90 mL
1	egg, slightly beaten	1
1 cup	fresh or frozen blueberries	250 mL
½ cup	fresh or frozen raspberries	125 mL

◆ *Preheat oven to 400°F (200°C)*
◆ *Muffin tin, greased or paper-lined*

1. In a bowl sift together cornmeal, flour, sugar, baking powder and salt. Make a well in the center.

2. In another bowl combine buttermilk, butter and egg. Add to dry ingredients; stir just until moist and blended. Fold in blueberries and raspberries.

3. Spoon batter into prepared muffin tin, filling three-quarters full. Bake in preheated oven for 20 to 25 minutes or until golden brown.

Raspberry Pecan Streusel Muffins

PECAN STREUSEL TOPPING		
¼ cup	chopped pecans	50 mL
¼ cup	packed brown sugar	50 mL
¼ cup	all-purpose flour	50 mL
2 tbsp	butter or margarine, melted	25 mL
MUFFINS		
1½ cups	all-purpose flour	375 mL
½ cup	granulated sugar	125 mL
2 tsp	baking powder	10 mL
½ cup	milk	125 mL
½ cup	melted butter or margarine	125 mL
1	egg, beaten	1
1 cup	fresh or frozen raspberries, unsweetened	250 mL

◆ *Preheat oven to 375°F (190°C)*
◆ *12-cup muffin tin, greased*

1. In a bowl combine pecans, brown sugar and flour. Add butter; mix until crumbly. Set aside.
2. In a bowl combine flour, sugar and baking powder. Make a well in the center.
3. In another bowl combine milk, butter and egg; mix well. Add to flour mixture; stir just until moist.
4. Spoon batter into prepared muffin tin, filling half full. Add a few raspberries. Top with remaining batter. Sprinkle with streusel topping. Bake in preheated oven for 25 to 30 minutes or until browned.

Best Ever Rhubarb Pecan Muffins

2 cups	all-purpose flour	500 mL
¾ cup	granulated sugar	175 mL
1½ tsp	baking powder	7 mL
½ tsp	baking soda	2 mL
1 tsp	salt	5 mL
¾ cup	chopped pecans	175 mL
1	egg	1
¼ cup	vegetable oil	50 mL
2 tsp	grated orange zest	10 mL
¾ cup	orange juice	175 mL
1¼ cups	finely chopped fresh rhubarb	300 mL

◆ *Preheat oven to 350°F (180°C)*
◆ *12-cup muffin tin, lightly greased*

1. In a bowl combine flour, sugar, baking powder, baking soda, salt and pecans.
2. In another bowl beat egg. Add oil, orange zest and orange juice. Add to flour mixture; stir just until moist and blended. Add rhubarb.
3. Spoon batter into prepared muffin tin, filling to top. Bake in preheated oven for 25 to 30 minutes.

Strawberry Cheesecake Muffins

4 oz	softened cream cheese	125 g
1/4 cup	sifted icing sugar	50 mL
2 1/2 cups	all-purpose flour	625 mL
1 tbsp	baking powder	15 mL
1/2 tsp	salt	2 mL
1	egg	1
1 1/4 cups	milk	300 mL
1/2 cup	lightly packed brown sugar	125 mL
1/3 cup	melted butter or margarine	75 mL
1 tsp	grated lemon zest	5 mL
1/4 tsp	almond extract	1 mL
1/4 cup	strawberry jam	1 mL

- *Preheat oven to 375°F (190°C)*
- *12-cup muffin tin, greased or paper-lined*

1. In a bowl combine cream cheese and icing sugar; beat until smooth. Set aside.
2. In a bowl combine flour, baking powder and salt.
3. In another bowl combine egg, milk, brown sugar, butter, lemon zest and almond extract. Add to flour mixture; stir just until moist and blended.
4. Spoon batter into prepared muffin tin, filling half full. Add 1 tbsp (15 mL) cream cheese mixture and 1 tsp (5 mL) jam. Top with remaining batter. Bake in preheated oven for about 20 minutes or until lightly browned.

Variation

- You can use any type of jam such as apricot, peach, grape, etc.

Strawberry Tea Muffins

1¼ cups	all-purpose flour	300 mL
⅔ cup	oat bran	150 mL
1½ tsp	baking powder	7 mL
½ tsp	baking soda	2 mL
½ cup	granulated sugar	125 mL
2	eggs	2
4 tbsp	butter, melted	50 mL
1 cup	buttermilk	250 mL
½ cup	strawberry preserves	125 mL
¼ cup	sliced almonds	50 mL

♦ *Preheat oven to 400°F (200°C)*
♦ *Muffin tin, greased or paper-lined*

1. In a bowl combine flour, oat bran, baking powder, baking soda and sugar. Make a well in the center.

2. In another bowl whisk together eggs, butter and buttermilk. Add to flour mixture; stir just until moist and blended.

3. Spoon batter into prepared muffin tin, filling half full. Add 1 heaping tbsp (15 mL) strawberry preserves. Top with remaining batter. Sprinkle with sliced almonds. Bake in preheated oven for 15 to 20 minutes or until golden brown.

Applesauce Carrot Muffins

3 cups	all-purpose flour	750 mL
2½ tsp	baking powder	12 mL
1 tsp	baking soda	5 mL
½ tsp	salt	2 mL
3 tsp	cinnamon	15 mL
1 tsp	ground cloves	5 mL
½ tsp	nutmeg	2 mL
1½ cups	brown sugar	375 mL
1 cup	oil	250 mL
1 cup	applesauce	250 mL
3 cups	grated carrots	750 mL
3	eggs, slightly beaten	3

◆ *Preheat oven to 400°F (200°C)*
◆ *Muffin tin, greased or paper-lined*

1. In a bowl sift together flour, baking powder, baking soda, salt, cinnamon, cloves and nutmeg. Add brown sugar, oil, applesauce, carrots and eggs; mix well.
2. Spoon batter into prepared muffin tin, filling three-quarters full. Bake in preheated oven for 18 to 20 minutes.

Carrot Cake Muffins

1 cup	all-purpose flour	250 mL
¾ cup	quick-cooking rolled oats	175 mL
1½ tsp	baking powder	7 mL
1 tsp	baking soda	5 mL
1 tsp	cinnamon	5 mL
¾ cup	raisins or chopped dates	175 mL
1	egg, beaten	1
1¼ cups	sweetened condensed skim milk	300 mL
1½ cups	grated carrots	375 mL
½ cup	drained crushed pineapple	125 mL
2 tbsp	vegetable oil	25 mL
2 tsp	grated orange zest	10 mL

◆ *Preheat oven to 375°F (190°C)*
◆ *Muffin tin, greased or paper-lined*

1. In a bowl combine flour, oats, baking powder, baking soda, cinnamon and raisins.
2. In another bowl combine egg, milk, carrots, pineapple, oil and orange zest. Add to dry ingredients; stir just until blended.
3. Spoon batter into prepared muffin tin, filling three-quarters full. Bake in preheated oven for 20 to 25 minutes or until toothpick inserted in center comes out clean and dry.

Coconut Pecan Carrot Muffins

2¼ cups	all-purpose flour	550 mL
⅔ cup	brown sugar	150 mL
½ cup	shredded coconut	125 mL
½ cup	pecans	125 mL
½ cup	raisins	125 mL
1 tbsp	baking powder	15 mL
1 tsp	salt	5 mL
1 tsp	cinnamon	5 mL
1½ cups	grated carrots	375 mL
⅔ cup	milk	150 mL
¼ cup	vegetable oil	50 mL
1 tsp	vanilla	5 mL
1	egg	1

♦ *Preheat oven to 375°F (190°C)*
♦ *12-cup muffin tin, greased or paper-lined*

1. In a bowl combine flour, brown sugar, coconut, pecans, raisins, baking powder, salt and cinnamon. Add carrots.

2. In another bowl combine milk, oil, vanilla and egg. Add to flour mixture; stir just until moist.

3. Spoon batter into prepared muffin tin, dividing evenly. Bake in preheated oven for 40 to 45 minutes.

Corn Carrot Muffins

1 cup	shredded raw carrots	250 mL
1 cup	yellow cornmeal	250 mL
1 cup	milk	250 mL
2	eggs, slightly beaten	2
2 tbsp	oil	25 mL
1 cup	all-purpose flour	250 mL
2½ tsp	baking powder	12 mL
1 tsp	salt	5 mL

♦ *Preheat oven to 400°F (200°C)*
♦ *12-cup muffin tin, greased*

1. In a bowl combine carrots and cornmeal.

2. In a saucepan over medium-high heat, bring milk to a boil. Add to carrot mixture. Cool to room temperature. Add eggs and oil.

3. In another bowl combine flour, baking powder and salt. Add to carrot mixture; blend well.

4. Spoon batter into prepared muffin tin, dividing evenly. Bake in preheated oven for 20 minutes.

Carrot Pineapple Muffins

1½ cups	all-purpose flour	375 mL
⅔ cup	granulated sugar	150 mL
1 tsp	baking powder	5 mL
1 tsp	baking soda	5 mL
½ tsp	salt	2 mL
1 tsp	cinnamon	5 mL
Pinch	nutmeg	Pinch
⅔ cup	vegetable oil	150 mL
2	eggs	2
1 cup	grated carrots	250 mL
1 tsp	vanilla	5 mL
½ cup	crushed pineapple, with juice	125 mL

- *Preheat oven to 350°F (180°C)*
- *12-cup muffin tin, greased*

1. In a bowl whisk together flour, sugar, baking powder, baking soda, salt, cinnamon and nutmeg. Make a well in the center.
2. In another bowl combine oil, eggs, carrots, vanilla and pineapple. Add to dry mixture; stir just until blended.
3. Spoon batter into prepared muffin tin, dividing evenly. Bake in preheated oven for 25 to 30 minutes.

Spicy Traditional Pineapple Carrot Muffins

1¼ cups	all-bran cereal	300 mL
1	can (14 oz/398 mL) crushed pineapple, with juice	1
¼ cup	milk	50 mL
1	egg	1
½ cup	packed brown sugar	125 mL
⅓ cup	oil	75 mL
1 cup	shredded carrots	250 mL
2 cups	all-purpose flour	500 mL
1 tbsp	baking powder	15 mL
2½ tsp	cinnamon	12 mL
1 tsp	ginger	5 mL
1 tsp	salt	5 mL
½ cup	raisins	125 mL

- *Preheat oven to 400°F (200°C)*
- *12-cup muffin tin, greased*

1. In a bowl combine cereal, pineapple (with juice) and milk. Let stand for 5 minutes. Add egg, brown sugar, oil and carrots.
2. In another bowl combine flour, baking powder, cinnamon, ginger and salt. Add cereal mixture and raisins; stir just until moist.
3. Spoon batter into prepared muffin tin, filling to top. Bake in preheated oven for 20 to 25 minutes or until tops are firm to the touch.

Pineapple Walnut Carrot Muffins

1½ cups	all-purpose flour	375 mL
1½ cups	shredded carrots	375 mL
¼ cup	granulated sugar	50 mL
3½ oz	coarsely chopped walnuts	90 g
1 tsp	cinnamon	5 mL
1 tsp	baking soda	5 mL
¼ tsp	baking powder	1 mL
¼ tsp	salt	1 mL
¼ tsp	nutmeg	1 mL
3	egg whites, lightly beaten	3
2 cups	drained crushed pineapple	500 mL
¼ cup	water	50 mL
2 tbsp + 2 tsp	frozen apple juice concentrate, thawed	25 mL + 10 mL
1 tbsp + 2 tsp	vegetable oil	15 mL + 10 mL

- ◆ *Preheat oven to 400°F (200°C)*
- ◆ *Muffin tin, greased or paper-lined*

1. In a bowl combine flour, carrots, sugar, walnuts, cinnamon, baking soda, baking powder, salt and nutmeg.
2. In another bowl combine egg whites, pineapple, water, apple juice concentrate and oil. Add to flour mixture; mix with a fork just until blended. Do not overmix.
3. Spoon batter into prepared muffin tin, dividing evenly. Bake in preheated oven for 25 to 30 minutes.

Corn Muffins

1 cup	yellow cornmeal	250 mL
1 cup	all-purpose flour	250 mL
2 tbsp	granulated sugar	25 mL
4 tsp	baking powder	20 mL
½ tsp	salt	2 mL
1 cup	milk	250 mL
¼ cup	shortening	50 mL
1	egg	1

◆ *Preheat oven to 425°F (220°C)*
◆ *12-cup muffin tin, greased*

1. In a bowl combine cornmeal, flour, sugar, baking powder, salt, milk, shortening and egg; stir until well blended.
2. Spoon batter into prepared muffin tin, filling two-thirds full. Bake in preheated oven for 15 minutes or until golden brown.

Zucchini and Carrot Muffins

1½ cups	all-purpose flour	375 mL
¾ cup	packed brown sugar	175 mL
1 tsp	baking powder	5 mL
½ tsp	ginger	2 mL
¼ tsp	baking soda	1 mL
2	eggs, slightly beaten	2
1½ cups	shredded carrots	375 mL
1 cup	shredded zucchini	250 mL
½ cup	raisins	125 mL
½ cup	chopped walnuts	125 mL
½ cup	oil	125 mL
¼ cup	honey	50 mL
1 tsp	vanilla	5 mL
CITRUS CREAM CHEESE FROSTING		
8 oz	light cream cheese	250 g
½ cup	icing sugar	125 mL
2 tbsp	orange juice	25 mL
1 tbsp	finely shredded orange or lemon zest	15 mL

◆ *Preheat oven to 375°F (190°C)*
◆ *Muffin tin, paper-lined*

1. In a bowl combine flour, brown sugar, baking powder, ginger and baking soda.
2. In another bowl combine eggs, carrots, zucchini, raisins, walnuts, oil, honey and vanilla. Add to flour mixture; stir just until blended.
3. Spoon batter into prepared muffin tin, filling three-quarters full. Bake in preheated oven for 15 to 20 minutes.
4. In a bowl combine cream cheese, icing sugar, orange juice and zest; beat on medium speed until fluffy. Spread over cooled muffins.

Cornmeal Muffins

½ cup	all-purpose flour	125 mL
1 tbsp	granulated sugar	15 mL
1 tbsp	baking powder	15 mL
¾ tsp	salt	4 mL
1½ cups	white cornmeal	375 mL
¼ cup	melted butter or margarine	50 mL
1	egg, well beaten	1
1 cup	milk	250 mL

MUFFIN STUFF: Most recipes call for yellow cornmeal but try this one using white cornmeal.

◆ *Preheat oven to 425°F (220°C)*
◆ *12-cup muffin tin, greased*

1. In a bowl sift together flour, sugar, baking powder and salt. Mix in cornmeal. Make a well in the center.
2. In another bowl combine butter, egg and milk. Add to flour mixture; stir until well blended. Do not overmix.
3. Spoon batter into prepared muffin tin, filling three-quarters full. Bake in preheated oven for 20 to 25 minutes or until golden brown.

Buttermilk Cornmeal Muffins

1 cup	cornmeal	250 mL
1½ cups	buttermilk	375 mL
1¼ cups	all-purpose flour	300 mL
1½ tsp	baking powder	7 mL
1 tsp	baking soda	5 mL
1 tsp	salt	5 mL
½ cup	granulated sugar	125 mL
1	egg	1
⅓ cup	melted butter, cooled	75 mL

◆ *Preheat oven to 400°F (200°C)*
◆ *12-cup muffin tin, greased or paper-lined*

1. In a bowl combine cornmeal and buttermilk. Set aside.
2. In another bowl combine flour, baking powder, baking soda, salt and sugar.
3. In another bowl whisk together egg and butter. Add cornmeal mixture; stir well. Add to flour mixture; stir just until blended. Do not overmix.
4. Spoon batter into prepared muffin tin, filling two-thirds full. Bake in preheated oven for 15 minutes.

Golden Cheddar Corn Muffins

1 cup	cornmeal	250 mL
1 cup	shredded old Cheddar cheese	250 mL
1 cup	all-purpose flour	250 mL
½ tsp	baking soda	2 mL
½ tsp	salt	2 mL
3	eggs	3
1	can (10 oz/284 mL) creamed corn	1
1 cup	buttermilk	250 mL
¼ cup	vegetable oil	50 mL
2 tbsp	chopped fresh parsley	25 mL

◆ *Preheat oven to 400°F (200°C)*
◆ *12-cup muffin tin, well-greased*

1. In a bowl combine cornmeal, cheese, flour, baking soda and salt.
2. In another bowl whisk together eggs, corn, buttermilk and oil. Add to dry ingredients; stir well. Add parsley; stir just until blended.
3. Spoon batter into prepared muffin tin, filling three-quarters full. Bake in preheated oven for 25 to 30 minutes or until tops are firm to the touch.

Mexican-Style Corn Muffins

½ cup + 1 tbsp	all-purpose flour	125 mL + 15 mL
1½ oz	yellow cornmeal	40g
2 tsp	granulated sugar	10 mL
1½ tsp	baking powder	7 mL
¼ tsp	salt	1 mL
¼ cup	skim milk	50 mL
1	egg, lightly beaten	1
2 tbsp	water	25 mL
1 tbsp	vegetable oil	15 mL
½ cup	canned Mexican-style corn, drained	125 mL
1 tbsp	chopped green chilies	15 mL

◆ *Preheat oven to 400°F (200°C)*
◆ *6-cup muffin tin, paper-lined*

1. In a bowl combine flour, cornmeal, sugar, baking powder and salt.
2. In another bowl combine milk, egg, water and oil. Add to flour mixture; stir to blend well. Add corn and chilies; stir just until blended.
3. Spoon batter into prepared muffin tin, dividing evenly. Bake in preheated oven for 15 to 20 minutes.

Double Corn Pepper Muffins

1½ cups	all-purpose flour	375 mL
¾ cup	cornmeal	175 mL
¼ cup	granulated sugar	50 mL
1 tbsp	chili powder	15 mL
½ tsp	salt	2 mL
½ tsp	baking soda	2 mL
¼ tsp	dried crushed chilies	1 mL
3	eggs	3
⅔ cup	buttermilk or sour milk	150 mL
2 tbsp	vegetable oil	25 mL
1 cup	frozen corn kernels, thawed or 1 can (12 oz/375 g) corn niblets, drained	250 mL
½ cup	chopped red or green bell peppers	125 mL

♦ *Preheat oven to 375°F (190°C)*
♦ *12-cup muffin tin, greased or paper-lined*

1. In a bowl combine flour, cornmeal, sugar, chili powder, salt, baking soda and chilies.
2. In another bowl combine eggs, buttermilk and oil; mix well. Add corn and chopped peppers; blend well. Add to flour mixture; mix just enough to moisten.
3. Spoon batter into prepared muffin tin, dividing evenly. Bake in preheated oven for 15 to 18 minutes or until golden brown. Serve warm.

Oatmeal Corn Muffins

1 cup	all-purpose flour	250 mL
1 tsp	baking powder	5 mL
¾ tsp	salt	4 mL
½ cup	yellow cornmeal	125 mL
½ cup	old-fashioned oats	125 mL
1 cup	buttermilk	250 mL
1	egg	1
⅓ cup	packed light brown sugar	75 mL
½ cup	melted butter or margarine	125 mL

♦ *Preheat oven to 400°F (200°C)*
♦ *12-cup muffin tin, greased or paper-lined*

1. In a bowl combine flour, baking powder and salt.
2. In another bowl combine cornmeal, oats and buttermilk. Add egg, brown sugar and butter; beat with a spoon until well blended. Add flour mixture; stir just until blended.
3. Spoon batter into prepared muffin tin, dividing evenly. Bake in preheated oven for about 25 minutes or until golden brown.

Bell Pepper Muffins

¼ cup	butter or margarine	50 mL
¼ cup	finely chopped red bell peppers	50 mL
¼ cup	finely chopped yellow bell peppers	50 mL
¼ cup	finely chopped green bell peppers	50 mL
2 cups	all-purpose flour	500 mL
2 tbsp	granulated sugar	25 mL
1 tbsp	baking powder	15 mL
¾ tsp	salt	4 mL
½ tsp	dried basil leaves	2 mL
1 cup	milk	250 mL
2	eggs	2

♦ *Preheat oven to 400°F (200°C)*
♦ *12-cup muffin tin, greased or paper-lined*

1. In a skillet heat butter over medium-high heat. Cook red, yellow and green peppers for 3 minutes or until bright and tender-crisp. Set aside.

2. In a bowl combine flour, sugar, baking powder, salt and basil.

3. In another bowl combine milk and eggs; blend well. Add to flour mixture; stir just until moist. Add peppers.

4. Spoon batter into prepared muffin tin, dividing evenly. Bake in preheated oven for 15 minutes or until golden brown.

Ham, Pepper and Onion Muffins

¼ cup	butter or margarine	50 mL
¾ cup	finely chopped onions	175 mL
¾ cup	finely chopped ham	175 mL
2 cups	all-purpose flour	500 mL
2 tbsp	granulated sugar	25 mL
1 tbsp	baking powder	15 mL
1 tsp	coarsely ground black pepper	5 mL
½ tsp	salt	2 mL
1 cup	milk	250 mL
1	large egg	1

♦ *Preheat oven to 400°F (200°C)*
♦ *Muffin tin, greased or paper-lined*

1. In a frying pan heat butter over medium-high heat. Add onions; cook for about 2 minutes. Set aside.

2. In a bowl combine ham, flour, sugar, baking powder, pepper and salt; blend well.

3. In another bowl combine milk, egg and onions. Add to flour mixture; stir just until moist.

4. Spoon batter into prepared muffin tin, dividing evenly. Bake in preheated oven for 20 to 25 minutes.

Turkey Ham, Cheese and Pepper Muffins

¼ cup	butter or margarine	50 mL
½ cup	minced sweet onions	125 mL
¼ cup	minced green bell peppers	50 mL
1	garlic clove, minced or pressed	1
2 cups	all-purpose flour	500 mL
1 tbsp	baking powder	15 mL
1 tsp	salt	5 mL
½ tsp	pepper	2 mL
1 cup	milk	250 mL
2	eggs	2
1 cup	finely diced turkey ham	250 mL
½ cup	diced Cheddar cheese	125 mL
¼ cup	shelled roasted sunflower seeds	50 mL

♦ *Preheat oven to 375°F (190°C)*
♦ *Muffin tin, well-greased*

1. In a skillet heat butter over medium-high heat. Add onions, green peppers and garlic. Cook, stirring, for 5 to 7 minutes or until onions are translucent.

2. In a bowl combine flour, baking powder, salt and pepper.

3. In another bowl combine milk and eggs; beat well. Add to flour mixture; mix well. Add vegetables with drippings, turkey and cheese; stir just until moist.

4. Spoon batter into prepared muffin tin, dividing evenly. Sprinkle with sunflower seeds. Bake in preheated oven for 25 to 30 minutes.

Onion-Parsley Muffins

2 cups	all-purpose flour	500 mL
1 tbsp	granulated sugar	15 mL
3 tsp	baking powder	15 mL
1½ tsp	salt	7 mL
¼ cup	vegetable oil	50 mL
1 cup	milk	250 mL
4	green onions, chopped	4
¼ cup	chopped parsley	50 mL

♦ *Preheat oven to 400°F (200°C)*
♦ *Muffin tin, greased*

1. In a bowl sift together flour, sugar, baking powder and salt.

2. In another bowl combine oil, milk, green onions and parsley. Add to dry ingredients; mix just until well-blended.

3. Spoon batter into prepared muffin tin, filling three-quarters full. Bake in preheated oven for 20 to 25 minutes or until toothpick inserted in center comes out clean.

Chili-Pepper Corn Muffins

1 cup	all-purpose flour	250 mL
1 cup	yellow cornmeal	250 mL
1 tbsp	baking powder	15 mL
1½ tsp	ground cumin	7 mL
1 tsp	crushed red bell pepper	5 mL
½ tsp	salt	2 mL
⅔ cup	sour cream	150 mL
⅔ cup	milk	150 mL
2 tbsp	butter or margarine, melted	25 mL
1	large egg	1
1¾ cups	finely shredded sharp Cheddar cheese	425 mL
⅓ cup	finely diced seeded hot chili peppers or jalapeno peppers	75 mL
⅓ cup	finely chopped green onions	75 mL
⅓ cup	canned whole kernel corn, drained	75 mL

◆ *Preheat oven to 375°F (190°C)*
◆ *12-cup muffin tin, greased or paper-lined*

1. In a bowl combine flour, cornmeal, baking powder, cumin, red pepper and salt.
2. In another bowl combine sour cream, milk, butter and egg; whisk until blended. Add cornmeal mixture; mix well. Add cheese, chili peppers, green onions and corn; blend well.
3. Spoon batter into prepared muffin tin, filling to top. Bake in preheated oven for 25 to 30 minutes or until toothpick inserted in center comes out clean.

Easy Orange Cornmeal Muffins

1 cup	yellow cornmeal	250 mL
1 cup	all-purpose flour	250 mL
⅓ cup	granulated sugar	75 mL
4 tsp	baking powder	20 mL
¼ tsp	salt	1 mL
1	egg, slightly beaten	1
1 cup	milk	250 mL
¼ cup	vegetable oil	50 mL
1 tbsp	grated orange or lemon zest	15 mL

◆ *Preheat oven to 425°F (220°C)*
◆ *Muffin tin, greased*

1. In a bowl combine cornmeal, flour, sugar, baking powder and salt.
2. In another bowl combine egg, milk, oil and orange zest. Add to cornmeal mixture; stir just until blended.
3. Spoon batter into prepared muffin tin, filling three-quarters full. Bake in preheated oven for about 15 minutes or until lightly browned.

Cornmeal Sausage Gems

8 oz	bulk beef or pork sausage, formed into 12 small patties	250 g
1 cup	all-purpose flour	250 mL
1 cup	cornmeal	250 mL
2 tsp	baking powder	10 mL
1/2 tsp	salt	2 mL
1 tbsp	granulated sugar	15 mL
1	egg	1
1 cup	milk	250 mL
2 tbsp	sausage drippings	25 mL

♦ *Preheat oven to 425°F (220°C)*
♦ *12-cup muffin tin, greased*

1. In a frying pan over medium-high heat, brown patties. Pour off drippings, saving as they accumulate.
2. In a bowl sift together flour, cornmeal, baking powder, salt and sugar.
3. In another bowl beat egg. Add milk and sausage drippings; mix well. Add to flour mixture; stir just until flour is dampened.
4. Place 1 patty in bottom of each muffin cup. Top with batter. Bake in preheated oven for 20 minutes.

Sunny Corn Muffins

1 1/4 cups	yellow cornmeal	300 mL
3/4 cup	sunflower seed	175 mL
1/2 cup	all-purpose flour	125 mL
2 tbsp	granulated sugar	25 mL
2 tsp	baking powder	10 mL
3/4 tsp	salt	4 mL
1 cup	milk	250 mL
1	egg	1
3 tbsp	oil	45 mL

♦ *Preheat oven to 425°F (220°C)*
♦ *12-cup muffin tin, greased*

1. In a bowl combine cornmeal, sunflower seed, flour, sugar, baking powder and salt.
2. In another bowl combine milk, egg and oil. Add to dry ingredients; stir to combine well (batter will be thin).
3. Spoon batter into prepared muffin tin, dividing evenly. Bake in preheated oven for 25 minutes.

Golden Squash Muffins

2¼ cups	all-purpose flour	550 mL
⅓ cup	granulated sugar	75 mL
2½ tsp	baking powder	12 mL
¼ tsp	salt	1 mL
⅓ cup	softened butter or margarine	75 mL
1	egg	1
¾ cup	mashed cooked winter squash	175 mL
1 tsp	grated orange zest	5 mL
1 cup	milk	250 mL
¼ cup	golden raisins	50 mL

◆ *Preheat oven to 400°F (200°C)*
◆ *12-cup muffin tin, greased or lined with foil cups*

1. In a bowl combine flour, sugar, baking powder and salt. With a pastry blender or 2 knives, cut in butter until mixture is crumbly.
2. In another bowl beat egg. Add squash, orange zest and milk; blend well. Add to flour mixture; stir just until blended. Fold in raisins.
3. Spoon batter into prepared muffin tin, filling three-quarters full. Bake in preheated oven for 20 to 25 minutes.

Best Zucchini Muffins

1 cup	all-purpose flour	250 mL
1 cup	whole wheat flour	250 mL
1½ tsp	baking powder	7 mL
½ tsp	baking soda	2 mL
1 tsp	cinnamon	5 mL
½ tsp	allspice	2 mL
1 tsp	salt	5 mL
1	egg	1
¼ cup	vegetable oil	50 mL
½ cup	granulated sugar	125 mL
1 cup	grated zucchini	250 mL
½ cup	milk	125 mL

◆ *Preheat oven to 400°F (200°C)*
◆ *12-cup muffin tin, greased*

1. In a bowl combine all-purpose flour, whole wheat flour, baking powder, baking soda, cinnamon, allspice and salt. Make a well in the center.
2. In another bowl beat egg. Add oil, sugar, zucchini and milk; blend well. Add to dry ingredients; stir just until moist (batter will be lumpy).
3. Spoon batter into prepared muffin tin, filling three-quarters full. Bake in preheated oven for 20 to 25 minutes.

Chocolate Zucchini Muffins

1 cup	all-purpose flour	250 mL
½ cup	whole wheat flour	125 mL
⅓ cup	quick-cooking rolled oats	75 mL
1 tsp	baking soda	5 mL
½ cup	softened butter	125 mL
½ cup	granulated sugar	125 mL
2	eggs	2
2 tbsp	sour cream or plain yogurt	25 mL
1 tsp	vanilla	5 mL
½ tsp	grated lemon zest	2 mL
2 cups	packed grated zucchini	500 mL
4 oz	grated bittersweet chocolate	125 g
½ cup	chopped pecans (optional)	125 mL

- ◆ *Preheat oven to 400°F (200°C)*
- ◆ *Muffin tin, greased*

1. In a bowl combine all-purpose flour, whole wheat flour, oats and baking soda.
2. In another bowl combine butter and sugar; cream until fluffy. Add eggs, sour cream, vanilla and lemon zest; beat well. Add flour mixture alternately with zucchini; blend well. Add chocolate and pecans; beat well.
3. Spoon batter into prepared muffin tin, filling three-quarters full. Bake in preheated oven for about 20 minutes or until toothpick inserted in center comes out clean and dry.

Lemon Zucchini Muffins

2 cups	all-purpose flour	500 mL
2 tsp	baking powder	10 mL
½ tsp	baking soda	2 mL
½ tsp	salt	2 mL
⅛ tsp	freshly grated nutmeg	.5 mL
¾ cup	granulated sugar	175 mL
1	egg	1
½ cup	milk	125 mL
½ cup	vegetable oil	125 mL
2 tbsp	freshly squeezed lemon juice	25 mL
1 cup	grated unpeeled zucchini, squeezed dry	250 mL
	Grated zest of 1 lemon	

- ◆ *Preheat oven to 400°F (200°C)*
- ◆ *Muffin tin, greased*

1. In a bowl combine flour, baking powder, baking soda, salt, nutmeg and sugar; stir with a fork until well blended.
2. In another bowl beat together egg, milk, oil and lemon juice. Add to flour mixture; blend well. Add zucchini and lemon zest; stir with a fork just until blended (batter will be thick).
3. Spoon batter into prepared muffin tin, filling three-quarters full. Bake in preheated oven for 20 to 25 minutes.

Zucchini Nut Muffins

4	eggs	4
1 cup	granulated sugar	250 mL
½ tsp	vanilla	2 mL
1 cup	vegetable oil	250 mL
2 cups	grated unpeeled zucchini	500 mL
3 cups	all-purpose flour	750 mL
1½ tsp	baking powder	7 mL
1 tsp	baking soda	5 mL
1 tsp	salt	5 mL
1 tsp	cinnamon	5 mL
1 cup	chopped walnuts	250 mL

◆ *Preheat oven to 375°F (190°C)*
◆ *Muffin tin, greased or paper-lined*

1. In a bowl combine eggs, sugar and vanilla; beat for 2 minutes. Slowly add oil; beat for 2 minutes. Add zucchini.

2. In another bowl combine flour, baking powder, baking soda, salt and cinnamon. Add walnuts; blend well. Add zucchini mixture; stir just until blended.

3. Spoon batter into prepared muffin tin, filling three-quarters full. Bake in preheated oven for 25 to 30 minutes.

Spiced Zucchini Muffins

1 cup	all-purpose flour	250 mL
1 cup	whole wheat flour	250 mL
1½ tsp	baking powder	7 mL
½ tsp	baking soda	2 mL
1 tsp	cinnamon	5 mL
½ tsp	allspice	2 mL
1 tsp	salt	5 mL
1	egg	1
¼ cup	oil	50 mL
½ cup	granulated sugar	125 mL
1 cup	grated zucchini	250 mL
½ cup	milk	125 mL

◆ *Preheat oven to 400°F (200°C)*
◆ *12-cup muffin tin, greased*

1. In a bowl combine all-purpose flour, whole wheat flour, baking powder, baking soda, cinnamon, allspice and salt. Make a well in the center.

2. In another bowl beat egg. Add oil, sugar, zucchini and milk; blend well. Add to dry ingredients; stir just until blended (batter will be lumpy).

3. Spoon batter into prepared muffin tin, filling three-quarters full. Bake in preheated oven for 20 to 25 minutes.

Whole Wheat Zucchini Muffins

1 cup	whole wheat flour	250 mL
½ tsp	baking powder	2 mL
½ tsp	baking soda	2 mL
1 tsp	cinnamon	5 mL
⅓ cup	chopped nuts	75 mL
1	egg	1
½ cup	granulated sugar	125 mL
½ cup	oil	125 mL
1 tsp	vanilla	5 mL
1 cup	grated zucchini	250 mL

◆ *Preheat oven to 400°F (200°C)*
◆ *12-cup muffin tin, greased or paper-lined*

1. In a bowl combine flour, baking powder, baking soda, cinnamon and nuts. Make a well in the center.

2. In another bowl combine egg, sugar, oil, vanilla and zucchini. Add to dry ingredients; mix just until blended.

3. Spoon batter into prepared muffin tin, filling three-quarters full. Bake in preheated oven for 20 to 25 minutes or until toothpick inserted in center comes out clean and dry.

Make-Ahead Muffins

continued on next page

All-Bran Breakfast Muffins

1 cup	bran flakes cereal	250 mL
1 cup	boiling water	250 mL
2½ cups	all-purpose flour	625 mL
2½ tsp	baking soda	12 mL
1 tsp	salt	5 mL
½ cup	shortening	125 mL
1 cup	granulated sugar	250 mL
2	eggs	2
2½ cups	buttermilk	625 mL
2 cups	all-bran cereal	500 mL
1 cup	raisins	250 mL

MUFFIN STUFF: This batter will keep for 3 to 4 weeks in the refrigerator if covered tightly.

◆ *Muffin tin, greased or paper-lined*

1. In a bowl combine cereal and boiling water. Set aside to cool.
2. In another bowl combine flour, baking soda and salt. Set aside.
3. In another bowl cream together shortening and sugar. Add eggs, one at a time, beating well each time. Add dry ingredients to this mixture alternatively with buttermilk; stir until blended.
4. Add cooled bran bud mixture, all-bran cereal and raisins; cover bowl tightly. Let stand overnight in refrigerator; do not stir. Spoon batter into prepared muffin tin. Bake at 400°F (200°C) for 30 minutes.

Applesauce Whole Wheat Muffins

¾ cup	all-purpose flour	175 mL
½ cup	whole wheat flour	125 mL
1 cup	uncooked quick-cooking rolled oats	250 mL
½ cup	packed brown sugar	125 mL
1 tsp	baking powder	5 mL
½ tsp	baking soda	2 mL
½ tsp	cinnamon	2 mL
¼ tsp	salt	1 mL
¾ cup	buttermilk	175 mL
¼ cup	applesauce	50 mL
¼ cup	vegetable oil	50 mL
1	egg, beaten	1
¼ cup	raisins	50 mL

MUFFIN STUFF: Batter will keep, refrigerated, for 2 to 3 weeks.

◆ *Muffin tin, greased or paper-lined*

1. In a bowl combine all-purpose flour, whole wheat flour, oats, brown sugar, baking powder, baking soda, cinnamon and salt.
2. In a bowl combine buttermilk, applesauce, oil and egg; mix well. Add to dry ingredients; stir just until moistened. Fold in raisins. Cover bowl tightly; refrigerate overnight.
3. Spoon batter into prepared muffin tin. Bake at 400°F (200°C) for 18 to 20 minutes.

Blueberry Bran Muffins

6	eggs	6
1½ cups	firmly packed dark brown sugar	375 mL
¼ cup	light molasses	50 mL
¼ cup	honey	50 mL
4 cups	buttermilk	1 L
1½ cups	vegetable oil	375 mL
1 tsp	vanilla	5 mL
2½ cups	unprocessed bran flakes	625 mL
2 cups	wheat germ	500 mL
1¾ cups	finely chopped pecans or walnuts	425 mL
2 cups	fresh or frozen blueberries, partially thawed	500 mL
4½ cups	all-purpose flour	1.125 L
4 tsp	baking powder	20 mL
4 tsp	baking soda	20 mL
1 tsp	cinnamon	5 mL
¼ tsp	salt	1 mL

◆ *Muffin tin, paper-lined*

1. In a bowl beat together eggs, brown sugar, molasses and honey until well blended. Add buttermilk, oil and vanilla; stir well. Add bran, wheat germ and 1¼ cups (300 mL) pecans. Let stand for 10 minutes; stir in berries.

2. In another bowl combine flour, baking powder, baking soda, cinnamon and salt. Add to batter, mixing just until blended. Cover bowl tightly; refrigerate overnight.

3. Spoon batter into prepared muffin tin. Sprinkle tops evenly with remaining pecans. Bake at 400°F (200°C) for about 25 minutes.

MUFFIN STUFF: Batter can be stored in the refrigerator or frozen.

Coffee 'n' Bran Muffins

½ cup	butter or margarine, soft or melted	125 mL
1 cup	granulated sugar	250 mL
2	eggs	2
1 cup	black coffee	250 mL
2 cups	buttermilk	500 mL
2½ cups	all-purpose flour	625 mL
2½ tsp	baking soda	12 mL
3 cups	wheat bran cereal	750 mL

◆ *Muffin tin, greased or paper-lined*

1. In a bowl whisk together butter, sugar and eggs. Add coffee and buttermilk; whisk until mixture looks curdled. Add flour and baking soda; beat to blend well. Stir in bran. Cover bowl tightly; refrigerate.

2. When ready to bake, stir mixture well. Spoon batter into prepared muffin tin. Bake at 400°F (200°C) for 20 minutes.

Golden Honey Bran Muffins

6 cups	all-bran cereal	1.5 L
2 cups	boiling water	500 mL
1 cup	honey	250 mL
5 cups	all-purpose flour	1.25 L
2 tbsp	baking soda	25 mL
2 tsp	cinnamon	10 mL
1 tsp	salt	5 mL
1 cup	shortening	250 mL
1 cup	granulated sugar	250 mL
1 cup	lightly packed brown sugar	250 mL
4	eggs	4
4 cups	buttermilk	1 L
2 cups	raisins or chopped dates	500 mL

◆ *Muffin tin, greased or paper-lined*

1. In a bowl cover bran cereal with boiling water. Add honey; stir well. Set aside.
2. In another bowl combine flour, baking soda, cinnamon and salt.
3. In another bowl cream together shortening, granulated sugar, brown sugar, eggs, buttermilk and soaked cereal. Add flour mixture; mix well. Stir in raisins. Pour batter into a container; cover tightly. Store in refrigerator for up to 2 months.
4. When ready to bake, spoon batter into prepared muffin tin, filling three-quarters full. Bake at 375°F (190°C) for 20 to 25 minutes.

Convenient Raisin Bran Muffins

1 cup	natural bran	250 mL
1 cup	boiling water	250 mL
½ cup	butter or margarine	125 mL
¾ cup	brown sugar	175 mL
3	eggs	3
2½ cups	all-purpose flour	625 mL
2½ tsp	baking soda	12 mL
½ tsp	salt	2 mL
2 cups	raisin bran cereal	500 mL
2 cups	buttermilk	500 mL
1 cup	raisins	250 mL
1 cup	coarsely chopped walnuts	250 mL

◆ *Muffin tin, greased or paper-lined*

1. In a bowl cover bran with boiling water; set aside 20 minutes.
2. In a food processor combine butter, brown sugar, eggs and soaked bran; process until smooth.
3. In a bowl combine bran mixture, flour, baking soda, salt, cereal and buttermilk; beat well. Fold in raisins and walnuts.
4. Pour batter into a container; cover tightly. Store in the refrigerator for up to 6 weeks.
5. When ready to bake, spoon batter into prepared muffin tin, filling three-quarters full. Bake at 375°F (190°C) for 20 minutes.

Oat Bran Refrigerator Muffins

⅔ cup	wheat germ	150 mL
1½ cups	natural bran	375 mL
1½ cups	uncooked oat bran	375 mL
3 cups	all-bran cereal	750 mL
3 cups	boiling water	750 mL
1 cup	margarine	250 mL
1 cup	firmly packed brown sugar	250 mL
½ cup	granulated sugar	125 mL
½ cup	molasses	125 mL
4	eggs	4
4 cups	buttermilk	1 L
2 cups	raisins and/or dates	500 mL
3 cups	all-purpose flour	750 mL
2 cups	whole wheat flour	500 mL
3 tbsp	baking soda	45 mL
1 tsp	salt	5 mL

♦ *Muffin tin, greased or paper-lined*

1. In a bowl combine wheat germ, natural bran, oat bran and bran cereal. Add boiling water; mix well. Set aside to cool.
2. In another bowl cream together margarine, brown sugar and granulated sugar; add molasses. Beat in eggs one at a time. Add buttermilk; mix well. Stir in raisins.
3. In another bowl combine all-purpose flour, whole wheat flour, baking soda and salt. Add to creamed mixture; mix well. Stir in bran mixture; blend well.
4. Pour batter into a container; cover tightly. Store in the refrigerator for at least 24 hours before baking.
5. When ready to bake, spoon batter into prepared muffin tin, filling three-quarters full. Bake at 375°F (190°C) for 25 to 30 minutes.

Oldtime Six Week Bran Muffins

4 cups	bran	1 L
2 cups	bran flakes cereal	500 mL
2 cups	boiling water	500 mL
1 cup	butter	250 mL
1 cup	granulated sugar	250 mL
2 cups	brown sugar	500 mL
4	eggs	4
4 cups	buttermilk	1 L
1/2 cup	molasses	125 mL
5 cups	flour	1.25 L
2 tbsp	baking soda	25 mL
1 tbsp	baking powder	15 mL
1 tsp	salt	5 mL
2 cups	raisins	500 mL

- ◆ *Muffin tin, greased or paper-lined*

1. In a bowl combine bran and bran flakes. Cover with boiling water; mix well. Set aside.
2. In another bowl cream together butter, granulated sugar and brown sugar. Beat in eggs one at a time. Add buttermilk and molasses; mix well.
3. In another bowl combine flour, baking soda, baking powder, salt and raisins. Add to buttermilk mixture; stir just until blended. Add bran mixture; mix well.
4. Pour batter into a container; cover tightly. Store in the refrigerator for up to 6 weeks.
5. When ready to bake, spoon batter into prepared muffin tin, filling three-quarters full. Bake at 400°F (200°C) for 20 to 25 minutes or until firm and springy to the touch.

Pineapple Bran Muffins

2 cups	all-bran cereal	500 mL
2 cups	buttermilk	500 mL
2	eggs, slightly beaten	2
1	can (19 oz/540 mL) crushed pineapple, not drained	1
1/2 cup	melted butter or margarine	125 mL
2 1/2 cups	all-purpose flour	625 mL
3/4 cup	packed dark brown sugar	175 mL
2 tsp	salt	10 mL
2 tsp	baking soda	10 mL
1 cup	toasted chopped almonds	250 mL

- ◆ *Muffin tin, greased*

1. In a bowl combine bran and buttermilk; let stand for 5 minutes. Add eggs, pineapple and butter; stir well.
2. In another bowl combine flour, brown sugar, salt, baking soda and almonds. Add to bran mixture; stir just until blended (batter will be lumpy).
3. Pour batter into a container; cover tightly. Store in the refrigerator for up to 3 weeks.
4. When ready to bake, spoon batter into prepared muffin tin, filling three-quarters full. Bake at 375°F (190°C) for 25 minutes.

All 'Round Muffin Mix

7 cups	all-purpose flour	1.75 L
1⅓ cups	non-fat dry milk	325 mL
¾ cup	granulated sugar	175 mL
¼ cup	double-acting baking powder	50 mL
1 tbsp	salt	15 mL

1. In a large bowl with a fork, combine flour, milk, sugar, baking powder and salt. Store in an airtight container in a cool, dry place.

Plain Muffins

2 cups	All 'Round Muffin Mix (see recipe above)	500 mL
1	egg, slightly beaten	1
1 cup	water	250 mL
3 tbsp	butter or margarine, melted	45 mL

◆ *Preheat oven to 400°F (200°C)*
◆ *12-cup muffin tin, greased*

1. Put muffin mix in a large bowl. In another bowl combine egg, water and melted butter. Add all at once to muffin mixture and stir just until moistened.
2. Spoon batter into prepared muffin tin, filling cups two-thirds full. Bake in preheated oven for 20 to 25 minutes.

Variations

◆ *Cheese Muffins:* Add a small piece of Cheddar cheese in the center of each muffin before baking.

◆ *Jelly Muffins:* Fill cups only half full with batter. Put 1 tsp (5 mL) of your favorite jelly in center of each muffin and top with remaining batter. Bake as directed.

Biscuit Mix No. 1

12 cups	all-purpose flour	3 L
4 tsp	cream of tartar	20 mL
4 tsp	baking soda	20 mL
4 tbsp	baking powder	60 mL
4 tbsp	granulated sugar	60 mL
1⅔ cups	powdered milk	400 mL
1 lb	lard or shortening	500 g
3 tsp	salt	15 mL

1. In a bowl combine flour, cream of tartar, baking soda, baking powder, sugar, powdered milk, lard and salt. Mix with fingers or pastry blender until coarse crumbs form.
2. Store mix in an airtight container in a cool, dry place. Use as you would any commercial mix.

Biscuit Mix No. 2

9 cups	all-purpose flour	2.25 L
1 tbsp	salt	15 mL
4 tbsp	baking powder	50 mL
2 cups	shortening (1 lb/500 g)	500 mL

1. In a large bowl mix together flour, salt and baking powder. Add shortening, working in with a pastry blender (or fingers) until texture resembles coarse crumbs.
2. Store mix in an airtight container in a cool, dry place. Use as you would any commercial mix.

Biscuit Mix No. 3

6 cups	sifted pastry flour or 5¼ cups (1.3 L) all-purpose flour	1.5 L
3 tbsp	baking powder	45 mL
1½ tsp	salt	7 mL
1 cup	shortening (8 oz/250 g)	250 mL

1. In a large bowl sift together flour, baking powder and salt 2 or 3 times to distribute evenly. Cut in shortening until mixture resembles coarse crumbs.
2. Store mix in an airtight tin or jar. Makes about 7½ to 8 cups (1.875 to 2 L) and will keep 4 to 6 weeks at room temperature.

Oat or Bran Muffins

1	egg	1
2 tbsp	vegetable oil or shortening, melted	25 mL
1 cup	soured skim milk	250 mL
½ tsp	baking soda	2 mL
⅔ cup	all-bran cereal or rolled oats	150 mL
1⅓ cups	homemade or packaged biscuit mix	325 mL
⅓ cup	packed brown sugar	75 mL

HINT: Use a packaged muffin mix, or one of your homemade mix recipes, to make a good quick coffee cake. Bake in a square pan and top with cinnamon and sugar.

◆ *Preheat oven to 400°F (200°C)*
◆ *Muffin tin, greased*

1. In a large bowl beat egg. Add oil, milk, baking soda and bran, mixing well. Add Biscuit Mix and brown sugar.
2. Spoon batter into prepared muffin tin, filling cups two-thirds full. Bake in preheated oven for 18 to 20 minutes.

Variation

◆ *Orange Muffins:* Add a little grated orange zest, plus 2 to 3 tbsp (25 to 45 mL) sugar for a sweeter muffin.

Bran and Whole-Wheat Mix

3 cups	whole-wheat flour	750 mL
3 cups	all-purpose flour	750 mL
2½ cups whole-bran cereal		625 mL
1½ cups non-fat dry milk		375 mL
1½ cups packed brown sugar or granulated sugar		375 mL
4 tbsp	baking powder	60 mL
1 tbsp	salt	15 mL
1½ cups shortening		375 mL

1. In a large bowl using a pastry blender or your fingers, mix together whole-wheat flour, all-purpose flour, cereal, dry milk, brown sugar, baking powder, salt and shortening. Blend well until mixture resembles fine crumbs.
2. Store mix in an airtight container in a cool, dry place for up to 3 months. Makes 12 cups (3 L).

Nutty Bran and Whole-Wheat Muffins

4½ cups Bran and Whole-Wheat Mix (see recipe above)		1.125 L
1¼ cups water		300 mL
1	egg, slightly beaten	1
½ cup	chopped nuts	125 mL

◆ *Preheat oven to 400°F (200°C)*
◆ *Muffin tin, greased*

1. In a large bowl combine mix, water, egg and nuts. Stir just to moisten.
2. Spoon batter into prepared muffin tin. Bake in preheated oven for 15 to 20 minutes or until toothpick inserted in center comes out clean and dry.

Cinnamon Raisin Bran Muffin Mix

6 cups	all-purpose flour	1.5 L
4 cups	raisins	1 L
3 cups	bran flakes cereal	750 mL
3 cups	wheat bran	750 mL
2 cups	packed brown sugar	500 mL
2 tbsp	baking soda	25 mL
2 tbsp	cinnamon	25 mL
2 tsp	salt	10 mL

1. In a large bowl combine flour, raisins, cereal, bran, brown sugar, baking soda, cinnamon and salt.
2. Store mix in an airtight container in a cool, dry place for up to 4 weeks. Makes about $13\frac{1}{2}$ cups (3.375 L).

Breakfast Muffins

$2\frac{1}{4}$ cups	Cinnamon Raisin Bran Mix (see recipe above)	550 mL
$\frac{1}{2}$ cup	low-fat plain yogurt	125 mL
$\frac{1}{2}$ cup	milk	125 mL
3 tbsp	vegetable oil	45 mL

- *Preheat oven to 400°F (200°C)*
- *6-cup muffin tin, greased or paper-lined*

1. Put muffin mix in a large bowl. In another bowl, whisk together yogurt, milk and oil. Stir into mix just until moistened.
2. Spoon batter into prepared muffin tin, filling cups to the top. Bake in preheated oven for 20 to 25 minutes or until firm to the touch.

Corn Muffin Mix

4 cups	all-purpose flour	1 L
4 cups	cornmeal	1 L
2 cups	non-fat dry milk	500 mL
¾ cup	granulated sugar	175 mL
¼ cup	double-acting baking powder	50 mL
1 tbsp	salt	15 mL

1. In a large bowl combine flour, cornmeal, milk, sugar, baking powder and salt. Mix with your hands, lifting mixture and letting it fall through your fingers.
2. Store mix in an airtight container in a cool, dry place. Makes 9½ cups (2.375 L).

Corn Muffins

1	egg	1
1 cup	water	250 mL
2⅓ cups	Corn Muffin Mix (see recipe above)	575 mL
¼ cup	butter or margarine, melted or bacon or sausage fat	50 mL

◆ *Preheat oven to 425°F (220°C)*
◆ *12-cup muffin tin, greased*

1. In a bowl with a fork mix together egg and water until blended. Add Corn Muffin Mix and melted butter, stirring just to blend.
2. Spoon batter evenly into prepared muffin tin. Bake in preheated oven for 20 minutes or until golden brown.

> **HINT:** To check baking powder for freshness, stir 1 tsp (5 mL) baking powder into ½ cup (125 mL) boiling water. If the mixture does not fizz and bubble, the baking powder has lost its leavening power and should be thrown out.

Granola Mix

4 cups	quick or old-fashioned rolled oats	1 L
1 cup	coarsely chopped walnuts	250 mL
¾ cup	hulled sunflower seeds	175 mL
½ cup	slivered almonds	125 mL
½ cup	coarsely chopped pecans	125 mL
½ cup	wheat germ	125 mL
½ cup	natural wheat and barley cereal	125 mL
⅓ cup	sesame seeds	75 mL
1½ cups	shredded coconut	375 mL
1 cup	packed light brown sugar	250 mL
⅔ cup	vegetable oil	150 mL
⅔ cup	water	150 mL
½ cup	honey	125 mL
2 tsp	vanilla	10 mL
1 tsp	cinnamon	5 mL
½ tsp	ground nutmeg	2 mL
1½ cups	raisins	375 mL

◆ *Preheat oven to 300°F (150°C)*
◆ *Two large roasting pans*

1. In a large bowl combine oats, walnuts, sunflower seeds, almonds, pecans, wheat germ, cereal, sesame seeds and coconut. Set aside.

2. In a large saucepan over low heat, combine brown sugar, oil, water, honey, vanilla, cinnamon and nutmeg. Heat, stirring occasionally, for 15 to 20 minutes or until sugar dissolves. Do not allow to boil. Pour over dry ingredients and stir until well coated.

3. Divide batter evenly between the 2 pans. Bake in preheated oven for 25 to 30 minutes (or 10 minutes more if you want a crunchier texture). Set aside to cool.

4. When cool, break into pieces. Stir in raisins. Store mix in airtight containers in a cool, dry place for up to 6 months. Makes about 14 cups (3.5 L) mix.

Granola Muffins

1 cup	Multipurpose Mix, (preferably Whole-Wheat, see page 200)	250 mL
½ cup + 2 tbsp	Granola Mix (see recipe above)	125 mL + 25 mL
2 tbsp	packed light brown sugar	25 mL
½ cup	milk	125 mL
1	egg, slightly beaten	1

◆ *Preheat oven to 400°F (200°C)*
◆ *6-cup muffin tin, greased*

1. In a large bowl combine Multipurpose Mix, ½ cup (125 mL) Granola Mix and sugar. Add milk and egg, stirring just until moistened.

2. Spoon batter into prepared muffin tin, filling cups two-thirds full. Sprinkle tops with remaining 2 tbsp (25 mL) Granola mix. Bake in preheated oven for 20 to 25 minutes or until golden brown.

Just-a-Minute Mix

10 cups	all-purpose flour	2.5 L
⅓ cup	baking powder	75 mL
1 tbsp	salt	15 mL
2⅓ cups shortening (1 lb/500 g)		575 mL

MUFFIN STUFF: A quick and easy recipe that really just takes a minute!

1. In a large mixing bowl, combine flour, baking powder and salt, mixing well. With a pastry blender or 2 knives, cut in shortening until mixture resembles coarse crumbs.
2. Store mix in an airtight container in a cool, dry place. Makes about 16 cups (4 L).

Just-a-Minute Muffins

2½ cups	Just-a-Minute Mix (see recipe above)	625 mL
3 tbsp	granulated sugar	45 mL
¾ cup	milk	175 mL
1	egg, beaten	1

MUFFIN STUFF: You can add raisins, blueberries or any other fruits, as well as chocolate chips – whatever you have on hand.

HINT: If you have saved egg yolks from previous recipes, use them in place of whole eggs. Use 2 yolks for every whole egg.

- ◆ *Preheat oven to 400°F (200°C)*
- ◆ *12-cup muffin tin, greased*

1. In a large bowl combine mix and sugar. Add milk and egg, stirring just until moistened. Batter will be lumpy.
2. Spoon batter into prepared muffin tin. Bake in preheated oven for 20 to 25 minutes.

Multipurpose Mix

10 cups	all-purpose flour	2.5 L
1/2 cup	granulated sugar	125 mL
1/3 cup	baking powder	75 mL
1 tbsp	salt	15 mL
2 cups	shortening	500 mL

1. In a large bowl combine flour, sugar, baking powder and salt, mixing well. With a pastry blender or 2 knives, cut in shortening until mixture resembles coarse crumbs.
2. Store in an airtight container in a cool, dry place for up to 3 months. Makes about 13 cups (3.25 L).

Variation
- *Whole-Wheat Multipurpose Mix:* Use 5 cups (1.25 L) all-purpose flour and 5 cups (1.25 L) whole-wheat flour.

Cornmeal Muffins

1 1/2 cups	Multipurpose Mix (see recipe above)	375 mL
3/4 cup	cornmeal	175 mL
2 tbsp	granulated sugar	25 mL
1 cup	milk	250 mL
1	egg, slightly beaten	1

- *Preheat oven to 400°F (200°C)*
- *12-cup muffin tin, greased*

1. In a bowl combine mix, cornmeal and sugar. Add milk and egg, stirring just until moistened.
2. Spoon batter into prepared muffin tin. Bake in preheated oven for 25 to 30 minutes.

Rolled Oats Mix

4 cups	all-purpose flour	1 L
4 cups	quick-cooking oats (not instant)	1 L
1½ cups	dry non-fat milk	375 mL
4 tbsp	double-acting baking powder	60 mL
1 tbsp	salt	15 mL
1½ cups	solid vegetable shortening	375 mL

1. In a large bowl combine flour, oats, milk, baking powder and salt. With a pastry blender, cut in shortening until mixture resembles coarse crumbs.
2. Store in an airtight container and keep in a cool, dry place. Makes about 10 cups (2.5 L).

Oat Muffins

2¼ cups	Rolled Oats Mix (see recipe above)	550 mL
¼ cup	raisins (optional)	50 mL
2 tbsp	granulated sugar	25 mL
⅔ cup	water	150 mL
1	egg, beaten	1

- *Preheat oven to 425°F (220°C)*
- *12-cup muffin tin, greased*

1. In a large bowl combine mix, raisins (if using), sugar, water and egg. Stir just until moistened. Do not overmix.
2. Spoon batter into prepared muffin tin. Bake in preheated oven for about 20 minutes.

Whole-Wheat Mix

4 cups	whole-wheat flour	1 L
4 cups	all-purpose flour	1 L
1½ cups	non-fat dry milk	375 mL
1½ cups	granulated sugar	375 mL
½ cup	wheat germ	125 mL
4 tbsp	double-acting baking powder	50 mL
1 tbsp	salt	15 mL
1½ cups	solid vegetable shortening	375 mL

1. In a large bowl combine whole-wheat flour, all-purpose flour, milk, sugar, wheat germ, baking powder and salt. With a pastry blender or 2 knives, cut in shortening until mixture is crumbly.

2. Store mix in an airtight container in a cool, dry place. Makes about 14 cups (3.5 L).

Whole-Wheat Muffins

1	egg	1
1¼ cups	water	300 mL
4½ cups	Whole-Wheat Mix (see recipe above)	1.125 L

- ◆ *Preheat oven to 400°F (200°C)*
- ◆ *12-cup muffin tin, greased*

1. In a large bowl beat egg slightly with water. Stir in mix just until moistened.

2. Spoon batter into prepared muffin tin. Bake in preheated oven for 15 to 20 minutes.

Bacon Muffins

2 cups	homemade or packaged biscuit mix	500 mL
2 tbsp	granulated sugar	25 mL
1	egg	1
2/3 cup	cold water or milk	150 mL
6	slices bacon, fried crisp and crumbled (about 1/4 cup/50 mL)	6

- *Preheat oven to 400°F (200°C)*
- *12-cup muffin tin, greased*

1. In a large bowl combine biscuit mix, sugar, egg and water. With a fork, beat vigorously for 1 minute. Stir in bacon, mixing just until blended.
2. Spoon batter into prepared muffin tin, filling cups two-thirds full. Bake in preheated oven for 15 minutes.

Quick Banana Muffins

4 cups	homemade or packaged biscuit mix	1 L
1 cup	granulated sugar	250 mL
1/2 cup	all-purpose flour	125 mL
1/2 tsp	baking soda	2 mL
4	eggs, beaten	4
1 cup	sour cream	250 mL
2 cups	mashed ripe bananas (about 4 medium)	500 mL
1 cup	chopped walnuts	250 mL

HINT: To shell walnuts, soak overnight in salt water before gently cracking. This will remove the nutmeat intact.

- *Preheat oven to 400°F (200°C)*
- *Muffin tin, greased*

1. In a large bowl combine biscuit mix, sugar, flour and baking soda.
2. In another bowl combine eggs and sour cream. Stir into dry ingredients. Add mashed banana and fold in chopped nuts.
3. Spoon batter into prepared muffin tin, filling cups three-quarters full. Bake in preheated oven for 15 to 20 minutes or until toothpick inserted in center comes out clean.

Blueberry Cornbread Muffins

1	pkg blueberry muffin mix (such as Duncan Hines)	1
1 cup	yellow cornmeal	250 mL
1 cup	water	250 mL
1	egg	1

♦ *Preheat oven to 400°F (200°C)*
♦ *Muffin tin, greased or paper-lined*

1. In a large bowl combine mix and cornmeal.
2. In another bowl mix together water and egg. Add to the dry ingredients, blending with a fork just until moistened. Fold in packaged blueberries.
3. Spoon batter into prepared muffin tin, filling cups three-quarters full. Bake in preheated oven for 20 to 25 minutes.

Blueberry Pancake Muffins

2 cups	pancake mix	500 mL
½ cup	granulated sugar or packed brown sugar	125 mL
2	eggs, beaten	2
1 cup	milk	250 mL
½ cup	butter or margarine, melted	125 mL

♦ *Preheat oven to 400°F (200°C)*
♦ *Muffin tin, paper-lined*

1. In a large bowl combine pancake mix and sugar. Add eggs, milk and melted butter. Stir just to moisten, but do not overmix.
2. Spoon batter into prepared muffin tin. Bake in preheated oven for 15 to 20 minutes or until golden brown.

Blueberry Cinnamon Treats

1	pkg wild blueberry muffin mix (such as Betty Crocker)	1
2 tbsp	vegetable oil	25 mL
2 tbsp	milk	25 mL
1/2 tsp	cinnamon	2 mL
1	egg	1
LEMON BUTTER FROSTING		
1 1/2 cups	icing sugar	375 mL
2 tbsp	softened butter or margarine	25 mL
1/2 tsp	lemon zest	2 mL
1 tsp	lemon juice	5 mL
1 tbsp	milk	15 mL

◆ *Preheat oven to 375°F (190°C)*
◆ *Cookie sheet*

1. In a large bowl combine muffin mix, oil, milk, cinnamon and egg. Fold in packaged blueberries.
2. Drop dough by teaspoonfuls (5 mL), 2 inches (5 cm) apart onto ungreased cookie sheet. Bake in preheated oven for 10 minutes or until edges are golden brown. Remove from cookie sheet immediately.
3. In a bowl mix together icing sugar and butter. Stir in lemon zest and lemon juice. Then add milk 1 tsp (5 mL) at a time until desired consistency is reached. Frost cookies and serve.

Blueberry Miniatures

2 cups	homemade or packaged biscuit mix	500 mL
1 tbsp	granulated sugar	15 mL
1	egg	1
2 tbsp	butter or margarine, melted	25 mL
3/4 cup	milk	175 mL
1 cup	blueberries, washed and stemmed	250 mL
1 tbsp	Sugar-Cinnamon Mix (page 357)	15 mL

◆ *Preheat oven to 400°F (200°C)*
◆ *Miniature muffin tin, greased*

1. In a large bowl combine biscuit mix and sugar.
2. In another bowl beat egg slightly. Stir in melted butter and milk. Add to biscuit mixture all at once and stir just until moistened. Fold in blueberries.
3. Spoon batter into prepared muffin tin. Sprinkle with Sugar-Cinnamon Mix. Bake in preheated oven for 10 minutes or until golden brown. Remove from pans and serve hot.

Blueberry Nut Muffins

1	egg	1
½ cup	milk	125 mL
1	pkg wild blueberry muffin mix	1
½ cup	chopped nuts	125 mL

◆ *Preheat oven to 400°F (200°C)*
◆ *12-cup muffin tin, greased or paper-lined*

1. In a large bowl blend together egg and milk. Stir in muffin mix just until blended. Batter should be lumpy. Fold in packaged blueberries and nuts.
2. Spoon batter into prepared muffin tin. Bake in preheated oven for 15 to 20 minutes.

Frosted Brownie Fudge Muffins

1	pkg hot fudge brownie mix (such as Betty Crocker)	1
½ cup	creamy chocolate frosting	125 mL
½ cup	whipped cream	125 mL

◆ *Preheat oven to 350°F (180°C)*
◆ *6-cup muffin tin, greased*

1. Prepare brownie mix according to package instructions. Spoon half the batter into prepared muffin tin.
2. Before opening hot fudge pouch, squeeze until fudge is softened, about 20 to 25 times. Squeeze fudge evenly over batter in cups. Spoon remaining batter over fudge. Bake in preheated oven for about 25 to 30 minutes. Set aside to cool slightly.
3. Warm frosting in microwave on High for 30 seconds. Drizzle over warm muffins and top with whipped cream.

Easy Buttermilk Muffins

1 cup	buttermilk baking mix	250 mL
3 tbsp	granulated sugar	45 mL
1	egg	1
⅓ cup	water	75 mL

- *Preheat oven to 400°F (200°C)*
- *Muffin tin, greased or paper-lined*

1. In a large bowl combine buttermilk mix, sugar, egg and water. Whisk together for about 30 seconds.
2. Spoon batter into prepared muffin tin, filling cups three-quarters full. Bake in preheated oven for 15 to 20 minutes.

Variations

- *Buttermilk Nut Muffins:* Add ¼ cup (50 mL) chopped nuts.
- *Buttermilk Date Muffins:* Add ¼ cup (50 mL) chopped dates.

Buttermilk Corn Muffins

½ cup	buttermilk mix	125 mL
½ cup	yellow cornmeal	125 mL
2 tbsp	granulated sugar	25 mL
1	egg	1
¼ tsp	salt	50 mL
⅓ cup	water	75 mL
2 tbsp	butter, melted	25 mL

- *Preheat oven to 400°F (200°C)*
- *Muffin tin, greased or paper-lined*

1. In a medium bowl combine buttermilk mix, cornmeal, sugar, egg, salt and water. Mix in melted butter, blending well.
2. Spoon batter into prepared muffin tin, filling cups three-quarters full. Bake in preheated oven for 15 to 20 minutes.

Cheddar Beer Muffins

3 cups	homemade or packaged biscuit mix	750 mL
¼ cup	granulated sugar	50 mL
1	egg	1
¾ cup + ⅓ cup	milk	175 mL + 75 mL
2 tbsp	beer	25 mL
½ cup	grated Cheddar cheese	125 mL

MUFFIN STUFF: If desired, increase the beer to ⅓ cup (75 mL).

- ◆ *Preheat oven to 400°F (200°C)*
- ◆ *Muffin tin, greased or paper-lined*

1. In a large bowl combine biscuit mix and sugar. Stir with a fork until no lumps remain.
2. In another bowl whisk together egg, milk and beer. Pour into dry ingredients. Add cheese, stirring just until moistened. Do not overmix.
3. Spoon batter into prepared muffin tin, filling cups three-quarters full. Bake in preheated oven for 12 to 15 minutes.

Chive Dinner Muffins

2 cups	homemade or packaged biscuit mix	500 mL
2 tbsp	shortening	25 mL
1	egg	1
⅔ cup	milk or water	150 mL
¼ cup	snipped chives	50 mL

- ◆ *Preheat oven to 400°F (200°C)*
- ◆ *12-cup muffin tin, greased*

1. In a bowl with a fork, combine mix, shortening, egg, milk and chives. Beat vigorously for 1 minute.
2. Spoon batter into prepared muffin tin, filling cups three-quarters full. Bake in preheated oven for 15 minutes.

Quick Cocoa Bran Muffins

1	pkg bran and honey muffin mix	1
¼ cup	cocoa	50 mL
1	egg, slightly beaten	1
¾ cup	water	175 mL
½ cup	raisins	125 mL
¼ cup	finely chopped nuts (optional)	50 mL

- ◆ *Preheat oven to 400°F (200°C)*
- ◆ *Muffin tin, greased or paper-lined*

1. In a large bowl combine muffin mix and cocoa, blending well. Stir in egg and water just until blended. Add raisins and, if using, nuts.
2. Spoon batter into prepared muffin tin, filling cups three-quarters full. Bake in preheated oven for 15 to 17 minutes. Serve warm.

Bacon, Chive and Corn Muffins

1	pkg (12 oz/340 g) corn muffin mix	1
2 tsp	minced fresh chives or dried chives	10 mL
Dash	black pepper	Dash
1	egg	1
⅔ cup	milk	150 mL
½ cup	crumbled crisp bacon	125 mL

- ◆ *Preheat oven to 400°F (200°C)*
- ◆ *12-cup muffin tin, greased*

1. In a large bowl combine corn muffin mix, chives and pepper. Add egg and milk and mix according to package directions. Fold in bacon.
2. Spoon batter into prepared muffin tin. Bake in preheated oven for 15 to 20 minutes. Serve hot.

Double Corn Muffins

1	pkg (12 oz/340 g) corn muffin mix	1
1	can (16 oz/473 mL) whole kernel corn, drained	1
1	can (2¼ oz/64 g) deviled ham	1

◆ *Preheat oven to 375°F (190°C)*
◆ *Muffin tin, greased or paper-lined*

1. Prepare muffin mix according to package directions. Stir in corn.
2. Spoon batter into prepared muffin tin, filling cups two-thirds full. Drop a spoonful of deviled ham in center of each muffin. Bake in preheated oven for 20 minutes.

Spicy Corn Muffins

2	eggs	2
¾ cup	milk	175 mL
2	pkgs (each 8½ oz/ 251 mL) corn muffin mix	2
1 cup	shredded Cheddar cheese	250 mL
1 cup	thawed frozen corn	250 mL
¼ cup	drained sliced jalapeno peppers	50 mL

◆ *Preheat oven to 400°F (200°C)*
◆ *Muffin tin, greased or paper-lined*

1. In a small bowl lightly beat together eggs and milk.
2. In a large bowl combine muffin mix, cheese, corn and peppers. Stir in milk mixture and stir just until blended. Batter will be lumpy. Let stand for 5 minutes.
3. Spoon batter into prepared muffin tin, filling cups to the top. Bake in preheated oven for 20 minutes or until golden brown.

Creamy Cottage Cheese Muffins

1/3 cup	granulated sugar	75 mL
3 tbsp	butter or margarine	45 mL
1/2 cup	cream-style cottage cheese	125 mL
1 tsp	grated lemon zest	5 mL
1	egg	1
1¾ cups	homemade or packaged biscuit mix	425 mL
1/2 cup	milk	125 mL

- ◆ *Preheat oven to 400°F (200°C)*
- ◆ *Muffin tin, greased or paper-lined*

1. In a large bowl cream together sugar and butter. Beat in cottage cheese and lemon zest. Add egg, beating well. Stir in biscuit mix and milk just until moistened.

2. Spoon batter into prepared muffin tin, filling cups three-quarters full. Bake in preheated oven for 20 minutes.

> **HINT:** When you are creaming butter and sugar together, it is a good idea to rinse the bowl with boiling water first. They will cream faster.

Festive Cranberry Date Muffins

3/4 cup	chopped almonds, pecans or walnuts	175 mL
1	pkg date and orange loaf and muffin mix	1
1/2 cup	milk	125 mL
2	eggs, lightly beaten	2
3 tbsp	butter, melted	45 mL
1 cup	fresh or frozen cranberries, cut in half	250 mL

- ◆ *Preheat oven to 350°F (180°C)*
- ◆ *Muffin tin, greased or paper-lined*

1. Toast nuts in preheated oven for 5 minutes or until slightly browned. Set aside.

2. Into a large bowl pour muffin mix and make a well in the center. Add milk, eggs and butter, stirring just until blended. Fold in nuts and cranberries.

3. Spoon batter into prepared muffin tin, filling cups three-quarters full. Bake in preheated oven for 15 to 20 minutes or until a toothpick inserted in center comes out clean and dry.

Devil's Food Muffins

1	pkg devil's food cake mix	1
3	eggs	3
1⅓ cups water		325 mL
½ cup	vegetable oil	125 mL

> **MUFFIN STUFF:** For an extra special treat, ice muffin tops with vanilla or chocolate icing, or put vanilla icing on half of muffin top and chocolate on the other half.

- *Preheat oven to 400°F (200°C)*
- *Muffin tin, paper-lined*

1. Into a large bowl pour cake mix and make a well in the center.
2. In another bowl with a mixing spoon, beat together eggs, water and oil. Add to cake mix and stir just until moistened.
3. Spoon batter into prepared muffin tin, filling cups to the top. Bake in preheated oven for 15 to 20 minutes.

Fruit Muffin Buns

2 cups	buttermilk baking mix	500 mL
1 tbsp	granulated sugar	15 mL
⅛ tsp	ground nutmeg	0.5 mL
¾ cup	milk	175 mL
½ cup	softened butter or margarine	125 mL
	Fruit pie filling or stewed fruit, drained	

- *Preheat oven to 375°F (190°C)*
- *12-cup muffin tin, greased*

1. In a large bowl combine buttermilk mix, sugar and nutmeg. Add milk and stir until mixture stiffens. Turn out on a floured board and roll out to ⅛ inch (2 mm) thick.
2. Spread with ¼ cup (50 mL) butter. Fold dough in half and spread with remaining butter. Fold again and roll into a rectangle. Cut into twelve 3-inch (7.5 cm) squares.
3. Place squares in prepared muffin tin. Spoon in fruit filling. Pull corners of dough together and pinch to seal. Bake in preheated oven for 25 minutes.

Variation
- *Dried Fruit Filling:* Poach until soft, drain and chop 6 dried apricots, 3 dried prunes and 1 dried peach. Set aside. In a bowl beat together 1 egg, ½ cup (125 mL) sugar, 1 tsp (5 mL) lemon juice and ½ tsp (2 mL) cinnamon. Stir in fruit.

Grandma's Muffins

2 cups	pancake and waffle mix	500 mL
½ cup	lightly packed brown sugar	125 mL
1 tsp	cinnamon	5 mL
¾ cup	milk	175 mL
1 tsp	vanilla	5 mL
1	egg, slightly beaten	1
¼ cup	vegetable oil	50 mL
¾ cup	raisins (optional)	175 mL

1. In a large bowl mix together pancake mix, brown sugar and cinnamon.
2. In another bowl combine milk, vanilla, egg and oil. Stir into dry ingredients just until blended. Fold in raisins, if using.
3. Spoon batter into prepared muffin tin, dividing evenly. Bake in preheated oven for 18 to 20 minutes.

Ham and Cheddar Muffins

2 cups	homemade or packaged biscuit mix	500 mL
2 tsp	dry mustard or 2 tbsp (25 mL) granulated sugar	10 mL
1	egg, beaten	1
½ cup	milk	125 mL
1	can (6.5 oz/184 g) flaked ham	1
1½ cups	grated Cheddar cheese	375 mL

- *Preheat oven to 400°F (200°C)*
- *12-cup muffin tin, greased or paper-lined*

1. In a medium bowl with a fork, combine mix, dry mustard, egg and milk. Stir in ham and cheese just until blended.
2. Spoon batter into prepared muffin tin, dividing evenly. Bake in preheated oven for about 20 minutes.

Hawaiian Hula Muffins

2 cups	homemade or packaged biscuit mix	500 mL
¾ cup	finely crushed hard candies, butterscotch flavored	175 mL
¾ cup	milk	175 mL
¼ cup	vegetable oil	50 mL
1 cup	sour cream	250 mL
1	can (13½ oz/385 g) crushed pineapple, drained	1

HINT: Use reserved juice from drained pineapple to retain the bright fresh coloring of sliced apples, bananas, avocados and mushrooms. The juice prevents darkening without adding an overpowering flavor.

◆ *Preheat oven to 350°F (180°C)*
◆ *8-cup muffin tin, greased or paper-lined*

1. In a bowl combine biscuit mix and ¼ cup (50 mL) of the candy.
2. In a small bowl combine milk and oil. Add to biscuit mixture, stirring just until moistened.
3. Spoon batter into prepared muffin tin. Bake in preheated oven for 10 to 12 minutes.
4. Split warm muffins and spread bottom sections with half the sour cream. Spoon on half the pineapple and half the remaining candy. Replace muffin tops and cover with remaining sour cream, pineapple and candy.

Marmalade Breakfast Muffins

2¼ cups	buttermilk baking mix	550 mL
2 tbsp	granulated sugar	25 mL
1	egg, slightly beaten	1
½ tsp	vanilla	2 mL
¼ cup	all-fruit orange marmalade spread	50 mL

MUFFIN STUFF: In place of the egg, you can use ¼ cup (50 mL) egg substitute plus 1 cup (250 mL) water.

◆ *Preheat oven to 400°F (200°C)*
◆ *Muffin tin, greased or paper-lined*

1. In a large bowl combine buttermilk mix and sugar. Add egg and vanilla, mixing just until blended.
2. Spoon batter into prepared muffin tin, filling cups half full. Top each with 1 tsp (5 mL) orange marmalade. Spoon remaining batter evenly over marmalade. Bake in preheated oven for 12 to 15 minutes or until a toothpick inserted in center comes out clean.

Meal-in-One Muffin

1 tbsp	butter or margarine	15 mL
2 tbsp	finely chopped onion	25 mL
2 tbsp	finely chopped celery	25 mL
2 tbsp	shredded carrot	25 mL
1	can (4½ oz/128 mL) deviled ham	1
2 cups	packaged or homemade biscuit mix	500 mL
1 tbsp	granulated sugar	15 mL
½ cup	shredded Cheddar cheese	125 mL
1	egg	1
⅔ cup	milk	150 mL

◆ *Preheat oven to 400°F (200°C)*
◆ *Muffin tin, greased or paper-lined*

1. In a small frying pan heat butter over medium heat. Add onion, celery and carrot, cooking until tender but not brown. Allow to cool. Stir in ham and set aside.

2. In a medium bowl combine biscuit mix, sugar, cheese, egg and milk. Beat with a fork for 1 minute. Spoon into prepared muffin tin, filling cups two-thirds full.

3. Make an indentation in center of each and spoon in ham mixture. Bake in preheated oven for 18 to 20 minutes or until browned.

Quick 'n' Easy Oatmeal Raisin Muffins

2 cups	buttermilk baking mix	500 mL
½ cup	quick-cooking rolled oats (not instant)	125 mL
½ cup	raisins	125 mL
2 tbsp	granulated sugar	25 mL
1	egg	1
⅔ cup	milk	150 mL
	Butter or margarine	

MUFFIN STUFF: These muffins are delicious served warm. Split them and spread with butter or any other favorites.

◆ *Preheat oven to 400°F (200°C)*
◆ *Muffin tin, greased or paper-lined*

1. In a large bowl combine buttermilk mix, oats, raisins and sugar.

2. In another bowl beat together egg and milk. Pour into dry ingredients and stir until well blended.

3. Spoon batter into prepared muffin tin, filling cups three-quarters full. Bake in preheated oven for 15 minutes.

Crunchy Onion Muffins

3 cups	homemade or packaged biscuit mix	750 mL
1 tsp	onion salt	5 mL
3/4 cup	shredded Cheddar cheese	175 mL
1	can (3 1/2 oz/100 mL) french fried onion rings, crumbled	1
1 cup	milk	250 mL
1	egg	1

◆ *Preheat oven to 400°F (200°C)*
◆ *Muffin tin, greased or paper-lined*

1. In a large bowl combine biscuit mix, onion salt, cheese, crumbled onion rings, milk and egg. Mix until well blended, but do not overmix.
2. Spoon batter into prepared muffin tin, filling cups to the top. Bake in preheated oven for 15 minutes or until golden brown.

> **HINT:** If you shake an egg and you hear a rattle, the egg is most likely bad. Don't use it.

Glazed Orange Muffins

1	pkg bran with fruit and muffin mix (such as Duncan Hines)	1
1	egg	1
1 1/2 cups water		375 mL
1/4 cup	orange marmalade	50 mL
GLAZE		
1/3 cup	orange juice	75 mL
1/4 cup	granulated sugar	50 mL
1 tbsp	grated orange zest	15 mL

◆ *Preheat oven to 400°F (200°C)*
◆ *12-cup muffin tin, greased or paper-lined*

1. In a bowl combine muffin mix, egg and water, mixing well.
2. Spoon just enough batter into prepared tin to cover bottoms. Add 1 tsp (5 mL) marmalade to each. Fill with remaining batter. Bake in preheated oven for about 20 minutes.
3. In a small saucepan over low heat, combine orange juice, sugar and zest. Cook until sugar dissolves.
4. Place warm muffins on a rack with waxed paper underneath. Drizzle hot glaze over muffins.

Orange Date Nut Muffins

1	pkg date-and-orange loaf cake mix (such as Robin Hood)	1
2	eggs	2
1 cup	sour cream	250 mL
2 tbsp	vegetable oil	25 mL
½ cup	chopped nuts	125 mL
¼ cup	lightly packed brown sugar	50 mL
¼ cup	chopped nuts	50 mL

◆ *Preheat oven to 375°F (190°C)*
◆ *Muffin tin, greased or paper-lined*

1. In a large bowl combine cake mix, eggs, sour cream, oil and nuts. Mix together just until moistened and blended.

2. Spoon batter into prepared muffin tin, filling cups three-quarters full. Sprinkle with brown sugar and chopped nuts. Bake in preheated oven for 20 to 25 minutes.

Deluxe Pizza Muffins

2 cups	homemade or packaged biscuit mix	500 mL
¾ cup	milk	175 mL
FILLING		
1	jar (15½ oz/458 mL) spaghetti sauce	1
1	can (4 oz/115 g) sliced mushrooms, drained	1
1	small green pepper, chopped	1
1	pkg (3 oz/75 g) sliced pepperoni, cut into quarters	1
1 cup	shredded Mozzarella cheese	250 mL

◆ *Preheat oven to 400°F (200°C)*
◆ *12-cup muffin tin, sprayed with vegetable spray*

1. In a bowl blend together biscuit mix and milk to form a soft dough. Turn out onto a floured surface and knead about 20 times. Roll dough into a rectangle, about ⅛ inch (2 mm) thick. With a cookie cutter or inverted glass, cut out twelve 4-inch (10 cm) circles. Press the circles into bottom and up sides of muffin cups.

2. In a large bowl combine spaghetti sauce, mushrooms, green pepper and pepperoni. Spoon over dough circles and then sprinkle with cheese. Bake in preheated oven for 15 minutes or until browned.

Polka Dot Muffins

1 cup	chopped fresh cranberries or frozen cranberries, thawed	250 mL
½ cup	granulated sugar	125 mL
1 tsp	grated orange zest	5 mL
1	egg, beaten	1
¼ cup	granulated sugar	50 mL
½ cup	orange juice	125 mL
2 tbsp	vegetable oil	25 mL
2 cups	homemade or packaged biscuit mix	500 mL

◆ *Preheat oven to 400°F (200°C)*
◆ *Muffin tin, greased or paper-lined*

1. In a bowl combine cranberries, ½ cup (125 mL) sugar and orange zest. Set aside.

2. In another bowl combine egg, ¼ cup (50 mL) sugar, orange juice and oil. Add biscuit mix and stir just until moistened. Fold in cranberry mixture.

3. Spoon batter into prepared muffin tin, filling cups three-quarters full. Bake in preheated oven for 25 minutes or until browned.

HINT: Try this for a quick and easy supper. Kids, especially, will love it!

MUFFIN-TIN SUPPER: Grease 2 large size muffin pans. Fill one with corn muffin mix prepared as directed on the package. Fill the other with corned-beef hash. Make an indentation in center of hash mound and drop an egg into it. Bake at temperature recommended for muffins.

Raspberry Buttermilk Balls

1	pkg buttermilk baking mix	1
	Raspberry jam	

◆ *Preheat oven to 450°F (230°C)*
◆ *10- to 12-cup muffin tin*

1. Prepare baking mix as directed on package. Roll out dough to ½ inch (1 cm) thick. With a floured cookie cutter or inverted glass, cut into 10 to 12 circles. Reserve remaining dough. Place a circle in each muffin cup.

2. Make a depression in center of each cup of batter. Fill each with 1 tsp (5 mL) raspberry jam.

3. Shape remaining dough into 10 to 12 balls and place on top of jam. Bake in preheated oven for 10 minutes or until lightly browned.

Sesame Cheese Muffins

1½ cups	homemade or packaged biscuit mix	375 mL
1 cup	shredded sharp processed cheese	250 mL
1 tbsp	vegetable oil	15 mL
½ cup	chopped onions	125 mL
1	egg, beaten	1
½ cup	milk	125 mL
1 tbsp	toasted sesame seeds	15 mL
2 tbsp	butter or margarine, melted	25 mL

◆ *Preheat oven to 400°F (200°C)*
◆ *Muffin tin, greased or paper-lined*

1. In a large bowl combine biscuit mix and half of the cheese.
2. In a small skillet heat oil over medium heat. Cook onions just until tender.
3. In a bowl combine egg, milk and onions. Add all at once to biscuit mixture and stir just until moistened.
4. Spoon batter into prepared muffin tin, filling cups three-quarters full. Sprinkle with remaining cheese and sesame seeds. Drizzle melted butter over top. Bake in preheated oven for 15 to 20 minutes.

Stuffed Bacon Cheese Muffins

2 cups	homemade or packaged biscuit mix	500 mL
5	slices bacon, cooked crisp and crumbled	5
¾ cup	milk	175 mL
1	egg, beaten	1
12	cubes (½ inch/1 cm) Swiss cheese	12

◆ *Preheat oven to 400°F (200°C)*
◆ *12-cup muffin tin, greased*

1. In a bowl combine biscuit mix and bacon. Add milk and egg, stirring just until blended.
2. Spoon half of the batter evenly into prepared muffin tin. Add a cheese cube to each and top with remaining batter. Bake in preheated oven for 25 minutes or until golden brown. Serve hot.

Wheat Germ Muffins

2 cups	wheat germ pancake mix	500 mL
½ cup	margarine	125 mL
½ cup	granulated sugar	125 mL
1	large egg	1
1¼ cups milk		300 mL

◆ *Preheat oven to 375°F (190°C)*
◆ *Muffin tin, greased or paper-lined*

1. Into a large bowl pour pancake mix. With a pastry blender cut in margarine until mixture resembles coarse crumbs. Add sugar.
2. In another bowl beat egg. Add milk and beat well. Pour into dry ingredients and stir slowly, just until moistened and blended. Batter should be lumpy.
3. Spoon batter into prepared muffin tin, filling cups to the top. Bake in preheated oven for 25 minutes.

Microwave
Muffins

Microwave Muffins

MUFFINS BAKED IN A MICROWAVE OVEN CAN BE JUST AS DELICIOUS AS those made the traditional way. The main difference is the speed at which they can be prepared.

Most conventional-oven recipes can easily be adapted for use in a microwave. Try to choose recipes that you know well, at first, until you become more familiar with adapting recipes. It is much easier to work out changes required if you know what the final result should be. If you did not enjoy a particular muffin prepared in the conventional way, you will probably not like it any better when baked in the microwave.

◆ Most foods cook faster in a microwave than in a conventional oven. This is particularly true of baked products, like muffins, which cook in a very short time (in fact, you can have piping hot muffins ready to eat in 5 minutes). As a result, however, they do not surface brown. You can improve their appearance by frosting, or using a topping such as cinnamon or nuts.

◆ Liquid ingredients slow down microwave cooking, whereas sugars and fatty ingredients will cook more rapidly. Therefore, to adapt a conventional recipe to the microwave, you must adjust the amount of liquid and fat to obtain the right balance between the two.

◆ Timing is very important. Just 2 or 3 minutes of extra cooking will dehydrate and toughen many foods in the microwave.

◆ A "carry-over" cooking time is required for almost every item cooked in the microwave. This is a few minutes during which the food rests, after being removed from the microwave, to allow it to finish cooking. Allow muffins 1 or 2 minutes. Follow your recipe. It is surprising how much cooking occurs during this carry-over time.

◆ Frozen muffins can be easily defrosted in the microwave when needed; reheating helps food retain the flavor often lost with conventional reheating.

◆ Keep your microwave oven clean; any food left on the walls or bottom will absorb microwave energy and therefore increase cooking times.

◆ The inside of the microwave oven stays cool, so spills won't bake on and can be wiped clean with a damp cloth or paper towel. If any food should stick on the oven walls, place 1 cup (250 mL) of water in the oven and heat for 2½ to 3 minutes. This produces steam which will soften the spills so that they can then be wiped clean.

◆ Cleaning baking dishes after microwave cooking is easier and quicker because food does not stick to them as it does in conventional cooking.

◆ Microwave cooking is more efficient; it requires only about half the electrical energy used in conventional cooking. With microwave cooking, the food gets hot but the kitchen, oven, baking dishes, utensils – and you, the cook – stay cool. And because the dish or container doesn't get hot, foods cooked in a microwave also cool down fast.

- Never use any container made of metal in the microwave, or one that has a metal trim. Glass, glass ceramic, heat-resistant glass or plastic containers can be used.
- The muffin maker, or cupcaker pan, is designed especially for microwave oven use. If it has a cup in the center, do not use it, since microwave energy is least efficient in the center of the oven and that muffin will not be properly cooked.

> **HINT:** If you do not have a cupcaker (microwave muffin pan) or glass ramekins, use the lower part of a paper cup for hot drinks. Cut it down to size and line it with a paper baking cup. Place the cups in a circle on a flat microwave-safe plate, and use as you would ramekins.

- To determine if a dish or container is suitable for use in the microwave oven, place 1 cup (250 mL) of tap water in the empty dish or container to be tested. Place it in the oven. Heat for 30 to 60 seconds. If the water becomes hot and the dish does not, then it is suitable for microwave use. If the dish becomes hot, it can't be used for microwave cooking.
- Shallow containers produce better results than deep ones. Round shapes are better than square or rectangular containers. (Food has a tendency to overcook in the corners because more microwave energy is absorbed there.)
- The cooking pattern in foods cooked in microwave ovens tends to be circular, with a hole in the middle, similar to a doughnut. The center of the dish receives the least amount of microwave energy and thus is slower to cook. It is often recommended that a glass be placed right-side up in the center of the dish so that there will be no uncooked spot in the center.
- Use large baking cups and fill them two-thirds full. If you put more batter in, they may overflow during baking and the muffins could be undercooked. The cooking time given in most microwave muffin recipes is correct for the amount of batter that fits comfortably into this size of baking cup. Cups of a different size will not yield as good results.
- To ensure even cooking, give the muffin pan a half turn during the cooking period. Another technique for even cooking is to place your muffin or dish on a rack. For example, if you put 6 ramekins with muffin batter in the microwave oven, they should be arranged in a ring and their position changed during cooking time. The individual cups are not rotated. The circle of ramekins is turned for better distribution of heat energy.
- When muffins are done, tiny bubbles will pop on the surface (as on the tops of pancakes when they are ready to turn). The muffins may be slightly moist on top, but when scratched with a toothpick, the dough will be done beneath the surface and the small moist spots will disappear when the muffins stand for a few minutes.

> **HINT:** For mini-micro muffins, line a paper (but not recycled paper) or styrofoam egg carton with mini paper baking cups. Fill only two-thirds full also. Microwave on High for 1 to 1 1/2 minutes or until tops are dry.

WITH TECHNOLOGY CHANGING SO RAPIDLY, EACH YEAR NEWER AND BETTER microwave ovens are appearing on the market, so always read the instruction booklet very carefully. If your microwave oven comes with a revolving turntable, it is still wise to shift or rotate your muffin pan halfway during cooking, unless you know for certain that there are no hot spots and that the heat is distributed evenly. In most ovens, there are hot spots, so shifting or rotating will ensure even cooking.

A simple test to see where the hot spots are in your oven is to lay slices of bread out to cover the bottom or turntable. Place pieces of cheese to cover the bread slices. Cook on High for about 2 minutes. You will be able to identify the hot spots in your oven by where the cheese is melting.

Get to know your microwave. Ovens range in wattage from 500 to 720 watts (or more). The higher wattage ovens heat foods faster; if you have a lower wattage, cooking times will be longer. If you don't know the wattage of your oven, check the back of the oven to see if there is a silver plate with the number on it. Failing that, a quick way to estimate the wattage is to see how long it takes to bring 1 cup (250 mL) of tap water to a boil in a glass measure. It should take $2\frac{1}{2}$ to 3 minutes in a 600- to 720-watt oven, 4 minutes in a 500- to 600-watt oven, and 5 minutes in a 400- to 500-watt oven.

Microwaves, like radio waves, pass through food but are stopped when they encounter moisture. The wave cause the water molecules to vibrate at a tremendous rate, which causes friction and thus heat. This cooks the food. Most microwave recipes give you a range of cooking times. Choose the lesser amount, then check for doneness, otherwise overcooking may be a problem.

Being a creature of habit, I do most of my muffin baking in a regular oven and therefore don't have an abundance of recipes for the microwave oven, but I hope you will enjoy the ones I have included in this chapter, and that you will try adapting some of your recipes.

HINT: For a quick café-au-lait with your muffins, microwave 1 cup (250 mL) milk on High for 2 to 3 minutes. Pour in $\frac{1}{4}$ cup (50 mL) espresso coffee or 1 tsp (5 mL) instant coffee.

Deluxe Pizza Muffins ➤
(page 217)

Micro-Tips

To shell nuts:
- Pour 1 cup (250 mL) nuts (brazil, walnuts, almonds or pecans) into a large bowl. Cover with 1 cup (250 mL) water and heat on High 3 to 4 minutes, or until water boils. Let stand for 1 minute. Pour off water and arrange nuts on paper towel to cool. Use a nutcracker to shell the nuts, being careful that you aren't burned by any hot water that may still be inside the shell.

To soften brown sugar:
- Put the brown sugar in a covered container and microwave on High for 50 seconds. *Or:*

- Put the hard block of sugar into a heavy plastic bag. Add a little water, or a quarter of an apple, or a slice of bread. Tie a piece of string loosely around the opening and heat on High for 20 seconds. Check to see if sugar has softened. If not, repeat once or twice, as necessary, being sure not to let sugar melt. When the sugar has softened sufficiently, take it out of the oven and allow to stand for about 5 minutes. Remove apple or bread and throw away, then stir to remove lumps. *Or:*

- Remove hard brown sugar from package and place on a plate with an apple wedge. Cover and cook on High for 20 to 30 seconds. Let stand 30 seconds, then uncover and stir to remove lumps.

To extract juice from a lemon:
- Microwave the whole lemon on High for 30 seconds, then roll firmly on a flat surface, using the palm of your hand.

To thaw frozen juice concentrate:
- Place frozen concentrated juice in a small bowl (never microwave in metal can) and microwave on High for 1 minute.

To melt chocolate:
- Place chocolate in a glass measuring cup. Microwave on Medium-High for 1 minute, then stir and repeat until melted completely. It will take about 2 minutes to melt 1 cup (250 mL) of chocolate chips.

To melt butter or margarine:
- Place in a glass dish. Cover with wax paper or a paper towel to avoid splattering. Heat on High for 30-second intervals until fully melted.

To soften butter:
- Cover $\frac{1}{4}$ cup (50 mL) butter with waxed paper. Microwave on Defrost for 30 seconds.

To liquefy solid honey:
- Place in a glass cup or container, Cook on High for 30 seconds, then stir to dissolve the crystals; repeat procedure, stirring often, until the honey is liquid.

For spreadable crystallized honey:
- Remove lid from jar and microwave on High for 1 to 2 minutes.

To soften cream cheese:
- For spreads and dips, or baking — microwave, uncovered, on Defrost for 1 to 2 minutes.

To bring cheese to room temperature:
- Place 8 oz (250 g) cold cheese on a microwave-safe plate. Microwave on Medium for 45 to 60 seconds until surface no longer feels chilled.

To plump raisins (or other dried fruits):
- Microwave 1 cup (250 mL) raisins or dried fruits in $\frac{1}{2}$ cup (125 mL) water, covered, on High for 2 minutes or until boiling. Let stand, covered, for 10 minutes. *Or:*

- Place raisins or dried fruits in a small bowl and sprinkle with water or other liquid. Cook, uncovered, on High for 15 to 30 seconds, depending on amount.

Apple Spice Muffins

¼ cup	shortening	50 mL
¾ cup	granulated sugar	175 mL
2	eggs	2
¾ cup	applesauce	175 mL
¼ cup	milk	50 mL
1 tbsp	lemon juice	15 mL
1½ cups	flour	375 mL
1 tsp	salt	5 mL
1 tsp	baking soda	5 mL
1 tsp	cinnamon	5 mL
¼ tsp	ground nutmeg	1 mL
¼ tsp	ground cloves	1 mL
¼ cup	floured raisins	50 mL
¼ cup	chopped walnuts	50 mL

◆ *Microwave muffin pan, paper-lined*

1. In a bowl cream together shortening and sugar. Add eggs and mix well. Add applesauce, milk and lemon juice.
2. In another bowl sift together flour, salt and baking soda. Add cinnamon, nutmeg and cloves. Pour this dry mixture gradually into the liquid mixture. Add raisins and nuts and mix together.
3. Spoon batter into prepared muffin pan. Bake on High for 2 to 2½ minutes, turning halfway through cooking time. Let stand for 3 to 5 minutes.

Banana Oatmeal Muffins

¼ cup	butter or margarine, softened	50 mL
¾ cup	packed brown sugar	175 mL
1	egg, beaten	1
1 cup	buttermilk	250 mL
1 cup	rolled oats	250 mL
1 cup	all-purpose flour	250 mL
1 tbsp	baking powder	15 mL
½ tsp	salt	2 mL
½ tsp	ground allspice	2 mL
2	medium bananas, chopped	2

◆ *Ramekins or microwave muffin pan, paper-lined*

1. In a bowl cream together butter and brown sugar. Mix in egg and buttermilk.
2. In another bowl, combine oats, flour, baking powder, salt and allspice; mix well. Add to the creamed mixture and stir in the bananas.
3. Spoon batter into prepared ramekins or muffin pan, filling cups one-half to two-thirds full. (If using ramekins, arrange in microwave in a circle.) Microwave on High for about 2 minutes, rotating after 1 minute. A toothpick inserted in the center should come out clean and dry. Let muffins stand for 3 to 5 minutes before removing from pan.

Banana Pecan Oat Muffins

1 cup	all-purpose flour	250 mL
1/4 cup	oat bran	50 mL
1/4 cup	packed brown sugar	50 mL
1/4 cup	chopped pecans	50 mL
1/2 tsp	baking soda	2 mL
Pinch	salt	Pinch
1 cup	mashed bananas (about 3 medium)	250 mL
1	egg	1
1/2 cup	oil	125 mL
TOPPING		
3 tbsp	chopped pecans	45 mL
3 tbsp	packed brown sugar	45 mL
1/4 tsp	cinnamon	1 mL

◆ *Microwave muffin pan, paper-lined*

1. In a large bowl combine flour, oat bran, sugar, pecans, baking soda and salt.
2. In a smaller bowl beat together bananas, egg and oil. Stir this mixture into the flour mixture just until blended. Spoon batter into prepared muffin pan, filling cups two-thirds full.
3. In a bowl combine pecans, sugar and cinnamon and sprinkle evenly over muffins.
4. Bake on High, rotating twice, for 2 minutes or until toothpick inserted in center comes out clean and dry. Let stand for 3 to 5 minutes.

Blueberry Quick Oat Muffins

1/2 cup	granulated sugar	125 mL
1 1/4 cups	all-purpose flour	300 mL
1 cup	uncooked quick oats	250 mL
1 1/2 tsp	baking powder	7 mL
1/2 tsp	baking soda	2 mL
3/4 cup	sour cream	175 mL
1/3 cup	margarine, melted	75 mL
1/3 cup	milk	75 mL
1	egg, beaten	1
1/2 tsp	vanilla	2 mL
1 cup	fresh blueberries (or frozen, thawed)	250 mL
	Sugar-Cinnamon Mix (see recipe, page 357)	

◆ *Ramekins or microwave muffin pan, paper-lined*

1. In a large bowl combine sugar, flour, oats, baking powder and baking soda.
2. In a smaller bowl combine sour cream, margarine, milk, egg and vanilla; mix well. Stir this mixture into the dry ingredients, mixing just until moist. Fold in the blueberries.
3. Spoon batter into prepared ramekins or muffin pan, filling cups two-thirds full. Sprinkle with Sugar-Cinnamon Mix. Bake uncovered on High for 2 1/2 to 3 minutes. A toothpick inserted in the center should come out clean and dry. Let muffins stand for 3 to 5 minutes.

Chocolate Chip Bran Muffins

¾ cup	milk	175 mL
¼ cup	oil	50 mL
1	egg, beaten	1
1 cup	bran	250 mL
1 cup	all-purpose flour	250 mL
2½ tsp	baking powder	12 mL
½ tsp	salt	2 mL
3 tbsp	cocoa	45 mL
½ cup	granulated sugar	125 mL
½ cup	chocolate chips	125 mL

♦ *Microwave muffin pan, paper-lined*

1. In a bowl combine milk, oil and egg. Stir in bran.
2. In another bowl mix together flour, baking powder, salt and cocoa.
3. Add sugar to the liquid mixture. Stir in flour mixture and add chocolate chips.
4. Spoon batter into prepared muffin pan, filling cups two-thirds full. Place pan on a rack in the microwave. Bake on High for 2 to 2½ minutes, rotating pan halfway through cooking time. Let stand for 3 to 5 minutes before removing from pan.

All Spicy Muffins

1½ cups	all-purpose flour	375 mL
½ cup	granulated sugar	125 mL
2 tsp	baking powder	10 mL
½ tsp	salt	2 mL
½ tsp	ground nutmeg	2 mL
½ tsp	ground coriander	2 mL
½ tsp	ground allspice	2 mL
½ cup	milk	125 mL
⅓ cup	butter or margarine, melted	75 mL
1	egg	1
¼ cup	granulated sugar	50 mL
1 tsp	ground cinnamon	5 mL
¼ cup	butter or margarine, melted	50 mL

♦ *Microwave muffin pan, double paper-lined*

1. In a large bowl combine flour, ½ cup (125 mL) sugar, baking powder, salt, nutmeg, coriander and allspice.

2. In a small bowl combine milk, ⅓ cup (75 mL) butter and egg. Stir into flour mixture just until moist.

3. Spoon batter into prepared muffin pan, filling three-quarters full. (Baking may have to be done in batches.) Microwave on High for 2½ to 4½ minutes, rotating halfway through cooking time.
A toothpick inserted in center should come out clean and dry. Let muffins stand for 5 minutes before removing from pan.

4. Meanwhile, in a small dish combine ¼ cup (50 mL) sugar and cinnamon. Roll warm muffins in the ¼ cup (50 mL) melted butter and then the sugar-cinnamon mixture. These muffins are best served warm.

Currant Nut Whole-Wheat Muffins

¾ cup	all-purpose flour	175 mL
¾ cup	whole-wheat flour	175 mL
⅓ cup	unprocessed wheat bran (Miller's bran), or oat bran	75 mL
1 tsp	baking soda	5 mL
½ tsp	cinnamon	2 mL
¼ tsp	ground ginger	1 mL
¼ tsp	salt	1 mL
1 cup	low-fat vanilla yogurt	250 mL
¼ cup	vegetable oil	50 mL
1	large egg	1
¼ cup	packed dark brown sugar	50 mL
⅓ cup	chopped walnuts	75 mL
⅓ cup	currants	75 mL

◆ *Microwave muffin pan, double paper-lined*

1. In a large bowl mix together all-purpose flour, whole-wheat flour, bran, baking soda, cinnamon, ginger and salt.

2. In a blender or food processor combine yogurt, oil, egg and sugar; process until smooth. Add half the flour mixture and process until blended. Scrape down sides of container and add remaining flour mixture; process until smooth.

3. Pour batter back into bowl and stir in walnuts and currants. Spoon batter into prepared pan, filling cups three-quarters full. (Baking may have to be done in batches.) Microwave on High for 3 to 4 minutes, rotating muffin pan a quarter-turn twice. Tops should spring back when gently pressed. Let stand for 3 to 5 minutes.

"Kentucky" Biscuit Muffins

2 cups	all-purpose flour	500 mL
2½ tsp	baking powder	12 mL
½ tsp	baking soda	2 mL
Pinch	salt	Pinch
1 tbsp	granulated sugar	15 mL
½ cup	butter or margarine or shortening	125 mL
¾ cup	buttermilk	175 mL
1 tbsp	butter, melted	15 mL
	Poppyseeds or fennel seeds, for garnish	

◆ *Microwave muffin pan*

1. In a large bowl mix together flour, baking powder, baking soda, salt and sugar. Using a pastry blender, cut in butter until mixture resembles coarse crumbs. Add buttermilk and mix quickly to make a soft dough.

2. Turn dough out onto a lightly floured board and knead a few times to make a soft dough. Do not overknead or the muffins will be hard and dry.

3. Roll the dough out to a square and cut out round biscuits with a glass or cookie cutter; place each in pan. Brush with melted butter and sprinkle with seeds.

4. Bake on High for about 1½ minutes. Let sit for a few minutes and then bake on High for another 1½ minutes. Serve warm. These muffins are great with honey, jam or just butter.

Orange Cinnamon Muffins

2 cups	all-purpose flour	500 mL
½ cup	packed brown sugar	125 mL
3 tsp	baking powder	15 mL
½ tsp	salt	2 mL
½ tsp	cinnamon	2 mL
1 tsp	finely grated orange zest	5 mL
2	eggs	2
½ cup	orange juice	125 mL
½ cup	vegetable oil	125 mL
TOPPING		
3 tbsp	granulated sugar	45 mL
1 tsp	finely grated orange zest	5 mL
½ tsp	cinnamon	2 mL

◆ *Microwave muffin pan, paper-lined*

1. In a large bowl combine flour, brown sugar, baking powder, salt, cinnamon and orange zest. Mix well.
2. In a smaller bowl whisk together eggs, orange juice and oil. Pour into flour mixture and stir just until moist.
3. Spoon batter into prepared muffin pan, filling cups two-thirds full. In a bowl combine sugar, zest and cinnamon; sprinkle over muffins. Bake uncovered on High for 2 to 2½ minutes, rotating pan halfway through cooking time. A toothpick inserted in the center should come out clean and dry. Let muffins stand for 3 to 5 minutes before removing from pan.

Peanut Butter Banana Muffins

1½ cups	all-purpose flour	375 mL
½ cup	granulated sugar	125 mL
2 tbsp	baking powder	25 mL
½ tsp	salt	2 mL
1	egg, slightly beaten	1
½ cup	milk	125 mL
⅓ cup	vegetable oil	75 mL
¾ cup	mashed banana	175 mL
1 cup	peanut butter chips	250 mL
¼ cup	raisins	50 mL
¼ cup	graham cracker crumbs	50 mL

◆ *Ramekins, double paper-lined*

1. In a large bowl combine flour, sugar, baking powder and salt. Make a well in the center and add egg, milk, oil and mashed banana; stir just until moist. Stir in peanut butter chips and raisins.
2. Spoon batter into prepared ramekins, filling each half full. Sprinkle with crumbs. (Baking may have to be done in batches.) Arrange ramekins in a circle on rack in microwave and bake on High for 2 minutes. Rotate circle of ramekins and bake for 1 minute or until done.

Pineapple Carrot Nutty Muffins

1½ cups	whole-wheat flour	375 mL
½ cup	packed brown sugar	125 mL
½ cup	granulated sugar	125 mL
1 cup	Grape Nuts cereal	250 mL
1½ tsp	baking soda	7 mL
¾ tsp	baking powder	4 mL
2 tsp	cinnamon	10 mL
1 cup	well-drained crushed pineapple	250 mL
2	eggs, beaten	2
2 cups	shredded carrots	500 mL
1 tsp	vanilla	5 mL
¾ cup	margarine, melted	175 mL

◆ *Microwave muffin pan, double paper-lined*

1. In a large bowl combine flour, brown sugar, granulated sugar, cereal, baking soda, baking powder and cinnamon.
2. In a smaller bowl combine pineapple, eggs, carrots, vanilla and margarine. Stir into the dry ingredients, mixing just until moistened. The batter will be quite thick.
3. Spoon batter into prepared muffin pan, filling cups two-thirds full. Bake, uncovered, on High for 2 to 2½ minutes, rotating halfway through cooking time. Let muffins stand for 3 to 5 minutes before removing from pan.

Quick Poppy Cheese Muffins

2½ cups	all-purpose biscuit mix	625 mL
1 cup	shredded sharp Cheddar cheese	250 mL
1 tsp	poppy seeds	5 mL
1	egg	1
1 cup	milk	250 mL

HINT: An extra apple or two hanging around? A baked apple takes 4 minutes in the microwave. Fill the middle with ice cream and drizzle liqueur on top. A delicious dessert that looks like you spent all day in the kitchen.

◆ *Ramekins or microwave muffin pan, paper-lined*

1. In a large bowl combine biscuit mix, cheese, poppyseeds, egg and milk; stir just to moisten.
2. Spoon batter into prepared ramekins or pan, filling cups two-thirds full. If using ramekins, arrange them in a circle. Bake on High for 2½ minutes, rotating ramekins or pan halfway through cooking time. Let muffins stand for 3 to 5 minutes.

Refrigerator Micro-Bran Muffins

1½ cups	bran flakes	375 mL
1½ cups	cooking bran	375 mL
½ cup	boiling water	125 mL
2	eggs, slightly beaten	2
¼ cup	molasses	50 mL
1¾ cups	buttermilk or sour milk	425 mL
¼ cup	oil	50 mL
1 to 2 tsp	browning sauce (such as Crosse and Blackwell)	5 to 10 mL
1 cup	raisins or dates or currants or prunes	250 mL
2½ tsp	baking soda	12 mL
1 tsp	baking powder	5 mL
¼ tsp	salt	1 mL
½ cup	firmly packed dark brown sugar	125 mL
2 cups	whole-wheat flour	500 mL

◆ *Microwave muffin pan, paper-lined*

1. In a large bowl combine bran flakes and cooking bran. Add boiling water and stir to moisten evenly. Set aside to cool. Then add molasses, buttermilk, oil, browning sauce and dried fruit; blend together well.

2. In another bowl combine baking soda, baking powder, salt, sugar and flour. Add to bran mixture and stir just until moist.

3. Spoon batter into prepared muffin pan, filling cups two-thirds full. Bake on a rack for 2½ to 3 minutes on High, rotating pan once during cooking time. Let stand for 3 to 5 minutes before removing muffins from pan.

> **HINT:** For a special treat to keep kids happy while you're busy micro-baking, take simple chocolate or vanilla wafers and place a marshmallow on top of each. Microwave for 15 seconds. The marshmallows will fluff up to a fantastic size and the kids love it.

Vegetable Corn Muffins

1 cup	all-purpose flour	250 mL
½ cup	cornmeal	125 mL
1 tbsp	granulated sugar	15 mL
1 tbsp	baking powder	15 mL
½ tsp	salt	2 mL
¾ tsp	Italian seasoning	4 mL
⅛ tsp	garlic powder	0.5 mL
2	eggs, beaten	2
1 tbsp	vegetable oil	15 mL
½ cup	drained corn kernels	125 mL
⅓ cup	milk (can use skim)	75 mL
⅓ cup	chopped green peppers	75 mL
¼ cup	finely chopped onions	50 mL

♦ *Ramekins or microwave muffin pan, double paper-lined*

1. In a large bowl combine flour, cornmeal, sugar, baking powder, salt, Italian seasoning, garlic powder, eggs, oil, corn, milk, peppers and onions. Stir just until blended. Do not overmix.

2. Spoon batter into prepared ramekins or pan. Microwave on a rack on High for 2½ to 3 minutes, rotating once halfway through cooking time. A toothpick inserted in the center of each muffin should come out clean and dry. Let stand for 3 to 5 minutes.

Whole-Wheat Honey Muffins

1¾ cups	whole-wheat flour	425 mL
4 tsp	baking powder	20 mL
½ tsp	salt	2 mL
1	egg, beaten	1
¾ cup	milk	175 mL
⅓ cup	honey	75 mL
¼ cup	vegetable oil	50 mL
⅓ cup	chopped walnuts	75 mL

♦ *Microwave muffin pan, paper-lined*

1. In a large bowl combine whole-wheat flour, baking powder and salt.

2. In another bowl blend together egg, milk, honey, oil and walnuts.

3. Pour egg mixture into dry ingredients and stir until well moistened. The batter should be a bit lumpy.

4. Spoon batter into prepared pan, filling cups two-thirds full. (Baking may have to be done in batches.) Place muffin pan on a rack in the microwave. Bake on High for 2½ minutes, rotating pan once during cooking. Let muffins stand for 3 to 5 minutes.

Special Yam Muffins

1 cup	all-purpose flour	250 mL
1/4 cup	granulated sugar	50 mL
1 tbsp	baking powder	15 mL
1 cup	yellow cornmeal	250 mL
1/2 tsp	salt	2 mL
1 1/4 tsp	cinnamon	6 mL
2	eggs	2
1/2 cup	cold strong coffee	125 mL
1/4 cup	butter or margarine, melted	50 mL
1/2 tsp	Tabasco sauce	2 mL
1 cup	mashed yams or sweet potatoes	250 mL

◆ *Ramekins or microwave muffin pan, double paper-lined*

1. In a large bowl combine flour, sugar, baking powder, cornmeal, salt and cinnamon. Make a well in the center.

2. In a medium bowl beat eggs. Stir in coffee, butter, Tabasco sauce and yams. Add to flour mixture and stir just until moistened.

3. Spoon batter into prepared ramekins or pan, filling cups two-thirds full. (Baking may have to be done in batches.) If using ramekins, arrange in a circle. Microwave on High for 4 to 5 1/2 minutes, rotating pan or rearranging ramekins halfway through cooking time. A toothpick inserted in the center of each muffin should come out clean and dry. Let stand for 5 minutes. These muffins are delicious served warm.

Buffins, Cuffins and Puffins

Buffins

2 cups	milk	500 mL
½ cup	butter or margarine	125 mL
4 tbsp	granulated sugar	60 mL
1 tsp	salt	5 mL
1 tbsp	granular yeast	15 mL
¼ cup	very warm water	50 mL
2	eggs, beaten	2
4 cups	all-purpose flour	1 L

- *Preheat oven to 400°F (200°C)*
- *Muffin tin, greased*

1. In a saucepan over medium heat, scald the milk. Add butter, sugar and salt. Set aside to cool.
2. Dissolve yeast in the very warm water. Add to scalded milk mixture. Add beaten eggs and flour, beating until smooth. Let rise for 1½ hours.
3. Beat batter down and spoon into prepared muffin tin, filling cups no more than half full. Set aside and let rise again for ½ hour. Bake in preheated oven for 12 to 15 minutes. This recipe should yield 16 to 24 buffins.

Apple Doughnut Buffins

1½ cups	all-purpose flour	375 mL
½ cup	granulated sugar	125 mL
1¾ tsp	baking powder	9 mL
½ tsp	salt	2 mL
½ tsp	ground nutmeg	2 mL
⅓ cup	shortening	75 mL
1	egg	1
¼ cup	milk	50 mL
½ cup	grated apple	125 mL
TOPPING		
½ cup	butter, melted	125 mL
½ cup	granulated sugar	125 mL
1½ tsp	cinnamon	7 mL

- *Preheat oven to 350°F (180°C)*
- *Muffin tin, greased*

1. In a large bowl sift together flour, sugar, baking powder, salt and nutmeg. With a pastry blender, cut in shortening.
2. In another bowl combine egg, milk and grated apple. Add to flour mixture.
3. Spoon batter into prepared muffin tin, filling cups two-thirds full. Bake in preheated oven for 20 to 25 minutes. Remove from pan.
4. In a bowl combine butter, sugar and cinnamon. Roll buffins in topping. Serve warm.

Caraway Rye Buffins

2	pkgs active dry yeast	2
½ cup	warm water	125 mL
½ tsp	granulated sugar	2 mL
3 cups	all-purpose flour	750 mL
1½ cups	rye flour	375 mL
2 tsp	salt	10 mL
¼ tsp	baking soda	1 mL
2 tbsp	caraway seeds	25 mL
8 oz	low-fat plain yogurt	250 g
½ cup	butter or margarine, melted	125 mL
2	eggs	2
GLAZE		
1	egg white mixed with 1 tbsp (15 mL) water	1
TOPPING		
	Additional caraway seeds	

◆ *Preheat oven to 350°F (180°C)*
◆ *Two 12-cup muffin tins, greased*

1. In a large bowl sprinkle yeast over warm water and sugar. Let stand for 5 minutes to allow yeast to soften.

2. In another bowl combine all-purpose flour, rye flour, salt, baking soda and seeds.

3. In another bowl whisk together yogurt, butter and eggs. Add to yeast mixture and mix until blended. Add half of flour mixture and beat on medium-high speed for 1 minute. Add remaining flour and continue beating until well blended. Cover with a towel and place in a warm spot away from drafts. Let rise for 1 hour or until doubled in size.

4. Punch down dough. Divide evenly into prepared muffin tins. Cover again and let rise in warm spot for 45 minutes or until doubled.

5. Brush tops with glaze. Sprinkle with caraway seeds. Bake in preheated oven for 20 to 25 minutes or until golden brown.

Baked 'Donut' Buffins

¼ cup	butter or margarine	50 mL
6 tbsp	granulated sugar	90 mL
1	egg	1
½ tsp	vanilla	2 mL
1¼ cups	all-purpose flour	300 mL
2 tsp	baking powder	10 mL
Dash	salt	Dash
¼ tsp	ground nutmeg	1 mL
⅓ cup	milk	75 mL
SUGAR-CINNAMON MIX		
½ cup	sugar	125 mL
1 to 1½ tsp	cinnamon	5 to 7 mL

- *Preheat oven to 375°F (190°C)*
- *Muffin tin, greased or paper-lined*

1. In a large bowl cream together butter and sugar. Add egg and vanilla, then flour, baking powder, salt, nutmeg and milk. Mix only until blended.
2. Spoon batter into prepared muffin tin. Bake in preheated oven for 15 minutes.
3. In a small bowl mix together sugar and cinnamon until well blended. Remove muffins from tins and roll in topping.

Praline Buffins

½ cup	butter	125 mL
½ cup	packed brown sugar	125 mL
	Cinnamon	
36	pecan or walnut halves	36
2 cups	biscuit baking mix	500 mL
⅓ cup	applesauce	75 mL
⅓ cup	milk	75 mL

HINT: To get walnut meats out whole, soak nuts overnight in salt water before cracking.

- *Preheat oven to 450°F (230°C)*
- *12-cup muffin tin*

1. Put 2 tsp (10 mL) butter in each muffin cup. Heat in preheated oven until butter is melted. Stir 2 tsp (10 mL) brown sugar and a pinch of cinnamon into butter in each cup. Add 3 nut halves to each.
2. In a large bowl combine biscuit mix, applesauce and milk. Mix well until a dough forms. Spoon batter into muffin cups. Bake in preheated oven for 10 minutes.
3. Invert whole pan immediately onto a plate and let sit for 5 minutes, allowing syrup to run down over buffins. Remove the pan and serve warm.

Citrus Upside-Down Buffins

2 cups	undrained canned grapefruit sections	500 mL
1	can (10 oz/284 mL) mandarin orange sections, undrained	1
½ cup	packed brown sugar	125 mL
3 tbsp	all-purpose flour	45 mL
3 tbsp	butter or margarine	45 mL
1 cup	all-purpose flour	250 mL
1 tbsp	granulated sugar	15 mL
1½ tsp	baking powder	7 mL
¼ tsp	salt	1 mL
4 tbsp	butter or margarine	60 mL
	Milk	
1	egg, slightly beaten	1
	Granulated sugar	
	Cinnamon	

♦ *Preheat oven to 425°F (220°C)*
♦ *Large ramekins*

1. In a small bowl mix together the undrained grapefruit and mandarin orange sections. Spoon evenly into ramekins.

2. In another small bowl mix together brown sugar and 3 tbsp (45 mL) flour. Sprinkle over fruit and dot with 3 tbsp (45 mL) butter. Bake in preheated oven for 15 minutes.

3. In a large bowl combine flour, sugar, baking powder and salt. Cut in 4 tbsp (50 mL) butter.

4. In a measuring cup add enough milk to beaten egg to make ½ cup (125 mL). Add to flour mixture. Stir until well blended.

5. Drop batter by spoonfuls over hot fruit cups to form biscuits. Sprinkle with sugar and cinnamon. Bake in preheated oven for 20 to 25 minutes or until golden brown. Serve warm.

Miniature Strawberry Buffins

½ cup	strawberry-flavored drink mix	125 mL
¾ cup	milk	175 mL
1	egg	1
2 tbsp	vegetable oil	25 mL
2 cups	biscuit mix	500 mL
	Icing sugar	

◆ *Preheat oven to 400°F (200°C)*
◆ *Miniature muffin tin, greased*

1. In a small bowl combine drink mix, milk, egg and oil. Beat with a fork until well blended.

2. In a large bowl combine biscuit mix and wet ingredients. Stir just until biscuit mix is completely moistened. The batter will be soft.

3. Spoon batter into prepared muffin tin, filling cups two-thirds full. Bake in preheated oven for 10 minutes or until delicately golden but not browned.

4. Remove buffins from pan and sprinkle tops with icing sugar. Serve hot.

Wheat Germ Cornmeal Buffins

2	eggs, slightly beaten	2
2 tbsp	milk	25 mL
1	pkg active dry yeast	1
¼ cup	very warm water (not boiling)	50 mL
¼ cup	granulated sugar	50 mL
¼ cup	butter, melted	50 mL
½ tsp	salt	2 mL
¼ cup	yellow cornmeal	50 mL
½ cup	dry currants or raisins	125 mL
1 cup	milk	250 mL
¼ cup	wheat germ	50 mL
2¼ cups	all-purpose flour	550 mL

HINT: When making any recipe requiring egg whites only, drop the yolks into a pan of boiling, salted water. Use these hard-cooked yolks for salads or sandwich fillings.

◆ *Preheat oven to 375°F (190°C)*
◆ *Muffin tin, greased*

1. In a small bowl combine 2 tbsp (25 mL) of the beaten egg with 2 tbsp (25 mL) milk. Set aside.

2. In a large mixing bowl dissolve yeast in warm water. Let stand for 5 minutes. Mix in the remaining egg, sugar, butter, salt, cornmeal and currants. Stir in milk and wheat germ, blending well. Add flour gradually and beat until smooth. Cover loosely with a towel or waxed paper and place in a warm spot. Let rise for 1 hour or until doubled in size.

3. Punch dough down or beat well. Spoon into pre-pared muffin tin. Cover again and let rise in a warm spot for 30 minutes or until muffin tin is full.

4. Lightly beat the reserved egg and milk and brush over tops. Sprinkle with additional wheat germ, if desired. Bake in preheated oven for 15 to 20 minutes or until browned.

Cuffins

1/3 cup	softened shortening	75 mL
2 cups	sifted cake flour	500 mL
1 cup	granulated sugar	250 mL
2 1/2 tsp	baking powder	12 mL
3/4 tsp	salt	4 mL
3/4 cup	milk	175 mL
1	egg, slightly beaten	1
1 tsp	vanilla	5 mL

◆ *Preheat oven to 400°F (200°C)*
◆ *Muffin tin, paper-lined*

1. In a large bowl cream shortening until well softened. Add cake flour, sugar, baking powder and salt, mixing until blended. Add half the milk and egg, mixing until flour is dampened. Add remaining milk and vanilla and stir just until moistened and well blended (or beat for 2 minutes with a hand mixer).
2. Spoon batter evenly into prepared muffin tin. Bake in preheated oven for 20 minutes or until done.

Apple Spice Cuffins

2	apples, pared, cored and diced	2
1/4 cup	water	50 mL
1 1/4 cups	all-purpose flour	300 mL
2 tbsp	unsweetened cocoa	25 mL
1/2 cup	granulated sugar	125 mL
1/2 tsp	baking powder	2 mL
1 tsp	baking soda	5 mL
1/2 tsp	salt	2 mL
1/2 tsp	cinnamon	2 mL
1/2 tsp	ground allspice	2 mL
2	egg yolks	2
1/4 cup	raisins	50 mL

◆ *Preheat oven to 350°F (180°C)*
◆ *Two 8-cup muffin tins, paper-lined*

1. In a small saucepan over medium heat, combine apples and water. Simmer, covered, for 5 minutes or until tender. Set aside to cool.
2. In a large bowl combine flour, cocoa, sugar, baking powder, baking soda, salt, cinnamon and allspice. Add apples and egg yolks, beating until blended. Fold in raisins.
3. Spoon batter into prepared muffin tins, dividing evenly. Bake in preheated oven for about 30 minutes.

Banana Nut Cuffins

2 cups	all-purpose flour	500 mL
1²⁄₃ cups	granulated sugar	400 mL
1¼ tsp	baking powder	6 mL
1¼ tsp	baking soda	6 mL
1 tsp	salt	5 mL
²⁄₃ cup	shortening	150 mL
²⁄₃ cup	buttermilk	150 mL
3	eggs	3
1¼ cups	mashed bananas	300 mL
½ cup	chopped walnuts or pecans	125 mL
	Icing sugar	

- *Preheat oven to 350°F (180°C)*
- *Two 12-cup muffin tins, paper-lined*

1. In a large bowl combine flour, sugar, baking powder, baking soda, salt, shortening, buttermilk, eggs, bananas and walnuts. Mix at low speed, scraping sides, then beat on high speed for 3 minutes.
2. Spoon batter into prepared muffin tins, filling cups three-quarters full. Bake in preheated oven for 20 to 25 minutes. When cuffins cool, dust with icing sugar.

> **HINT:** To separate eggs use a small funnel, cracking egg open over the funnel. The white will run through while the yoke will remain in the funnel.

Black Bottom Cuffins

1½ cups	all-purpose flour	375 mL
½ tsp	baking powder	2 mL
½ tsp	baking soda	2 mL
¼ cup	unsweetened cocoa	50 mL
1 cup	granulated sugar	250 mL
½ tsp	salt	2 mL
1 cup	water	250 mL
1 tsp	vanilla	5 mL
6 tbsp	vegetable oil	90 mL
FILLING		
4 oz	softened cream cheese	125 g
1	egg, beaten	1
6 tbsp	granulated sugar	90 mL
½ cup	semi-sweet chocolate chips	125 mL

- *Preheat oven to 400°F (200°C)*
- *Muffin tin, paper-lined*

1. In a large bowl mix together flour, baking powder, baking soda, cocoa, sugar and salt.
2. In another bowl combine water, vanilla and oil. Pour into dry ingredients and stir well. Spoon batter into prepared muffin tin, about 2 tbsp (25 mL) each.
3. In another bowl mix together cream cheese, egg, sugar and chocolate chips. Spoon 1 tbsp (15 mL) over batter and top with remaining batter. Bake in preheated oven for 20 minutes or until toothpick inserted in center comes out clean.

Brownie Chip Cuffins

3	squares semi-sweet baking chocolate	3
½ cup	butter	125 mL
2	eggs	2
1½ cups	packed light brown sugar	375 mL
1½ tsp	vanilla	7 mL
1 tbsp	strong black coffee	15 mL
1 tsp	cinnamon	5 mL
1	mashed ripe banana	1
1 cup	all-purpose flour	250 mL
1 cup	white chocolate chips (optional)	250 mL

◆ *Preheat oven to 350°F (180°C)*
◆ *Muffin tin, paper-lined*

1. In a small saucepan over low heat, melt chocolate with butter, stirring gently. Set aside to cool.
2. In a large bowl whisk together eggs, sugar, vanilla, coffee and cinnamon. Add mashed banana and drizzle with chocolate, stirring lightly. Add flour, stirring just until moistened and blended. Fold in chocolate chips.
3. Spoon batter into prepared muffin tin, filling cups three-quarters full. Bake in preheated oven for 20 to 25 minutes or until a toothpick inserted in the center comes out dry and clean.

Cherry Cuffins

3	eggs	3
½ cup	shortening, melted	125 mL
¾ cup	milk	175 mL
1 tsp	vanilla	5 mL
1½ cups	all-purpose flour	375 mL
1¼ cups	granulated sugar	300 mL
2 tsp	baking powder	10 mL
Pinch	salt	Pinch
1 lb	cherries, pitted and chopped	500 g

◆ *Preheat oven to 400°F (200°C)*
◆ *Muffin tin, paper-lined*

1. In a bowl combine eggs, shortening, milk and vanilla. Mix well.
2. In a large bowl combine flour, sugar, baking powder and salt. Add cherries and stir into egg mixture. Do not overmix.
3. Spoon batter into prepared muffin tin, filling cups two-thirds full. Bake in preheated oven for about 25 minutes.

Old-Fashioned Chocolate Cuffins

½ cup	shortening	125 mL
1 cup	granulated sugar	250 mL
2	eggs, separated and beaten	2
2 cups	all-purpose flour	500 mL
2 tsp	baking powder	10 mL
¼ tsp	salt	1 mL
¼ tsp	baking soda	1 mL
¾ cup	milk	175 mL
1 tsp	vanilla	5 mL
2½	squares unsweetened chocolate, melted	2½

◆ *Preheat oven to 375°F (190°C)*
◆ *Muffin tin, greased or paper-lined*

1. In a large bowl cream together shortening and sugar. Add beaten egg yolks.

2. In another bowl combine flour, baking powder, salt and baking soda. Add to creamed mixture alternately with milk. Add vanilla and melted chocolate.

3. In another bowl beat egg whites until stiff. Fold into mixture and blend well.

4. Spoon batter into prepared muffin tin, filling each cup to the top. Bake in preheated oven for 25 minutes or until done.

Chocolate Chip Cuffins

⅓ cup	softened shortening	75 mL
¾ cup	granulated sugar	175 mL
2	eggs	2
1 tsp	vanilla	5 mL
2¼ cups	sifted cake flour	550 mL
3 tsp	double-acting baking powder	15 mL
1 tsp	salt	5 mL
⅔ cup	milk	150 mL
1	pkg (8 oz/250 g) chocolate chips	1

◆ *Preheat oven to 375°F (190°C)*
◆ *Muffin tin, paper-lined*

1. In a large bowl cream together shortening and sugar. With a spoon, mix in eggs one at a time. Add vanilla.

2. In another bowl combine flour, baking powder and salt. Add to the shortening mixture alternately with milk.

3. Spoon batter into prepared muffin tin, filling cups half full. Sprinkle with half the chocolate chips. Top with remaining batter and sprinkle with remaining chocolate chips. Bake in preheated oven for 20 to 25 minutes.

Chocolate Cream Cheese Cuffins

1	pkg (8 oz/250 g) softened cream cheese	1
1	egg	1
1/3 cup	granulated sugar	75 mL
1 cup	chocolate chipits	250 mL
3 cups	all-purpose flour	750 mL
2 cups	granulated sugar	500 mL
1/2 cup	instant chocolate drink powder	125 mL
1 tsp	salt	5 mL
2 tsp	baking soda	10 mL
2 tsp	vanilla	10 mL
2 tbsp	vinegar	25 mL
2 cups	water	500 mL
2/3 cup	vegetable oil	150 mL

- *Preheat oven to 350°F (180°C)*
- *Two 12-cup muffin tins, greased or paper-lined*

1. In a small bowl mix together cream cheese, egg and sugar. Add chipits and blend well. Set aside.
2. In a large bowl combine flour, sugar, chocolate powder, salt and baking soda, mixing well. Add vanilla, vinegar, water and oil. Beat on low speed just until well blended.
3. Spoon batter into prepared muffin tins, filling cups two-thirds full. Drop 1 heaping tsp (5 mL) cheese mixture into each prepared muffin cup. Bake in preheated oven for 20 to 25 minutes.

Variations

- For a quick version of this recipe, use 1 pkg chocolate cake mix (the 2 layer size). Mix according to package directions and bake as above.
- You can use chocolate pieces or chunks in place of the chipits.

Cocoa Raisin Cuffins

1¼ cups	all-purpose flour	300 mL
1 cup	granulated sugar	250 mL
¾ tsp	baking soda	4 mL
½ tsp	cinnamon	2 mL
¼ tsp	ground nutmeg	1 mL
¼ tsp	salt	1 mL
¼ cup	butter or margarine, melted (about 1 stick)	50 mL
¼ cup	cocoa	50 mL
¾ cup	applesauce	175 mL
1	egg, slightly beaten	1
½ cup	raisins	125 mL

- *Preheat oven to 350°F (180°C)*
- *Muffin tin, greased or paper-lined*

1. In a large bowl mix together flour, sugar, baking soda, cinnamon, nutmeg and salt. Make a well in the center.
2. In another bowl blend together butter and cocoa. Add applesauce and pour into flour mixture. Add egg, stirring just until moistened and blended. Fold in raisins.
3. Spoon batter into prepared muffin tin, filling cups three-quarters full. Bake in preheated oven for 20 minutes.

Coconut Chiffon Cuffins

2¼ cups	sifted cake-and-pastry flour	550 mL
1½ cups	granulated sugar	375 mL
3 tsp	baking powder	15 mL
1 tsp	salt	5 mL
⅓ cup	vegetable oil	75 mL
1 cup	milk	250 mL
1½ tsp	vanilla	7 mL
2	eggs, separated	2
1 cup	flaked coconut	250 mL

- *Preheat oven to 400°F (200°C)*
- *Muffin tin, paper-lined*

1. In a large mixer bowl combine flour, 1 cup (250 mL) sugar, baking powder and salt. Make a well in the center. Add oil, half the milk and vanilla. Beat for 1 minute on medium speed. Add remaining milk and egg yolks. Beat again for 1 minute.
2. In a small mixer bowl beat egg whites until soft peaks form. Gradually add remaining ½ cup (125 mL) sugar and beat until stiff peaks form. Fold into the batter.
3. Spoon batter into prepared muffin tin, filling cups three-quarters full. Top with coconut. Bake in preheated oven for about 15 minutes.

Fudgey Cuffins

⅔ cup	packed brown sugar	150 mL
⅓ cup	milk	75 mL
2	squares unsweetened chocolate	2
⅓ cup	softened shortening	75 mL
⅔ cup	packed brown sugar	150 mL
1 tsp	vanilla	5 mL
2	eggs	2
1⅓ cups	all-purpose flour	325 mL
1 tsp	baking soda	5 mL
½ tsp	salt	2 mL
½ cup	milk	125 mL

◆ *Preheat oven to 375°F (190°C)*
◆ *Muffin tin, paper-lined*

1. In a saucepan over very low heat, combine ⅔ cup (150 mL) brown sugar, ⅓ cup (75 mL) milk and chocolate, stirring until chocolate melts. Set aside to cool.
2. In a large bowl cream together shortening and ⅔ cup (150 mL) brown sugar until light and fluffy. Add vanilla and eggs, one at a time. Beat well after each addition.
3. In another bowl combine flour, baking soda and salt. Add to creamed mixture alternately with ½ cup (125 mL) milk, beating after each addition. Add chocolate mixture.
4. Spoon batter into prepared muffin tin, filling cups three-quarters full. Bake in preheated oven for about 20 minutes.

Lemon Cream Cuffin Tarts

1	roll refrigerated sugar cookie dough	1
1	pkg lemon pudding and pie filling	1
1 tsp	grated lemon zest	5 mL
	Sweetened whipped cream	
	Strawberries, washed and hulled	

◆ *Preheat oven to 375°F (190°C)*
◆ *Muffin tin, foil-lined*

1. Unwrap cookie dough and cut into 36 slices. Press into bottoms and up sides of prepared muffin tins. Bake in preheated oven for 10 minutes or until golden brown. Cool completely and then carefully peel off the foil. Set aside.
2. In a bowl prepare pudding mix according to package directions. Stir in lemon zest and place in refrigerator.
3. When filling is chilled, spoon 1 tbsp (15 mL) into each cup. Return to refrigerator.
4. To serve, spoon some whipped cream on top. Place a whole strawberry, hull-side down, on top.

Lemon Streusel Cuffins

2¼ cups	sifted cake-and-pastry flour	550 mL
2 tsp	baking powder	10 mL
½ tsp	salt	2 mL
1¾ cups	granulated sugar	425 mL
1 tbsp	fresh lemon juice	15 mL
1 tsp	grated lemon zest	5 mL
8 oz	non-fat plain yogurt	250 g
3 tbsp	vegetable oil	45 mL
½ tsp	vanilla	2 mL
4	large egg whites	4
STREUSEL TOPPING		
¼ cup	firmly packed brown sugar	50 mL
¼ cup	uncooked oats	50 mL
¼ tsp	cinnamon	1 mL

◆ *Preheat oven to 350°F (180°C)*
◆ *Two 12-cup muffin tins, paper-lined*

1. In a large mixer bowl combine flour, baking powder and salt.
2. In another bowl beat together sugar, juice, zest, yogurt, oil and vanilla. Pour into flour mixture and beat on low speed just until well blended.
3. In a small bowl beat egg whites until stiff peaks form. Fold into batter.
4. In another bowl combine brown sugar, oats and cinnamon.
5. Spoon batter into prepared muffin tins, filling cups three-quarters full. Sprinkle with streusel topping. Bake in preheated oven for 35 to 40 minutes.

MUFFIN STUFF: I usually make the streusel topping first by mixing all the ingredients together in a bowl and then set it aside until needed.

HINT: When you buy cello-wrapped cupcakes or muffins and the wrapper is stuck to the frosting, hold the package under cold water for 1 minute. The wrapper will come off clean.

Lemon Sugar-Topped Cuffins

TOPPING

1 tbsp	granulated sugar	15 mL
½ tsp	grated lemon zest	2 mL

CUFFINS

1 cup	self-rising flour	250 mL
½ cup	granulated sugar	125 mL
½ cup	milk	125 mL
⅓ cup	salad oil	75 mL
1 tsp	grated lemon zest	5 mL
1	egg	1
½ tsp	vanilla	2 mL

◆ *Preheat oven to 425°F (220°C)*
◆ *Muffin tin, paper-lined*

1. In a small bowl combine sugar and grated lemon zest. Set aside.
2. In a large bowl combine flour and sugar. Make a well in the center. Add milk, oil, lemon zest, egg and vanilla. Mix together until just moistened.
3. Spoon batter into prepared muffin tin. Sprinkle with topping. Bake in preheated oven for 15 minutes.

Variations

◆ *Jam Cuffins:* Omit lemon zest and topping. Spoon batter into muffin tins and top each with 1 tsp (5 mL) seedless red raspberry jam. Swirl a thin knife or toothpick through batter and bake as above.

◆ *Mocha Chip Cuffins:* Omit lemon zest and topping. Reduce milk to ¼ cup (50 mL). Dissolve 2 tsp (10 mL) instant coffee in ¼ cup (50 mL) hot water and combine with the milk. Fold in ⅓ cup (75 mL) mini chocolate chips and bake as above.

◆ *Sour Cream 'n' Spice Cuffins:* Omit lemon zest and topping. Add ½ tsp (2 mL) cinnamon, pinch of cloves and nutmeg to the dry ingredients. Decrease the milk to ¼ cup (50 mL) and combine with ¼ cup (50 mL) sour cream. Make a topping of ½ cup (125 mL) chopped walnuts, 1 tbsp (15 mL) sugar and ¼ tsp (1 mL) cinnamon. Sprinkle on top of each cuffin and bake as above.

Peanut Butter Cuffins

2 cups	all-purpose flour	500 mL
2 tsp	baking powder	10 mL
½ tsp	salt	2 mL
½ cup	peanut butter	125 mL
⅓ cup	softened shortening	75 mL
1 tsp	vanilla	5 mL
1½ cups	packed brown sugar	375 mL
2	eggs	2
¾ cup	milk	175 mL

MUFFIN STUFF: You can frost the cuffins with peanut butter and sprinkle with icing sugar.

◆ *Preheat oven to 375°F (190°C)*
◆ *Muffin tin, paper-lined*

1. In a large bowl mix together flour, baking powder and salt.

2. In another bowl cream together peanut butter, shortening and vanilla. Gradually add brown sugar, beating with a spoon until light and fluffy. Add eggs, one at a time, beating well after each addition. Add to flour mixture alternately with milk.

3. Spoon batter into prepared muffin tin, filling cups three-quarters full. Bake in preheated oven for 20 minutes.

Peanut Butter Chocolate Cuffins

2 cups	all-purpose flour	500 mL
2 cups	granulated sugar	500 mL
¾ cup	dry cocoa	175 mL
1 tsp	baking soda	5 mL
1 tsp	salt	5 mL
½ tsp	baking powder	2 mL
¾ cup	shortening	175 mL
¾ cup	buttermilk	175 mL
¾ cup	water	175 mL
2	eggs	2
1 tsp	vanilla	5 mL

PEANUT BUTTER CREAM ICING

6 oz	softened cream cheese	175 g
⅔ cup	creamy peanut butter	150 mL
¼ cup	milk	50 mL
1 tsp	vanilla	5 mL
3 cups	icing sugar	750 mL

MUFFIN STUFF: To make this cuffin even more special, take a pastry bag with a large star tip and fill with icing. Insert the tip into the center of each cuffin. Pipe some icing into the cuffin and add a swirl on top.

◆ *Preheat oven to 350°F (180°C)*
◆ *Muffin tin, paper-lined*

1. In a large mixer bowl combine flour, sugar, cocoa, baking soda, salt and baking powder. Make a well in the center. Add shortening, buttermilk, water, eggs and vanilla. Beat on low speed for 30 seconds, scraping sides of bowl. Then beat on high speed for 3 minutes.

2. Spoon batter into prepared muffin tin, filling cups three-quarters full. Bake in preheated oven for 20 minutes or until toothpick inserted in center comes out dry. Remove from pan and cool completely.

3. Meanwhile, in a large bowl beat together cream cheese and peanut butter. Add milk and vanilla, beating well. Gradually add icing sugar and beat until smooth. (If necessary, add additional milk until a smooth consistency is reached.) Spread over cooled cuffins.

Pumpkin Nut Cuffins

2¼ cups	all-purpose flour	550 mL
3 tsp	baking powder	15 mL
½ tsp	baking soda	2 mL
½ tsp	salt	2 mL
¾ tsp	ground ginger	4 mL
½ tsp	cinnamon	2 mL
½ tsp	ground nutmeg	2 mL
½ cup	softened butter or margarine	125 mL
1⅓ cups	granulated sugar	325 mL
2	eggs, well beaten	2
1 cup	canned pumpkin purée or cooked pumpkin, mashed	250 mL
¾ cup	milk	175 mL
¾ cup	chopped pecans or walnuts	175 mL

◆ *Preheat oven to 375°F (190°C)*
◆ *Muffin tin, greased or paper-lined*

1. In a large bowl combine flour, baking powder, baking soda, salt, ginger, cinnamon and nutmeg.
2. In another bowl cream together butter and sugar until light and fluffy. Stir in eggs and pumpkin. Pour into dry ingredients alternately with milk, blending until smooth. Fold in the nuts.
3. Spoon batter into prepared muffin tin, filling cups three-quarters full. Bake in preheated oven for 25 minutes or until a toothpick inserted in center comes out clean.

MUFFIN STUFF: These cuffins are not very sweet, so if you have a sweet tooth, top them with your favorite frosting.

HINT: If you are using fresh pumpkin in a recipe, a 5 lb (2.5 kg) pumpkin yields about 4½ cups (1.125 L) mashed pumpkin.

Sweet Chocolate Cuffins

2 cups	sifted cake-and-pastry flour	500 mL
2 tsp	baking powder	10 mL
½ tsp	salt	2 mL
¼ cup	butter	50 mL
3	squares unsweetened chocolate	3
2	eggs, separated	2
1½ cups	granulated sugar	375 mL
1⅓ cups	milk	325 mL
2½ tsp	vanilla	12 mL
	Icing sugar	

◆ *Preheat oven to 375°F (190°C)*
◆ *Muffin tin, paper-lined*

1. In a large bowl mix together flour, baking powder and salt.
2. In top of a double boiler over hot (not boiling) water, melt butter and chocolate.
3. In a small bowl beat together egg yolks and sugar until well blended and lemon colored. Add chocolate mixture and blend well. Pour into flour mixture alternately with milk and vanilla. Beat on low speed until blended.
4. In another small bowl beat egg whites until stiff peaks form. Fold gently into the batter.
5. Spoon batter into prepared muffin tin, filling cups to the top. Bake in preheated oven for about 20 minutes. Remove from pan and set aside to cool. Dust tops with icing sugar.

Applesauce Puffins

2 cups	packaged biscuit mix	500 mL
1/4 cup	granulated sugar	50 mL
1 tsp	cinnamon	5 mL
1/2 cup	applesauce	125 mL
1/4 cup	milk	50 mL
1	egg, beaten	1
2 tbsp	vegetable oil	25 mL
TOPPING		
2 tbsp	butter or margarine, melted	25 mL
1/4 cup	granulated sugar	50 mL
1/4 tsp	cinnamon	1 mL

◆ *Preheat oven to 400°F (200°C)*
◆ *Muffin tin, greased or paper-lined*

1. In a large bowl mix together biscuit mix, sugar and cinnamon. Add applesauce, milk, egg and oil. Beat with a spoon for about 1 minute.
2. Spoon batter into prepared muffin tin, filling cups two-thirds full. Bake in preheated oven for 12 minutes or until golden brown. Cool slightly before removing from tins.
3. Dip slightly cooled puffins into melted butter, then into sugar and cinnamon.

MUFFIN STUFF: Try making these in a mini or petite muffin pan.

Apple Streusel Puffins

1/4 cup	butter, melted	50 mL
1/2 cup	granulated sugar	125 mL
1	egg, slightly beaten	1
1/2 cup	milk	125 mL
1 1/2 cups	all-purpose flour	375 mL
1 tbsp	baking powder	15 mL
1/2 tsp	salt	2 mL
1/2 tsp	cinnamon	2 mL
1 cup	grated apple	250 mL
TOPPING		
1/4 cup	granulated sugar	50 mL
1/2 tsp	cinnamon	2 mL
1/4 cup	chopped walnuts	50 mL

◆ *Preheat oven to 375°F (190°C)*
◆ *Muffin tin, greased or paper-lined*

1. In a large bowl cream together butter and sugar. Stir in egg and milk. Add flour, baking powder, salt and cinnamon. Fold in apple.
2. Spoon batter into prepared muffin tin, filling cups two-thirds full.
3. In a bowl combine sugar, cinnamon and walnuts and sprinkle over puffins. Bake in preheated oven for about 20 minutes.

Lemon Cream Cuffin Tarts   ➤
(page 249)

Cheese Puffin Popovers

1 cup	all-purpose flour	250 mL
½ tsp	salt	2 mL
2	eggs	2
1 cup	milk	250 mL
½ cup	grated Cheddar cheese	125 mL

◆ *Preheat oven to 425°F (220°C)*
◆ *Six ramekins, greased*
◆ *Cookie sheet*

1. In a bowl combine flour and salt. Add eggs, milk and cheese, stirring until just smooth.
2. Spoon batter into ramekins, filling only half full. Set cups on cookie sheet.
3. Bake in preheated oven for 45 minutes or until golden brown. Do not open oven before done or the puffins will fall. Serve hot.

Chocolate Peanut Puffins

2 cups	biscuit mix	500 mL
2 tbsp	granulated sugar	25 mL
½ cup	creamy peanut butter	125 mL
¾ cup	chocolate-covered peanuts	175 mL
1	egg	1
¾ cup	milk	175 mL
2 tbsp	vegetable oil	25 mL

◆ *Preheat oven to 400°F (200°C)*
◆ *Muffin tin, paper-lined*

1. In a large bowl combine biscuit mix and sugar. Cut in peanut butter until mixture is crumbly. Add peanuts, mixing well.
2. In a small bowl beat egg slightly. Add milk and oil. Pour into peanut mixture and stir just until moistened.
3. Spoon batter into prepared muffin tin, filling cups three-quarters full. Bake in preheated oven for 20 minutes or until golden brown. Serve hot.

◄ "Candy Apple" Muffins
(page 287)

Double Chocolate Puffins

3	squares unsweetened chocolate	3
¾ cup	milk	175 mL
6 tbsp	softened butter or margarine	90 mL
¾ cup	granulated sugar	175 mL
2	eggs	2
1 tsp	vanilla	5 mL
¾ cup	all-purpose flour	175 mL
1½ tsp	baking powder	7 mL

NOTE: For an added treat, whip ½ cup (125 mL) whipping cream and gradually stir in ½ cup (125 mL) slightly softened chocolate ice cream. Spoon over the inverted puffins.

◆ *Preheat oven to 350°F (180°C)*
◆ *Ramekins or muffin tin, greased*

1. In a saucepan over low heat, combine chocolate and milk until smooth. Set aside to cool.

2. In a large bowl cream together butter and sugar. Add eggs, one at a time, mixing well. Add vanilla and stir in flour and baking powder. Stir in chocolate mixture.

3. Spoon batter into prepared ramekins. Bake in preheated oven for 20 to 25 minutes. Remove from oven and invert cups over a plate so that puffins are upside-down.

Cinnamon Puffs

1 cup	all-purpose flour	250 mL
½ tsp	salt	2 mL
1 tsp	cinnamon	5 mL
3	eggs	3
1 cup	milk	250 mL
3 tbsp	butter or margarine, melted	45 mL

◆ *Preheat oven to 425°F (220°C)*
◆ *Muffin tin, greased*

1. In a blender combine flour, salt, cinnamon, eggs, milk and melted butter. Blend just until smooth.

2. Spoon batter into prepared muffin tin, filling cups three-quarters full. Bake in preheated oven for 15 to 20 minutes.

French Breakfast Puffins

⅓ cup	softened shortening	75 mL
½ cup	granulated sugar	125 mL
1	egg	1
1½ cups	all-purpose flour or cake-and-pastry flour	375 mL
1½ tsp	baking powder	7 mL
½ tsp	salt	2 mL
¼ tsp	ground nutmeg	1 mL
½ cup	milk	125 mL
TOPPING		
½ cup	granulated sugar	125 mL
1 tsp	cinnamon	5 mL
½ cup	butter or margarine, melted	125 mL

- *Preheat oven to 350°F (180°C)*
- *Muffin tin, greased*

1. In a large bowl cream shortening with ½ cup (125 mL) sugar and egg, blending well. Stir in flour, baking powder, salt and nutmeg alternately with milk.

2. Spoon batter into prepared muffin tin, filling cups two-thirds full. Bake in preheated oven for 20 to 25 minutes.

3. In a bowl combine ½ cup (125 mL) sugar and cinnamon. As soon as puffins are ready, remove from pan. Roll in melted butter, then into the sugar-cinnamon mixture. Serve immediately.

Ginger Lemon Puffins

4 tbsp	softened butter	60 mL
½ cup	granulated sugar	125 mL
1	egg	1
1 tsp	grated lemon zest	5 mL
2 cups	all-purpose flour	500 mL
4 tsp	baking powder	20 mL
½ tsp	salt	2 mL
¼ tsp	ground nutmeg	1 mL
1 cup	milk	250 mL
¾ cup	granulated sugar	175 mL
2 tsp	ground ginger	10 mL
½ cup	melted butter	125 mL

- *Preheat oven to 375°F (190°C)*
- *Muffin tin, greased*

1. In a bowl cream together butter and ½ cup (125 mL) sugar. Beat in egg and lemon zest.

2. In a large bowl combine flour, baking powder, salt and nutmeg. Add creamed mixture alternately with milk, beating after each addition.

3. Spoon batter into prepared muffin tin, filling cups three-quarters full. Bake in preheated oven for 15 to 20 minutes.

4. Meanwhile, in a bowl combine ¾ cup (175 mL) sugar and ginger. When puffins come out of the oven, immediately dip in melted butter, then in sugar-ginger mixture. Serve while warm.

Herbed Puffin Popovers

1 cup	all-purpose flour	250 mL
½ tsp	dried thyme	2 mL
¼ tsp	nutmeg	1 mL
¼ tsp	salt	1 mL
1 cup	milk	250 mL
½ tsp	Dijon mustard	2 mL
2 tbsp	vegetable oil	25 mL
2	eggs	2

MUFFIN STUFF: For this particular recipe it is best not to preheat the oven but to turn it on as you are placing the muffin tins inside.

♦ *Muffin tin, greased or paper-lined*

1. In a large bowl combine flour, thyme, nutmeg and salt. Make a well in the center.
2. In another bowl whisk together milk, mustard, oil and eggs. Pour into flour mixture, whisking until smooth and blended.
3. Spoon batter into prepared muffin tin, filling cups three-quarters full. Bake at 450°F (230°C) for 15 minutes. Reduce heat to 375°F (190°C) and bake for 20 to 25 minutes or until crusty and golden brown.

Lemon Nutmeg Puffins

1 cup	whole-wheat bread flour	250 mL
½ tsp	grated nutmeg	2 mL
¼ tsp	salt	1 mL
3	eggs	3
1 cup	milk	250 mL
1 tbsp	vegetable oil	15 mL
	Grated zest of 1 lemon	
2 tsp	butter or margarine	10 mL

MUFFIN STUFF: If you are not serving these immediately, puncture tops with a sharp knife to release the steam inside. Return pan to the turned-off oven, leaving door partially open, until you are ready to serve.

♦ *Preheat oven to 450°F (230°C)*
♦ *6-cup muffin tin, greased*

1. In a bowl combine flour, nutmeg and salt.
2. In a blender process eggs. Gradually add flour mixture alternately with milk. Add oil and zest, blending until smooth. The batter should be thick.
3. Heat prepared muffin tins in preheated oven for a few minutes. Cut butter into 6 pieces and place a piece in each muffin cup. Return to oven until sizzling.
4. Spoon batter into muffin tin, filling cups two-thirds full. Bake in oven for 25 minutes.

Orange Bran Puffins

1 cup	all-purpose flour	250 mL
1/2 tsp	baking powder	2 mL
3/4 tsp	baking soda	4 mL
1 tsp	salt	5 mL
3 tbsp	granulated sugar	45 mL
1 cup	bran	250 mL
1 tsp	grated orange zest	5 mL
1	egg	1
1 cup	buttermilk	250 mL
1 tbsp	butter or margarine, melted	15 mL

◆ *Preheat oven to 400°F (200°C)*
◆ *Muffin tin, greased*

1. In a large bowl combine flour, baking powder, baking soda, salt and sugar. Stir in bran and grated orange zest.
2. In another bowl beat egg slightly with buttermilk and melted butter. Add all at once to the flour mixture and stir just until moistened. Do not overmix. The batter will be lumpy.
3. Spoon batter into prepared muffin tin, filling cups three-quarters full. Bake in preheated oven for 15 minutes or until golden brown. Best served warm.

> **HINT:** When making iced tea from a mix, add a little hot water and then cold water so that the crystals will dissolve more completely.

Parmesan Cheese Puffins

4	eggs	4
1 cup	milk	250 mL
2/3 cup	all-purpose flour	150 mL
1/2 cup	grated Parmesan cheese	125 mL
1/2 tsp	salt	2 mL

◆ *Preheat oven to 425°F (220°C)*
◆ *Muffin tin or ramekins, greased*

1. In a large mixer bowl beat together eggs and milk. Add flour, cheese and salt, beating until well blended.
2. Spoon batter into prepared muffin tin, filling cups two-thirds full. Bake in preheated oven for 35 to 40 minutes.

Peanut Orange Breakfast Puffins

2 cups	all-purpose flour	500 mL
1 tbsp	baking powder	15 mL
1 tsp	salt	5 mL
¼ cup	granulated sugar	50 mL
1	egg, beaten	1
1 cup	milk	250 mL
¼ cup	peanut oil	50 mL
½ cup	chopped salted peanuts	125 mL
TOPPING		
¼ cup	granulated sugar	50 mL
1 tsp	grated orange zest	5 mL
¼ cup	butter or margarine, melted	50 mL

◆ *Preheat oven to 425°F (220°C)*
◆ *Muffin tin or ramekins, greased*

1. In a large bowl combine flour, baking powder, salt and sugar.
2. In another bowl combine egg, milk and peanut oil. Pour into flour mixture and stir just until moistened. Fold in peanuts.
3. Spoon batter into prepared muffin tin, filling cups two-thirds full. Bake in preheated oven for 15 to 20 minutes or until lightly brown.
4. In a bowl combine sugar and zest until crumbly. Dip puffin tops, hot from the oven, into melted butter and then into sugar mixture. Serve warm.

Pecan Lemon Honey Puffins

1 cup	all-purpose flour	250 mL
½ tsp	salt	2 mL
2	eggs	2
1 cup	milk (room temperature)	250 mL
3 tbsp	finely chopped pecans	45 mL
LEMON HONEY BUTTER		
6 tbsp	softened butter	90 mL
6 tbsp	honey	90 mL
	Finely grated zest of 1 lemon	

> **MUFFIN STUFF:** Try other flavored spreads with these puffins.

◆ *Preheat oven to 425°F (220°C)*
◆ *6-cup muffin tin or six ramekins, greased*

1. In a large bowl combine flour and salt. Make a well in the center.
2. In another bowl beat together eggs and milk. Pour into flour mixture, beating just until smooth. Fold in pecans.
3. Spoon batter into prepared muffin tin, filling cups two-thirds full. (If using custard cups, place them on a cookie sheet.) Bake in preheated oven for 25 to 30 minutes or until they puff up and are well browned.
4. In a bowl combine butter, honey and zest. Spread over warm puffins. Serve.

Poppin' Puffins

2	eggs	2
1 cup	milk	250 mL
1 cup	all-purpose flour	250 mL
½ tsp	salt	2 mL
1 tbsp	vegetable oil	15 mL

◆ *Preheat oven to 450°F (230°C)*
◆ *Six to eight ramekins, greased*
◆ *Cookie sheet*

1. In a large bowl blend together eggs and milk. Beat in flour and salt. Add oil and beat another ½ minute. Do not overmix.

2. Spoon batter into prepared ramekins, filling cups only half full. Place cups on a cookie sheet. Bake in preheated oven for 10 minutes or until puffins pop. Then reduce heat to 350°F (180°C) and bake for 25 to 30 minutes or until firm and browned.

3. A few minutes before removing from oven, prick each puffin with a fork, allowing steam to escape. If you want puffins dry inside, turn off oven, keep door ajar and leave cups in for 30 minutes.

Variations

◆ *Cheese Puffins:* Mix ½ cup (125 mL) grated cheese into batter before filling cups.

◆ *Stuffed Puffins:* Split the puffins in half and fill with creamed vegetables, scrambled eggs or anything you like.

◆ *Whole-Wheat Puffins:* Replace half the all-purpose flour with whole-wheat flour.

Red Cherry Puffins

2½ cups	chopped canned red cherries (reserve ½ cup/125 mL juice)	625 mL
½ cup	granulated sugar	125 mL
2 tbsp	quick-cooking tapioca	25 mL
2	egg whites	2
Dash	salt	Dash
¼ tsp	cream of tartar	1 mL
2	egg yolks	2
⅓ cup	granulated sugar	75 mL
⅓ cup	sifted cake-and-pastry flour	75 mL

MUFFIN STUFF: Delicious served warm with ice cream.

- ◆ *Preheat oven to 350°F (180°C)*
- ◆ *Muffin tin, paper-lined*

1. In a saucepan over medium heat, combine cherries, cherry juice, sugar and tapioca. Simmer for 5 minutes, stirring constantly. Set aside.
2. In a small bowl beat egg whites until foamy. Add salt and cream of tartar. Beat until stiff peaks form.
3. In another bowl beat egg yolks until thick and lemon-colored. Gradually add sugar, beating well. Fold into egg whites. Stir in flour.
4. Spoon cherry mixture into prepared muffin tin and pour batter over top. Bake in preheated oven for 25 to 30 minutes.

Baked Salmon Puffins

3	eggs, separated	3
1	can (16 oz/455 mL) salmon	1
¾ cup	bread crumbs	175 mL
1 tbsp	finely chopped onion	15 mL
1 tbsp	lemon juice	15 mL
½ tsp	salt	2 mL
Dash	black pepper	Dash

MUFFIN STUFF: There are all kinds of prepared dips available in supermarkets that would be great with these puffins, especially one with sour cream, dill, onion, etc.

- ◆ *Preheat oven to 300°F (150°C)*
- ◆ *Four to six ramekins, greased*
- ◆ *Baking pan*

1. In a small bowl beat egg whites until stiff peaks form. Set aside.
2. Drain salmon and remove any skin or small bones. Flake with a fork.
3. In a large bowl beat egg yolks slightly. Add salmon, bread crumbs, onion, lemon juice, salt and pepper, mixing well. Fold in beaten egg whites.
4. Spoon batter into prepared ramekins. Place in baking pan with 1 inch (2.5 cm) boiling water. Bake in preheated oven for 45 to 50 minutes or until a knife inserted in the center of a puffin comes out clean.

Strawberry Drop Puffins

2 cups	miniature marshmallows	500 mL
¼ cup	granulated sugar	50 mL
1 cup	sour cream	250 mL
1 cup	water	250 mL
½ cup	butter or margarine	125 mL
1 cup	all-purpose flour	250 mL
¼ tsp	salt	1 mL
4	eggs	4
4 cups	fresh strawberries, washed and hulled	1 L

MUFFIN STUFF: These are like an elegant, dressed-up version of a cream puff!
HINT: To keep strawberries fresh and firm, wash and remove caps (hull) just before using, not when storing, or they will absorb too much water and become mushy. Washing removes the natural protective covering. The hull protects the berry and helps preserve flavor, texture and nutrients.

◆ *Baking sheet, greased*

1. In a bowl combine marshmallows, sugar and sour cream. Cover and chill for several hours.

2. In a large saucepan over medium-high heat, bring water to a boil. Add butter, stirring until melted. Add flour and salt, stirring vigorously until mixture forms a ball. Remove from heat and cool slightly. Add eggs one at a time, beating after each addition.

3. Drop batter by heaping tablespoons (15 mL), about 3 inches apart on prepared baking sheet. Bake at 450°F (230°C) for 15 minutes. Reduce heat to 325°F (160°C) and bake for 25 minutes. Set aside to cool. Split puffins in half and remove any webbing inside.

4. In a bowl crush 2 cups (500 mL) strawberries. Slice the remaining 2 cups (500 mL) strawberries. Fold all berries into chilled sour cream mixture. Spoon ¼ cup (50 mL) filling into bottom half of each split puffin. Cover puffins with tops and spread with 1 tbsp (15 mL) filling.

Variation

◆ *Strawberry Sundae Puffins:* Fill split puffin halves with whipped cream and sliced fresh strawberries. Drizzle with a prepared fudge sauce and cover with the puffin tops. Dust lightly with icing sugar.

Tuna Mushroom Puffins

4	eggs, slightly beaten	4
2 cups	soft bread crumbs	500 mL
1 tsp	salt	5 mL
1 tbsp	prepared mustard	15 mL
1 tbsp	minced onion	15 mL
2 cups	milk	500 mL
1	can (6 oz/170 g) chunky-style tuna	1
SAUCE		
1	can (10 oz/284 mL) cream of mushroom soup	1
2 tbsp	butter	25 mL

◆ *Preheat oven to 400°F (200°C)*
◆ *Ramekins, greased*

1. In a large bowl combine eggs, bread crumbs, salt, mustard, onion, milk and tuna. Pour evenly into prepared custard cups. Place cups in a large pan of hot water. Bake in preheated oven for 35 to 40 minutes.

2. In a saucepan over medium heat, combine cream of mushroom soup and butter. Spoon over puffins and serve warm.

Potato Cheese Puffins

1¼ cups	all-purpose flour	300 mL
¼ cup	granulated sugar	50 mL
3 tsp	baking powder	15 mL
1 tsp	salt	5 mL
1 cup	instant potato flakes	250 mL
1	egg	1
1 cup	milk	250 mL
¼ cup	vegetable oil	50 mL
½ cup	grated Cheddar cheese	125 mL

HINT: Keep oils in a squeeze bottle for when you need only a small amount of oil.

◆ *Preheat oven to 400°F (200°C)*
◆ *Muffin tin or ramekins, greased*

1. In a large bowl mix together flour, sugar, baking powder, salt and ¾ cup (175 mL) potato flakes.

2. In a smaller bowl combine egg, milk and oil. Beat slightly until well blended. Pour into flour mixture and stir just until moistened and blended.

3. Spoon batter into prepared tin, filling cups two-thirds full. Sprinkle tops with grated cheese and remaining potato flakes. Bake in preheated oven for 15 to 20 minutes or until browned.

Specially for Kids

Specially for Kids

THIS CHAPTER IS SPECIALLY WRITTEN FOR KIDS. IT CONTAINS RECIPES FOR muffins that kids will enjoy eating and making. The recipe on the opposite page is a basic, easy, plain muffin recipe – great for young cooks or anyone who has never baked muffins. The variations show you how to make a few changes and/or substitutions, and create a wide range of different flavored muffins. Following this recipe are other easy-to-make muffin recipes which I hope you will try to bake – and enjoy. When baking, keep the following tips in mind.

- Make sure your oven racks are in the right position.

- Set the oven to the temperature called for in your recipe so that the oven will be preheating and ready to use by the time you have mixed your muffin batter.

- Grease your muffin tins, or line them with large-size paper baking cups and set aside.

- In a large bowl, measure out all of your dry ingredients, for example, flour, sugar, baking powder, baking soda, salt, etc.

- Make a well (hole) in the centre of these dry ingredients and set aside.

- In a smaller bowl, combine your liquid ingredients, for example, milk, beaten eggs, oil, etc.

- Add the smaller bowl of liquid ingredients all at once to the larger bowl of dry ingredients and stir only until the dry ingredients are just moistened. Do not overmix.

- Spoon the batter into the tins, filling them three-quarters full, or fill the tins to the top for larger muffins.

- Bake as directed in your recipe.

To measure dry ingredients:
- Use plastic or metal measuring cups that come in sets of different sizes. Spoon the dry ingredient into the right size cup until heaping, holding the cup over the canister it came in, or an empty bowl, not over the mixing bowl you are using to prepare the recipe.

- Level the ingredient by scraping a knife across the top, allowing the excess amount to fall back into the canister or empty bowl. Do not tap the cup on the counter. Level measuring spoons containing a dry ingredient the same way.

To measure liquid ingredients:
- To measure any liquid, use a measuring cup with a spout and amounts marked on the side of the cup. Place the cup on a counter and pour the liquid into the cup, bending down to read the measurements properly.

- To measure small amounts, pour into measuring spoon until full, holding spoon away from your mixing bowl.

Fruits and vegetables:
- Always wash any fruits and vegetables before using them in your recipe.

Plain Muffins

2 cups	all-purpose flour	500 mL
3 tsp	baking powder	15 mL
1/4 cup	granulated sugar	50 mL
1/2 tsp	salt	2 mL
1 cup	milk	250 mL
1	egg, beaten	1
1/4 cup	vegetable oil	50 mL
1/2 tsp	vanilla	2 mL

HINT: Once you feel confident in making plain muffins as in the recipe above, and adding different variations, you can start baking all kinds of delicious muffins using all kinds of ingredients. So, happy baking!

- *Preheat oven to 400°F (200°C)*
- *Muffin tin, greased or paper-lined*

1. In a large bowl combine flour, baking powder, sugar and salt. Make a well in the center.
2. In a smaller bowl combine milk, beaten egg, oil and vanilla. Add liquid ingredients all at once to dry ingredients. Stir only until moistened and slightly lumpy.
3. Spoon batter into prepared muffin tin, filling cups three-quarters full. Bake in preheated oven for 20 to 25 minutes or until golden brown.

Variations

- *Orange Muffins:* Replace half or all of the milk with orange juice and add 1 tsp (5 mL) grated orange zest.
- *Cheese Muffins:* Reduce sugar to 2 tbsp (25 mL), add 1 cup (250 mL) grated cheese to the dry ingredients, and use 2 tbsp (25 mL) of oil instead of the 1/4 cup (50 mL).
- *Raisin Muffins:* Add 1/2 cup (125 mL) raisins to the dry ingredients.
- *Blueberry Muffins:* Fold in 1 cup (250 mL) fresh blueberries, or 3/4 cup (175 mL) thawed, well-drained frozen blueberries into the batter before spooning into the muffin tins.

Apple Muffins

1¾ cups	all-purpose flour	425 mL
3½ tsp	baking powder	17 mL
½ tsp	salt	2 mL
¼ cup	granulated sugar	50 mL
½ tsp	ground nutmeg	2 mL
1 cup	milk	250 mL
1	egg, beaten	1
⅓ cup	vegetable oil	75 mL
1 tsp	grated lemon zest	5 mL
¾ cup	shredded peeled apple	175 mL

◆ *Preheat oven to 400°F (200°C)*
◆ *Muffin tin, greased or paper-lined*

1. In a large bowl combine flour, baking powder, salt, sugar and nutmeg. Make a well in the center.
2. In a small bowl combine milk, beaten egg and oil. Add this mixture, all at once, to dry ingredients and stir just until moist. Fold in lemon zest and apple with just a few strokes. The batter will be a bit lumpy.
3. Spoon batter into prepared muffin tin, filling cups two-thirds full. Bake in preheated oven for 25 to 30 minutes.

Apple Cheddar Muffins

½ cup	butter or margarine	125 mL
½ cup	brown sugar	125 mL
2	eggs	2
1⅔ cups	whole-wheat flour	410 mL
½ tsp	salt	2 mL
1 tsp	baking soda	5 mL
½ cup	rolled oats	125 mL
1 cup	apple pie filling	250 mL
½ cup	finely chopped, aged Cheddar cheese	125 mL
¼ cup	milk or water	50 mL

◆ *Preheat oven to 400°F (200°C)*
◆ *Muffin tin, greased or paper-lined*

1. In a large bowl cream together margarine and sugar. Add eggs and mix well. Add flour, salt and baking soda and mix. Add oats, pie filling and cheese and mix well. Stir in milk.
2. Spoon batter into prepared muffin tin, filling cups three-quarters full. Bake in preheated oven for 20 minutes.

> **HINT:** If children (or adults) are sick in bed, serve their meals in a muffin tin. The cups hold assorted foods, even a small glass of milk or juice, and you will avoid sliding and spilling.

Apple Honey Muffins

1 cup	applesauce	250 mL
1/3 cup	orange juice	75 mL
1/4 cup	honey	50 mL
1/4 cup	vegetable oil	50 mL
1	egg	1
1 cup	all-purpose flour	250 mL
3/4 cup	rolled oats	175 mL
1 tbsp	baking powder	15 mL
1/2 tsp	cinnamon	2 mL

◆ *Preheat oven to 400°F (200°C)*
◆ *Muffin tin, greased or paper-lined*

1. In a small bowl mix together applesauce, orange juice, honey, oil and egg.
2. In a large bowl mix together flour, rolled oats, baking powder and cinnamon. Make a well in the center.
3. Pour liquid ingredients into dry ingredients and stir just to moisten. Do not overmix. Spoon batter into prepared muffin tin. Bake in preheated oven for 25 to 30 minutes.

Apple Nut Muffins

2/3 cup	apple juice or milk	150 mL
1/2 cup	vegetable oil	125 mL
1 tsp	vanilla	5 mL
1	egg	1
2 cups	all-purpose flour	500 mL
1/4 cup	granulated sugar	50 mL
1/4 cup	firmly packed brown sugar	50 mL
1 tbsp	baking powder	15 mL
1/2 tsp	salt	2 mL
1/2 cup	chopped nuts	125 mL
1	chopped peeled apple	1
	Sugar-Cinnamon Mix (see recipe, page 357)	

◆ *Preheat oven to 400°F (200°C)*
◆ *Muffin tin, greased or paper-lined*

1. In a large bowl beat together juice, oil, vanilla and egg. Stir in flour, granulated sugar, brown sugar, baking powder and salt. Mix just until moistened. (Batter will be lumpy.) Stir in nuts and apple.
2. Spoon batter into prepared muffin tin, filling cups three-quarters full. Sprinkle with Sugar-Cinnamon Mix. Bake in preheated oven for 20 minutes or until golden brown.

HINT: To soften rock-hard brown sugar, put a piece of cut apple in the container. Leave for one day, remove, and fluff up the sugar with a fork.

Special Banana Muffins

1 cup	granulated sugar	250 mL
2	eggs	2
1/2 cup	softened margarine	125 mL
2 cups	all-purpose flour	500 mL
2 tsp	baking soda	10 mL
3	medium bananas, mashed	3

◆ *Preheat oven to 425 °F (220°C)*
◆ *Muffin tin, paper-lined*

1. In a large bowl, cream together sugar and eggs until well mixed. Add margarine and blend well. Add flour and baking soda and blend until mixture resembles a loose dough. Add bananas and stir just until moist and blended.

2. Spoon batter into prepared muffin tin, filling cups to the top. Bake in preheated oven for 15 to 20 minutes or until golden brown.

Banana Split Muffins

2	egg whites	2
1/3 cup	granulated sugar	75 mL
2/3 cup	flaked coconut	150 mL
2 cups	packaged biscuit mix	500 mL
1/4 cup	granulated sugar	50 mL
2/3 cup	milk	150 mL
2 tbsp	shortening, melted	25 mL
2	egg yolks, beaten	2
Half	small banana, cut into 12 cubes	Half
12	maraschino cherries, halved	12
12	walnut halves	12

◆ *Preheat oven to 400°F (200°C)*
◆ *12-cup muffin tin, greased or paper-lined*

1. In a small bowl beat egg whites until soft peaks form. Gradually add 1/3 cup (75 mL) sugar and continue beating until stiff peaks form. Fold in coconut and set aside.

2. In a large bowl mix together biscuit mix and 1/4 cup (50 mL) sugar.

3. In another bowl combine milk, shortening and egg yolks. Add this mixture all at once to dry ingredients. Stir just until moistened.

4. Spoon 1 1/2 tbsp (20 mL) batter into the bottom of each prepared cup. Place a banana cube, cherry half and walnut half on top of batter. Cover with 1 tbsp (15 mL) more batter. Spoon 1 1/2 tbsp (20 mL) meringue mixture on each muffin. Top with remaining cherries. Bake in preheated oven for 15 to 20 minutes.

Banana Walnut Muffins

1½ cups all-purpose flour		375 mL
¾ cup	granulated sugar	175 mL
¾ cup	chopped walnuts (about 3 oz/75 g)	175 mL
1½ tsp	baking soda	7 mL
¼ tsp	salt	1 mL
1¼ cups mashed ripe bananas		300 mL
½ cup	melted unsalted butter (1 stick)	125 mL
1	egg	1
2½ tbsp	milk	35 mL

HINT: For a nice thick milkshake to enjoy with your muffins, put half a banana, ½ cup (125 mL) each of 2% milk, plain yogurt and sliced strawberries (or blueberries) in a blender and purée.

- ◆ *Preheat oven to 350°F (180°C)*
- ◆ *Muffin tin, greased or paper-lined*

1. In a large bowl combine flour, sugar, chopped walnuts, baking soda and salt.

2. In another bowl combine mashed bananas, melted butter, egg and milk. Add to dry ingredients and stir just until moistened. Do not overmix.

3. Spoon batter into prepared muffin tin, filling cups three-quarters full. Bake in preheated oven for 25 minutes or until a toothpick inserted in center of muffin comes out dry.

Barbecue Muffins

1	pkg (10 oz/284 mL) refrigerated buttermilk biscuits	1
½ cup	tomato ketchup	125 mL
3 tbsp	packed brown sugar	45 mL
1 tbsp	cider vinegar	15 mL
½ tsp	chili powder	2 mL
1 lb	ground beef	500 g
1 cup	shredded Cheddar cheese	250 mL

◆ *Preheat oven to 375°F (190°C)*
◆ *Muffin tin, greased*

1. Remove dough from package and separate into 10 biscuits. With the palm of your hand or a small rolling pin, flatten each biscuit into 5-inch (12.5 cm) circles. Press dough into the bottom and up the sides of each prepared cup. Set aside.

2. In a small bowl combine ketchup, brown sugar, vinegar and chili powder, stirring until smooth.

3. In a skillet over medium-high heat, brown the ground beef. Drain the fat and add ketchup mixture, mixing well.

4. Divide meat equally among the biscuit-lined muffin cups, about ¼ cup (50 mL) each. Sprinkle with cheese. Bake in preheated oven for 20 minutes or until golden brown. Allow to cool before serving.

Blueberry Breakfast Gems

2 cups	all-purpose flour	500 mL
3 tbsp	packed brown sugar	45 mL
1 tbsp	baking powder	15 mL
½ tsp	salt	2 mL
1 cup	milk	250 mL
1	egg	1
¼ cup	butter or margarine, melted	50 mL
1 cup	fresh blueberries (or frozen)	250 mL
2 tbsp	granulated sugar	25 mL

◆ *Preheat oven to 425°F (220°C)*
◆ *Muffin tin, greased or paper-lined*

1. In a large bowl mix together flour, brown sugar, baking powder and salt.
2. In a small bowl combine milk, egg, and butter; mix until well blended. Add to the flour mixture and stir just until moistened. Do not overmix. Fold in the blueberries.
3. Spoon batter into prepared muffin tin. Sprinkle sugar over tops. Bake in preheated oven for 20 to 25 minutes or until golden brown.

Blueberry Cheese Muffins

1½ cups	all-purpose flour	375 mL
¼ cup	granulated sugar	50 mL
3 tsp	baking powder	15 mL
1 tsp	salt	5 mL
1 cup	yellow cornmeal	250 mL
2 cups	grated sharp Cheddar cheese	500 mL
2 cups	fresh blueberries, rinsed and drained	500 mL
1 cup	milk	250 mL
1	egg, beaten	1
¼ cup	butter or margarine, melted	50 mL

◆ *Preheat oven to 400°F (200°C)*
◆ *Muffin tin, greased or paper-lined*

1. In a large bowl mix together flour, sugar, baking powder, salt, cornmeal, cheese and blueberries.
2. In another bowl beat together milk, egg and melted butter. Add all at once to the flour mixture, stirring just until blended.
3. Spoon batter into prepared muffin tin, filling cups three-quarters full. Bake in preheated oven for 20 to 25 minutes.

Blueberry Cornmeal Muffins

1 cup	all-purpose flour	250 mL
1 cup	yellow cornmeal	250 mL
1/4 cup	granulated sugar	50 mL
1 tsp	baking soda	5 mL
1 tsp	baking powder	5 mL
1/2 tsp	salt	2 mL
2 tsp	finely grated lemon zest	10 mL
1 1/2 cups	buttermilk	375 mL
1	egg	1
1/4 cup	butter or margarine, melted	50 mL
1 tsp	vanilla	5 mL
1 1/2 cups	fresh blueberries (or frozen)	375 mL

- ◆ *Preheat oven to 400°F (200°C)*
- ◆ *Muffin tin, greased or paper-lined*

1. In a large bowl combine flour, cornmeal, sugar, baking soda, baking powder, salt and lemon zest.
2. In another bowl whisk together buttermilk, egg, butter and vanilla. Pour into flour mixture and stir just until moistened. Do not overmix. Fold in blueberries.
3. Spoon batter into prepared muffin tin, filling cups three-quarters full. Bake in preheated oven for 20 to 25 minutes or until golden brown.

Easy Blueberry Muffins

1 3/4 cups	all-purpose flour	425 mL
1/3 cup	granulated sugar	75 mL
3 tsp	baking powder	15 mL
3/4 tsp	salt	4 mL
3/4 cup	milk	175 mL
1/3 cup	vegetable oil	75 mL
1	egg	1
1 cup	fresh blueberries (or thawed and drained frozen blueberries)	250 mL

- ◆ *Preheat oven to 400°F (200°C)*
- ◆ *Muffin tin, greased or paper-lined*

1. In a large bowl mix together flour, sugar, baking powder and salt until blended.
2. In another bowl beat together milk, oil and egg. Add to the flour mixture and stir only until moistened. Do not overmix. Gently fold in blueberries.
3. Spoon batter into prepared muffin tin, filling cups three-quarters full. Bake in preheated oven for 20 to 25 minutes. Delicious served warm.

HINT: When your friends come over to visit, if their parents (or your parents) want them sent home at a certain time, set the kitchen timer – just as you do in baking. When the buzzer sounds, home they go. Moms will be happy.

More Blueberry Muffins

2 cups	all-purpose flour	500 mL
2 tsp	baking powder	10 mL
1/4 tsp	salt	1 mL
1/2 cup	softened butter	125 mL
1 cup	granulated sugar	250 mL
2	eggs	2
3/4 cup	milk	175 mL
1 1/2 cups	blueberries	375 mL

- *Preheat oven to 375°F (190°C)*
- *Muffin tin, greased or paper-lined*

1. In a large bowl mix together flour, baking powder and salt. Make a well in the center.
2. In another bowl cream together butter and sugar, then beat in eggs one at a time. Gradually stir in milk. The mixture may look curdled. Pour into the flour mixture and stir just until moistened. Gently fold in blueberries.
3. Spoon batter into prepared muffin tin, filling cups to the top. Bake in preheated oven for 25 to 30 minutes or until toothpick inserted in center of a muffin comes out clean and dry.

Blueberry Oat Muffins

1 cup	quick-cooking rolled oats	250 mL
1 cup	water	250 mL
1 cup + 3 tbsp	oat bran cereal	250 mL + 45 mL
1 tsp	baking powder	5 mL
1/2 tsp	baking soda	2 mL
1/2 tsp	sea salt	2 mL
3/4 cup	packed brown sugar	175 mL
1	egg, beaten	1
1/4 cup	vegetable oil	50 mL
1 1/4 cups	fresh or frozen blueberries	300 mL

- *Preheat oven to 400°F (200°C)*
- *Muffin tin, greased or paper-lined*

1. In a medium bowl combine quick-cooking oats and water. Set aside.
2. In a large bowl mix together oat bran cereal, baking powder, baking soda, sea salt and brown sugar Add egg and oil and mix only until blended. Add the oats and mix only until blended. Fold in blueberries and stir only until moistened. Do not overmix.
3. Spoon batter into prepared muffin tin, filling cups three-quarters or to the top. Bake in preheated oven for 20 to 25 minutes or until done.

Blueberry Orange Muffins

2 cups	all-purpose flour	500 mL
1 tbsp	baking powder	15 mL
½ tsp	cinnamon	2 mL
½ cup	vegetable oil	125 mL
2	eggs	2
⅓ cup	honey	75 mL
¼ cup	milk	50 mL
¼ cup	orange juice	50 mL
1½ cups fresh blueberries		375 mL

◆ *Preheat oven to 400°F (200°C)*
◆ *Muffin tin, paper-lined*

1. In a large bowl combine flour, baking powder and cinnamon. Make a well in the center.
2. In another bowl beat together oil, eggs, honey, milk and orange juice. Pour into flour mixture and blend just until moistened. Fold in blueberries.
3. Spoon batter into prepared muffin tin, filling cups three-quarters full. Bake in preheated oven for 20 to 25 minutes or until golden brown.

Quick Breakfast Muffins

2 cups	all-purpose flour	500 mL
4 tsp	baking powder	20 mL
4 tbsp	granulated sugar	50 mL
Pinch	salt	Pinch
1	egg	1
1 cup	milk	250 mL
2 tbsp	vegetable oil or melted butter	25 mL

◆ *Preheat oven to 375°F (190°C)*
◆ *Muffin tin, paper-lined*

1. In a large bowl mix together flour, baking powder, sugar and salt. Make a well in the center.
2. In another bowl whisk together egg, milk and oil. Pour into dry ingredients and stir only until moistened. Do not overmix.
3. Spoon batter into prepared muffin tin, filling cups to the top. Bake in preheated oven for 20 to 25 minutes or until done.

MUFFIN STUFF: If you want to save time in the morning, mix the dry ingredients the night before, cover and set aside on the counter. Blend together the liquid ingredients and set aside in the fridge until the morning. Then, all you have to do for a really quick breakfast muffin is pour the liquid ingredients into the dry ingredients and bake as above.

Bran Cereal Muffins

1¼ cups	all-purpose flour	300 mL
3 tsp	baking powder	15 mL
½ tsp	salt	2 mL
½ cup	granulated sugar	125 mL
1½ cups	all-bran cereal	375 mL
1¼ cups	milk	300 mL
1	egg	1
⅓ cup	vegetable oil	75 mL

◆ *Preheat oven to 400°F (200°C)*
◆ *12-cup muffin tin, paper-lined*

1. In a large bowl mix together flour, baking powder, salt and sugar. Set aside.

2. In another bowl combine cereal and milk. Stir well and let stand for 1 to 2 minutes or until the cereal has softened. Add the egg and oil to this cereal mixture and beat well. Pour into the flour mixture and stir just until moistened.

3. Spoon batter evenly into prepared muffin tin. Bake in preheated oven for 25 minutes or until lightly browned.

Variations

◆ Add ½ cup (125 mL) raisins to the batter.

◆ Substitute 3 cups (750 mL) raisin bran cereal, or 2½ cups (625 mL) bran flakes cereal in place of the all-bran cereal.

Chili Muffins

1 lb	lean ground beef	500 g
¾ cup	salsa (medium)	175 mL
1 tsp	chili powder	5 mL
½ tsp	salt	2 mL
¼ tsp	pepper	1 mL
1	can (14 oz/398 mL) red kidney beans, rinsed and drained	1
½ cup	shredded Cheddar cheese (or Monterey Jack, etc.)	125 mL

HINT: Make mini meat loaves by patting meat mixture into muffin pan cups. Brush each generously with barbecue sauce and bake.

◆ *Preheat oven to 400°F (200°C)*
◆ *8-cup muffin tin*

1. In a large bowl break up the beef with a fork. Mix in ¼ cup (50 mL) of the salsa, chili powder, salt and pepper. Divide evenly into 8 muffin cups. Press into the center of each to form a well and press into the bottom and up sides of each cup. Bake in preheated oven for 10 minutes or until the meat is no longer pink.

2. In another bowl combine beans and remaining salsa. Spoon into the muffin cups. Sprinkle with cheese. Bake for 7 or 8 minutes or until the beans are hot and the cheese is melted.

Chocolate Muffins

1²⁄₃ cups	all-purpose flour	400 mL
¾ cup	granulated sugar	175 mL
⅓ cup	cocoa	75 mL
3½ tsp	baking powder	17 mL
½ tsp	salt	2 mL
1	egg	1
1 cup	milk	250 mL
¼ cup	vegetable oil or shortening, melted	50 mL

◆ *Preheat oven to 400°F (200°C)*
◆ *Muffin tin, greased or paper-lined*

1. In a large bowl combine flour, sugar, cocoa, baking powder and salt.
2. In another bowl beat together egg, milk and oil. Pour into the flour mixture and stir just until combined. Do not overmix.
3. Spoon batter into prepared muffin tin, filling cups three-quarters full. Bake in preheated oven for 20 to 25 minutes.

Variation
◆ Chocolate Nut Muffins: Add ½ cup (125 mL) chopped walnuts to the batter and bake as above.

Chocolate Chip Muffins

1	egg	1
1 cup	sour cream	250 mL
½ cup	milk	125 mL
1¾ cups	all-purpose flour	425 mL
2 tbsp	granulated sugar	25 mL
1 tsp	baking powder	5 mL
½ tsp	baking soda	2 mL
1 tsp	salt	5 mL
1 cup	chocolate chips	250 mL

◆ *Preheat oven to 400°F (200°C)*
◆ *Muffin tin, greased or paper-lined*

1. In a bowl beat egg. Stir in sour cream and milk.
2. In a large bowl combine flour, sugar, baking powder, baking soda and salt. Pour egg mixture into flour mixture and stir just until moistened. Fold in chocolate chips.
3. Spoon batter into prepared muffin tin, filling cups three-quarters full. Bake in preheated oven for 20 to 25 minutes.

Chocolate Chip Banana Muffins

2	ripe bananas	2
1 tsp	baking soda	5 mL
1 tsp	hot water	5 mL
½ cup	margarine or vegetable oil	125 mL
¾ cup	granulated sugar	175 mL
1	egg, beaten	1
1 tsp	vanilla	5 mL
1½ cups	all-purpose flour	375 mL
1 tsp	baking powder	5 mL
1 tsp	salt	5 mL
5 oz	chocolate chips	150 g

+ *Preheat oven to 425°F (220°C)*
+ *Muffin tin, greased or paper-lined*

1. In a medium bowl mash bananas. Add baking soda and hot water and set aside.
2. In a large bowl cream together margarine and sugar. Add egg and vanilla; mix well. Add flour, baking powder and salt. Add banana mixture and blend together. Add chocolate chips; stir just until moistened.
3. Spoon batter into prepared muffin tin. Bake in preheated oven for 15 to 20 minutes.

Chocolate Chunk Banana Muffins

1 cup	mashed overripe bananas (about 2 medium)	250 mL
1 cup	low-fat Miracle Whip	250 mL
½ cup	granulated sugar	125 mL
½ tsp	vanilla	2 mL
2 cups	all-purpose flour	500 mL
2 tsp	baking soda	10 mL
½ cup	chocolate chunks (or cut up a plain chocolate bar)	125 mL

+ *Preheat oven to 375°F (190°C)*
+ *Muffin tin, greased or paper-lined*

1. In a large bowl combine bananas, Miracle Whip, sugar and vanilla.
2. In another bowl whisk together flour and baking soda. Fold into the banana mixture and stir just until blended. Fold in chocolate chunks.
3. Spoon batter into prepared muffin tin. Bake in preheated oven for 20 minutes or until golden brown.

MUFFIN STUFF: You could use chocolate chips in place of the chocolate chunks. Using the Miracle Whip means you don't have to add an egg to this recipe, and the muffins are nice and moist.

Chocolate Lovers' Delight

3	squares unsweetened chocolate	3
1/3 cup	vegetable oil	75 mL
2	eggs	2
1 tsp	vanilla	5 mL
1 1/3 cups	milk	325 mL
2 cups	all-purpose flour	500 mL
1/2 cup	granulated sugar	125 mL
2 tsp	baking soda	10 mL
1 cup	semi-sweet chocolate chips	250 mL

HINT: An ice-cream scoop makes filling muffin cups a breeze. To make muffins mushroom out, use an oiled scoop.

- ◆ *Preheat oven to 400°F (200°C)*
- ◆ *Muffin tin, paper-lined*

1. In a saucepan over low heat, melt the chocolate with the oil (or microwave on Medium for 2 minutes). Remove from heat and add eggs, vanilla and milk; blend well.
2. In a large bowl combine flour, sugar and baking soda. Add the chocolate mixture and half the chocolate chips, stirring only until moistened.
3. Spoon batter into prepared muffin tin, filling cups two-thirds full. Sprinkle with remaining chocolate chips. Bake in preheated oven for 20 to 25 minutes or until a toothpick inserted in the center comes out clean.

Double Chocolate Muffins

1 cup	semi-sweet chocolate chips	250 mL
1 tbsp	instant coffee crystals	15 mL
1/4 cup	margarine	50 mL
1 1/4 cups	milk	300 mL
1	egg	1
2 1/2 cups	all-purpose flour	625 mL
1/3 cup	granulated sugar	75 mL
1 tbsp	baking powder	15 mL
1/2 tsp	salt	2 mL

HINT: To avoid the mess of serving ice-cream at children's parties, prepare the ice-cream in balls. Put them into muffin tins and store in freezer until it is time to serve them. This makes dishing it out easier and faster and avoids the usual "he/she got more than I did!"

- ◆ *Preheat oven to 400°F (200°C)*
- ◆ *Muffin tin, paper-lined*

1. In a saucepan over low heat, melt 1/2 cup (125 mL) of the chocolate chips, coffee, margarine and milk, stirring to blend well. Set aside. When mixture cools, beat in egg.
2. In a large bowl combine flour, sugar, baking powder and salt. Stir in chocolate mixture, stirring just until moistened. Fold in the remaining 1/2 cup (125 mL) chocolate chips.
3. Spoon batter into prepared muffin tin, filling cups to the top. Bake in preheated oven for 20 minutes or until a toothpick inserted in center of a muffin comes out clean and dry.

Peanut Butter Cornmeal Muffins

1 cup	all-purpose flour	250 mL
½ tsp	salt	2 mL
3 tsp	baking powder	15 mL
1 tbsp	granulated sugar	15 mL
½ cup	cornmeal	125 mL
1 cup	milk	250 mL
1	egg, beaten	1
¼ cup	peanut butter	50 mL
1 tbsp	butter or shortening, melted	15 mL

◆ *Preheat oven to 400°F (200°C)*
◆ *Muffin tin, greased or paper-lined*

1. In a large bowl combine flour, salt, baking powder and sugar. Stir in cornmeal.

2. In another bowl combine milk, egg, peanut butter and melted butter. Add the milk mixture, stirring only until moistened. Do not overmix.

3. Spoon batter into prepared muffin tin, filling cups three-quarters full. Bake in preheated oven for 20 to 25 minutes or until done.

Surprise Cornmeal Muffins

1 cup	yellow cornmeal	250 mL
1¼ cups	cake-and-pastry flour	300 mL
1 tsp	baking soda	5 mL
2 tsp	baking powder	10 mL
½ tsp	salt	2 mL
½ cup	shortening or butter	125 mL
½ cup	granulated sugar	125 mL
1	egg	1
1 cup	milk	250 mL
½ cup	plain yogurt	125 mL
¼ cup	filling (such as softened cream cheese, jam etc.)	50 mL

◆ *Preheat oven to 400°F (200°C)*
◆ *12-cup muffin tin, paper-lined*

1. In a large bowl combine cornmeal, flour, baking soda, baking powder and salt.

2. In another bowl cream together shortening and sugar. Beat in egg, milk and yogurt. Pour into dry ingredients and stir just until moistened.

3. Spoon half the batter evenly into prepared muffin tin. Top each with 1 tsp (5 mL) filling and then spoon remaining batter evenly over top. Bake in preheated oven for 20 to 25 minutes or until golden brown.

Corn-on-the-Cob Muffins

1 cup	all-purpose flour	250 mL
¾ cup	yellow cornmeal	175 mL
2 tbsp	granulated sugar	25 mL
2 tsp	baking powder	10 mL
¾ tsp	salt	4 mL
1	egg, beaten	1
¾ cup	milk	175 mL
¼ cup	butter or margarine, melted	50 mL
½ cup	cooked corn, cut off the cob	125 mL
2 tbsp	minced green onion (optional)	25 mL

◆ *Preheat oven to 425°F (220°C)*
◆ *Muffin tin, paper-lined*

1. In a large bowl combine flour, cornmeal, sugar, baking powder and salt.
2. In a small bowl combine egg, milk, butter, corn and onion. Pour into dry ingredients and stir just until moistened and blended.
3. Spoon batter into prepared muffin tin. Bake in preheated oven for 20 minutes or until lightly browned.

HINT: Top hot, baked muffins (or cupcakes) with a marshmallow and put back in oven until marshmallows melt and brown lightly.

Egg Bread Muffins

1	loaf of bread (white or brown)	1
	Cheddar cheese slices, about ½ inch (1 cm) thick	
	Eggs	
	Toppings (see above)	

◆ *Preheat oven to 350°F (180°C)*
◆ *Muffin tin, greased*

1. Arrange bread slices on a cutting board. Cut out circles the same size as bottom of muffin tin cups, using a cookie cutter or top of a glass. Make as many as you want.
2. Place circles of bread in bottom of each prepared muffin cup. Place cheese slices on top of each bread circle. Break an egg over top. Add your choice of toppings.
3. Bake in preheated oven until tops turn golden brown or longer if you want a firmer yolk. Serve immediately.

Fudgey Nut Muffins

1 cup	all-purpose flour	250 mL
1⅓ cups	granulated sugar	325 mL
1¼ tsp	baking powder	6 mL
½ tsp	salt	2 mL
¼ tsp	baking soda	1 mL
1 cup	milk	250 mL
3 tbsp	butter or shortening, melted	45 mL
1	egg	1
½ tsp	vanilla	2 mL
3	squares unsweetened chocolate, melted and cooled	3
1	pkg (6 oz/175 g) semi-sweet chocolate chips	1
½ cup	chopped walnuts	125 mL

◆ *Preheat oven to 400°F (200°C)*
◆ *Muffin tin, greased or paper-lined*

1. In a large bowl combine flour, sugar, baking powder, salt and baking soda. Make a well in the center. Add milk, butter, egg, vanilla and melted chocolate; stir just until moistened and blended. Fold in the chocolate chips and walnuts.

2. Spoon batter into prepared muffin tin, filling cups three-quarters full or to the top if a larger muffin is desired. Bake in preheated oven for 20 to 25 minutes or until toothpick inserted in center of a muffin comes out clean and dry.

HINT: Hey kids! Get Mom to buy your favorite cake mix. Prepare the batter as directed on the package. Use flat-bottomed ice-cream cones. Fill one-quarter full with the batter. Bake at 375°F (190°C) for 20 minutes or until done. Frost and decorate with chocolate chips, miniature marshmallows, candy, raisins or whatever you happen to have on hand.

"Candy Apple" Muffins

2 cups	all-purpose flour	500 mL
1/2 cup	granulated sugar	125 mL
1 tbsp	baking powder	15 mL
1/2 tsp	salt	2 mL
1/4 tsp	ground nutmeg	1 mL
1/2 cup	milk	125 mL
1/4 cup	butter or margarine, melted	50 mL
2	eggs	2
1 tsp	vanilla	5 mL
1	apple, chopped	1
DIP		
1/2 cup	honey	125 mL
1/2 cup	packed dark brown sugar	125 mL
3/4 cup	finely chopped walnuts	175 mL

MUFFIN STUFF: You can use a miniature muffin tin and bake for 12 to 15 minutes.

HINT: Put medium-sized apples into muffin tins. Bake as in any baked apple recipe.

- *Preheat oven to 400°F (200°C)*
- *Muffin tin, greased*
- *Wooden skewers or popsicle sticks*

1. In a large bowl mix together flour, sugar, baking powder, salt and nutmeg.

2. In another bowl combine milk, butter, eggs and vanilla until well blended. Pour into dry ingredients and stir until just moistened. Fold in apple. Do not overmix.

3. Spoon batter into prepared muffin tin, filling cups two-thirds full. Bake in preheated oven for 15 to 20 minutes or until lightly browned. Cool slightly and remove from pan.

4. In a saucepan over medium heat, bring honey and brown sugar to a boil. Stir until sugar is dissolved. Pour walnuts onto a plate.

5. Spear warm muffins with a skewer or popsicle stick and dip quickly into the honey/brown sugar mixture, then into chopped nuts.

Halloween Monster Muffins

1½ cups	all-purpose flour	375 mL
2 tsp	baking powder	10 mL
½ tsp	salt	2 mL
1 tsp	cinnamon	5 mL
½ tsp	ground ginger	2 mL
¼ tsp	ground cloves	1 mL
¼ tsp	ground nutmeg	1 mL
½ cup	packed brown sugar	125 mL
½ cup	raisins (optional)	125 mL
1	egg	1
½ cup	milk	125 mL
½ cup	canned pumpkin purée	125 mL
¼ cup	vegetable oil	50 mL

- ◆ *Preheat oven to 400°F (200°C)*
- ◆ *Muffin tin, paper-lined*

1. In a large bowl combine flour, baking powder, salt, cinnamon, ginger, cloves, nutmeg and brown sugar. Mix in raisins, if using. Make a well in the center.

2. In a smaller bowl beat together egg, milk, pumpkin and oil. Pour into flour mixture and stir just until moistened. The batter will be lumpy.

3. Spoon batter into prepared muffin tin. Bake in preheated oven for about 20 minutes.

4. Decorate with vanilla or cream-cheese frosting or whipping cream. Use raisins, chipits, smarties, carrot or green bell pepper pieces, nuts, or whatever else you have on hand to make all kinds of scary monster faces on your muffin tops.

Funny Face Tuna Melts

1	can (6.5 oz/184 g) flaked tuna, drained	1
2 tbsp	mayonnaise	25 mL
1	celery stalk, chopped	1
¼ cup	grated Cheddar cheese	50 mL
	Black pepper	
2 or 3	English Muffins, split in half	2 or 3
	Pickle slices	
	Olives	
	Tomato slices	

- ◆ *Preheat broiler*
- ◆ *Small cookie sheet*

1. In a bowl combine tuna, mayonnaise, celery, cheese and pepper to taste. Divide mixture evenly over each muffin half.

2. Make "funny faces" on each half, using pickle slices for eyes, olives for the nose and half a tomato slice for smiling mouths. Use any other garnishes you have on hand as well. Place under the broiler for 3 to 5 minutes or until cheese melts.

MUFFIN STUFF: In place of the tuna, try canned salmon, turkey or chicken, or mashed hard-boiled eggs. You might also try using green or red bell peppers, raisins, mushrooms, or anything else you like to make the "funny faces."

Orange Upside-Down Muffins ➤
(*page 306*)

Ham and Cheddar Muffins

2 cups	biscuit mix	500 mL
2 tsp	dry mustard	10 mL
1	egg, beaten	1
1/2 cup	milk	125 mL
1	can (6.5 oz/184 g) flaked ham, flaked with a fork	1
1 1/2 cups	grated Cheddar cheese	375 mL

◆ *Preheat oven to 400°F (200°C)*
◆ *Muffin tin, greased or paper-lined*

1. In a medium bowl combine biscuit mix, mustard, egg and milk with a fork. Stir in flaked ham and cheese just until moistened.
2. Spoon batter into prepared muffin tin, filling cups three-quarters full. Bake in preheated oven for 20 to 25 minutes or until done.

Variation
◆ If you want a sweet muffin instead, use 2 tbsp (25 mL) sugar in place of the dry mustard.

Hamburger Muffins

18	slices white or brown bread	18
	Butter	
1 lb	lean ground beef	500 g
1 cup	canned mushroom soup	250 mL
1/4 cup	chopped onions	50 mL
1	egg, beaten	1
1/2 cup	grated Cheddar cheese	125 mL
1 tsp	Worcestershire sauce	5 mL
	Salt and pepper, to taste	

◆ *Preheat oven to 350°F (180°C)*
◆ *Muffin tin*

1. Trim the crusts off bread slices and flatten slightly with a rolling pin. Butter each slice on one side and place, buttered-side down, in muffin cups. Set aside.
2. In a bowl mix together meat, soup, onions, egg, cheese, Worcestershire sauce, salt and pepper. Spoon mixture evenly over bread slices. Bake in preheated oven for 35 to 45 minutes or until meat is well-cooked.

Hot Chocolate Puddings with Marshmallow Topping

1	pkg chocolate pudding and pie filling	1
2 cups	miniature marshmallows	500 mL

◆ *Six 6-oz (175 g) ramekins*

1. Prepare pudding as directed on package. Remove from heat and stir in 1½ cups (375 mL) of the marshmallows just until mixed, not melted. Pour into ramekins. Top with remaining marshmallows. Serve hot.

Jam-Filled Muffins

1¾ cups	all-purpose flour	425 mL
½ cup	granulated sugar	125 mL
1 tbsp	baking powder	15 mL
½ tsp	salt	2 mL
2	eggs	2
⅔ cup	milk	150 mL
⅓ cup	butter or margarine, melted	75 mL
1 tsp	grated lemon zest	5 mL
½ cup	strawberry or raspberry jam	125 mL

◆ *Preheat oven to 400°F (200°C)*
◆ *12-cup muffin tin, greased or paper-lined*

1. In a large bowl mix together flour, sugar, baking powder and salt.

2. In another bowl lightly beat eggs. Add milk, butter and lemon zest. Pour into flour mixture, stirring just until moistened and blended. Do not overmix.

3. Spoon half the batter into prepared muffin tin. Make a well in the center of each cup and add a spoonful of jam. Spoon remaining batter over jam. Bake in preheated oven for 20 to 25 minutes or until golden brown.

Little Miss Muffins

1	can (6.5 oz/184 g) flaked chicken or tuna, well-drained	1
¼ cup	mayonnaise	50 mL
1	tomato, peeled, seeded and chopped	1
1 tbsp	lemon juice	15 mL
	Salt and pepper to taste	
	Butter	
2	English muffins, split and toasted	2
1	small cucumber, scored and sliced	1
2	slices processed cheese, each cut diagonally in half	2
1	tomato, sliced	1

♦ *Preheat broiler*
♦ *Small cookie sheet*

1. In a bowl mix together chicken, mayonnaise, chopped tomato, lemon juice, salt and pepper.
2. Butter the toasted English muffins and put cucumber slices and chicken mixture on each half. Top with cheese and tomato slices. Broil for 2 to 3 minutes or until cheese melts.

> **HINT:** To peel a tomato, lower the tomato into boiling water for 5 seconds. Remove from water and the peel should come off easily. If not, repeat and try again.

Meal in a Muffin

8 oz	boiled ham, cut into chunks	250 g
1½	slices rye bread, crusts removed and torn into pieces	1½
2 tbsp	minced green onion	25 mL
2 tbsp	fresh parsley	25 mL
1	egg yolk	1
1 tbsp	unsweetened apricot jam	15 mL
1 tsp	honey mustard	5 mL

♦ *Preheat oven to 350°F (180°C)*
6-cup muffin tin

1. In a food processor combine ham, bread, onion, parsley, egg yolk and jam; process until ground.
2. Spoon mixture evenly into muffin cups. Bake in preheated oven for 30 minutes. Remove from oven and brush tops with mustard. Return to oven and bake for 5 more minutes. Remove from cups and cool just enough to eat.

Oatmeal Cinnamon Muffins

1 cup	all-purpose flour	250 mL
3½ tsp	baking powder	17 mL
½ tsp	salt	2 mL
½ tsp	cinnamon	2 mL
Pinch	ground nutmeg	Pinch
¾ cup	rolled oats	175 mL
½ cup	lightly packed brown sugar	125 mL
1	egg	1
1 cup	milk	250 mL
¼ cup	vegetable oil or shortening, melted	50 mL

◆ *Preheat oven to 400°F (200°C)*
◆ *Muffin tin, greased or paper-lined*

1. In a large bowl combine flour, baking powder, salt, cinnamon and nutmeg. Stir in rolled oats and brown sugar; blend together well.

2. In another bowl beat together egg, milk and oil. Add to flour mixture and stir only until moistened. Batter will be lumpy.

3. Spoon batter into prepared muffin tin, filling cups two-thirds full. Bake in preheated oven for 20 to 25 minutes or until done.

Miniature Orange Muffins

2 cups	all-purpose flour	500 mL
1 tsp	baking soda	5 mL
1 tsp	salt	5 mL
1 tsp	grated orange zest	5 mL
½ cup	butter, at room temperature	125 mL
1 cup	granulated sugar	250 mL
¾ cup	sour cream	175 mL
½ cup	raisins	125 mL
½ cup	chopped nuts	125 mL
DIP		
1 cup	granulated sugar	250 mL
½ cup	orange juice (juice of 1 orange)	125 mL

◆ *Preheat oven to 375°F (190°C)*
◆ *Miniature muffin tin, greased*

1. In a large bowl combine flour, baking soda, salt and zest.

2. In another bowl cream together butter and the 1 cup (250 mL) sugar. Add sour cream alternately with flour mixture, stirring just until moistened and blended. Fold in raisins and nuts.

3. Spoon batter into prepared muffin tin, filling cups to the top. Bake in preheated oven for 12 to 15 minutes.

4. In a small bowl, mix together sugar and orange juice. Dip warm muffins into dip mixture. Let cool before serving.

Orange Raisin Muffins

2 cups	all-purpose flour	500 mL
1/3 cup	granulated sugar	75 mL
1/2 tsp	salt	2 mL
3/4 tsp	baking soda	4 mL
1/2 cup	raisins	125 mL
1	egg, well-beaten	1
1/3 cup	orange juice	75 mL
1/2 tsp	grated orange zest	2 mL
2/3 cup	buttermilk or sour milk	150 mL
1/3 cup	shortening	75 mL

◆ *Preheat oven to 425°F (220°C)*
◆ *Muffin tin, greased*

1. In a large bowl mix together flour, sugar, salt and baking soda. Add raisins.
2. In a smaller bowl combine beaten egg, orange juice, zest, buttermilk and shortening. Pour into dry ingredients and stir just until moistened and blended.
3. Spoon batter into prepared muffin tin, filling cups three-quarters full. Bake in preheated oven for 25 minutes.

HINT: To make 1 cup (250 mL) of sour milk, measure 1 tbsp (15 mL) vinegar or lemon juice into a measuring cup. Then fill to 1 cup (250 mL) with milk. Let stand about 5 minutes before using in your recipe.

Peanut Butter Muffins

2 cups	all-purpose flour	500 mL
1 tbsp	baking powder	15 mL
1/2 tsp	salt	2 mL
1 1/4 cups	milk	300 mL
1	egg	1
3 tbsp	granulated sugar	45 mL
1/2 cup	peanut butter	125 mL

◆ *Preheat oven to 400°F (200°C)*
◆ *Muffin tin, paper-lined*

1. In a large bowl mix together flour, baking powder and salt. Make a well in the center.
2. In an electric blender combine milk, egg, sugar and peanut butter. Cover and blend until thoroughly mixed. Add all at once to dry ingredients and stir just until moistened. Do not overmix.
3. Spoon batter into prepared muffin tin, filling cups three-quarters full. Bake in preheated oven for 25 to 30 minutes or until golden brown.

Peanut Butter Banana Muffins

2 cups	all-purpose flour	500 mL
1/2 cup	packed brown sugar	125 mL
1 tbsp	baking powder	15 mL
1/4 tsp	salt	1 mL
1/2 cup	peanut butter (chunky or smooth)	125 mL
2 tbsp	vegetable oil	25 mL
2	eggs	2
3/4 cup	milk	175 mL
2	medium bananas, mashed	2

- *Preheat oven to 400°F (200°C)*
- *Muffin tin, greased or paper-lined*

1. In a large bowl combine flour, brown sugar, baking powder and salt.
2. In another bowl combine peanut butter, oil, eggs, milk and mashed bananas. Add to flour mixture, stirring just until moistened and blended.
3. Spoon batter evenly into prepared muffin tin. Bake in preheated oven for 20 minutes or until done.

Crunchy Peanut Butter and Jelly Muffins

2 cups	all-purpose flour	500 mL
1/2 cup	granulated sugar	125 mL
2 1/2 tsp	baking powder	12 mL
1/2 tsp	salt	2 mL
3/4 cup	crunchy peanut butter	175 mL
3/4 cup	milk	175 mL
2	eggs	2
1/4 cup	jam or jelly	50 mL

HINT: Use muffin tins to make extra-large ice cubes for punch.

- *Preheat oven to 400°F (200°C)*
- *Muffin tin, paper-lined*

1. In a large bowl mix together flour, sugar, baking powder and salt. With a pastry blender or two knives, cut in peanut butter until mixture resembles coarse crumbs. Add milk and eggs all at once, stirring just until moistened and blended.
2. Spoon 2 tbsp (25 mL) batter into each prepared cup. Put 1 tsp (5 mL) jam or jelly in center of each. Top with another 2 tbsp (25 mL) batter. Bake in preheated oven for about 20 minutes.

Peanut Butter Oat Muffins

1½ cups	whole-wheat flour	375 mL
1½ cups	rolled oats	375 mL
4 tsp	baking powder	20 mL
1 tsp	salt	5 mL
1 tsp	baking soda	5 mL
½ cup	raisins	125 mL
1 cup	plain yogurt	250 mL
¾ cup	liquid honey	175 mL
½ cup	peanut butter	125 mL
⅓ cup	vegetable oil	75 mL
3	eggs, lightly beaten	3
1 tsp	vanilla	5 mL

♦ *Preheat oven to 375°F (190°C)*
♦ *Muffin tin, greased or paper-lined*

1. In a large bowl combine flour, oats, baking powder, salt and baking soda. Stir in raisins.
2. In another bowl beat together yogurt, honey, peanut butter, oil, eggs and vanilla until smooth. Add to dry ingredients and stir just until moistened and blended. Do not overmix.
3. Spoon batter into prepared muffin tin, filling cups three-quarters full. Bake in preheated oven for 25 to 30 minutes or until done.

> **HINT:** For a special treat, spread peanut butter on butter cookies or vanilla wafers. Place a toasted marshmallow between two cookies or wafers and press together slightly and – voila! – a Peanut Butter Puff.

Peanut Pops

1 cup	finely crushed peanut brittle	250 mL
4 cups	vanilla ice cream	1 L
8 tbsp	peanut butter	125 mL

♦ *8-cup muffin tin*
♦ *Eight 5-oz (150 mL) paper drinking cups*
♦ *Eight plastic spoons*

1. Place a paper cup in each ungreased muffin tin cup. Add 1 tbsp (15 mL) peanut brittle to each. Spoon in some ice cream to half fill each cup. Add 1 tbsp (15 mL) peanut butter and then remaining ice cream. Top with remaining peanut brittle.
2. With the back of a spoon, pack mixture down firmly. Insert a plastic spoon, bowl-end down, into each cup. Wrap each cup in foil and place muffin tin in freezer.
3. When firm, peel off foil, lift out cups and eat ice cream on a stick. Or leave cups on, pull out spoon and enjoy an ice cream sundae.

Pepperoni Muffins

2½ cups	all-purpose flour	625 mL
¼ cup	grated Parmesan cheese	50 mL
2 tbsp	packed brown sugar	25 mL
1 tbsp	baking powder	15 mL
½ tsp	salt	2 mL
1 tsp	oregano or basil leaves	5 mL
1 cup	chopped pepperoni (casings removed)	250 mL
1	pkg (4 oz/125 g) softened cream cheese	1
1 cup	milk	250 mL
2	eggs	2
½ cup	margarine or butter, melted	125 mL

- *Preheat oven to 400°F (200°C)*
- *Muffin tin, greased or paper-lined*

1. In a large bowl combine flour, cheese, brown sugar, baking powder, salt, oregano and pepperoni.
2. In another bowl beat softened cream cheese, gradually adding milk. Add eggs, one at a time, and beat well. Stir in margarine. Add to flour mixture, stirring just until moistened.
3. Spoon batter into prepared muffin tin, filling cups to the top. Bake in preheated oven for about 20 minutes. Serve warm.

Pizza Muffins

1½ cups	chopped pepperoni sausage	375 mL
1	green pepper, seeded and finely chopped	1
1	can (10 oz/284 mL) sliced mushrooms	1
1	medium onion, finely chopped	1
1¼ cups	grated cheese (such as Monterey Jack)	300 mL
½ cup	pizza sauce	125 mL
2 tsp	garlic powder	10 mL
5	eggs	5
¼ cup	vegetable oil	50 mL
1¼ cups	all-purpose flour	300 mL
1 tbsp	baking powder	15 mL

- *Preheat oven to 375°F (190°C)*
- *Muffin tin, greased*

1. In a large bowl combine pepperoni, green pepper, mushrooms, onion, cheese, pizza sauce and garlic powder.
2. In another bowl beat eggs. Blend in oil, then flour and baking powder. Beat until smooth. Stir in pepperoni mixture and mix until well blended.
3. Spoon batter into prepared muffin tin. Bake in preheated oven for 20 to 25 minutes or until lightly browned.

Mini Pumpkin Muffins

1¾ cups	all-purpose flour	425 mL
½ cup	packed brown sugar	125 mL
1 tsp	baking powder	5 mL
½ tsp	baking soda	2 mL
½ tsp	salt	2 mL
½ tsp	cinnamon	2 mL
¼ tsp	ground nutmeg	1 mL
¾ cup	canned pumpkin	175 mL
½ cup	vegetable oil	125 mL
⅔ cup	milk	150 mL

◆ *Preheat oven to 350°F (180°C)*
◆ *Miniature muffin tin, greased*

1. In a large bowl mix together flour, brown sugar, baking powder, baking soda, salt, cinnamon and nutmeg.
2. In another bowl combine pumpkin, oil and milk until well-blended. Add to flour mixture and stir just until moistened and blended. Do not overmix.
3. Spoon batter into prepared miniature muffin tin, filling cups to the top. Bake in preheated oven for 12 to 15 minutes.

Puffed Wheat Morsels

¼ cup	butter or margarine	50 mL
¼ cup	packed brown sugar	50 mL
¼ cup	corn syrup	50 mL
3 cups	sugar-coated puffed wheat cereal (or puffed rice or corn)	750 mL

◆ *Muffin tin, greased or paper-lined*

1. In a heavy saucepan over medium heat, melt butter with sugar and corn syrup. Cook until bubbly and slightly thick. Be careful – it gets very hot. Remove from heat, holding onto handle tightly.
2. Pour in cereal and stir quickly with a wooden spoon. Drop by spoonfuls into prepared muffin tin. Allow to cool before serving.

Quick Mix Muffins

1 cup	buttermilk baking mix	250 mL
3 tbsp	granulated sugar	45 mL
1	egg	1
⅓ cup	water	75 mL

◆ *Preheat oven to 400°F (200°C)*
◆ *6- or 8-cup muffin tin, paper-lined*

1. In a large bowl mix together baking mix, sugar and egg. Add water and beat vigorously with a mixing spoon for 1 minute.
2. Spoon batter evenly into prepared muffin tin. Bake in preheated oven for 15 to 20 minutes.

Variation

◆ Add ¼ cup (50 mL) chopped nuts to batter before spooning into muffin tins.

Spicy Spice Muffins

2 cups	all-purpose flour	500 mL
3 tsp	baking powder	15 mL
1 tsp	salt	5 mL
1 tsp	ground ginger	5 mL
1 tsp	ground nutmeg	5 mL
1 tsp	cinnamon	5 mL
1	egg, well-beaten	1
½ cup	granulated sugar	125 mL
¼ cup	butter or margarine, melted	50 mL
1 cup	milk	250 mL

◆ *Preheat oven to 425°F (220°C)*
◆ *Muffin tin, greased or paper-lined*

1. In a large bowl combine flour, baking powder, salt, ginger, nutmeg and cinnamon.
2. In another bowl combine egg, sugar, melted butter and milk. Add to the flour mixture, stirring just until moistened and blended.
3. Spoon batter into prepared muffin tin, filling cups two-thirds to three-quarters full. Bake in preheated oven for 15 to 20 minutes or until toothpick inserted in the center of a muffin comes out clean and dry.

Special Occasion Muffins

continued on next page

Christmas Morning Muffins

2 cups	all-purpose flour	500 mL
1/2 cup	wheat germ	125 mL
4 tsp	baking powder	20 mL
1 tsp	baking soda	5 mL
1 tsp	salt	5 mL
1/2 cup	granulated sugar	125 mL
1 tsp	ground cardamom	5 mL
1/2 cup	chopped almonds	125 mL
1/2 cup	raisins	125 mL
1 cup	glazed mixed fruit	250 mL
2	eggs	2
1 cup	buttermilk	250 mL
1/2 cup	melted butter or margarine	125 mL

- ◆ *Preheat oven to 375°F (190°C)*
- ◆ *18-cup muffin tin, greased or paper-lined*

1. In a bowl combine flour, wheat germ, baking powder, baking soda, salt, sugar, cardamom, almonds, raisins and mixed fruit.
2. In another bowl whisk together eggs, buttermilk and butter. Add to dry ingredients; stir quickly just until ingredients are moist.
3. Spoon batter into prepared muffin tin, dividing evenly. Bake in preheated oven for 20 to 25 minutes.

Christmas Tea Muffins

2 cups	all-purpose flour	500 mL
1 tbsp	baking powder	15 mL
1/2 cup	granulated sugar	125 mL
1 tsp	salt	5 mL
3/4 cup	milk	175 mL
3 tbsp	maraschino cherry juice	45 mL
1/4 cup	oil	50 mL
1	egg	1
1/3 cup	chopped maraschino cherries	75 mL
1/4 cup	chopped almonds	50 mL

- ◆ *Preheat oven to 375°F (190°C)*
- ◆ *12-cup muffin tin, greased or paper-lined*

1. In a bowl sift together flour, baking powder, sugar and salt.
2. In another bowl whisk together milk, cherry juice, oil and egg. Add to dry ingredients; cherries and almonds. Stir just until blended.
3. Spoon batter into prepared muffin tin, dividing evenly. Bake in preheated oven for 25 minutes.

Traditional Cranberry Muffins

1½ cups	all-purpose flour	375 mL
½ cup	granulated sugar	125 mL
1 tbsp	baking powder	15 mL
¼ tsp	salt	1 mL
1	egg	1
1 cup	milk	250 mL
⅓ cup	melted butter or margarine	75 mL
1 cup	fresh cranberries or frozen cranberries, thawed and drained	250 mL
½ cup	chopped nuts	125 mL

- *Preheat oven to 375°F (190°C)*
- *12-cup muffin tin, greased*

1. In a bowl combine flour, sugar, baking powder and salt.
2. In another bowl whisk together egg, milk and butter. Add to dry ingredients; stir just until moist and blended. Fold in cranberries and nuts.
3. Spoon batter into prepared muffin tin, dividing evenly. Bake in preheated oven for 20 to 25 minutes.

Cranberry-Filled Almond Muffins

1½ cups	all-purpose flour	375 mL
½ cup	granulated sugar	125 mL
1 tsp	baking powder	5 mL
¼ tsp	baking soda	1 mL
¼ tsp	salt	1 mL
2	eggs	2
¼ cup	melted margarine	50 mL
½ cup	sour cream	125 mL
½ tsp	almond extract	2 mL
½ cup	sliced almonds	125 mL
FILLING		
½ cup	whole berry cranberry sauce	125 mL
¼ cup	sliced almonds	50 mL

- *Preheat oven to 375°F (190°C)*
- *Muffin tin, greased or paper-lined*

1. In a bowl combine flour, sugar, baking powder, baking soda and salt.
2. In another bowl whisk together eggs, margarine, sour cream and almond extract; blend well. Add almonds. Add to flour mixture; stir just until blended.
3. Spoon batter into prepared muffin tin, filling half full. Add 1 tbsp (15 mL) cranberry sauce to each; top with remaining batter. Sprinkle evenly with almonds. Bake in preheated oven for 30 to 35 minutes or until golden brown.

Cranberry Applesauce Muffins

1¾ cups	all-purpose flour	425 mL
¼ cup	granulated sugar	50 mL
1½ tsp	baking powder	7 mL
½ tsp	baking soda	2 mL
½ tsp	salt	2 mL
1	egg	1
¾ cup	milk	175 mL
¾ cup	sweetened applesauce	175 mL
¼ cup	melted butter or margarine	50 mL
1 cup	coarsely chopped cranberries	250 mL
2 tbsp	all-purpose flour	25 mL
TOPPING		
¼ cup	granulated sugar	50 mL
½ tsp	cinnamon	2 mL

◆ *Preheat oven to 400°F (200°C)*
◆ *12-cup muffin tin, greased*

1. In a bowl combine flour, sugar, baking powder, baking soda and salt. Make a well in the center.
2. In another bowl combine egg, milk, applesauce and butter; mix well. Add to flour mixture; stir quickly just until batter is moist.
3. In another bowl combine cranberries and flour; toss well. Fold into batter.
4. Spoon batter into prepared muffin tin, filling three-quarters full. Sprinkle tops with sugar and cinnamon. Bake in preheated oven for 20 to 25 minutes.

Apricot Cranberry Bran Muffins

1¾ cups	all-purpose flour	425 mL
⅓ cup	packed brown sugar	75 mL
2 tsp	baking powder	10 mL
½ tsp	salt	2 mL
2	eggs	2
⅔ cup	orange juice	150 mL
2 tsp	grated orange zest	10 mL
¼ cup	vegetable oil	50 mL
1 cup	all-bran cereal	250 mL
⅔ cup	chopped dried apricots	150 mL
¾ cup	whole berry cranberry sauce	175 mL

◆ *Preheat oven to 400°F (200°C)*
◆ *12-cup muffin tin, greased or paper-lined*

1. In a bowl combine flour, brown sugar, baking powder and salt. Make a well in the center.
2. In another bowl whisk together eggs, orange juice, orange zest and oil. Add cereal and apricots; blend well. Add to flour mixture; stir just until blended. Fold in cranberry sauce.
3. Spoon batter into prepared muffin tin, dividing evenly. Bake in preheated oven for 25 to 30 minutes or until golden brown.

Cranberry Banana Breakfast Muffins

2 cups	uncooked oat bran hot cereal	500 mL
½ cup	firmly packed brown sugar	125 mL
¼ cup	all-purpose flour	50 mL
2 tsp	baking powder	10 mL
½ tsp	salt	2 mL
½ tsp	cinnamon	2 mL
½ cup	finely chopped cranberries	125 mL
⅔ cup	cranberry juice	150 mL
½ cup	ripe mashed bananas	125 mL
2	egg whites, slightly beaten	2
3 tbsp	vegetable oil	45 mL

♦ *Preheat oven to 400°F (200°C)*
♦ *12-cup muffin tin, greased or paper-lined*

1. In a bowl combine oat bran, brown sugar, flour, baking powder, salt and cinnamon. Add cranberries; stir gently.

2. In another bowl combine cranberry juice, bananas, egg whites and oil. Add to dry ingredients; mix just until moist and blended.

3. Spoon batter into prepared muffin tin, filling to top. Bake in preheated oven for 20 to 25 minutes or until golden brown.

Cranberry Honey Muffins

⅓ cup	softened margarine	75 mL
⅓ cup	honey	75 mL
1	egg, well-beaten	1
1¼ cups	chopped cranberries or thick cranberry sauce	300 mL
	Grated zest of 1 orange	
⅔ cup	milk	150 mL
2 cups	all-purpose flour	500 mL
1 tbsp	baking powder	15 mL
1 tsp	salt	5 mL

♦ *Preheat oven to 400°F (200°C)*
♦ *Muffin tin, greased or paper-lined*

1. In a bowl cream together margarine and honey. Add egg, cranberries, orange zest and milk; mix well.

2. In another bowl combine flour, baking powder and salt. Add to cranberry mixture; stir just until ingredients are moist.

3. Spoon batter into prepared muffin tin, filling three-quarters full. Bake in preheated oven for about 20 minutes.

Cranberry Fruitcake Muffins

⅔ cup	all-purpose flour	150 mL
⅔ cup	whole wheat flour	150 mL
½ cup	rolled oats	125 mL
1½ tsp	baking soda	7 mL
1 tsp	ginger	5 mL
2	eggs	2
½ cup	honey	125 mL
⅓ cup	orange juice	75 mL
¼ cup	oil	50 mL
1 tsp	vanilla	5 mL
1 cup	cranberries	250 mL
¾ cup	shredded apples	175 mL

◆ *Preheat oven to 400°F (200°C)*
◆ *Muffin tin, greased or paper-lined*

1. In a bowl combine all-purpose flour, whole wheat flour, oats, baking soda and ginger.
2. In another bowl whisk together eggs, honey, orange juice, oil and vanilla. Add cranberries and apples; stir well. Add to flour mixture; stir just until blended.
3. Spoon batter into prepared muffin tin, filling three-quarters full. Bake in preheated oven for 15 to 20 minutes.

Cranberry Nut Muffins

2 cups	all-purpose flour	500 mL
¾ cup	granulated sugar	175 mL
½ cup	chopped nuts	125 mL
1 tsp	baking powder	5 mL
1 tsp	baking soda	5 mL
2 tsp	grated orange zest	10 mL
¾ cup	mayonnaise	175 mL
¼ cup	frozen undiluted orange juice concentrate, thawed	50 mL
2	eggs, beaten	2
2 cups	fresh or frozen whole cranberries	500 mL

◆ *Preheat oven to 350°F (180°C)*
◆ *12-cup muffin tin, greased*

1. In a bowl combine flour, sugar, nuts, baking powder, baking soda and orange zest.
2. In another bowl combine mayonnaise, orange juice, eggs and cranberries; mix well. Add to flour mixture; stir just until blended.
3. Spoon batter into prepared muffin tin, filling to top. Bake in preheated oven for 20 to 25 minutes.

Orange Upside-Down Cranberry Muffin

	Frozen orange juice concentrate	
	Granulated sugar	
2½ cups	all-purpose flour	625 mL
⅓ cup	granulated sugar	75 mL
1 tsp	salt	5 mL
1 tbsp	baking powder	15 mL
1 tsp	baking soda	5 mL
1 cup	chopped pecans	250 mL
	Grated zest of 2 oranges	
1 cup	whole berry cranberry sauce	250 mL
⅔ cup	orange juice	150 mL
1 tbsp	lemon juice	15 mL
2	eggs	2
¼ cup	oil	50 mL

- *Preheat oven to 375°F (190°C)*
- *15-cup muffin tin, sprayed with vegetable spray*

1. Into each prepared muffin cup spoon 1 tsp (5 mL) frozen concentrate and ½ tsp (2 mL) sugar. Set aside.
2. In a bowl combine flour, sugar, salt, baking powder, baking soda, pecans and orange zest. Make a well in the center.
3. In another bowl whisk together cranberry sauce, orange juice, lemon juice, eggs and oil. Add to flour mixture; stir quickly just until blended.
4. Spoon batter into muffin tin, dividing evenly. Bake in preheated oven for 25 to 30 minutes or until browned. Remove from oven; let stand for 5 minutes. Turn pans upside-down so orange mixture is on top. Spoon any remaining sauce over muffins.

Stuffed Orange Cranberry Muffins

1	large orange, seeds removed and quartered	1
¾ cup	boiling water	175 mL
¼ cup	oil	50 mL
1	egg	1
2 cups	all-purpose flour	500 mL
2 tsp	baking powder	10 mL
1 tsp	baking soda	5 mL
½ tsp	salt	2 mL
¾ cup + 2 tbsp	lightly packed brown sugar	175 mL + 25 mL
¾ cup	cranberries	175 mL
4 oz	cream cheese, cut into 12 pieces	125 g

♦ *Preheat oven to 375°F (190°C)*
♦ *12-cup muffin tin, paper-lined*

1. In a blender combine orange pieces and boiling water; blend until almost smooth. Add oil and egg; blend well.

2. In a bowl combine flour, baking powder, baking soda, salt, brown sugar and cranberries. Add orange mixture; stir quickly just until moist.

3. Spoon batter into prepared muffin tin, filling half full. Add 1 cream cheese piece; top with remaining batter. Bake in preheated oven for 20 to 25 minutes or until lightly browned.

Cranberry Streusel Muffins

STREUSEL TOPPING		
2 tbsp	all-purpose flour	25 mL
2 tbsp	granulated sugar	25 mL
1/4 tsp	cinnamon	1 mL
2 tbsp	butter or margarine	25 mL
MUFFINS		
1/4 cup	softened butter or margarine	50 mL
1/4 cup	granulated sugar	50 mL
1	egg	1
1 tsp	vanilla	5 mL
2 cups	all-purpose flour	500 mL
2 tsp	baking powder	10 mL
Pinch	salt	Pinch
1/2 cup	milk	125 mL
2 cups	coarsely chopped cranberries	500 mL
1/2 cup	icing sugar	125 mL

◆ *Preheat oven to 375°F (190°C)*
◆ *Muffin tin, greased or paper-lined*

1. In a bowl combine flour, sugar and cinnamon. Cut in butter until mixture is crumbly. Set aside.
2. In another bowl combine butter and sugar; cream until light and fluffy. Beat in egg and vanilla.
3. In a bowl combine flour, baking powder and salt. Add to creamed mixture alternately with milk; stir just until moist. In another bowl combine cranberries and icing sugar; fold into batter.
4. Spoon batter into prepared muffin tin, filling two-thirds full. Sprinkle with streusel topping. Bake in preheated oven for 25 to 30 minutes.

Cranberry Swirl Muffins

1/4 cup	shortening	50 mL
1/2 cup	granulated sugar	125 mL
2	egg whites	2
1 1/2 cups	all-purpose flour	375 mL
2 tsp	baking powder	10 mL
1/2 tsp	salt (optional)	2 mL
3/4 cup	milk	175 mL
1/2 cup	cranberry sauce	125 mL

◆ *Preheat oven to 400°F (200°C)*
◆ *12-cup muffin tin, paper-lined*

1. In a bowl cream together shortening and sugar. Add egg whites; beat until fairly smooth. Add flour, baking powder, salt and milk; stir just until blended. Add cranberry sauce; swirl with spatula through batter.
2. Spoon batter into prepared muffin tin, dividing evenly. Bake in preheated oven for 20 minutes or until golden brown.

Cranberry Tea Muffins

2 cups	cake flour	500 mL
1/3 cup	granulated sugar	75 mL
2 tsp	baking powder	10 mL
1/2 tsp	salt	2 mL
2	eggs	2
3/4 cup	milk	175 mL
1/4 cup	melted butter	50 mL
1 cup	freshly chopped whole cranberries	250 mL
1 tsp	grated orange zest	5 mL

◆ *Preheat oven to 400°F (200°C)*
◆ *18-cup muffin tin, greased or paper-lined*

1. In a bowl combine flour, sugar, baking powder and salt.
2. In another bowl whisk together eggs, milk and butter. Add to flour mixture; stir quickly just until blended. Fold in cranberries and orange zest.
3. Spoon batter into prepared muffin tin, dividing evenly. Bake in preheated oven for 20 to 25 minutes.

Cranberry Upside-Down Muffins

¾ cup	whole berry cranberry sauce	175 mL
¼ cup	chopped pecans	50 mL
2 tbsp	granulated sugar	25 mL
¼ tsp	ground nutmeg	1 mL
12	pecan halves	12
½ cup	butter or margarine (room temperature)	125 mL
½ cup	granulated sugar	125 mL
2 tsp	baking powder	10 mL
½ tsp	salt	2 mL
2	large eggs	2
2 cups	all-purpose flour	500 mL
½ cup	buttermilk	125 mL

HINT: Add a few teaspoons of sugar and cinnamon to an empty pie plate and slowly burn over the stove. Your home will smell like a bakery.

◆ *Preheat oven to 375°F (190°C)*
◆ *12-cup muffin tin, greased*

1. In a bowl mix together cranberry sauce, chopped pecans, sugar and nutmeg. Divide evenly amongst muffin tin cups. Press 1 pecan half into center of each cup. Set aside.

2. In a large mixer bowl beat together butter, sugar, baking powder and salt until pale and fluffy. Beat in eggs. Gently stir in flour alternately with buttermilk, beginning and ending with flour.

3. Spoon batter gently over cranberry mixture, filling cups to the top. Bake in preheated oven for about 20 minutes Cool slightly and then invert muffin pan over a plate.

Holiday Gingerbread Muffins

1½ cups all-purpose flour		375 mL
1½ cups whole wheat flour		375 mL
⅓ cup	firmly packed brown sugar	75 mL
3½ tsp	baking powder	17 mL
2 tsp	ginger	10 mL
¾ tsp	cinnamon	4 mL
½ tsp	salt	2 mL
1	egg	1
1¼ cups milk		300 mL
½ cup	molasses	125 mL
½ cup	melted margarine	125 mL

◆ *Preheat oven to 400°F (200°C)*
◆ *12-cup muffin tin, greased or paper-lined*

1. In a bowl combine all-purpose flour, whole wheat flour, brown sugar, baking powder, ginger, cinnamon and salt. Make a well in the center.
2. In another bowl whisk together egg, milk, molasses and margarine. Add to dry ingredients; stir just until moist.
3. Spoon batter into prepared muffin tin, filling to top. Bake in preheated oven for about 20 minutes.

Gingerbread Sour Cream Muffins

1½ cups all-purpose flour		375 mL
1 tsp	baking soda	5 mL
1 tsp	ground ginger	5 mL
¼ tsp	salt	1 mL
2	eggs	2
½ cup	sour cream	125 mL
½ cup	molasses	125 mL
¼ cup	packed brown sugar	50 mL
¼ cup	butter or margarine, melted	50 mL
	Sweetened whipped cream or lemon sauce	

◆ *Preheat oven to 400°F (200°C)*
◆ *Muffin tin, greased*

1. In a medium bowl combine flour, baking soda, ginger and salt.
2. In a large bowl beat eggs with a fork until light. Add sour cream, molasses, sugar and butter, blending well. Add flour mixture, stirring just until moistened and blended.
3. Spoon batter into prepared muffin tin, filling cups three-quarters full. Bake in preheated oven for 15 to 20 minutes. Serve warm topped with whipped cream or lemon sauce.

> **HINT:** No whipped cream? Beat egg whites until stiff and add 1 sliced banana per egg white. Beat again until bananas are dissolved.

Mincemeat Bran Muffins

2¼ cups	all-purpose flour	550 mL
1¼ cups	natural bran	300 mL
2 tsp	baking powder	10 mL
2 tsp	baking soda	10 mL
1 tsp	salt	5 mL
2	eggs, beaten	2
¾ cup	vegetable oil	175 mL
¾ cup	granulated sugar	175 mL
¼ cup	molasses or brown sugar	50 mL
2 cups	milk	500 mL
1½ cups	mincemeat	375 mL

◆ *Preheat oven to 375°F (190°C)*
◆ *2 12-cup muffin tins, greased*

1. In a bowl combine flour, bran, baking powder, baking soda and salt. Make a well in the center.
2. In another bowl beat together eggs, oil and sugar. Add molasses, milk and mincemeat; beat well. Add to dry ingredients; stir just until moist.
3. Spoon batter into prepared muffin tins, filling three-quarters full. Bake in preheated oven for 18 to 20 minutes.

Snow Muffins

2 cups	all-purpose flour	500 mL
1 cup	lightly packed brown sugar	250 mL
1 tbsp	baking powder	15 mL
1 tsp	salt	5 mL
3 tbsp	margarine, melted	45 mL
1 cup	milk	250 mL
1½ cups	snow	375 mL
¾ cup	raisins or currants	175 mL

◆ *Preheat oven to 375°F (190°C)*
◆ *12-cup muffin tin, greased*

1. In a bowl combine flour, brown sugar, baking powder and salt; mix well. Add margarine and milk; mixture will be lumpy. Quickly add snow and raisins; stir just until blended.
2. Spoon batter into prepared muffin tin, dividing evenly. Bake in preheated oven for 20 to 25 minutes or until lightly browned.

MUFFIN STUFF:
At first, when I was given this recipe, I thought it was an April fool's joke!

Before making muffins collect fresh, loosely packed snow.

Passover Apple Muffins

FILLING		
1/3 cup	granulated sugar	75 mL
1½ tsp	cinnamon	7 mL
1 tbsp	margarine, melted	15 mL
MUFFINS		
4	egg yolks	4
2/3 cup	granulated sugar	150 mL
2 cups	grated apples	500 mL
½ tsp	grated lemon zest	2 mL
1 tbsp	lemon juice	15 mL
1 cup	matzo meal	250 mL
½ tsp	cinnamon	2 mL
4	egg whites, stiffly beaten	4
Pinch	salt	Pinch

♦ *Preheat oven to 425°F (220°C)*
♦ *Muffin tin, greased*

1. In a bowl combine sugar, cinnamon and margarine; mix well. Set aside.
2. In another bowl beat together egg yolks and sugar. Add apples, lemon zest, lemon juice, matzo meal and cinnamon; mix well. Fold in egg whites and salt.
3. Spoon some of the batter into prepared muffin tin, filling half full. Sprinkle with filling. Top with remaining batter. Bake in preheated oven for 15 to 20 minutes.

Passover Blueberry Muffins

1 cup	granulated sugar	250 mL
½ cup	oil	125 mL
3	eggs	3
½ cup	cake meal	125 mL
¼ cup	potato starch	50 mL
¼ tsp	salt	1 mL
1	pkg (10 oz/300 g) frozen blueberries, thawed and drained	1
	Cinnamon (optional)	
	Granulated sugar (optional)	

♦ *Preheat oven to 350°F (180°C)*
♦ *Muffin tin, greased or paper-lined*

1. In a bowl combine sugar, oil and eggs; beat well.
2. In another bowl sift together cake meal, potato starch and salt. Add to egg mixture; stir until blended. Fold in blueberries.
3. Spoon batter into prepared muffin tin, filling to top. Sprinkle with cinnamon and sugar. Bake in preheated oven for 30 minutes or until browned.

Passover Cocoa Brownies

½ cup	cocoa powder	125 mL
½ cup	boiling water	125 mL
2	eggs	2
1 cup	granulated sugar	250 mL
½ cup	oil	125 mL
½ cup	cake meal	125 mL
1 tsp	instant coffee, dissolved in 2 tsp (10 mL) water	5 mL
½ cup	chopped walnuts	125 mL

◆ *Preheat oven to 400°F (200°C)*
◆ *Muffin tin, greased*

1. In a bowl combine cocoa and water; mix to form a paste. Set aside.
2. In a bowl combine eggs, sugar and oil; beat until well blended. Add cocoa paste; mix well. Add cake meal, coffee mixture and walnuts.
3. Spoon batter into prepared muffin tin, dividing evenly. Bake in preheated oven for 20 to 25 minutes.

Passover Popovers

½ cup	oil or shortening	125 mL
1½ cups	water	375 mL
2 tbsp	granulated sugar	25 mL
1½ cups	cake meal	375 mL
7	eggs	7

◆ *Preheat oven to 450°F (230°C)*
◆ *Muffin tin, greased*

1. In a saucepan over medium-high heat, combine oil, water and sugar; bring to a boil. Remove from heat. Add cake meal; cool slightly. Add eggs one at a time; beat after each addition.
2. In preheated oven heat prepared muffin tin. Spoon batter into cups, filling three-quarters full. Bake in preheated oven for 20 minutes. Lower heat to 350°F (180°C); bake for another 25 to 30 minutes.

Mashed Potato Muffins

10	medium-sized potatoes	10
1 tsp	salt	5 mL
½ tsp	pepper	2 mL
2 tbsp	oil	25 mL
4	eggs, beaten	4
2	onions, chopped	2

◆ *Preheat oven to 400°F (200°C)*
◆ *2 12-cup muffin tins, greased*

1. In a saucepan of boiling water, cook potatoes until soft. In a bowl combine cooked potatoes, salt, pepper and oil; mash until smooth. Add eggs; mix well.

2. In a frying pan over medium-high heat, cook onions for about 2 minutes. Add to potato mixture; stir well.

3. In preheated oven heat prepared muffin tins. Spoon batter into cups. Bake in preheated oven for 30 to 40 minutes.

Apple Streusel Pumpkin Muffins

STREUSEL TOPPING		
2 tbsp	all-purpose flour	25 mL
1/4 cup	granulated sugar	50 mL
1/2 tsp	cinnamon	2 mL
4 tsp	butter	20 mL
MUFFINS		
2 1/2 cups	all-purpose flour	625 mL
2 cups	granulated sugar	500 mL
1 tsp	baking soda	5 mL
1 tbsp	pumpkin pie spice	15 mL
1/2 tsp	salt	2 mL
2	eggs, beaten	2
1 cup	canned pumpkin	250 mL
1/2 cup	vegetable oil	125 mL
2 cups	finely chopped apples	500 mL

- ◆ *Preheat oven to 375°F (190°C)*
- ◆ *Muffin tin, greased or paper-lined*

1. In a bowl combine flour, sugar and cinnamon. Cut in butter; mix until coarse and crumbly. Set aside.
2. In another bowl combine flour, sugar, baking soda, pumpkin pie spice and salt. Make a well in the center.
3. In another bowl combine eggs, pumpkin and oil; stir just until blended. Add apples; blend well. Add to dry ingredients; stir just until moist.
4. Spoon batter into prepared muffin tin, filling three-quarters full. Sprinkle with topping. Bake in preheated oven for 25 to 30 minutes.

Traditional Pumpkin Muffins

1 cup	all-purpose flour	250 mL
1 cup	whole wheat flour	250 mL
1/2 cup	lightly packed brown sugar	125 mL
1 tbsp	baking powder	15 mL
1 1/2 tsp	cinnamon	7 mL
1/2 tsp	nutmeg	2 mL
2	egg whites	2
1/2 cup	milk	125 mL
1 cup	canned pumpkin	250 mL
1/4 cup	oil	50 mL
1/2 tsp	vanilla	2 mL
3/4 cup	raisins	175 mL

- ◆ *Preheat oven to 400°F (200°C)*
- ◆ *12-cup muffin tin, greased or paper-lined*

1. In a bowl combine all-purpose flour, whole wheat flour, brown sugar, baking powder, cinnamon and nutmeg; blend well. Make a well in the center.
2. In another bowl beat egg whites. Add milk, pumpkin, oil and vanilla; blend well. Add to dry ingredients; stir just until moist. Add raisins.
3. Spoon batter into prepared muffin tin, filling three-quarters full. Bake in preheated oven for 20 to 25 minutes or until browned.

Orange Pumpkin Muffins

1¾ cups	all-purpose flour	425 mL
2½ tsp	baking powder	12 mL
½ tsp	baking soda	2 mL
½ tsp	salt	2 mL
⅔ cup	brown sugar	150 mL
1 tsp	cinnamon	5 mL
¼ tsp	nutmeg	1 mL
Pinch	ginger	Pinch
Pinch	mace	Pinch
1	egg	1
¼ cup	melted butter or margarine, cooled	50 mL
½ cup	milk	125 mL
	Finely grated zest of 1 orange	
½ cup	orange juice	125 mL
¾ cup	canned pumpkin purée	175 mL

- *Preheat oven to 400°F (200°C)*
- *12-cup muffin tin, greased or paper-lined*

1. In a bowl combine flour, baking powder, baking soda, salt, brown sugar, cinnamon, nutmeg, ginger and mace. Make a well in the center.
2. In another bowl whisk together egg, butter, milk, orange zest, orange juice and pumpkin. Add to dry ingredients; stir just until blended.
3. Spoon batter into prepared muffin tin, filling three-quarters full. Bake in preheated oven for about 20 minutes.

Creamy Pumpkin Nut Muffins

CREAM CHEESE FILLING

4 oz	softened cream cheese	115 mL
2 tbsp	packed brown sugar	25 mL
1½ tsp	maple flavoring	7 mL

MUFFINS

2 cups	all-purpose flour	500 mL
¾ cup	packed brown sugar	175 mL
½ cup	chopped walnuts	125 mL
2 tsp	baking powder	10 mL
1 tsp	cinnamon	5 mL
½ tsp	baking soda	2 mL
¼ tsp	salt	1 mL
2	eggs	2
1 cup	pumpkin purée	250 mL
¾ cup	evaporated milk	175 mL
¼ cup	vegetable oil	50 mL
2 tsp	maple flavoring	10 mL

NUT TOPPING

2 tbsp	packed brown sugar	25 mL
¼ cup	chopped walnuts	50 mL

HINT: To keep a bowl from slipping on a working surface, place it on a folded wet towel.

◆ *Preheat oven to 400°F (200°C)*
◆ *Muffin tin, greased or paper-lined*

1. In a bowl mix together cream cheese, brown sugar and maple flavoring until smooth. Set aside.

2. In a large bowl mix together flour, sugar, nuts, baking powder, cinnamon, baking soda and salt. Make a well in the center.

3. In another bowl whisk together eggs, pumpkin, evaporated milk, oil and maple flavoring until well blended. Add to flour mixture, stirring just until moistened and blended. Do not overmix.

4. Spoon batter into prepared muffin tin, filling cups two-thirds full. Add 1 heaping tsp (5 mL) cream cheese filling to each cup. Sprinkle with brown sugar and walnuts. Bake in preheated oven for about 20 minutes.

Afternoon Tea Muffins

1½ cups	all-purpose flour	375 mL
½ cup	granulated sugar	125 mL
¼ tsp	salt	1 mL
2 tsp	baking powder	10 mL
1 tsp	baking soda	5 mL
1 tsp	cinnamon	5 mL
½ tsp	ground nutmeg	2 mL
1¼ cups	raisins	300 mL
2	eggs, beaten	2
1 cup	buttermilk	250 mL
2 tbsp	margarine, melted	25 mL

◆ *Preheat oven to 400°F (200°C)*
◆ *Muffin tin, greased or paper-lined*

1. In a large bowl mix together flour, sugar, salt, baking powder, baking soda, cinnamon and nutmeg. Fold in raisins.

2. In a small bowl whisk together eggs, milk and margarine. Add to dry ingredients, stirring quickly just until moistened. Batter will be lumpy.

3. Spoon batter into prepared muffin tin, filling cups three-quarters full. Bake in preheated oven for 20 to 25 minutes.

Almond Citrus Muffins

½ cup	whole natural almonds	125 mL
1¼ cups	all-purpose flour	300 mL
2 tsp	baking powder	10 mL
¼ tsp	salt	1 mL
1 cup	shredded wheat bran cereal	250 mL
¼ cup	packed brown sugar	50 mL
¾ cup	milk	175 mL
¼ cup	orange juice	50 mL
1 tsp	grated orange zest	5 mL
1	egg	1
¼ cup	vegetable oil or almond oil	50 mL

◆ *Preheat oven to 350°F (180°C)*
◆ *Muffin tin, greased or paper-lined*

1. Spread almonds in a single layer on baking sheet. Bake in preheated oven, stirring occasionally, for 12 to 15 minutes or until lightly toasted. Set aside to cool and then chop toasted almonds. Increase oven temperature to 400°F (200°C).

2. In a large bowl combine flour, baking powder and salt.

3. In a medium bowl combine cereal, sugar, milk, orange juice and zest. Let stand for 2 minutes or until cereal is softened. Add egg and oil, beating well. Stir in almonds. Add to flour mixture and stir until just moistened. Batter will be lumpy.

4. Spoon batter into prepared muffin tin. Bake in preheated oven for 20 minutes or until lightly browned.

Apple Almond Muffins

½ cup	butter (room temperature)	125 mL
½ cup	granulated sugar	125 mL
2 tsp	baking powder	10 mL
½ tsp	salt	2 mL
2	large eggs	2
2 cups	all-purpose flour	500 mL
½ cup	buttermilk	125 mL
1	can (8 oz/250 g) almond paste	1
1 cup	chopped peeled apples	250 mL
	Thin apple slices	
	Warmed honey	

- *Preheat oven to 375°F (190°C)*
- *Muffin tin, greased or paper-lined*

1. In a large mixer bowl beat together butter, sugar, baking powder and salt until pale and fluffy. Beat in eggs. Fold in flour alternately with buttermilk, beginning and ending with flour. Stir until well blended but do not overmix.

2. Crumble almond paste over batter and sprinkle with chopped apples. Stir just until blended.

3. Spoon batter into prepared muffin tin, filling cups two-thirds full. Top each with 2 thin slices of apple. Bake in preheated oven for 20 minutes or until a toothpick inserted in the center comes out dry and clean. Brush tops with 2 tbsp (25 mL) warmed honey.

Apple Cider Muffins

½ cup	packed brown sugar	125 mL
½ cup	vegetable oil	125 mL
¼ cup	molasses	50 mL
1	egg	1
¾ cup	sweet apple cider	175 mL
2	apples, peeled and finely chopped	2
1½ cups	all-purpose flour	375 mL
¾ cup	natural bran	175 mL
1 tbsp	baking powder	15 mL
1 tsp	baking soda	5 mL
½ tsp	salt	2 mL
½ tsp	ground nutmeg	2 mL
1 cup	raisins	250 mL
½ cup	chopped walnuts	125 mL

- *Preheat oven to 400°F (200°C)*
- *Muffin tin, greased or paper-lined*

1. In a bowl mix together sugar, oil, molasses and egg. Stir in cider and apples. Set aside.

2. In a large bowl combine flour, bran, baking powder, baking soda, salt and nutmeg. Add apple mixture, stirring just until blended. Fold in raisins and walnuts.

3. Spoon batter into prepared muffin tin, filling cups three-quarters full. Bake in preheated oven for 15 to 20 minutes.

Mocha Walnut Frosted Muffins ➤
(page 336)

Striped Apple Cinnamon Muffins

2 cups	all-purpose flour	500 mL
¼ cup	granulated sugar	50 mL
3 tsp	baking powder	15 mL
¾ tsp	salt	4 mL
½ cup	finely chopped tart apple	125 mL
1	egg, beaten	1
¾ cup	milk	175 mL
¼ cup	vegetable oil	50 mL
TOPPING		
3 tbsp	granulated sugar	45 mL
1 tsp	cinnamon	5 mL
½ tsp	nutmeg	2 mL
1 cup	thinly sliced tart apple	250 mL

♦ *Preheat oven to 400°F (200°C)*
♦ *Muffin tin, greased or paper-lined*

1. In a large bowl combine flour, sugar, baking powder and salt. Stir in chopped apple.
2. In another bowl combine egg, milk and oil. Add to flour mixture and stir until just moistened and blended. Spoon batter into prepared muffin tin.
3. In a bowl mix together sugar, cinnamon and nutmeg. Coat apple slices with this topping and arrange slices over batter to make stripes. Bake in preheated oven for 20 to 25 minutes.

HINT: To prevent peeled or cut apples or other fruits from turning brown, brush surfaces with lemon juice.

Applesauce Crunch Muffins

1½ cups	all-purpose flour	375 mL
¼ cup	granulated sugar	50 mL
3 tsp	baking powder	15 mL
½ tsp	salt	2 mL
½ tsp	cinnamon	2 mL
1	egg	1
¾ cup	milk	175 mL
3 tbsp	vegetable oil or shortening, melted	45 mL
	Applesauce	
TOPPING		
⅔ cup	lightly packed brown sugar	150 mL
⅓ cup	all-purpose flour	75 mL
2 tbsp	softened butter or margarine	25 mL

♦ *Preheat oven to 400°F (200°C)*
♦ *Muffin tin, paper-lined*

1. In a large bowl sift together flour, sugar, baking powder, salt and cinnamon.
2. In another bowl beat together egg, milk and oil. Pour into flour mixture. Stir just until moistened. Batter will be lumpy.
3. Spoon batter into prepared muffin tin, filling cups two-thirds full. Top each with 1 tsp (5 mL) applesauce.
4. In a small bowl, mix together brown sugar, flour and butter. Sprinkle over batter. Bake in preheated oven for 18 to 20 minutes or until golden brown.

◄ Counter-clockwise from upper right:
Apple and Plum Butter (page 349)
Strawberry Rhubarb Jam *(page 352)*
Orange Marmalade *(page 354)*

Applesauce Snackin' Muffins

¾ cup	all-purpose flour	175 mL
⅔ cup	whole-wheat flour	150 mL
¾ tsp	baking soda	4 mL
1 tsp	cinnamon	5 mL
½ tsp	ground ginger	2 mL
Pinch	ground cloves	Pinch
⅛ tsp	salt	.5 mL
1 cup	applesauce	250 mL
¼ cup	packed brown sugar	50 mL
¼ cup	fancy molasses	50 mL
¼ cup	vegetable oil	50 mL
2	eggs	2
1 cup	raisins	250 mL
ICING (OPTIONAL)		
⅔ cup	icing sugar	150 mL
1 tbsp	apple juice	15 mL

◆ *Preheat oven to 375°F (190°C)*
◆ *Muffin tin, paper-lined*

1. In a large bowl combine all-purpose flour, whole-wheat flour, baking soda, cinnamon, ginger, cloves and salt.
2. In another bowl whisk together applesauce, sugar, molasses, oil and eggs. Fold in raisins. Add to dry ingredients, stirring just until moistened and blended.
3. Spoon batter into prepared muffin tin, filling cups three-quarters full. Bake in preheated oven for 15 to 20 minutes.
4. In a bowl whisk together icing sugar and apple juice. Drizzle over cooled muffins.

Apricot Muffins

1¾ cups	all-purpose flour	425 mL
2½ tsp	baking powder	12 mL
½ tsp	baking soda	2 mL
½ tsp	salt	2 mL
½ cup	chopped pecans	125 mL
2	eggs	2
¼ cup	vegetable oil	50 mL
½ cup	lightly packed brown sugar	125 mL
1	can (14 oz/398 mL) apricots, puréed	1
1 tsp	orange extract	5 mL

◆ *Preheat oven to 400°F (200°C)*
◆ *Muffin tin, greased or paper-lined*

1. In a large bowl combine flour, baking powder, baking soda, salt and pecans.
2. In another bowl beat eggs lightly. Add oil, brown sugar, puréed apricots and orange extract. Add to flour mixture, stirring just until blended. Batter will be lumpy.
3. Spoon batter into prepared muffin tin, filling cups to the top. Bake in preheated oven for 20 to 25 minutes.

HINT: Out of muffin pans? Use aluminum foil muffin or cupcake liners, or custard cups. Place on a cookie sheet and bake as usual.

Chocolate Chip Banana Muffins

2	ripe bananas, mashed	2
1 tsp	baking soda	5 mL
1 tsp	hot water	5 mL
1/2 cup	margarine or vegetable oil	125 mL
3/4 cup	granulated sugar	175 mL
1	egg, beaten	1
1 tsp	vanilla	5 mL
1 1/2 cups	all-purpose flour	375 mL
1 tsp	baking powder	5 mL
1 tsp	salt	5 mL
2/3 cup	chocolate chips	150 mL

◆ *Preheat oven to 425°F (220°C)*
◆ *12-cup muffin tin, greased or paper-lined*

1. In a bowl combine bananas, baking soda and hot water. Set aside.
2. In a large bowl cream together margarine and sugar. Add egg and vanilla. Stir in flour, baking powder and salt, mixing until well blended. Add banana mixture and fold in chocolate chips.
3. Spoon batter into prepared muffin tin, filling cups three-quarters full. Bake in preheated oven for 15 to 20 minutes.

Corn Flakes 'n' Banana Muffins

1 1/4 cups	all-purpose flour	300 mL
1 tbsp	baking powder	15 mL
1/2 tsp	salt	2 mL
1/2 tsp	cinnamon	2 mL
1/4 tsp	ground nutmeg	1 mL
1/2 cup	firmly packed brown sugar	125 mL
2 cups	lightly crushed Corn Flakes	500 mL
1	egg	1
1/3 cup	milk	75 mL
1/4 cup	vegetable oil	50 mL
1 cup	mashed ripe bananas	250 mL

◆ *Preheat oven to 400°F (200°C)*
◆ *Muffin tin, greased*

1. In a medium bowl sift together flour, baking powder, salt, cinnamon, nutmeg, brown sugar and crushed Corn Flakes.
2. In a large bowl combine egg, milk and oil. Stir in banana. Add flour mixture and stir just until blended.
3. Spoon batter into prepared muffin tin, filling cups to the top. Bake in preheated oven for 20 to 25 minutes or until lightly brown.

HINT: Freeze ripe bananas for later use. Peel them and wrap in plastic wrap. Store them in freezer bags.

Banana Crumble Muffins

TOPPING

½ cup	banana nut crunch cereal	125 mL
1 tbsp	packed brown sugar	15 mL
1 tsp	cinnamon	5 mL

MUFFINS

1 tsp	vegetable oil	5 mL
1¼ cups	all-purpose flour	300 mL
1 tbsp	baking powder	15 mL
⅛ tsp	salt	0.5 mL
1	egg	1
½ cup	milk	125 mL
⅓ cup	firmly packed brown sugar	75 mL
3 tbsp	vegetable oil	45 mL
1½ cups	banana nut crunch cereal	375 mL
1 cup	finely chopped bananas	250 mL

HINT: Ripen green bananas by wrapping in a wet dish towel and placing in a paper bag.

◆ *Preheat oven to 400°F (200°C)*
◆ *Muffin tin, greased or paper-lined*

1. In a bowl mix together cereal, brown sugar and cinnamon. Drizzle with oil and mix until topping is crumbly. Set aside.

2. In a large bowl combine flour, baking powder and salt. Make a well in the center.

3. In another bowl whisk egg. Add milk, brown sugar and oil, blending well. Pour into flour mixture and stir just until moistened and blended. Do not overmix. Fold in cereal and bananas.

4. Spoon batter into prepared muffin tin, filling cups three-quarters full. Sprinkle with topping. Bake in preheated oven for 15 to 20 minutes or until lightly browned.

Berry Special Muffins

2 cups	all-purpose flour	500 mL
½ cup	granulated sugar	125 mL
1½ tsp	baking powder	7 mL
½ tsp	baking soda	2 mL
½ tsp	salt	2 mL
1	egg	1
½ cup	orange juice	125 mL
1½ tsp	grated orange zest	7 mL
½ cup	butter or margarine, melted	125 mL
1 cup	coarsely chopped fresh or frozen berries	250 mL

◆ *Preheat oven to 400°F (200°C)*
◆ *Muffin tin, paper-lined*

1. In a large bowl combine flour, sugar, baking powder, baking soda and salt. Make a well in the center.

2. In another bowl whisk together egg, orange juice, zest and margarine until well blended. Add to flour mixture and stir just until moistened and blended. Fold in berries.

3. Spoon batter into prepared muffin tin, filling cups to the top. Bake in preheated oven for 20 minutes or until golden brown.

Coffee Cake Blueberry Muffins

TOPPING

2 tbsp	softened margarine	25 mL
1/2 cup	packed brown sugar	125 mL
1 1/2 tsp	cinnamon	7 mL
1 tbsp	all-purpose flour	15 mL

MUFFINS

3/4 cup	softened margarine	175 mL
3/4 cup	granulated sugar	175 mL
1	egg	1
1 cup	sour cream	250 mL
1 tsp	vanilla	5 mL
2 cups	all-purpose flour	500 mL
1 tsp	baking powder	5 mL
1 tsp	baking soda	5 mL
1/4 tsp	salt	1 mL
2 cups	fresh blueberries or frozen blueberries, thawed and well drained	500 mL

- ◆ *Preheat oven to 400°F (200°C)*
- ◆ *12-cup muffin tin, greased or paper-lined*

1. In a small bowl mix together margarine, brown sugar, cinnamon and flour. Set aside.
2. In a large mixer bowl cream margarine and sugar until light and fluffy. Add egg and blend well on low speed. Stir in sour cream and vanilla. Add flour, baking powder, baking soda and salt. Stir just until moistened and blended.
3. Spoon batter into prepared muffin tin, filling cups half full. Add blueberries and top with remaining batter. Sprinkle with topping. Bake in preheated oven for 15 to 20 minutes or until golden brown.

Spiced Buttermilk Muffins

2 cups	whole-wheat flour	500 mL
2/3 cup	all-purpose flour	150 mL
2/3 cup	packed brown sugar	150 mL
2 tsp	baking soda	10 mL
1 tsp	pumpkin pie spice	5 mL
2 cups	buttermilk	500 mL
3/4 cup	raisins	175 mL

- ◆ *Preheat oven to 350°F (180°C)*
- ◆ *Muffin tin, greased*

1. In a large bowl combine whole-wheat flour, all-purpose flour, sugar, baking soda and pumpkin pie spice. Add buttermilk, stirring just until moistened. Fold in raisins.
2. Spoon batter into prepared muffin tin, filling cups two-thirds full. Bake in preheated oven for 35 to 40 minutes or until toothpick inserted in center comes out clean and dry.

Blueberry Walnut Streusel Muffins

1½ cups	all-purpose flour	375 mL
2 tsp	baking powder	10 mL
½ tsp	salt	2 mL
6 tbsp	softened butter	90 mL
½ cup	granulated sugar	125 mL
1	egg	1
1 tsp	vanilla	5 mL
½ cup	milk	125 mL
1½ cups fresh blueberries		375 mL
WALNUT STREUSEL TOPPING		
2 tbsp	melted butter	25 mL
2 tbsp	packed brown sugar	25 mL
¼ tsp	cinnamon	1 mL
¼ cup	chopped walnuts	50 mL

◆ *Preheat oven to 400°F (200°C)*
◆ *Muffin tin, greased or paper-lined*

1. In a medium bowl combine flour, baking powder and salt.
2. In a large bowl cream butter and sugar until light and fluffy. Beat in egg and vanilla. Add flour mixture alternately with milk. Stir just until moistened and blended. Fold in blueberries.
3. Spoon batter into prepared muffin tin, filling cups two-thirds full. In a bowl combine butter, brown sugar, cinnamon and walnuts. Sprinkle topping over batter. Bake in preheated oven for about 20 minutes.

Lemon Oat Blueberry Muffins

1 cup	all-purpose flour	250 mL
3 tsp	baking powder	15 mL
½ tsp	salt	2 mL
¼ tsp	nutmeg	1 mL
¾ cup	packed brown sugar	175 mL
¾ cup	rolled oats	175 mL
	Finely grated zest of 1 lemon	
1	egg	1
¼ cup	vegetable oil	50 mL
1 cup	milk	250 mL
1	can (14 oz/398 mL) blueberries, drained and patted dry	1

◆ *Preheat oven to 400°F (200°C)*
◆ *Muffin tin, greased or paper-lined*

1. In a large bowl combine flour, baking powder, salt, nutmeg and brown sugar. Stir with a fork until well blended. Add oats and lemon zest.
2. In another bowl whisk together egg, oil and milk. Add to flour mixture, stirring just until blended and moistened. Fold in blueberries.
3. Spoon batter into prepared muffin tin, filling cups three-quarters full. Bake in preheated oven for 15 to 20 minutes.

Caramel Nut-Topped Muffins

TOPPING

½ cup	firmly packed brown sugar	125 mL
¼ cup	margarine	50 mL
½ cup	chopped pecans or walnuts	125 mL

MUFFINS

2	eggs	2
¾ cup	milk	175 mL
½ cup	margarine, melted	125 mL
1½ cups	all-purpose flour	375 mL
1 cup	whole-wheat flour	250 mL
⅓ cup	granulated sugar	75 mL
1 tbsp	baking powder	15 mL
1 tsp	cinnamon	5 mL
½ tsp	salt	2 mL
1 tbsp	baking powder	15 mL
1 tsp	cinnamon	5 mL
½ tsp	salt	2 mL

- ◆ *Preheat oven to 400°F (200°C)*
- ◆ *12-cup muffin tin*

1. Into each muffin cup measure 2 tsp (10 mL) brown sugar and 1 tsp (5 mL) margarine. Place in preheated oven for 2 minutes to melt. Remove from oven and add 2 tsp (10 mL) nuts to each cup. Set aside.

2. In a bowl beat eggs with a fork. Blend in milk and melted margarine.

3. In a large bowl combine all-purpose flour, whole-wheat flour, sugar, baking powder, cinnamon and salt. Add liquid mixture, stirring just until moistened and blended. Do not overmix.

4. Spoon batter into muffin tin. Bake in preheated oven for about 20 minutes. Invert pan onto a plate so caramel nut topping is on top. Serve warm.

Cream Cheese Carrot Muffins

1	pkg (8 oz/250 g) softened cream cheese	1
⅓ cup	granulated sugar	75 mL
1	egg	1
1½ cups	all-purpose flour	375 mL
1 tsp	baking powder	5 mL
1 tsp	baking soda	5 mL
½ tsp	cinnamon	2 mL
½ cup	packed brown sugar	125 mL
⅓ cup	vegetable oil	75 mL
2	eggs	2
⅔ cup	plain yogurt	150 mL
1 cup	finely grated carrots	250 mL
½ cup	finely chopped walnuts	125 mL

- ◆ *Preheat oven to 350°F (180°C)*
- ◆ *12-cup muffin tin, greased or paper-lined*

1. In a small bowl whisk together cream cheese, sugar and 1 egg. Set aside.

2. In a large bowl combine flour, baking powder, baking soda and cinnamon.

3. In another bowl combine brown sugar, oil, 2 eggs and yogurt. Stir in carrots and walnuts. Add to flour mixture and stir just until moistened.

4. Spoon about 2 tbsp (25 mL) batter into muffin tin. Top with heaping spoonfuls of cream cheese mixture and top with remaining batter. Bake in preheated oven for about 20 minutes.

Mini Cheesecakes

2	pkgs (8 oz/250 g each) softened cream cheese	2
1/2 cup	granulated sugar	125 mL
1 tsp	vanilla	5 mL
2	eggs	2
12	vanilla wafers	12
	Jam, nuts, chocolate curls etc.	

♦ *Preheat oven to 325°F (160°C)*
♦ *12-cup muffin tin, foil-lined*

1. In a large mixer bowl combine cheese, sugar and vanilla. Blend on medium speed until smooth. Add eggs, blending well.
2. Put 1 vanilla wafer in each cup. Spoon cheese mixture over wafers, filling cups three-quarters full. Bake in preheated oven for 25 minutes. Set aside to cool. Remove from tin and chill in refrigerator before serving. Top with whatever you like.

Variation

♦ For a special flavor, use 1/2 tsp (2 mL) rum or almond flavoring in place of the vanilla.

Cheese Muffin Ring

1 1/2 cups	sifted cake flour	375 mL
2 tsp	baking powder	10 mL
1/2 tsp	salt	2 mL
3/4 cup	grated cheese (any type)	175 mL
1	egg, well beaten	1
1/2 cup	milk	125 mL
1 tbsp	butter or shortening, melted	15 mL

♦ *Preheat oven to 425°F (220°C)*
♦ *Ring mold, greased*

1. In a large bowl sift together flour, baking powder and salt. Add cheese and blend together well.
2. In another bowl combine egg, milk and melted butter. Add to dry ingredients, stirring just until moistened and blended.
3. Spoon batter into prepared ring mold. Bake in preheated oven for 25 minutes.

MUFFIN STUFF: Serve with scrambled eggs or vegetables.

Chocolate Cinnamon Muffins

½ cup	softened butter or margarine	125 mL
½ cup	granulated sugar	125 mL
2 tsp	baking powder	10 mL
½ tsp	salt	2 mL
2	eggs	2
2 cups	all-purpose flour	500 mL
1 tsp	cinnamon	5 mL
½ cup	buttermilk	125 mL
1 cup	melted semi-sweet chocolate chips	500 mL
4 oz	cream cheese, cut-up	125 g
2 tbsp	granulated sugar	25 mL
½ tsp	cinnamon	2 mL

◆ *Preheat oven to 375°F (190°C)*
◆ *Muffin tin, greased or paper-lined*

1. In a large mixer bowl beat together butter, sugar, baking powder and salt until pale and fluffy. Beat in eggs.

2. In another bowl mix together flour and cinnamon. Slowly stir into butter mixture alternately with buttermilk just until moistened and blended. Do not overmix. Fold in melted chocolate just until blended.

3. Spoon batter into prepared muffin tin, filling cups two-thirds full. Press pieces of cream cheese into top of batter in each cup. Sprinkle with sugar and cinnamon. Bake in preheated oven for about 20 minutes.

Mini Cinnamon Breakfast Muffins

1½ cups	all-purpose flour	375 mL
½ cup	granulated sugar	125 mL
2 tsp	baking powder	10 mL
½ tsp	salt	2 mL
½ tsp	ground allspice	2 mL
½ tsp	ground nutmeg	2 mL
1	egg, lightly beaten	1
½ cup	milk (2% or skim)	125 mL
⅓ cup	butter or margarine, melted	75 mL

◆ *Preheat oven to 400°F (200°C)*
◆ *Muffin tin, greased or paper-lined*

1. In a large bowl mix together flour, sugar, baking powder, salt, allspice and nutmeg. Make a well in the center.

2. In another bowl combine egg, milk and margarine, beating until well blended. Add to dry ingredients, stirring only until moistened and blended. Do not overmix.

3. Spoon batter into prepared muffin tin, filling cups to the top. Bake in preheated oven for 12 to 14 minutes or until muffins are done.

MUFFIN STUFF: For an extra delicious muffin, melt ¼ cup (50 mL) margarine and brush over tops of warm muffins. Mix together ½ tsp (2 mL) cinnamon and 2 tbsp (25 mL) sugar and sprinkle over tops.

Morning Glory Corn Muffins

1 cup	all-purpose flour	250 mL
¾ cup	yellow cornmeal	175 mL
3 tbsp	granulated sugar	45 mL
1 tbsp	double-acting baking powder	15 mL
1 tsp	salt	5 mL
1	egg	1
¾ cup	milk	175 mL
⅓ cup	butter or margarine, melted	75 mL

◆ *Preheat oven to 400°F (200°C)*
◆ *Muffin tin, greased or paper-lined*

1. In a large bowl with a fork combine flour, cornmeal, sugar, baking powder and salt. Make a well in the center.
2. In another bowl with a fork mix together egg, milk and butter. Add to flour mixture, stirring just until flour is moistened. Do not overmix.
3. Spoon batter into prepared muffin tin, filling cups three-quarters full. Bake in preheated oven for 20 minutes or until lightly browned.

Kernel Krunch Corn Muffins

¾ cup	softened unsalted butter	175 mL
¾ cup	granulated sugar	175 mL
3	large eggs	3
1⅔ cups	all-purpose flour	400 mL
1⅔ cups	yellow cornmeal	400 mL
4 tsp	baking powder	20 mL
½ tsp	salt	2 mL
2 cups	milk	500 mL
1 cup	drained whole corn kernels	250 mL

HINT: Never double the amount of salt when you double a recipe. Season according to taste.

◆ *Preheat oven to 425°F (220°C)*
◆ *Muffin tin, greased or paper-lined*

1. In a large bowl cream together butter and sugar until fluffy. Beat in eggs one at a time, beating well after each addition.
2. In another bowl mix together flour, cornmeal, baking powder and salt. Add to creamed mixture alternately with milk, mixing on low speed, beginning and ending with dry ingredients. Fold in corn.
3. Spoon batter into prepared muffin tin, filling cups to the top. Bake in preheated oven for 20 minutes.

Old-Fashioned Corn Bread Muffins

1½ cups	yellow cornmeal	375 mL
1½ tsp	baking powder	7 mL
1 tsp	salt	5 mL
¾ tsp	baking soda	4 mL
1	egg	1
1½ cups	buttermilk	375 mL
¼ cup	shortening, melted	50 mL

> **MUFFIN STUFF:** These are made with cornmeal only, no flour. It makes them crispy outside and moist inside.

♦ *Preheat oven to 425°F (220°C)*
♦ *12-cup muffin tin, greased*

1. In a large bowl combine cornmeal, baking powder, salt and baking soda until well blended. Make a well in the center.
2. In another bowl beat together egg and buttermilk. Add to dry ingredients, stirring until thin and smooth. Stir in melted shortening.
3. Heat muffin tin in preheated oven. Spoon batter into hot tin and then bake for 18 to 20 minutes or until crusty and golden brown. Serve hot.

Creamy Muffin Curls

2 cups	all-purpose flour	500 mL
4 tsp	baking powder	20 mL
½ tsp	salt	2 mL
4 tbsp	shortening	60 mL
⅔ cup	milk	150 mL
3 tbsp	creamed butter	45 mL
½ cup	packed brown sugar	125 mL

> **MUFFIN STUFF:** Centers of rolls curl up and will be glazed on edges.

♦ *Preheat oven to 375°F (190°C)*
♦ *Muffin tin, greased*

1. In a large bowl with a fork mix together flour, baking powder and salt. Add shortening and then milk, blending to make a soft dough. Knead slightly and then roll out to ¼ inch (5 mm) thick.
2. Spread with creamed butter and sprinkle with brown sugar. Roll up like a jelly roll. Cut into 1-inch (2.5 cm) pieces. Stand rolls on end in prepared muffin tin. Bake in preheated oven for 30 minutes.

Cinnamon Coffee Cake Muffins

FILLING

¼ cup	all-purpose flour	50 mL
2 tbsp	granulated sugar	25 mL
½ tsp	cinnamon	2 mL
2 tbsp	butter or margarine	25 mL

MUFFINS

1⅓ cups	all-purpose flour	325 mL
1 cup	whole-wheat flour	250 mL
½ cup	packed brown sugar	125 mL
1 tbsp	baking powder	15 mL
1 tbsp	cinnamon	15 mL
½ tsp	salt	2 mL
⅓ cup	butter or margarine	75 mL
2	eggs	2
1½ cups	milk	375 mL
½ cup	raisins	125 mL

> **MUFFIN STUFF:** Cutting in butter produces a lighter, cake-like texture in these muffins.

- *Preheat oven to 400°F (200°C)*
- *Muffin tin, greased or paper-lined*

1. In a small bowl mix together flour, sugar and cinnamon. With a pastry blender or 2 knives, cut in 2 tbsp (25 mL) butter until mixture resembles coarse crumbs. Set aside.

2. In a large bowl combine all-purpose flour, whole-wheat flour, brown sugar, baking powder, cinnamon and salt. Cut in butter. Make a well in the center.

3. In another bowl whisk together eggs and milk until blended. Add to flour mixture, stirring only until moistened. Fold in raisins.

4. Spoon batter into prepared muffin tin, filling cups only half full. Add 1 tbsp (15 mL) filling to each and top with remaining batter. Sprinkle any remaining filling on top. Bake in preheated oven for 20 minutes or until firm to the touch.

Island Fruit Muffins

2¼ cups	oat bran	550 mL
⅔ cup	all-purpose flour	150 mL
⅔ cup	whole-wheat flour	150 mL
1 tsp	baking powder	5 mL
2½ tsp	baking soda	12 mL
¼ tsp	salt	1 mL
1½ cups	golden raisins	375 mL
1¼ cups	shredded coconut	300 mL
2	eggs	2
1 cup	buttermilk	250 mL
½ cup	vegetable oil	125 mL
1 cup	mashed bananas	250 mL
½ cup	honey	125 mL

- *Preheat oven to 375°F (190°C)*
- *Muffin tin, greased or paper-lined*

1. In a large bowl combine oat bran, all-purpose flour, whole-wheat flour, baking powder, baking soda, salt, raisins and coconut.
2. In another bowl whisk together eggs, buttermilk, oil, bananas and honey. Add to dry ingredients, stirring just until moistened and blended. Do not overmix.
3. Spoon batter into prepared muffin tin, filling cups three-quarters full. Bake in preheated oven for 20 to 25 minutes or until browned.

HINT: To tint coconut, place 1⅓ cups (325 mL) flaked coconut in a jar. Add a few drops of food coloring, screw on lid and shake well.

Fresh Fruit Muffins

2 cups	all-purpose flour	500 mL
½ cup	granulated sugar	125 mL
⅓ cup	skim milk powder	75 mL
1 tbsp	baking powder	15 mL
½ tsp	salt	2 mL
1	egg	1
½ cup	margarine, melted	125 mL
½ cup	milk (2% or skim)	125 mL
1 cup	chopped fresh fruit	250 mL
1 tsp	lemon juice	5 mL
½ tsp	grated lemon zest	2 mL

- *Preheat oven to 400°F (200°C)*
- *12-cup muffin tin, lightly greased*

1. In a large bowl combine flour, sugar, skim milk powder, baking powder and salt.
2. In another bowl whisk together egg, margarine and milk until blended. Add fruit, lemon juice and zest. Add to flour mixture, stirring just until blended. Batter will be lumpy.
3. Spoon batter evenly into prepared muffin tin. Bake in preheated oven for 15 to 20 minutes or until golden brown.

HINT: The key to tender muffins is not to overmix. Just mix ingredients until no flour is visible.

Lemon Berry Streusel Muffins

TOPPING

¼ cup	butter or margarine, melted	50 mL
½ cup	all-purpose flour	125 mL
2 tbsp	granulated sugar	25 mL
1½ tsp	finely grated lemon zest	7 mL

MUFFINS

2½ cups	all-purpose flour	625 mL
2 tsp	baking powder	10 mL
1 tsp	baking soda	5 mL
1¼ cups	granulated sugar	300 mL
1 tbsp	finely shredded lemon	15 mL
1	egg	1
1 cup	buttermilk	250 mL
½ cup	butter or margarine, melted	125 mL
1 tbsp	lemon juice	15 mL
1½ cups	frozen berries (any kind), coated with 1 tbsp (15 mL) flour	375 mL

- *Preheat oven to 400°F (200°C)*
- *Muffin tin, paper-lined*

1. In a bowl mix together butter, flour, sugar and zest. Set aside.
2. In a large bowl combine flour, baking powder, baking soda, sugar and lemon zest.
3. In another bowl whisk together egg, buttermilk, melted butter and lemon juice. Add to dry ingredients, stirring just until moistened and blended. Fold in berries.
4. Spoon batter into prepared muffin tin, filling cups two-thirds full. Crumble reserved topping over tops. Bake in preheated oven for 20 minutes or until lightly browned.

Lemon Pepper Muffins

2 cups	all-purpose flour	500 mL
½ cup	granulated sugar	125 mL
2 tsp	baking powder	10 mL
½ tsp	baking soda	2 mL
½ tsp	salt	2 mL
¾ tsp	freshly ground black pepper	4 mL
	Finely grated zest of 1 lemon	
1 cup	milk	250 mL
	Juice of 1 lemon	
1	egg	1
⅓ cup	butter, melted	75 mL

HINT: Freeze grated zest from lemons and oranges in small plastic yogurt cups.

◆ *Preheat oven to 400°F (200°C)*
◆ *Muffin tin, greased or paper-lined*

1. In a large bowl combine flour, sugar, baking powder, baking soda, salt and pepper. Stir until well blended. Add lemon zest and mix until well coated. Make a well in the center.
2. In another bowl whisk together milk, lemon juice and egg. Add to dry ingredients at once. (Milk mixture may look curdled.) Stir just until well blended. Add butter and blend together.
3. Spoon batter into prepared muffin tin, filling cups three-quarters full. Bake in preheated oven for 15 to 20 minutes or until toothpick inserted in center comes out clean.

Mexican Muffins

1 cup	milk	250 mL
¼ cup	butter, melted	50 mL
2	eggs, beaten	2
2 cups	all-purpose flour	500 mL
2 tsp	baking powder	10 mL
2 tsp	ground cumin	10 mL
½ tsp	salt	2 mL
½ cup	chopped fresh cilantro	125 mL

◆ *Preheat oven to 400°F (200°C)*
◆ *Muffin tin, greased*

1. In a medium bowl whisk together milk, butter and eggs.
2. In another bowl combine flour, baking powder, cumin and salt. Add to milk mixture and stir just until blended. Stir in cilantro.
3. Spoon batter into prepared muffin tin, filling cups to the top. Bake in preheated oven about 15 minutes or until toothpick inserted in center comes out clean and dry.

Mocha Walnut Frosted Muffins

½ cup	softened butter or margarine	125 mL
1 cup	granulated sugar	250 mL
2 cups	all-purpose flour	500 mL
3 tsp	baking powder	15 mL
¼ tsp	salt	1 mL
½ cup	cold strong coffee	125 mL
¾ cup	chopped walnuts	175 mL
3	egg whites, stiffly beaten	3
FROSTING		
3 tbsp	softened butter	45 mL
1 cup	icing sugar	250 mL
1 tbsp	powdered cocoa	15 mL
2 tbsp	strong coffee	25 mL

HINT: To make icing with a smooth glazed surface, use liquid hot.

♦ *Preheat oven to 350°F (180°C)*
♦ *Muffin tin, greased or paper-lined*

1. In a large bowl cream butter thoroughly. Add sugar gradually, beating well.
2. In another bowl mix together flour, baking powder and salt. Add to creamed mixture alternately with coffee. Stir thoroughly until well blended. Add chopped walnuts. Fold in egg whites.
3. Spoon batter into prepared muffin tin, filling cups two-thirds full. Bake in preheated oven for 25 minutes.
4. In a bowl cream together butter and 2 tbsp (25 mL) icing sugar. Add coffee, remaining icing sugar and cocoa. Beat until light and fluffy. Spread over cooled muffins.

Cocoa Nut Oatmeal Muffins

½ cup	margarine, melted	125 mL
2	eggs	2
1 cup	milk	250 mL
1 tsp	vanilla	5 mL
1¼ cups	all-purpose flour	300 mL
¾ cup	oats	175 mL
1 cup	granulated sugar	250 mL
⅓ cup	cocoa	75 mL
1 tbsp	baking powder	15 mL
1 tsp	salt	5 mL
1 cup	chopped nuts	250 mL

HINT: Try ice cream muffins! Soften 2 or 3 different flavors of ice cream. Fill muffin tins one-third full with one flavor. Smooth out into bottoms of cups and then layer with the other flavors. Freeze, unmold and then decorate as you wish.

♦ *Preheat oven to 400°F (200°C)*
♦ *Muffin tin, greased or paper-lined*

1. In a small bowl whisk together margarine, eggs, milk and vanilla.
2. In a large bowl mix together flour, oats, sugar, cocoa, baking powder and salt. Add egg mixture, stirring just until moistened and blended. Fold in chopped nuts.
3. Spoon batter into prepared muffin tin, filling cups to the top. Bake in preheated oven for 15 to 20 minutes or until toothpick inserted in the center comes out clean and dry.

Almond Orange Muffins

2¼ cups	all-purpose flour	550 mL
½ cup	granulated sugar	125 mL
2½ tsp	baking powder	12 mL
½ tsp	baking soda	2 mL
¼ cup	sliced almonds	50 mL
½ cup	skim milk	125 mL
½ cup	orange juice	125 mL
¼ cup	butter or margarine, melted	50 mL
2	egg whites	2
1 tsp	grated orange zest	5 mL

♦ *Preheat oven to 375°F (190°C)*
♦ *Muffin tin, lightly greased or paper-lined*

1. In a large bowl combine flour, sugar, baking powder and baking soda. Stir in almonds.
2. In a small bowl combine milk, orange juice, melted butter, egg whites and orange zest. Mix until well blended. Add to flour mixture, stirring lightly just until moistened and blended. Batter will be lumpy.
3. Spoon batter into prepared muffin tin, dividing equally. Bake in preheated oven for 15 to 20 minutes.

Miniature Orange-Dipped Muffins

½ cup	softened butter	125 mL
1 cup	granulated sugar	250 mL
2 cups	all-purpose flour	500 mL
1 tsp	baking soda	5 mL
1 tsp	salt	5 mL
1 tsp	grated orange zest	5 mL
¾ cup	sour cream	175 mL
½ cup	raisins	125 mL
½ cup	chopped nuts	125 mL
DIP		
1 cup	granulated sugar	250 mL
½ cup	orange juice	125 mL

HINT: Soften butter quickly by grating it.

♦ *Preheat oven to 375°F (190°C)*
♦ *Miniature muffin tins, well-greased*

1. In a large bowl cream together butter and sugar until smooth.
2. In another bowl combine flour, baking soda, salt and zest. Add to creamed mixture alternately with sour cream, stirring just until blended. Do not overmix. Fold in raisins and chopped nuts.
3. Spoon batter into prepared muffin tins. Bake in preheated oven for 12 to 15 minutes.
4. In a bowl combine sugar and orange juice. Dip warm muffins into this mixture.

Orange Sunbursts

5	oranges	5
½ cup	snipped dates	125 mL
¼ cup	flaked coconut	50 mL
Dash	aromatic bitters	Dash
	Marshmallows	

HINT: To cut sticky ingredients like prunes, dates or marshmallows, dip kitchen shears in hot water often, or rub the blades with vegetable oil.

◆ *Preheat oven to 325°F (160°C)*
◆ *Oblong baking dish*

1. Cut tops off oranges with a grapefruit knife. Scoop out pulp and chop.
2. In a bowl combine pulp, dates, coconut and bitters. Spoon mixture into orange shells and place in baking dish. Pour a little water around oranges.
3. Bake in preheated oven for 25 minutes. Top each orange with a marshmallow and continue baking for 8 to 10 minutes or until marshmallows are golden.

Spicy Orange and Sweet Potato Muffins

1 cup	all-purpose flour	250 mL
1 cup	whole-wheat flour	250 mL
2 tsp	baking powder	10 mL
2 tsp	baking soda	10 mL
1 tsp	cinnamon	5 mL
½ tsp	ground nutmeg	2 mL
½ tsp	ground allspice	2 mL
1	can (16 oz/455 mL) sweet potatoes, drained	1
⅔ cup	firmly packed brown sugar	150 mL
2	eggs	2
1 cup	orange juice	250 mL
1	carrot, shredded	1
1 tsp	vanilla	5 mL

HINT: For long-term storage of eggs, crack them open into an ice-cube tray. When completely frozen, put egg cubes in a sealed freezer bag and use as needed.

◆ *Preheat oven to 400°F (200°C)*
◆ *Muffin tin, greased or paper-lined*

1. In a medium bowl combine all-purpose flour, whole-wheat flour, baking powder, baking soda, cinnamon, nutmeg and allspice.
2. In a large bowl mash sweet potatoes. Add brown sugar, eggs, orange juice, carrot and vanilla. Mix together until well blended. Add flour mixture, stirring just until moistened and blended. Do not overmix.
3. Spoon batter into prepared muffin tin, filling cups to the top. Bake in preheated oven for 15 to 20 minutes or until golden brown. Serve warm.

Orange Tea Muffins

1½ cups	all-purpose flour	375 mL
½ cup	granulated sugar	125 mL
2 tsp	baking powder	10 mL
½ tsp	salt	2 mL
½ cup	butter or margarine, melted	125 mL
	Grated zest of 1 orange	
½ cup	fresh orange juice	125 mL
2	eggs	2
1 cup	fresh or frozen raspberries (optional)	250 mL
½ cup	sweetened flaked coconut (optional)	125 mL

* *Preheat oven to 375°F (190°C)*
* *12-cup muffin tin, greased or paper-lined*

1. In a large bowl, combine flour, sugar, baking powder and salt.
2. In another bowl, combine melted butter, orange zest, orange juice and eggs, mixing well. If desired, add raspberries and coconut. Add to flour mixture, stirring just until moist and blended.
3. Spoon batter into prepared muffin tin, dividing evenly. Bake in preheated oven for 15 to 20 minutes (22 to 25 if using raspberries and coconut) or until lightly browned.

Peanut Butter Surprise Muffins

1 cup	all-purpose flour	250 mL
½ tsp	salt	2 mL
3 tsp	baking powder	15 mL
1 tbsp	granulated sugar	15 mL
½ cup	cornmeal	125 mL
1 cup	milk	250 mL
1	egg, beaten	1
¼ cup	peanut butter	50 mL
1 tbsp	shortening, melted	15 mL

* *Preheat oven to 375°F (190°C)*
* *12-cup muffin tin, greased or paper-lined*

1. In a large bowl combine flour, salt, baking powder and sugar. Stir in cornmeal, mixing to blend well.
2. In a small bowl combine milk, egg, peanut butter and melted shortening. Add to dry ingredients, stirring until moistened and blended.
3. Spoon batter into prepared muffin tin, filling cups three-quarters full. Bake in preheated oven for about 20 minutes.

Cinnamon Pear Muffins

3 cups	diced peeled pears	750 mL
¾ cup	granulated sugar	175 mL
½ cup	vegetable oil	125 mL
2	eggs	2
2 tsp	vanilla	10 mL
2 cups	all-purpose flour	500 mL
2 tsp	baking soda	10 mL
2 tsp	cinnamon	10 mL
1 tsp	ground nutmeg	5 mL
1 tsp	salt	5 mL
1 cup	raisins	250 mL
1 cup	chopped walnuts or pecans	250 mL

- *Preheat oven to 400°F (200°C)*
- *Muffin tin, greased or paper-lined*

1. In a bowl combine pears and sugar.
2. In a large bowl whisk together oil, eggs and vanilla. Add pear mixture and blend well.
3. In another bowl combine flour, baking soda, cinnamon, nutmeg and salt. Add to oil mixture and stir just until moistened and blended. Do not overmix. Fold in raisins and walnuts.
4. Spoon batter into prepared muffin tin, filling cups to the top. Bake in preheated oven for about 20 minutes.

HINT: Check spices for freshness by sniffing for aroma. The stronger the aroma, the fresher and more flavorful they will be.

Potato Pudding Muffins

12	medium potatoes	12
2	grated medium onions	2
4	eggs, well-beaten	4
1 cup	all-purpose flour	250 mL
1 tbsp	salt	15 mL
½ tsp	pepper	2 mL
½ tsp	savory	2 mL
1 tsp	baking powder	5 mL
8 tbsp	bacon fat or butter, melted	125 mL

- *Preheat oven to 375°F (190°C)*
- *Muffin tin, lightly greased*

1. Peel potatoes and grate over a bowl of cold water. Drain, pressing out as much water as possible. In a large bowl combine grated potatoes, onions and eggs.
2. In another bowl combine flour, salt, pepper, savory and baking powder. Add to potato mixture and mix well. Stir in melted fat.
3. Spoon batter into prepared muffin tin, filling cups to the top. Bake in preheated oven for 1 hour or until brown and crusty. Let stand for 30 minutes on a cake rack, then run a knife around edges and remove from pan.

HINT: To freeze, place muffins on a baking sheet, freeze, and then put into freezer bags.

Raspberry Corn Muffins

¾ cup	fresh raspberries	175 mL
1½ cups	all-purpose flour	375 mL
¾ cup	granulated sugar	175 mL
¾ cup	yellow cornmeal	175 mL
1 tbsp	baking powder	15 mL
½ tsp	salt	2 mL
2	eggs	2
1 cup	milk	250 mL
1 tsp	vanilla	5 mL
4 tbsp	melted butter	60 mL

◆ *Preheat oven to 400°F (200°C)*
◆ *12-cup muffin tin, lightly greased*

1. In a small bowl gently toss together raspberries and 2 tbsp (25 mL) flour.
2. In a large bowl combine remaining flour, sugar, cornmeal, baking powder and salt. Make a well in the center.
3. In another bowl whisk together eggs, milk and vanilla. Add to dry ingredients along with melted butter. Stir quickly just to moisten and blend.
4. Spoon 2 tbsp (25 mL) batter into each prepared muffin cup. Scatter 3 or 4 floured raspberries into each cup and spoon remaining batter over top. Bake in preheated oven for 15 minutes or until golden brown.

Kiwi Raspberry Muffins

1 cup	all-purpose flour	250 mL
1 cup	whole-wheat flour	250 mL
1 tbsp	baking powder	15 mL
½ tsp	baking soda	2 mL
2	peeled chopped kiwi	2
½ cup	fresh raspberries (or frozen)	125 mL
1	egg, lightly beaten	1
¼ cup	margarine or butter	50 mL
⅓ cup	skim milk	75 mL
1 tsp	vanilla	5 mL

◆ *Preheat oven to 400°F (200°C)*
◆ *Muffin tin, greased or paper-lined*

1. In a large bowl mix together all-purpose flour, whole-wheat flour, baking powder and baking soda. Add kiwi and raspberries, mixing well. Make a well in the center.
2. In another bowl combine egg, margarine, milk and vanilla. Add to the flour mixture, stirring only until moistened and blended. Do not overmix.
3. Spoon batter into prepared muffin tin, filling cups to the top. Bake in preheated oven for 15 to 20 minutes.

Smoked Sausage Corn Muffins

8 oz	smoked sausage	250 g
1 cup	all-purpose flour	250 mL
¾ cup	yellow cornmeal	175 mL
¼ cup	granulated sugar	50 mL
1 tbsp	baking powder	15 mL
1 cup	buttermilk	250 mL
¼ cup	vegetable oil	50 mL
2	eggs, beaten	2

MUFFIN STUFF: Delicious with scrambled eggs in place of toast.

♦ *Preheat oven to 375°F (190°C)*
♦ *Muffin tin, paper-lined*

1. Cut sausage into quarters lengthwise, then cut crosswise into ¼-inch (5 mm) pieces. In a skillet over medium heat, lightly brown sausage. Remove from skillet and drain on paper towels.

2. In a large bowl combine flour, cornmeal, sugar and baking powder. Add buttermilk, oil, eggs and sausage, stirring just until blended.

3. Spoon batter into prepared muffin tin, filling cups three-quarters full. Bake in preheated oven for 15 minutes or until golden brown.

Salmon Lunch Muffins

1	can (6 oz/175 mL) skinless, boneless salmon, not drained	1
2	eggs	2
½ cup	chopped celery	125 mL
½ cup	quick-cooking rolled oats	125 mL
½ tsp	baking powder	2 mL
¼ cup	evaporated milk	50 mL
2 tsp	lemon juice	10 mL
¾ tsp	salt	4 mL
¼ tsp	black pepper	1 mL

MUFFIN STUFF: For a tangier muffin, add 1 or 2 drops of Tabasco sauce.

HINT: Run a cut-up lemon (or other citrus fruit) through your garbage disposal to freshen the air in your kitchen.

♦ *Preheat oven to 350°F (180°C)*
♦ *6-cup muffin tin, lightly greased*

1. In a food processor combine salmon (and juice), eggs, celery, oats, baking powder, milk, lemon juice, salt and pepper. Purée until well blended.

2. Spoon batter into prepared muffin tin, dividing evenly. Bake in preheated oven for 30 minutes or until golden brown. Serve warm.

Sweet Potato Muffins

²⁄₃ cup	cooked sweet potatoes, well-drained	150 mL
¼ cup	butter or margarine	50 mL
½ cup	granulated sugar	125 mL
1	egg	1
¾ cup	all-purpose flour	175 mL
2 tsp	baking powder	10 mL
½ tsp	salt	2 mL
½ tsp	cinnamon	2 mL
¼ tsp	ground nutmeg	1 mL
½ cup	milk	125 mL
¼ cup	chopped pecans or walnuts	50 mL
¼ cup	chopped raisins	50 mL

♦ *Preheat oven to 400°F (200°C)*
♦ *Muffin tin, greased*

1. In a blender or food processor purée sweet potatoes.
2. In a large bowl cream together butter and sugar. Beat in egg and puréed sweet potatoes.
3. In another bowl combine flour, baking powder, salt, cinnamon and nutmeg. Add to sweet potato mixture alternately with milk and mix just until moistened and blended. Fold in chopped nuts and raisins.
4. Spoon batter into prepared muffin tin, filling cups three-quarters full. If desired, sprinkle with sugar and cinnamon. Bake in preheated oven for about 20 minutes.

Parmesan Tomato Muffins

1¾ cups	all-purpose flour	425 mL
⅓ cup	grated Parmesan cheese	75 mL
2 tbsp	granulated sugar	25 mL
2 tsp	baking powder	10 mL
¼ tsp	baking soda	1 mL
⅛ tsp	garlic powder	.5 mL
½ tsp	crushed dried rosemary	2 mL
Dash	black pepper	Dash
1	egg, lightly beaten	1
½ cup	milk	125 mL
½ cup	tomato sauce	125 mL
⅓ cup	olive oil or vegetable oil	75 mL
	Grated Parmesan cheese	

♦ *Preheat oven to 350°F (180°C)*
♦ *Muffin tin, lightly greased*

1. In a large bowl combine flour, cheese, sugar, baking powder, baking soda, garlic powder, rosemary and pepper. Make a well in the center.
2. In another bowl mix together egg, milk, tomato sauce and oil. Add to dry ingredients, stirring just until moistened and blended. Do not overmix.
3. Spoon batter into prepared muffin tin, filling cups to the top. Bake in preheated oven for 20 to 25 minutes or until lightly browned.

Strawberry Pecan Muffins

STREUSEL TOPPING

¼ cup	all-purpose flour	50 mL
¼ cup	finely chopped pecans	50 mL
¼ cup	light brown sugar	50 mL
2 tbsp	softened butter or margarine	25 mL

MUFFINS

2 cups	all-purpose flour	500 mL
⅓ cup	granulated sugar	75 mL
2½ tsp	baking powder	12 mL
1 tsp	grated lemon zest	5 mL
¼ tsp	salt	1 mL
⅔ cup	milk	150 mL
¼ cup	butter or margarine, melted	50 mL
1	egg	1
2 cups	finely chopped fresh strawberries	500 mL

♦ *Preheat oven to 400°F (200°C)*
♦ *Muffin tin, paper-lined*

1. In a small bowl combine flour, pecans, brown sugar and softened butter. Mix with your fingers until crumbly. Set aside.

2. In a large bowl combine flour, sugar, baking powder, lemon zest and salt. Make a well in the center.

3. In another bowl whisk together milk, melted butter and egg until blended. Add to flour mixture and stir just until moistened. Do not overmix. The batter will be lumpy. Fold in strawberries.

4. Spoon batter into prepared muffin tin, filling cups two-thirds full. Sprinkle with streusel topping. Bake in preheated oven for 20 to 25 minutes.

HINT: Save margarine tubs for storing baking ingredients such as raisins, cinnamon, baking soda, nuts, etc.

Pepper, Corn and Zucchini Muffins

¾ cup	all-purpose flour	175 mL
⅓ cup	yellow cornmeal	75 mL
1 tbsp	firmly packed light brown sugar	15 mL
2 tsp	baking powder	10 mL
½ tsp	salt	2 mL
½ cup	skim milk	125 mL
1	egg	1
⅓ cup	margarine, melted	75 mL
1½ cups	shredded zucchini	375 mL
½ cup	chopped roasted red peppers	125 mL

◆ *Preheat oven to 400°F (200°C)*
◆ *Muffin tin, paper-lined*

1. In a large bowl combine flour, cornmeal, sugar, baking powder and salt. Make a well in the center.
2. In another bowl whisk together milk, egg and melted margarine. Add to dry ingredients, stirring just until moistened and blended. Do not overmix. Stir in zucchini and peppers.
3. Spoon batter into prepared muffin tin. Bake in preheated oven for 20 to 25 minutes.

Cocoa Nut Zucchini Muffins

¾ cup	butter or margarine	175 mL
2 cups	granulated sugar	500 mL
2 tsp	vanilla	10 mL
3	eggs	3
1½ cups	all-purpose flour	375 mL
1 cup	whole-wheat flour	250 mL
½ cup	cocoa	125 mL
2½ tsp	baking powder	12 mL
1½ tsp	baking soda	7 mL
1 tsp	cinnamon	5 mL
2 cups	grated zucchini	500 mL
½ cup	milk	125 mL
1 cup	chopped nuts	250 mL

◆ *Preheat oven to 375°F (190°C)*
◆ *Muffin tin, greased*

1. In a large bowl cream together butter, sugar and vanilla. Add eggs one at a time, beating well after each addition.
2. In another bowl combine all-purpose flour, whole-wheat flour, cocoa, baking powder, baking soda and cinnamon. Add to the creamed mixture alternately with zucchini and milk, mixing well. Do not overmix. Fold in nuts.
3. Spoon batter into prepared muffin tin, filling cups to the top. Bake in preheated oven for 25 minutes.

HINT: To clean oven spills, sprinkle with automatic dishwashing powder, cover with wet paper towels and let stand for a few hours. Wipe with a damp sponge.

Graham Muffin Gems

1 cup	all-purpose flour	250 mL
¾ tsp	salt	4 mL
4 tsp	baking powder	20 mL
4 tbsp	packed brown sugar	50 mL
1 cup	graham flour	250 mL
1 cup	milk	250 mL
1	egg, slightly beaten	1
4 tbsp	butter or margarine, melted	50 mL

- *Preheat oven to 425°F (220°C)*
- *Muffin tin, greased or paper-lined*

1. In a large bowl mix together all-purpose flour, salt and baking powder. Add brown sugar and graham flour. Add milk, egg and melted butter, stirring just until blended.

2. Spoon batter into prepared muffin tin, filling cups to the top. Bake in preheated oven for about 20 minutes.

Variation
- *Pecan Muffins:* Add ½ cup (125 mL) chopped pecan nuts to the dry ingredients. Put a half pecan on each muffin top before baking.

Spreads and Toppings

Spreads and Toppings

THERE ARE NUMEROUS WAYS TO ADD FLAVOR, VARIETY AND A LITTLE intrigue to your muffins. Warm sliced muffins are delicious topped with any of the following recipes. Whether added before or after baking, toppings make an extra special treat.

Toppings you can sprinkle on top of muffins before baking:

- Sesame or poppy seeds
- Grated Cheddar cheese
- Sugar mixed with lemon or orange zest

Toppings you can sprinkle on top of muffins after baking:

- Marmalade, jelly or jam
- Dip tops in melted butter and then in sugar or cinnamon
- Icing sugar
- Chocolate sauce (in a bowl blend together 1 can sweetened condensed milk, 2 squares semi-sweet chocolate, 2 tbsp (25 mL) butter and 1 tsp (5 mL) butter. Heat over low heat.)

Some of the following recipes may seem to yield a large amount, but you will want to have plenty on hand to serve with different flavors of muffins.

Some recipes call for pouring mixture into hot, sterilized jars and using a boiling water bath. Here's the why and how of the water bath. This process is recommended for acidic foods such as fruits, tomatoes and pickles. It helps to maintain color and flavor and to prevent spoilage. Choose a pan deep enough to allow 1 to 2 inches (2.5 to 5 cm) of water above tops of jars, plus a little extra space for boiling. A roasting pan may be good for this. (Do not use a pressure cooker.) The pan should have a tight-fitting cover and a wire rack to keep jars from touching each other or the sides of the pan. Before preparing your recipe, put pan of water over heat. The water should be boiling when the jars are put in. After jars are filled and lids tightened, immerse them in the hot water, cover pan tightly and bring water quickly back to boiling. Start counting processing time when water again comes to a boil after adding jars. Follow your recipe directions for timing. Set jars upright, 2 to 3 inches (5 to 7.5 cm) apart, on several thicknesses of towels or on a wire rack to cool.

Apple and Plum Butter

Makes 6 jars

4½ lbs	apples	2.25 kg
3 lbs	plums	1.5 kg
2 cups	water	500 mL
6 cups	granulated sugar	1.5 L
1 tsp	cinnamon	5 mL

1. Wash and chop apples and plums. In a saucepan over medium heat, combine chopped apples and plums (including peels and cores) with water and cook until fruit is tender.
2. In a food processor purée fruit mixture and then push through a sieve. Return to heat. Add sugar and cinnamon. Cook until thick and clear, stirring occasionally to prevent sticking. Fill sterilized jars and seal.

Cinnamon Butter

Makes ½ cup (125 mL) butter

3 tbsp	softened butter	45 mL
½ cup	icing sugar	125 mL
¼ tsp	cinnamon	1 mL

1. In a bowl cream together butter, sugar and cinnamon. Chill.

Honey Peach Butter

½ cup	softened butter	125 mL
6 tbsp	peach preserves	90 mL
2 tsp	honey	10 mL

1. In a bowl beat butter until fluffy. Mix in peach preserves and honey.

> **HINT:** Keep honey or molasses from sticking to the measuring cup by greasing cup first. If recipe calls for vegetable oil, measure that first.

Special Fruit Butter

1 cup	puréed baby fruit (any flavor)	250 mL
1 cup	softened butter	250 mL
2 tbsp	icing sugar	25 mL

1. In a bowl beat together puréed fruit and butter. Beat in sugar. Chill and serve.

Sweet Orange Butter

¼ cup	softened butter	50 mL
½ cup	icing sugar	125 mL
	Juice of half an orange	
	Grated zest of half an orange	

1. In a bowl mix together butter and icing sugar. Add juice and zest. Mix well and serve.

> **HINT:** For lump-free icing sugar, try sifting it through a tea strainer.

Apricot Raspberry Jam

2 lbs	fresh ripe apricots, peeled, pitted and washed	1 kg
2 cups	fresh raspberries, washed	500 mL
2 lbs 4 oz	granulated sugar	1.25 kg
¼ cup	water	50 mL
1 tbsp	lemon juice	15 mL

1. In a saucepan over medium heat, combine apricots, raspberries, sugar and water. Cook, stirring occasionally, until mixture is thick. (Test by putting a little on a cold plate. If syrup stiffens as soon as it is cool, the jam is done.)
2. Add lemon juice and mix together. Pour jam into hot, sterilized jars and seal with parafin wax.

> **HINT:** You can make your own jam with any fruit you like in small or large amounts.
>
> Use 1 lb (500 g) (weighed after fruit is prepared) to 1½ cups (375 mL) sugar.
>
> For apple plus another fruit, use 12 oz (375 g) apples and 4 oz (125 g) of another fruit such as peaches, apricots and raspberries.

Light Strawberry Jam

8 cups	halved strawberries	2 L
1 cup	granulated sugar	250 mL
½ cup	corn syrup	125 mL
2 tbsp	lemon juice	25 mL

> **HINT:** Ripen peaches and pears quickly. Place in a brown paper bag with a ripe apple. Keep in a cool place. Make sure there are a few holes in the bag. The apple gives off a gas which stimulates other fruit to ripen.

1. In a bowl crush 4 cups (1 L) strawberries with a potato masher.
2. In a saucepan over medium heat, combine crushed strawberries, remaining strawberries and ½ cup (125 mL) water; bring to a boil. Reduce heat and simmer, covered, for 10 minutes. Stir in sugar, corn syrup and lemon juice. Increase heat and bring to a boil, stirring constantly. Allow to boil hard, uncovered, for 15 to 20 minutes or until softly set.
3. Remove from heat. Skim off any foam that has risen to the surface. Pour into hot, sterilized jars, leaving ½ inch (1 cm) headspace. Seal and process in boiling water bath for 10 minutes.
4. Cool on racks. Store in a cool, dark place. Once jam jars are open, keep in refrigerator for up to 4 weeks.

Variation

◆ *Peach Apricot Jam:* Substitute 4 cups (1 L) each of chopped, peeled peaches and apricots for the strawberries. Reduce lemon juice to 1 tbsp (15 mL).

Grandma's Raspberry Jam

Makes 4 or 5 jars

4 cups	fresh ripe raspberries	1 L
1 tbsp	vinegar	15 mL
4 cups	granulated sugar	1 L

> **HINT:** Butter the bottom of the saucepan before starting to make jam to prevent it from sticking while cooking. Use a wooden spoon for stirring. Use a metal spoon to remove scum as it accumulates around edges of pan.

♦ *Preheat oven to 275°F (140°C)*

1. Put berries in a sieve and quickly run under cold water. (Not for too long as raspberries absorb water easily.) Remove stems.

2. Take 3 pie plates and divide the sugar equally between them. Heat pie plates with sugar on them in preheated oven for 20 minutes.

3. In a large saucepan over medium heat, combine berries and vinegar. Allow to boil, without stirring, for 5 minutes. Add hot sugar, one plate at a time. (Adding the hot sugar this way does not stop the boiling). Boil over high heat for exactly 2 minutes.

4. Pour jam into hot, sterilized jars. Wax and seal.

Strawberry Rhubarb Jam

3 cups	fresh strawberries	750 mL
2 cups	thickly sliced rhubarb	500 mL
3 cups	granulated sugar	750 mL
3 tbsp	lemon juice	45 mL

> **HINT:** To freeze fresh strawberries for making jam later, hull the amount required and freeze on a tray. Place frozen strawberries in freezer bag, remove air and seal. Instead, you could crush fresh berries with a potato masher and freeze in 4-cup (1 L) amounts.

1. In a large bowl crush strawberries 1 cup (250 mL) at a time with a potato masher. Transfer to a large, heavy saucepan. Add the rhubarb. Heat over medium-high heat for 10 minutes or until rhubarb is softened.

2. Reduce heat to low. Stir in sugar and lemon juice until sugar is dissolved. Increase heat to high and bring to a full rolling boil, stirring often. Boil hard, uncovered, for 8 minutes, stirring often. Remove from heat. Let jam cool for 5 minutes, skimming off foam and stirring often.

3. Spoon into jars, leaving 1/2 inch (1 cm) headspace. Cool slightly for 2 minutes. Seal with parafin wax. Tighten lids, cool and store in a cool, dry, dark place.

Three-Fruit Jam

3 cups	shredded fresh pineapple	750 mL
2 cups	diced peeled rhubarb	500 mL
4 cups	strawberries, washed and hulled	1 L
Pinch	salt	Pinch
	Juice of 1 lemon	
4½ cups granulated sugar		1.125 L

> **HINT:** When making jam, boil fruit gently until cooked before adding the sugar. If the sugar is added before fruit boils, much more is needed. Overboiling the fruit after adding the sugar will adversely affect the flavor, color and consistency.

◆ *Preheat oven to 325°F (160°C)*
◆ *Three pie plates*

1. In a Dutch oven cook pineapple over medium heat for 10 minutes. Add rhubarb, strawberries, salt and lemon juice. Boil gently for 20 minutes.
2. Meanwhile, spread sugar in bottom of pie plates. Heat in preheated oven until sugar is quite hot. (This is done so as not to stop the boiling when added to the fruit.) Add heated sugar to fruit mixture. Boil rapidly, stirring often, for 20 to 25 minutes. Skim off any foam.
3. Pour jam into hot, sterilized jars. Seal with hot wax, cover and store in a cool, dry, dark place.

Nectarine Marmalade

1	orange	1
1	lemon	1
1 cup	water	250 mL
	Juice of 1 lemon	
2 lbs	ripe nectarines or peaches	1 kg
5 cups	granulated sugar	1.25 L
Half	bottle liquid pectin	Half

1. In a blender or food processor grind orange and lemon with water. Transfer mixture to a saucepan and add juice. Bring to a boil over medium heat. Allow to boil, covered, for 20 minutes.
2. Into a pot of boiling water, drop nectarines. Allow to boil for 20 seconds, then remove from heat. Transfer to a bowl of cold water for half an hour or until cool. Remove nectarines, peel and chop. Add to citrus mixture and boil hard for 2 minutes. Add pectin and boil until a jelly thermometer reaches 221°F (112°C).
3. Remove from heat. Stir and skim off foam for about 10 minutes. Pour into hot, sterilized jars and seal.

Orange (Citrus) Marmalade

8	oranges, washed	8
2	lemons, washed	2
	Water	
2 cups	granulated sugar	500 mL

1. Cut the unpeeled oranges and lemons into quarters lengthwise and then slice very thinly crosswise. Measure the sliced fruit, transfer to a bowl and add twice as much water as fruit and juice. Let stand overnight.

2. The next day, transfer mixture to a pot and bring to a boil. Cook for 1 hour, then set aside for 24 hours.

3. After 24 hours, stir well and measure out 2 cups (500 mL) juice and fruit. Put into a Dutch oven pot. Add sugar. Bring to a full rolling boil and boil for 9 minutes.

4. Pour into hot, sterilized jars and cool. When cold, cover with melted parafin wax. Seal with tight lids. Repeat procedure with any remaining fruit.

Variation

◆ *Amber Marmalade:* Substitute 1 grapefruit, 1 orange and 1 lemon in place of the fruit listed. Use the same amount of sugar and water.

Creamy Berry Spread

1 cup	strawberries or raspberries	250 mL
8 oz	light cream cheese, at room temperature	250 g

1. In a bowl mash strawberries.
2. In another bowl beat softened cream cheese until fluffy. Stir in mashed berries. Spread on sliced muffins or toast.

Lemon Swirl Spread

1	pkg (3 oz/85 g) softened cream cheese	1
1/2 cup	softened butter	125 mL
4 cups	icing sugar	1 L
1 tsp	vanilla	5 mL
2 to 3 tsp	grated lemon zest	10 to 15 mL
3 tbsp	lemon juice	45 mL

1. In a bowl beat together cream cheese, butter, sugar, vanilla, zest and juice until fluffy and spreadable. If necessary, add more lemon juice, 1 tsp (5 mL) at a time. Store in refrigerator up to one week.

> **NOTE:** This makes a large amount, so halve the recipe if you're not planning on using much.
>
> **HINT:** For a quick topping or spread for muffins, place a soft caramel candy in the bottom of each muffin tin or ramekin. Pour batter over top. Bake as usual and then invert. You'll have a delicious caramel sauce!

Plum Cheese Spread

8 oz	cream cheese	250 g
1/2 cup	shredded mild Cheddar cheese	125 mL
2 tbsp	mayonnaise or plain yogurt	25 mL
2 tbsp	plum sauce	25 mL

1. In a blender or food processor cream together cream cheese and Cheddar cheese until smooth. Add mayonnaise and plum sauce and purée until creamy and thick, but not hard.

Special Holiday Spread

1 cup	raisins	250 mL
1/3 cup	rum	75 mL
1	pkg (8 oz/250 g) softened cream cheese	1
2 cups	grated sharp Cheddar cheese	500 mL
1/4 tsp	cinnamon	1 mL
1/4 tsp	ground ginger	1 mL

HINT: For a quick and easy, sweet spread that is terrific on muffins (or toast), combine equal amounts of softened butter or margarine and honey. Add a little vanilla. Start with a smaller amount, like 1/4 tsp (1 mL) and increase, if desired.

1. In a saucepan over low heat, combine raisins and rum. Heat slowly just until hot. Cool for 15 to 20 minutes.
2. In a large bowl, cream together cream cheese, Cheddar cheese, cinnamon and ginger. Drain raisins, reserving rum. Pour rum into cheese mixture and mix until well blended and smooth. Fold in raisins.
3. Put mixture into jar or container. Store, covered, in refrigerator up to 3 weeks.

Strawberry Cream Cheese Spread

4 oz	low-fat cream cheese	125 g
2 tbsp	strawberry jam	25 mL

NOTE: One tbsp (15 mL) low-fat cream cheese has only 50 calories.

1. In a small bowl mash cream cheese until softened. Stir in jam and mix well.

Variations

♦ *Orange:* Replace jam with 1 tbsp (15 mL) thawed frozen orange juice concentrate, and 1 tbsp (15 mL) honey.

♦ *Cinnamon Date:* Replace jam with 2 tbsp (25 mL) finely chopped dates and 1/4 tsp (1 mL) cinnamon.

♦ *Cinnamon Raisin:* Replace jam with 2 tbsp (25 mL) chopped raisins and 1/4 tsp (1 mL) cinnamon.

Nut Crunch Topping

¼ cup	firmly packed brown sugar	50 mL
¼ cup	chopped walnuts	50 mL
1 tbsp	all-purpose flour	15 mL
1 tbsp	softened margarine	15 mL
1 tsp	cinnamon	5 mL

1. In a bowl combine brown sugar, walnuts, flour, margarine and cinnamon. Sprinkle over batter. Bake as directed in muffin recipe.

MUFFIN STUFF: This recipe can also be used as a filling for muffins.

Sugar-Cinnamon Mix

⅓ cup	granulated sugar	75 mL
1½ tsp	cinnamon	7 mL
1 tbsp	margarine, melted	15 mL

1. In a bowl combine sugar, cinnamon and margarine. Sprinkle over batter. Bake as directed in muffin recipe.

HINT: Keep muffins hot longer by lining your basket (under the cloth or napkin) with a sheet of foil.

Chocolate, Sour Cream and Coconut Topping

1 cup	semi-sweet chocolate pieces	250 mL
1 cup	sour cream	250 mL
¼ cup	toasted coconut	50 mL
1 tsp	vanilla	5 mL

1. In top of a double boiler over hot water, melt chocolate. Add sour cream, stirring until well blended. Add coconut and vanilla and mix well.

HINT: Buy or make molded chocolate cups. Fill them with ice-cream, drizzle with a sauce or liqueur that compliments the ice cream flavor.

Crunchy Broiled Topping

¼ cup	softened butter	50 mL
⅔ cup	firmly packed brown sugar	150 mL
½ cup	finely chopped nuts	125 mL
½ cup	Whole Wheat Flakes cereal	125 mL
3 tbsp	milk	45 mL

1. In a bowl cream together butter and brown sugar. Add nuts and cereal, mixing well. Stir in milk, mixing until well blended.
2. Spread evenly over muffins, hot from the oven. Put under broiler for 3 minutes or until topping is bubbling and slightly browned.

Lemon Glaze Topping

1 cup	icing sugar	250 mL
2 to 3 tsp	grated lemon zest	10 to 15 mL
4 to 5 tsp	lemon juice	20 to 25 mL

1. In a bowl combine icing sugar and lemon zest. Add lemon juice gradually, mixing well until desired consistency is reached.

Peach Walnut Topping

1 cup	peach preserves	250 mL
1 tbsp	butter or margarine	15 mL
	Juice of 1 orange	
¼ cup	chopped walnuts	50 mL

1. In a small saucepan over low heat, combine peach preserves, butter and orange juice. Cook, stirring, until heated and blended. Stir in walnuts. Serve warm.

Streusel Topping

⅓ cup	softened butter or margarine	75 mL
⅓ cup	granulated sugar	75 mL
½ cup	all-purpose flour	125 mL
1 cup	ground dry cake or bread crumbs	250 mL
1 tsp	cinnamon	5 mL

1. In a bowl cream butter while gradually adding sugar. Mix well. Add flour, crumbs and cinnamon, stirring until well mixed and crumbly.
2. Spoon topping over batter. Bake as directed in muffin recipe.

HINT: If you want a quick and delicious icing for carrot muffins boil a small potato and mash it. Add icing sugar and vanilla.

Toffee Coffee Topping

1 cup	packed brown sugar	250 mL
2 tbsp	cornstarch	25 mL
Pinch	salt	Pinch
1¾ cups	hot strong coffee	425 mL
2 tbsp	butter or margarine	25 mL
2 tsp	vanilla	10 mL

1. In a heavy saucepan over low heat, combine brown sugar, cornstarch and salt. Add coffee and cook, stirring, until thickened. Remove from heat. Add butter and vanilla, stirring until well blended. Drizzle warm over muffins.

Whipped Cream Topping

1 cup	whipping (35%) cream	250 mL
2 to 4 tbsp	icing sugar	25 to 60 mL

1. In a bowl beat together cream and sugar until stiff.

Variations

♦ *Grand Marnier:* To unbeaten cream add 1 to 2 tbsp (15 to 25 mL) icing sugar and 2 tbsp (25 mL) orange liqueur. Beat until stiff.

♦ *Mocha:* To unbeaten cream add ¼ cup (50 mL) icing sugar, 3 tbsp (45 mL) unsweetened cocoa powder, 1 tsp (5 mL) instant coffee granules and ½ tsp (2 mL) vanilla. Beat until stiff.

♦ *Peppermint:* To unbeaten cream add 2 tbsp (25 mL) icing sugar, a drop of green food coloring and ¼ tsp (1 mL) peppermint extract. Beat until stiff.

♦ *Strawberry:* To unbeaten cream add a drop of red food coloring and 2 tbsp (25 mL) strawberry jam. Beat until stiff.

HINTS:

To test doneness of jam or jelly, place a small plate in the freezer section of your refrigerator for an hour before you start cooking. Place a small spoonful of the boiling jam or jelly on the cold plate. Let it cool for a few seconds. Hold plate up vertically. If jam stays on the plate, it is cooked.

Store your favorite muffin recipes neatly by slipping them between the clear plastic pages of a photo album. They are protected from spills and can be removed easily.

National Library of Canada Cataloguing in Publication

Brody, Esther
    500 best muffin recipes / Esther Brody.

Includes index.
Previously published under titles: The 250 best muffin recipes and
Another 250 best muffin recipes.
ISBN 0-7788-0071-7

1. Muffins.
I. Brody, Esther. Another 250 best muffin recipes.
II. Brody, Esther. 250 best muffin recipes.
III. Title. IV. Title: Five hundred best muffin recipes.

TX770.M83B763 2003   641.8'15   C2003-901459-2

Index

A

Afternoon tea muffins, 319
All 'round muffin mix, 192
All spicy muffins, 229
All-bran cereal
  apricot cranberry muffins, 303
  banana muffins, 141
  carrot muffins, 58
  Cheddar cheese muffins, 59, 76
  cottage cheese lemon muffins, 78
  cream cheese bran muffins, 60
  honey muffins, 189
  mincemeat muffins, 43
  muffins, 55, 120, 187, 194, 279
  peaches and cream muffins, 160
  peanut-banana muffins, 143
  pineapple carrot muffins, 171
  pineapple muffins, 131, 191
  and raisin muffins, 29
  refrigerator muffins, 190
  sour cream muffins, 60
  tangerine muffins, 64
  See also Bran
Almond paste
  apple muffins, 320
  raspberry muffins, 165
Almond(s)
  blueberry muffins, 147
  bran-sweet potato muffins, 65
  Christmas muffins, 301
  citrus muffins, 319
  cranberry-filled muffins, 302
  oat bran muffins, 82
  orange muffins, 337
  pineapple bran muffins, 191
  topping, 147
  two-tone muffins, 117

Amber marmalade, 354
Apple cider muffins, 320
Apple pie filling, Cheddar muffins, 270
Apple(s)
  almond muffins, 320
  applecrisp muffins, 136
  bran muffins, 56, 320
  bran streusel muffins, 67
  butter, 76
  "candy apple" muffins, 287
  carrot pecan oat bran muffins, 89
  cereal breakfast muffins, 64
  Cheddar cheese and bacon muffins, 135
  Cheddar cheese muffins, 72, 270
  cinnamon muffins, 24, 137, 321
  cranberry fruitcake muffins, 305
  crunch muffins, 26
  date oatmeal muffins, 95
  doughnut buffins, 238
  -filled bran muffins, 66
  johnny appleseed muffins, 128
  lemon-glazed oatmeal muffins, 100
  microwave baked, 233
  muffins, 135, 270
  nut muffins, 271
  passover muffins, 313
  and plum butter, 349
  to prevent browning, 321
  spice cuffins, 243
  spice muffins, 138
    bran, 136
  streusel
    muffins, 139
    puffins, 256
    pumpkin muffins, 316
    wheat germ muffins, 104

S

Salmon
  lunch muffins, 342
  melts, 288
  puffins, 264
Salsa, chili muffins, 280
Salt, to reduce in recipes, 100
Sauces
  butter, 73
  lemon, 73
  mushroom, 266
Sausage cornmeal gems, 180
Sausage corn muffins, 342
Savory yogurt muffins, 113
Self-iced muffins, 50
Sesame cheese muffins, 219
Shredded bran cereal, buttermilk bran
      muffins, 58
Shredded wheat bran cereal, almond
      citrus muffins, 319
Smoked sausage corn muffins, 342
Snow muffins, 312
Sour cream
  all-bran muffins, 60
  banana muffins, 203
  blueberry muffins, 150, 151
  chili-pepper corn muffins, 179
  chocolate and coconut topping, 357
  chocolate chip muffins, 281
  chocolate orange muffins, 38
  coffee cake blueberry muffins, 325
  gingerbread muffins, 311
  Hawaiian muffins, 214
  maple oat muffins, 92
  miniature orange muffins, 292
  'n' spice cuffins, 251
  orange marmalade wheat muffins, 107
  Parmesan muffins, 36
  pineapple coconut muffins, 162

  pineapple oatmeal muffins, 94
  poppy seed muffins, 46
  raisin bran muffins, 51
  -raisin muffins, 62
  rice muffins, 33
  strawberry puffins, 265
  upside-down honey bran muffins, 66
Sour milk
  apple bran muffins, 56
  applesauce bran muffins, 56
  bran and cheese muffins, 76
  carrot bran muffins, 58
  chocolate chip bran muffins, 59
  date bran muffins, 69
  to make, 293
  oat bran muffins, 88
  orange raisin muffins, 293
Southern biscuit muffins, 51
Spiced
  apple muffins, 226
    bran, 136
  bran-sweet potato muffins, 65
  buttermilk muffins, 325
  carrot bran muffins, 58
  coffee-raisin muffins, 40
  corn muffins, 210
  muffins, 229, 298
  orange and sweet potato muffins, 338
  pineapple carrot muffins, 171
  raisin muffins, 49
  whole wheat muffins, 105
  zucchini muffins, 183
Spinach, vegetable muffins, 116
Spreads
  creamy berry, 355
  holiday, 356
  lemon swirl, 355
  plum cheese, 355
  strawberry cream cheese, 355, 356
  and toppings, 349-59